To one of my favorite prese

Thank you for all o

you inspire. Happy 2012.

With love forever,

Anna

RADICAL ACTS

THEATRE AND FEMINIST PEDAGOGIES OF CHANGE

EDITED BY ANN ELIZABETH ARMSTRONG AND KATHLEEN JUHL

aunt lute books—san francisco

First Edition

Aunt Lute Books
P.O. Box 410687
San Francisco, CA 94141
www.auntlute.com

Senior Editor: Joan Pinkvoss
Managing Editor: Shay Brawn
Production: Erica Bestpitch, Andrea de Brito, Noelle de la Paz, Gina Gemello, Sarah Beth Graham, Shahara Godfrey, Rashida Harmon, Laura Kramp, Merri Kwan, Cloe Le Gall-Scoville, Soma Nath, Sabrina Peterson, Elisabeth Rohrbach, Jenna Varden, Ladi Youssefi

Cover and Text Design: Amy Woloszyn, Amymade Graphic Design
Typesetting: Amy Woloszyn, Amymade Graphic Design
Cover Photos (L-R): Photographer: 1. Norma Bowles   July 2001
Pictured: Alejandra Flores in a scene from Fringe Benefits' *Mitos, Ritos y Tonterias* (Myths, Rites and Silliness)
2. Photographer: Bret Brookshire   September 5, 2006
Pictured: Laurie Carlos directs the play HALF-BREED/southern fried/Check One by Florinda Bryant in Austin, TX
3. Photographer: Ann Elizabeth Armstrong   May 4, 2007
Pictured: Tour guides and participants in "Walk With Me: Freedom Summer Training at Western College Campus"
4. Photographer: Walston Warner   October 28, 2006
Pictured: Gene R. Rodgers and Sharon Ploeger in *Actual Lives*

ISBN 978-1-879960-75-6

Library of Congress Cataloging-in-Publication Data

Radical acts : theatre and feminist pedagogies of change / edited by Ann Elizabeth Armstrong and Kathleen Juhl. – 1st ed.
    p. cm.
  ISBN 978-1-879960-75-6
  1. Women in the theater. 2. Feminist theater. 3. Women in literature. 4. Drama–History and criticism. I. Armstrong, Ann Elizabeth. II. Juhl, Kathleen.
  PN1590.W64R33 2007
  792.082–dc22

                                                        2007025307

TABLE OF CONTENTS
RADICAL ACTS: THEATRE AND FEMINIST PEDAGOGIES OF CHANGE

1: POSITIONING OUR VOICES

2: ACTIVATING PRACTICE

3: ENGAGING COMMUNITY

DEAR GENTLE, PISSED OFF, UTOPIAN READER:

I'm wondering who you are and what your impulse was to pick up this book.

To voluntarily pick up a book, especially one entitled *Radical Acts*, goes beyond casual or even respectful curiosity. Suggesting discontent, it is actually a utopian gesture. You have dared to imagine, in itself a radical act. For in imagining lies the first step towards action.

As I write to you, with cell phone, email, and bottled water at hand (bottled water!), the world is changing in ways I would not have anticipated as a younger theatre artist and educator. Where I live, the temperature has risen 30 degrees over the past few hours as a result of global warming that is wreaking havoc on the environment worldwide.

Thousands of people have died or been wounded in a war declared by an illegally elected president. A war that has plundered social services and education and undermined the credibility of the United States around the world. Under the guise of security, we see the propagation of prisons, detention centers and border walls. We are living in an age of surveillance in which our precious liberties are increasingly invaded and challenged and rights for which we have long struggled, such as reproductive choice and comprehensive sex education, are under attack.

Much of the media is controlled by multi-national corporations that value the bottom line over truth. Disavowed of their own power and creativity, many of our students seek refuge in addictive behaviors, rampant consumerism, and obsession with celebrities.

And what of institutionalized racism? The impact of cultural genocide? Homophobia? Gender and class inequities? The general disregard and condescension towards those who are most vulnerable–children, people with disabilities, the sick, frail, elderly and poor?

This is the historical moment in which we find ourselves. It is one not necessarily of our individual making but we are culpable, nevertheless.

I could go on. But you know the score. You are probably as distressed as I am and similarly stunned to find yourself in this place. The wrongness of our world seems so large it is often overwhelming.

And yet, as this gorgeous collection of essays and interviews reminds us, in an age where the search for authentic connection can be as elusive as an honest politician, theatre continues to hold out possibility. Especially within its continually evolving forms, the vitality of performance is an antidote to the homogenization of so many of our media images and to our often profound isolation from each other. Theatre's embodied interdisciplinarity can speak across many channels to engage the senses, challenge assumptions, and to transgress.

A book like this inspires hope because it is about the profundity of the teaching moment, whether in a formal classroom, rehearsal hall, or in the wider community. Notably, it takes as its starting point the groundbreaking feminist pedagogical premise that as we teach each other, we learn as well. The roles of teacher and student morph, moving in and out, rejecting the illusory and exclusionary patriarchal notions of perfection and control that have lead to this sad state of affairs.

When I feel discouraged–and I often do in my struggles to balance individual agency and collectivity or to continue innovation in a culture that prefers repetition and the commercial–I am reminded that there are others taking risks in their classrooms or rehearsal halls. I feel especially encouraged by the stories here of experimentation gone awry. The generosity of these pages is in their sharing of our hard won histories, our triumphs and travails. We have the courage to try, fail, and find success in sharing failure with each other in the pursuit and enactment of a truly brave new world.

I am thrilled by this book and the possibilities it offers. Essay upon essay and interview after interview are lovingly and painstakingly written and edited. And they suggest a community of artists, academics, and activists simultaneously grounded in and existing beyond geography, posing questions and solutions. When we read this together, no matter where we may be, we consciously form a different kind of community, supported by a common text and an ethos of possibilities and hope.

No book can or should be a blueprint. But a book like this can generate a textual community, posing questions to generate the next crucial moment of dialogue.

This moment is crucial, indeed. In times like these, we must embrace our opportunities. This includes reclaiming the civil liberties we are guaranteed by the Bill of Rights. Rights that many of our sisters and brothers in our democratic process have nevertheless been denied–freedom of speech, the power of dissent, and the right to assemble and make our voices heard. To reclaim these rights, we must cherish the sanctity of our imaginations and trust in the infinite wisdom and the imperfection of art.

It is an exciting and terrifying time to be an educator, artist, and activist. But we are a polis, a community. And this beautiful book can help us in the quest to find our way.

Joan Lipkin
2007

ACKNOWLEDGMENTS

This collection, first of all, embodies a community of feminist theatre educators and artists who worked with us through many drafts and changes as this project evolved. Their important ideas have inspired us, spurred us on, and comprise the content and spirit of the work. Elly Donkin co-editor of *Upstaging Big Daddy: Directing Theatre as If Gender and Race Matter*, originally encouraged Juhl to make this book a reality. Her anthology, co-edited with Susan Clement, has been a source of inspiration and an invaluable resource. The Women and Theatre Program, a focus group in the Association for Theatre in Higher Education, motivated us to provide a place for the voices of many of the educators and artists in this book. The Women and Theatre Program also sponsored the successful acquisition of a Projects and Programs grant through the Association of Theatre for Higher Education that made the project possible. Many colleagues have supported this project in various capacities. We extend our gratitude in particular to: Carrie Ponder Ameling, Lisa Anderson, Leslie Bentley, Beth Berila, Jessica Berson, Rhonda Blair, Karen Bovard, Kathy DeVecka, William Doan, Jill Dolan, LeAnn Fields, Berenice Malka Fisher, Ann Fox, Rinda Frye, Sally Harrison-Pepper, Joan Herrington, Elizabeth Homan, Shirley Huston-Findley, Katie Johnson, Yuko Kurahashi, Karen Libman, Robert Lublin, Frances A. Maher, Rhona Justice Malloy, Kathy McHugh, Kate Mendeloff, Lisa Merrill, Claudia Tatinge Nascimento, Donna Marie Nudd, Ana Perea, Adrian Rodgers, Susan Russell, Eberhard Scheiffele, Judith Sebesta, Helen Stub, Kamala Viswesraran, Sara Warner, Beth Watkins, and Shannon Winnubst. And there were certainly many others along the way whose names we may have omitted. To our vast and supportive network of feminist colleagues, we are grateful. We also greatly appreciate student assistants who helped us, notably JiaYun Zhuang, Nicole Wilder, Samantha Brewer and Kinsey Keck. We would also like to thank our institutions, Southwestern University and Miami University of Ohio, for their support and resources that allowed us to complete the work. Most importantly, without the incredible women at Aunt Lute Books, especially editor Joan Pinkvoss, Shay Brawn, and our gracious, diligent, kind, and good-natured copy-editor Gina Gemello, all of whom believed in our work with inspirational enthusiasm, this project would not be a reality. Juhl would like to thank her partner Ruth Davis for her love and patience through all the time it took to conceive and complete this work. Ann Elizabeth would like to thank Robert and Kiefer Bell for sustenance, encouragement, and for not giving up on her.

And, of course, we must thank all the students who inspired the work represented in this volume, work that we developed with and for them.

CONSTRUCTING A MATRIX OF FEMINIST TEACHING IN AND WITH THEATRE
AN INTRODUCTION

Ann Elizabeth Armstrong with Kathleen Juhl

> Feminist pedagogy is...*teaching that engages students in political discussion of gender injustice.*
>
> —Berenice Malka Fisher, *No Angel in the Classroom*[1]

> We could use our positions as teachers and scholars to put the body back into thought, to think of pleasures like desire not as a space of absence that language can't lead us to, but as a space of social possibility to which our bodies lead us.
>
> —Jill Dolan, *Geographies of Learning*[2]

> The classroom, with all its limitations, remains a location of possibility. In that field of possibility we have the opportunity to labor for freedom, to demand of ourselves and our comrades, an openness of mind and heart that allows us to face reality even as we collectively imagine ways to move beyond boundaries, to transgress.
>
> —bell hooks, *Teaching to Transgress*[3]

Feminist pedagogy embraces a critical reflectiveness of dynamic and context-specific classroom strategies–those "radical acts" that we use to imagine, embody, and enact social justice through our teaching. Conscious of how power relations inform and shape the classroom, feminist pedagogies in theatre construct communities where knowledge emerges through our encounters, and especially through our confrontations, with one another. A feminist theatre pedagogy suggests that what we do with our bodies on the stage has the potential to reverberate and transform both the artists who make the representations and the community members who witness them. With this in mind, *Radical Acts* brings together the work of feminist professors, teachers, activists, and artists, acknowledging a wide variety of feminist theatre teaching as part of an important network through which participants sustain and support each other. The authors represented here work in large public institutions, private liberal arts colleges, high schools, professional theatre companies, and community-based organizations. Offering a diverse spectrum of locations and approaches, the contributors each share a commitment to feminist theatre practices that embrace gender and justice, transgress boundaries, and create spaces of social possibility. By emphasizing the importance of context and diversity, this volume strives to expand our definitions of feminism, theatre, and pedagogy as we reflect on our teaching, discuss practical classroom strategies, and consider the impact of our work in the wider community.

Why should we organize an anthology collection around "feminist" pedagogies instead of other politically progressive activist pedagogies? Feminist pedagogy includes more than the teaching of content about women and feminism. It is also more than a formal set of guidelines for teaching. While there are other important progressive and activist pedagogies, Fisher's call for engaging with "gender injustice" resonated with our sense of feminism's relationship to other political struggles. To organize a collection around categories of difference, highlighting gender as an important and dynamic part of that discussion, we consciously acknowledge the power of articulating the "women's work" of the educator/artist within the idioms of our own communities and embodied experiences. In doing this, we engage with a broad range of feminist locations, identities, and perspectives within the struggle for social justice. In many essays, these perspectives are further enriched vis-à-vis discourses like masculinity studies, disability studies, critical white studies, ethnic studies, and transnational studies. However, the collection also highlights the voices of artist/practitioners, acknowledging that many artists generate theory through their innovative practices. By expanding definitions of pedagogy in this way, we acknowledge that artistic work frequently generates paradigm shifts, creating consciousness-raising that changes the way we see ourselves and society.

In the current U.S. political climate, feminist teachers and theatre artists are uniquely qualified to speak to educational and social crises. Both feminism and theatre offer methods for speaking through and across differences, and as an artistic medium, theatre requires that we enter into an honest and authentic representation of conflict. It also provides collaborative methodologies that help us engage multiple voices. Significantly, many educators outside the discipline of theatre have recognized that theatre and performance offer productive ways of thinking about the student and teacher relationship that resist static hierarchies.[4] Furthermore, performance offers a way of thinking about relationships among students as they solve creative problems collaboratively, as well as the relationships between students and the world, as they engage the wider community when presenting their work. Indeed, feminist teaching of and with theatre offers a way to bridge the widening gap between the ivory tower and our broader communities. For those working in underrepresented communities, methods and approaches from feminism and activist theatre traditions offer opportunities to move beyond dominant narratives and engage the site-specific potential of theatrical creation.

Many contributors' essays emphasize how their teaching strategies relate to their specific locations. Consequently, *Radical Acts* consciously juxtaposes privilege with oppression, noting the tension and dissonance between the two. In doing this, we recognize that a strategy to confront oppression in one context might not be appropriate in another. For instance, the question of how a feminist pedagogy assists university students struggling to do improv without reinforcing stereotypes may seem less important, or even irrelevant, when juxtaposed with other questions in the volume, such as: how does theatre allow one to confront the genocide of one's ancestors, reclaim one's voice, or organize to enact social change? *Radical Acts* recognizes that the academy and theatre are both deeply entrenched within a history of elitism. It is therefore critical to articulate relationships between positions of privilege and oppression in order to open up new sites for resistance and intervention. This in turn expands the purposes of education and our definitions of theatre. For example, in one essay, we see how professional theatre artist and Ivy League professor Deb Margolin intervenes in the racism of students and expands on the ethical repercussions of their fictional representations. Then, if we consider the lengths to which Chris Strickling must go to accommodate a diverse, disabled group of actors and the theatrical presentation of their stories in a community setting, we begin to understand the consequences of *not* making interventions such as Margolin's. As Strickling and other contributors demonstrate, theatre has symbolically, economically, and physically become an act of exclusion rather than a practice of democracy. Can we imagine ways in which boundaries are reconfigured so that more voices are heard? How can feminist pedagogy help us explore the relationship between sites of practice, as well as generate alliances and strategies of transformation?

Ellen Donkin and Susan Clement's 1992 collection, *Upstaging Big Daddy: Directing Theatre As if Gender and Race Matter,* has served as an important source of inspiration for this collection and fuelled our desire to broaden the discussion it began. It provides a space where theatre professionals, academics, and activists engage in feminist inquiry, as does our other primary inspiration, the Women and Theatre Program (WTP).[5] Within WTP, we've found a home and a way to explore the vastly different ways of being a feminist in the theatre. It has introduced us to the joys and limits of theory, provided a fruitful site for cross-pollination with other disciplines, and given us a broader point of view that has helped us negotiate our own institutions. Most of all it has provided a space that has nurtured our activist impulses. WTP has been fraught with many of the same controversies that have troubled the U.S. feminist movement, but while grappling with issues such as the relationship between theory and practice or the classism and racism of academic theatre, among other controversies, this community has proven its relevance and resilience.[6] Our collection self-consciously builds upon the network we found through this organization, but, recognizing the need to broaden this base, we've also pushed to move beyond it. While some of the authors in this anthology have been important voices in WTP, others responded to a call for papers; others emerged through our own communities and collaborations. Most of the essays represent experiences within the U.S., though a few invite a comparison across national boundaries. We decided to focus this collection on North American experiences, though we look forward to future collections that will fully realize the global potential for a feminist pedagogy of theatre.

Radical Acts invites you to enter at multiple points. The anthology is organized into three sections, providing a path from the personal, through the creative, to the political. Various themes tend to cross over from section to section; however, we're aware that none of these concepts can be separated from each other. We begin with "Positioning Our Voices," autobiographical narratives that assist us in recognizing the diverse experiences of feminist teachers. Our autobiographical experiences frequently reveal our values and chart a path toward social justice, but they also mark silences and the struggle to represent ourselves and our work within oppressive traditions. As noted in several of these essays, feminist teachers struggle within the same educational system that has in part created us. Re-presenting our own experiences as teachers allows us to trace more clearly the source of our pedagogy. How do we separate our values from those of oppressive systems in order to create sites of resistance? How do we find and negotiate boundaries in order to transgress them? Here, the authors place personal narratives in dialogue with some of theatre's traditions and disciplinary practices. Each of these essays sheds light upon obstacles that feminist theatre practitioners encounter, and the importance of self-representing our personal experience and history—for both ourselves and our students.

The classroom and the rehearsal hall are spaces in which these charged political questions naturally emerge through the creative process. The second section, entitled "Activating Practice," interrogates specific creative philosophies and exercises in classroom and rehearsal contexts, noting how theatrical practice can activate us politically. These essays expose paradoxes and assumptions in our teaching and practice. For example, though some might conceive of the feminist classroom or rehearsal hall as a "safe" space for artistic exploration, others see it as a "safe" space to take dangerous risks and confront difference, and still others eschew the whole idea of "safety" in their pedagogy, instead focusing on generative confrontations and discomfort. Throughout this section, important themes such as danger and safety, political and creative freedom, the power of embodiment and improvisation, and the complex dynamics of collaboration and group process are developed.

While the second section highlights artistic choices, the final section, entitled "Engaging Community," looks at how theatrical performance can negotiate the boundaries between art and life to manifest social change. Essays in this section develop themes from the previous two sections while also pushing us to ask, what's at stake for a feminist pedagogy of theatre? Several essays utilize a historical lens, allowing the authors to articulate the specific links between theatre and activist movements or between theatre and the institutions within which they work. Other essays describe projects in which participants agitate for political changes in their communities. Some questions that arise from the projects represented in this section include: Can theatre persuade audience members to question their homophobic beliefs? Can performances by disabled actors lead to structural changes in theatres that will accommodate future generations of diverse bodies on the stage? How does a curriculum evolve to create a "dramaturgy of liberation" that reflects the identities of the students who study it? Can a performance about Civil Rights spur institutional changes? How do we measure "transformations," both the big and small results of our pedagogy and art? These essays examine the relationship between theatre, its creative processes, and its audiences, tracing how art can move us from conscious recognition toward a commitment to action. The three sections of *Radical Acts* mirror the construction of a classroom that offers porous zones through which to explore feminist engagements. Furthermore, by connecting some of the current discussions in feminist pedagogy and theatre/performance studies to the essays in *Radical Acts*, we can better see the intersections between them.

FEMINIST PEDAGOGY, POLITICS, EDUCATION, AND ACTIVISM

Women's Studies, an academic interdiscipline that began developing in the 1980s, has changed the landscape of knowledge production. Feminist teachers have pioneered innovative pedagogies that challenge both what we know and how we know it. Important concepts from feminist pedagogy that circulate in this volume include: the relationship between process and product, the focus on embodied over detached knowledges, the rich terrain between the personal and political, how to deal with resistance and failure in our work, the importance of emotions and witnessing, and how we perform the role of teacher or authority figure.

In *The Feminist Classroom*, Maher and Tetreault suggest that feminist pedagogy refers to an open and flexible praxis that is connected to the material being taught. They explicitly broaden the scope of feminist pedagogy beyond classroom practice to include "the entire process of creating knowledge, involving the innumerable ways in which students, teachers, and academic disciplines interact and redefine each other in the classroom, the educational institution, and the larger society" (57). Pedagogy is a dynamic process for Maher and Tetreault, and its specific character depends on who is participating, what material is being explored, and the location of a particular classroom. Any pedagogy can be defined as a practice that produces knowledge, but the processes through which that knowledge is produced will reflect and affect the material that teachers and students explore and interpret. We see this important relationship between how meaning is created and what is created in essays such as Joni L. Jones/Omi Osun Olomo's, in which she explains how director Laurie Carlos sets up and engages a non-traditional rehearsal process in order to create a "jazz aesthetic," a new language that more fully represents an African American experience; in Kathleen Juhl's interview with queer performance artists Kate Bornstein and Barbara Carrellas, who discuss exploring gender through a "language of paradox" and describe how they encourage students to experience the knowledge and wisdom of their bodies through kinesthetic processes; and in Amy Seham's innovative strategies for revising popular methods of comedy improv in order to explore alternative narratives of gender, race, and power. *Radical Acts* suggests throughout that feminists must discover new methods in order to allow new knowledges and new voices to be heard in the theatre.

Patriarchal traditions have valued "universal" knowledge over local, situated knowledge, and femininst pedagogy builds upon critiques of this tradition, such as that of Paolo Freire, who railed against the "banking system" of education, in which students are viewed as empty receptacles ready to be unquestioningly filled with knowledge (72). Similarly, Peter McLaren notes how schooling has become a "ritualized performance" that turns education into a process of indoctrination (1999). While we would like to think that theatre provides a space for resistance, we must also examine how theatre participates in such an indoctrination as well. Corinne Rusch-Drutz's article "Good Female Parts" critiques how academic theatre's acceptance of a "universal canon" creates standards that can lead to young women disciplining, erasing, or censoring their bodies and subjectivities through dieting or by "neutralizing" their accents. Paul Bryant-Jackson's article similarly explores how African American women of Spelman College have historically performed a canon that excluded them, but how, eventually, a "dramaturgy of liberation" has activated the voices of these students and helped them to place their experiences at the center of their representations. Ellen Margolis questions her own graduate education and consciously revises her theatre history classroom to move students from passive to active participants in the construction of history.

Though feminist teachers have created radically democratic learning processes, feminist pedagogies include trial and error. In early attempts to empower students, feminist pedagogy often devolved into classroom discussions that focused solely on students' experiences rather than a rigorous discourse in which students grapple with difficult new ideas. An important criticism of feminist pedagogy is that a myopic focus on the personal may stop short of political insight and activism and will reinforce individualism rather than collectivity and community. While it is important to acknowledge personal experience, feminist pedagogy also strives to move students beyond it.

In moving students beyond the personal, theatre can complement feminist pedagogies by actively engaging collaborative choices and requiring students to take points of view other than their own. Theatre processes create productive spaces for reflection. Within those spaces, students can negotiate differences, discover common ground, and move to a collective consciousness. We see how a creative process can force participants beyond themselves in Lisa Jo Epstein's interview with playwright Deb Margolin, in which Margolin describes pushing her playwriting students to put words in *others'* mouths and experiment with how an "irrelevant" comment can test the limits of a character and a dramatic situation. Chris Strickling describes a disabled female performer transforming a story about an intensely personal experience into a collective representation, turning it from a "sincere and eloquent lament" into an "irreverently comic piece" (297) that took on a larger political resonance. Domnica Radulescu shows how her American students who play Winnie in Beckett's *Happy Days* come to a collective recognition of their oppression as women, just as she had done in Romania many years before, and Jo Beth Gonzalez shares how one of her female high school students convinced a male peer to fully embrace the emotional depths available to him in his monologue about suicide. As Epstein remarks, theatre requires that we "collapse the boundaries" (112) between ourselves.

Yet collapsing these boundaries in the classroom and on the stage often means that students must acknowledge their own privileges and biases along with their moments of empowerment. Feminist educators must embrace and confront the difficult task of addressing these issues when they arise—and, importantly, must recognize their own prejudices, biases, and privileges as well. Rebecca Schneider, who states that "in every case fear is something our classrooms should be designed to explore" (260), illustrates this perfectly in her description of a class in which she exposed her students to danger by conducting her class outside, but also embraced the "danger" of exploring her own fears when a student challenged her to recognize her assumption of gendered binaries. Encouraging us to ask what's at stake in such moments, Schneider notes that even though we can't resolve all conflicts, we must be willing to engage them, despite the uncomfortable moments they may bring.

Feminist pedagogies also foreground the role of emotion and empathy in learning. Because emotions obscure boundaries, threatening to produce a reign of chaos and anarchy, patriarchal systems have long relegated emotion to the female sphere and out of the realm of discourse. In *Feeling Emotion*, Megan Boler articulates how education trains us to express the right emotions at the right time in front of the right people. But when incorporated into feminist pedagogy, Boler points out, emotions can open up a space between ideology and the privacy of internalized feeling (13). Empathy can also bridge gaps and create coalitional spaces; feminist teachers can engage both empathy and emotions in order to reveal sites of potential political resistance. Emotions and empathy should be considered from an audience standpoint as well. Ann Elizabeth Armstrong's essay describes a walking tour about Freedom Summer that she created with students at Miami University of Ohio, in which participants are guided through a re-enactment of the training that Civil Rights activists experienced on her campus in 1964. This performance project illustrates how an audience experience can generate not only powerful emotions and empathy, but also, Armstrong hopes, a similar commitment to social justice that carries over into the present.

As feminist educators, however, we must be cautious about the power of emotion and empathy in performance contexts. Like experience, emotions must be critically interpreted, even as they are valued and consciously directed towards strategies for changing the status quo. Many of the writers in *Radical Acts* address this when they evoke the power of witnessing. Witnessing values the importance of listening as well as the implication of the self in the other. bell hooks writes about a similar kind of listening in *Teaching Community*, where she describes the importance of a state of "interbeing" that makes one "aware of what is going on in your body, in your feelings, in our mind. When we practice interbeing in the classroom we are transformed not just by one individual's presence but by our collective presence. Experiencing the world of learning we can make together in community is the ecstatic moment that makes us come and come again to the present, to the now, to the place where we are real" (173-74). Here, hooks describes a pedagogy through which the performed embodiment of community takes place, fully engaging the emotions and bearing witness to each other's experiences. In the context of feminist pedagogy, witnessing demands an active response to injustice, as Norma Bowles illustrates when describing the internal conflict she sometimes experiences while acting as witness in her workshops. Bowles grapples with the "rules" for an ideal democratic learning space; although such a space ostensibly supports all stories and opinions, she recognizes one of the fundamental problems of witnessing: the impossibility of remaining neutral in the face of injustice. The feminist classroom is one in which students struggle among themselves to construct an ethical community, and this struggle assists in building larger communities with theatre audiences that also demand justice.

By working as both insider and outsider to the community, and by encouraging vulnerability, disclosure, and resistance in her role as witness, the feminist teacher becomes a kind of agent provocateur or trickster who utilizes classroom dynamics. Several articles in *Radical Acts* illustrate teachers playing tricksters as part of their pedagogies. Kathleen Juhl describes a playful method for teaching acting in which, rather than providing "master teacher" critiques in response to students' work, she encourages new ideas for performances by providing props, costumes, food, drink, lighting, sound effects, and side-coaching. Stacy Wolf shares exercises that playfully engage students in embodying a continuum of gendered behavior. Her exercises problematize and complicate students' conceptions of gender, while providing a space for them to reflect on it. The trickster/provocateur can also be seen in Ellen Margolis, who modeled her pedagogy for a theatre history class on a part-time teaching job she once had for a company called Traffic Safety Taught with Humor; in Becca Schneider's "tricking" students into questioning basic cultural assumptions; and in Norma Bowles moving between her teaching personas of Martha Stewart and Richard Simmons. Whether we identify with Laurie Carlos's "tough love" (98), Deb Margolin's impulse to mother students (129), or Kate Bornstein's wish to act as "crone" (183), we recognize that our teaching personas–and our tricks–are diverse and flexible.

The feminist teacher as trickster is constantly pushing at the limits of the classroom community, negotiating the boundaries of identity and acknowledging differences, contradictions, and subjugated knowledges that may be present. While this role might be seen as manipulative, we believe that it underscores the importance of ethical leadership to guide inquiry. It also emphasizes the centrality of the role of the teacher, who might not possess more knowledge than the students but instead destabilizes all knowledges. Many of the educators in *Radical Acts* destabilize their roles as teachers and the knowledge they provide. They offer students agency but provide limits. They destabilize power relations by providing constant variety, and they ask seemingly ridiculous questions that are ultimately unresolvable but stimulate conversation. They provoke laughter and subvert hierarchies. Their pedagogies dismantle the limits of traditional classroom protocol and learning becomes dialogical.[7]

When the feminist teacher engages pedagogical practices such as these, the classroom becomes a liminal space of performance, and one for performing new possibilities. But these new possibilities aren't approached uncritically, since the classroom is specifically situated within larger communities and within particular institutionalized hierarchies. Feminist teachers are aware of the porous boundaries between society and the classroom and the important limits placed on classroom work by structures such as curricula, policy, and institutional agendas. Macdonald and Sanchez-Casal note how "academic hierarchies consolidate power in dominant identity groups [to reveal] how institutional agendas tokenize, marginalize and appropriate radical curricula and radical teachers," making only narrow perimeters of change possible (14). While the curricula and the identities of students have become increasingly more diverse, pedagogical methods are not necessarily serving this diversity, and feminist teachers must be ever vigilant of institutional attempts to assimilate and co-opt it. Whether we experience our classrooms as what Gonzalez describes in her article as "fragile bubble[s]" (273), where external forces must be held at bay so that students can find their voices, or as Armstrong's "truth telling" spaces that reverberate through institutional structures with moral outrage (203), the feminist teacher takes on a role that extends beyond the classroom–to counteract institutional strategies of containment and form productive coalitions with colleagues, administrators, and other stakeholders who are working for change. The teaching and theatre-making explored in this volume exists within social and institutional structures, whether they be schools, universities, theatre companies, grant-making agencies, or communities. We have the power to influence dominant institutional histories and narratives. Theatre has proven its potential to change hearts and minds, but its ability to capitalize upon and influence the social webs within which it is situated has emerged only more recently, especially in community-based theatre.

Through feminist pedagogy, *Radical Acts* addresses a range of questions suggesting how we can move pedagogy and performance toward activism in a variety of ways. How can we challenge the hierarchies and values that exist within the mainstream professional theatre community and the traditional canon? How can feminist artist/teachers create liberating creative processes that challenge stereotypes and engage creative freedom? How can feminist pedagogy in theatre engage differences among students within classrooms, in workshops and rehearsals, and engender political consciousness about those differences? How can feminist pedagogies tear down the walls of the classroom, encouraging students to engage in civic dialogue with broader communities?

THEATRE PEDAGOGY AND METHODS OF THEATRE AS EDUCATION

It has been well known throughout history that theatre is a powerful method of educating audiences. In its early forms, in ancient Greece and in medieval church settings, this education was directed primarily toward teaching people to behave in ways that supported coercive, though purportedly "democratic," political systems and conservative religious doctrine. And, as many contemporary feminist theorists and historians have pointed out, throughout history and into the twentieth century, theatre has represented and upheld hegemonic versions of binary gender roles and heterosexism. Yet contemporary educators in multiple disciplines have discovered the rich possibilities of the theatrical process as a useful means for teaching about such hegemonic systems. Through its unique interdisciplinarity that brings together literature, politics, the visual arts, music, and ethnography, theatre and performance have influenced academic disciplines in productive ways. In 2001, Jill Dolan pointed out that "'[p]erformativity as a metaphor is used increasingly to describe the nonessentialized constructions of marginalized identities" (*Geographies* 65). Dolan notes that the *metaphorical* use of the term "performance" outside of theatre and performance studies had not resulted in an increased interest in theatrical performances "as located, historical sites for interventionist work in social identity constructions...[by those] disciplines, methods, and politics that borrow its terms" (65). The writers in *Radical Acts*, however, suggest ways that theatre teacher-scholars and practitioners can begin to participate actively in revising cultural constructions of gender and identity by developing interventionist pedagogies where theory and practice can be explored simultaneously along with theatre's invaluable interdisciplinarity.

Theatre artists, particularly those with a Marxist orientation, like Brecht,

have theorized spectator reception and theatrical process as a democratic praxis
for re-imagining the world and examining ethical dilemmas. Because theatre
offers a space for negotiating meaning, for engaging conflict, for raising consciousness, and for creating praxis, it has spawned countless pedagogical techniques and methods, such as Theatre of the Oppressed (TO), Drama in
Education (DIE or TIE), psychodrama, "teaching-in-role," sociodrama, and
community-based theatre, which reflect an exciting confluence of disciplinary
knowledges.[8] We can see the influence, for instance, of the work of women theatre teachers in the early twentieth century who had few or no outlets in professional theatre but created innovative approaches to using drama in one of the
few professional realms available to them: the classroom. These role models,
like Anne Cooke Reid, whose work is detailed in Paul Bryant-Jackson's essay,
and Viola Spolin, cited by several authors in this volume, combined their training in education with their love and knowledge of theatre to engage the whole
person in the classroom and in experiential learning.[9] However, historically the
work of these teachers has been labeled as mere "child's play" rather than
being viewed as important social and political work or sophisticated artistry that
it is. Sadly, the archetypal role of the mother as storyteller, who may potentially
pass down subversive knowledges to her children, is a dangerous threat to
patriarchial ways of knowing, and, consequently, she has been contained by
multiple disciplinary and artistic barriers that have limited her influence.

However, since the rise of performance studies, an academic interdiscipline
that brings together theatre, communication, anthropology, ethnography, autobiography, discourse analysis, and the study of literature through performance,
teachers in higher education have more readily explored the continuums
between art and everyday life including the application of theatre to education.
The study of community-based theatre in performance studies has expanded
ideas about theatre as a social ritual and has revolutionized the reach of theatre
as a means of knowing ourselves and our communities, and of inspiring social
change. Through community-based theatre, artists and community members
can devise performances in which multiple voices can be heard and individuals' stories can be told. The resistant performances developed through collaborations between theatre artists and communities are antidotes to conventional
theatre, which often reflects and supports coercive cultural values. Jan Cohen-
Cruz defines it this way: "Community-based performance relies on artists guiding the creation of original work or material adapted to, and with, people with
a primary relationship to the content, not necessarily to the craft" (*Local Acts* 2-
3). Such work might mythologize local experience, brainstorm strategies for
activism, or engage civic dialogue through theatre.

Many contributors to *Radical Acts* conceive their work in relation to communities. Cherríe Moraga describes a collaboration with students in her son's
second grade class in Oakland, California, in which they create a performance
revising the history of Christopher Columbus. Sharon Bridgforth, whose work

is featured prominently in Joni L. Jones/Omi Osun Olomo's essay, collaborates with women of color and professional artists to create performances based on writing and story-telling. Kate Bornstein and Barbara Carrellas work with various groups across the country creating community-based workshops and performances on gender and sexuality. Jo Beth Gonzalez, Chris Strickling, and Norma Bowles collaborate with students, public schools, people with disabilities, and with grassroots organizations to create performances that explore the continuums between art and everyday life.

Augusto Boal's body of methods known as Theatre of the Oppressed, which has inspired and is closely related to many community-based theatre techniques, has been influential to current feminist pedagogies in theatre, as well as to this volume. While many artists and educators, especially women and people of color, have pioneered similar techniques within their own local contexts, Boal has thoroughly recorded and systematized his approach, which has been disseminated globally. In critiques similar to many of those directed at Boal's ideological father, Paulo Freire, some feminists have noted that both the genealogy of ideas from women and the role of gender have at times been marginalized and decontextualized in Boal's work.[10] However, feminist theatre teachers and practitioners have used Theatre of the Oppressed to move beyond the often conservative paradigms of text-based theatre and to combine traditional principles of dramatic structure with improvised techniques so that they can devise performances that reflect upon and change our realities. Boal's techniques and theories figure prominently in the essays that follow, primarily because the clarity of his methods as a form of praxis and their relevance across many cultural boundaries make them adaptable to diverse locations, circumstances, purposes, and communities.[11]

It is important to include a discussion of context when considering the application of community-based pedagogical methods. The purpose of *Radical Acts* is not to simply provide a practical manual on feminist theatre pedagogy, but to engage in a reflection on the contexts of those methods. Within the artistic and academic boundaries of theatre, discussions have brought to the forefront several crises that shape feminist theatre pedagogies. The representation of women within the various facets of theatre disciplines has been one stumbling block, dividing women and men along a body/mind continuum that keeps women within the realms of acting, costuming, or education, while excluding them from the important roles of writing, directing, and producing theatre. Within the narrowly defined realm of professional Western text-based theatre, less than 17% of professional theatre is written or directed by women, a number that has only slowly increased since the 1980s and is always at risk of plateauing or backsliding (New York State Council on the Arts).[12] However, gender representation is merely *one* part of the larger crisis in professional theatre, which struggles with a dearth of funding and entrenched class and racial biases. When asking why theatre doesn't represent and serve diverse populations, we must recognize that traditional methods have narrowed audiences and the only way to truly open up the field is to invent new approaches to serve the particularities of concrete contexts and specific audiences. Looking more broadly at theatrical activity outside of the professional realm, there are many innovative possibilities for the application of theatre, but understanding the delicate and complex relationship of an artistic method to its audience and its context is an art in and of itself.

This collection also highlights relationships among teachers and artists working together in the academy. With little or no support for the arts in U.S. society, many feminist artists have benefited from either short-term residencies in educational venues or they have found themselves moving from the professional theatre world into full-time positions in the academy. The community of teachers and artists in this book demonstrate the important dialogue between teachers and artists, providing a fuller understanding of the genealogy of feminist pedagogies in theatre studies and artistic practice. Certainly there are tensions between artists and academics which have elicited heated, significant, and productive discussions, particularly within the Women and Theatre Program. This volume resists divisions between theory and practice. We believe that we cannot understand feminist pedagogical work in theatre without acknowledging the presence and labor of feminist artists who interact with the academy. We must acknowledge all our voices and pedagogical strategies and the differences among us. For this reason, we have included interviews with artists that allow us to embrace the tensions that fuel our exchanges and allow artists to speak in their own words.

The crises of theatre as an art form in our culture has led us to scrutinize how we teach it in our universities and pre-professional training programs. In her article, "Educating the Creative Theatre Artist," Sonja Kuftinec cites the Association for Theatre in Higher Education's Task Force on Expanding Roles of Theatre in Education, noting that when responding to the question of "what they wish they had been taught," professional artists working within diverse community-based contexts responded: "collaboration, ensemble-building, idea development, interdisciplinary approaches to creating art, listening, conflict resolution, community engagement, and application of artistic skills in a wide range of settings" (46). Each of these skills might suggest the usefulness of a feminist pedagogy in theatre studies that balances or challenges the traditional focus on canonical literature, artistic skills, and individual accomplishments. While artistic excellence in technique is still fundamental to producing effective theatre, and while technical training and familiarity with text-based work is still vital, devised work using community-based techniques can, as many of our contributors demonstrate, be particularly powerful and relevant.

In response to these tensions, theatre and performance studies curricula have undergone a number of transformations, many of which have been recently documented in collections like Stucky and Wimmer's *Teaching*

Performance Studies and Fliotsos and Medford's *Teaching Theatre Today.* As practitioners of a relatively young academic discipline, theatre teachers in higher education have just begun to reflect deeply on the need to develop innovative pedagogical approaches to theatre and theorize its place within an academic culture that has historically marginalized it. Many who teach in the liberal arts have discovered theatre's interdisciplinary potential to enhance humanities core courses and teach multiple skill sets. In disciplines such as languages and literatures in higher education, professors are discovering the potential of theatre as a pedagogical tool that can negotiate the boundaries of cultures, engage mind and body, employ multiple languages (verbal and non-verbal), and illuminate the semiotic production of meaning beyond the stage.[13] The techniques of performance studies have similarly been incorporated into multiple disciplinary practices, including performance ethnography, protest performance, the performance of literature, theology education, neuroscience, digital technology, and even government and business (Stucky and Wimmer). These multiple locations also include Women's Studies and other interdisciplinary programs that have discovered the potential of theatre to create classroom community, explore embodied knowledge, sustain public argument, acknowledge student difference and experience, and move toward action and real social change.

TRANSFORMATION THROUGH THEATRE

Margaret Wilkerson explains that theatre does not passively serve audiences, but rather maintains the active potential to transform them: "Theatre provides an opportunity for a community to come together and reflect on itself…. It is not only the mirror through which a society can reflect upon itself–it also helps to shape the perceptions of that culture through the power of its imagining" (239). *Radical Acts* documents the imaginative ways in which theatre and teaching work together in reshaping individuals, disciplinary knowledges, and culture in a quest for social justice. These essays chart a continuum of transformations and examine how the act of creative freedom can inform the goals of political freedom. As philosopher of aesthetic education Maxine Greene writes, freedom "…never occurs in a vacuum. Freedom cannot be conceived apart from a matrix of social, economic, cultural, and psychological conditions. It is within the matrix that selves take shape or are created through choice of action in the changing situations of life. The degree and quality of whatever freedom is achieved are functions of the perspectives available, and the reflectiveness on the choices made" (*The Dialectics of Freedom* 80).

Here we present a matrix that allows us to chart how feminist teachers, artists, and activists seek freedom by engaging multiple perspectives through theatre. Ultimately, Greene and other feminist theorists challenge us to continue to expand the perspectives and choices available, taking us out of our comfort zones as we use theatre to challenge the different situations within which we find ourselves and to create creative coalitions that bridge differences.

In her interview with Lisa Jo Epstein in this volume, Deb Margolin articulates the simultaneously delicate and radical development that can occur through theatre. She says,

> ...good art, is pre-political in its essence. It does not take place on a political continuum in its initial, tender budding impulses; it is profoundly personal, it is profoundly of the sentiment and the spirit, and then as it grows, develops, it is perforce political in its nature. And as it steps forward and presents itself to a group of people, it has a political valence that can be embraced, that is radical in its personal-ness, particularly when it is done by women, and people of color. (122-23)

The essays presented here move between the healing and therapeutic roles of theatre arts and the more politicized act of testifying and witnessing. Between these two impulses there is rich terrain in which feminist teachers, artists, and activists create egalitarian spaces for interaction, explore the permeable boundaries between art and life, engage ethical dilemmas, and challenge dominant ways of knowing.

NOTES

[1] Fisher 44.

[2] Dolan 17.

[3] hooks *Teaching to Transgress*, 207.

[4] For example, many educators have recognized that a feminist pedagogy that resists the authoritarian role of the teacher merely inverts the hierarchy, creating instead the tyranny of the student. However, the metaphor of performance allows educators to conceive of the relationship between teacher and student as dynamic and changing. Activist educators whose discussions have informed us include: Berenice Malka Fisher, Shauna Butterick and Jan Selman, Kevin Kumashiro, and Sondra Perl.

[5] The Women and Theatre Program is a focus group within the larger Association for Theatre in Higher Education. It sponsors an annual pre-conference and the Jane Chambers playwriting competition, among other activities. For more information, see www.athe.org/wtp.

[6] The organization began as the Women's Caucus of the American Theatre Association in the 1970s and later became the Women and Theatre Program (WTP). Members of the organization have become significant leaders in the Association for Theatre in Higher Education, and its history and conference proceedings have been chronicled in articles like Rhonda Blair's "A History of the Women and Theatre Program." (*Women & Performance: A Journal of Feminist Theory*, Vol. 4, No. 2, Summer 1989) and Juli Burk's "Shifting Positionalities: Interrogating Cultural Pluralism." *Theatre Topics*. 3.1 (March 1993): 71-75.

[7] For these insights, we are indebted to Mady Schutzman's essays, such as "Jok(er)ing: Joker Runs Wild" in *A Boal Companion* (New York: Routledge, 2006) where she notes that "community teaches...that paradox can be lived, endured, and offered up as an action not an object.... Community is thus flexible, humorous, capable of accommodating what challenges it without breaking" (139). Her insights on the joker as trickster illustrate how many feminist teachers build community through their teaching.

[8] *The Applied and Interactive Theatre Guide* provides comprehensive information on this family of techniques, which applies theatre arts outside of strictly artistic venues (http://www.tonisant.com/aitg/).

[9] There are many foremothers, such as Jane Addams, Winifred Ward, Dorothy Heathcote, and Cecily O'Neil, whose work as teachers led to innovations in drama education and liberatory education. This is not to suggest that men, like John Dewey for example, did not participate in advancing such libera-

tory educational methods. We want to emphasize, however, that women's contributions have been relegated to educational spheres and, even there, many of their contributions have been overlooked.

[10] For more on the tensions between feminism and Theatre of the Oppressed, see Armstrong, "Negotiating Feminist Identities in Theatre of the Oppressed" in *A Boal Companion*, edited by Schutzman and Cohen-Cruz.

[11] For more on the multiple resonances of Boal's work within disciplines and discourses such as race, postcolonialism, and therapy, consult *A Boal Companion*.

[12] The New York Arts Council's 2002 study of the presence of women in professional theatre reveals the more complex layers of this dismal statistic. Although the actual number of women directors or writers who have work produced in professional venues fluctuates each year, sadly, most of these plays are by the same two or three well-known women playwrights (Paula Vogel, Eve Ensler, or Suzan-Lori Parks, for example).

[13] The National Symposium of Theatre Educators, led by Domnica Radulescu at Washington and Lee University, for example, is one such group of educators devising theatrical methods of engagement from within their own disciplines. See Radulescu and Fox, *The Theater of Teaching and the Lessons of Theater*.

WORKS CITED

Blair, Rhonda. "A History of the Women and Theatre Program." *Women & Performance: A Journal of Feminist Theory.* 4.2 (Summer 1989): 5-13..

Armstrong, Ann Elizabeth. "Negotiating Feminist Identities in Theatre of the Oppressed." *A Boal Companion: Dialogues on Theatre and Cultural Politics.* Eds. Mady Schutzman and Jan Cohen Cruz. London and New York: Routledge, 2006: 173-184.

Aston, Elaine. *Feminist Theatre Practice; A Handbook.* New York: Routledge, 1999.

Berkely, Anne. "Phronesis or techne? Theatre studies as moral agency." *Research in Drama Education.* 10.2 (June 2005): 213-227.

Boal, Augusto. *Games for Actors and Non-Actors.* 2nd Ed. New York; Routledge, 2002.

Boler, Megan. *Feeling Emotion.* New York: Routledge, 1999.

Burk, Juli Thompson. "Shifting Positionalities: Interrogating Cultural Pluralism." *Theater Topics.* 3.1 (1995): 71-75.

Butterwick, Shauna and Jan Selman. "Telling Stories and creating Participatory Audience: Deep Listening in a Feminist Popular Theatre Project." Proceedings of the 41st Adult Education Research Conference, 2000. <http://www.edst.educ.ubc.ca/aerc/2000/butterwicks&selmanj-final.PDF>, 1 October 2005.

Cohen-Cruz, Jan. *Local Acts:Community-based Performance in the United States.* New Brunswick, NJ: Rutgers University Press, 2005.

Dolan, Jill. *Geographies of Learning: Theory and Practice, Activism and Performance.* Middletown, CT: Wesleyan UP, 2001.

Donkin, Ellen and Susan Clement, eds. *Upstaging Big Daddy: Directing Theatre as if Gender and Race Matter.* Ann Arbor: University of Michigan Press, 1992.

Fisher, Berenice Malka. *No Angel in the Classroom: Teaching Through Feminist Discourse.* Lanham, MD: Rowman & Littlefield Publishers, Inc., 2001.

Fliotsos, Anne L. and Gail S. Medford, eds. *Teaching Theatre Today: Pedagogical Views of Theatre in Higher Education.* New York: Palgrave Macmillan, 2004.

Freire, Paulo. *Pedagogy of the Oppressed.* New York: Continuum, 2003.

Greene, Maxine. *The Dialectic of Freedom.* New York: Teachers College Press, 1988.

hooks, bell. *Teaching to Transgress: Education as the Practice of Freedom.* New York: Routledge, 1994.

hooks, bell. *Teaching Community: A Pedagogy of Hope.* New York: Routledge, 2003.

Kuftinec, Sonja. "Educating the Creative Theatre Artist." *Theatre Topics.* 11.1 (March 2001): 43-53.

Kumashiro, Kevin. "Against Repetition: Addressing Resistance to Anti-Oppressive Change in the Practices of Learning, Teaching, Supervising, and Researching." *Race and Higher Education: Rethinking Pedagogy in Diverse College Classrooms.* Howell and Tuitt, eds. Cambridge, MA: Harvard University Press, 2003: 67-92.

Macdonald, Amie and Susan Sanchez-Casal, eds. *Twenty-First Century Feminist Classrooms: Pedagogies of Identity and Difference.* New York: Palgrave Macmillan, 2002.

Maher, Frances and Mary Kay Thompson Tetreault. *The Feminist Classroom.* Lanham, MD: Rowman & Littlefield, 2001.

McLaren, Peter. *Schooling as Ritualized Performance.* 3rd Ed. Lanham, MD: Rowman & Littlefield, 1999.

New York State Council On The Arts Theatre Program. "Report On The Status Of Women: A Limited Engagement? Executive Summary." 2002. <http://www.Americantheaterweb.Com/Nysca/Opening.Html>. 19 March 2006.

Perl, Sondra. "Teaching and Practice." *Race and Higher Education: Rethinking Pedagogy in Diverse College Classrooms.* Howell and Tuitt, eds. Cambridge, MA: Harvard University Press, 2003. 165-188.

Radulescu, Domnica and Maria Stadter Fox, eds. *The Theatre of Teaching and the Lessons of Theater.* Lanham, MD: Lexington Books, 2005.

Schutzman, Mady. "Jok(er)ing: Joker Runs Wild" *A Boal Companion: Dialogues on Theatre and Cultural Politics.* London and New York: Routledge, 2006. 133-145.

Spolin, Viola. *Improvisation for Theatre.* 3rd Ed. Chicago: Northwestern University Press, 1999.

Stucky, Nathan and Cynthia Wimmer, eds. *Teaching Performance Studies.* Carbondale, IL: Southern Illinois University Press., 2002.

Sant, Tony and Joel Plotkin, editors. "The Applied and Interactive Theatre Guide." <http://www.tonisant.com/aitg/>, 18 March 2006.

Wilkerson, Margaret. "Demographics and the Academy." *The Performance of Power: Theatrical Discourse and Politics.* Ed. Sue-Ellen Case nd Janelle Reinelt. Iowa City: University of Iowa Press, 1991. 238-41.

1 POSITIONING OUR VOICES

We begin by featuring autobiographical essays in which contributors position themselves as feminist teachers in classrooms, rehearsals, and institutions. When they activate their own voices as teachers, they encourage their students to do so as well. When they tell their own stories, they liberate themselves from positions of neutrality that many traditional educational systems value. Candidly revealing their biases and experiences, the feminist teachers represented in this section position themselves in relationship to their specific contexts and encourage their students to do likewise. Students, therefore, learn from a teacher who has the expertise to facilitate rather than indoctrinate. In this way, teachers and students enrich the educational conversation in a mutual production of knowledge.

Autobiography assists the writers as they recall their journeys through embodied collaborations in theatre. In "Winnie in the Attic," Domnica Radalescu's recalls her discovery of the value of the collaborative processes of theatre in communist Romania, where she acted in a production of Samuel Beckett's *Happy Days* for an experimental theatre company. When four women shared the role of Winnie, they inadvertently discovered female solidarity and a feminist rehearsal process. Radulescu later re-created her experience with this production with students in the United States, raising their feminist consciousness in intense and sometimes hilarious ways while revealing important cultural boundaries.

In "An Irrevocable Promise," Cherríe Moraga describes doing theatre with her son's second grade class in Oakland, California. Moraga discovered that second-graders were able to instinctively critique colonial history as they explored the sensual, visceral processes of theatre. Moraga's speech reminded us of why theatre is a powerful means of embodied remembering, and she illuminates how theatre comprises a powerful pedagogy of resistance as it re-enacts history, raises political consciousness and brings body and spirit in dialogue with community. In short, she awakens our passions and clarifies what's at stake in teaching and making theatre through feminist politics.

While Radulescu and Moraga focus on cultural hegemony, Ellen Margolis and Corinne Rusch-Drutz critique the myth of "objective institutions" that claim they are not participating in ideologies that perpetuate gendered oppression. In "Playing Out a Past, Recovering an Education," Margolis' stage is her classroom where she creates a pedagogy that takes on her own educational history. She, like Radulescu and Moraga, challenges the hegemony and tyranny of traditional pedagogies of theatre history by encouraging embodied learning and insisting on inflecting all of her pedagogy with the personal, whether it focuses on her own education or her experiences as a mother. In this way, she encourages her students to engage in embodied collaboration as a way undermining institutionalized disciplinary practices in teaching theatre history.

Corinne Rusch-Drutz in "Good Female Parts" looks at how pedagogy is institutionalized through autobiographical accounts of women graduates of Canadian theatre training programs. Rusch-Drutz describes the ways institutions often require women to neutralize their regional dialects and lose weight in order to be competitive in the Broadway "market." When institutions require these kinds of coercive voice and body altering practices, they are, of course, replicating a culturally driven "pedagogy of tyranny" and gendered and racialized sameness. She, like many of the authors in *Radical Acts*, calls for engaging students in devised projects that will have the potential to develop international and intercultural perspectives.

Early incarnations of feminist pedagogy were influenced by the consciousness raising groups of the early women's movement. In these groups, women met and talked about gender oppression in their personal and public lives, providing one another with support and planning activist strategies for change. However, when consciousness-raising was the model for feminist teaching during these early years, students' stories of oppression often overshadowed the important voices of teachers. Without negating the importance of students' voices in feminist teaching strategies, the four essays in this section establish a significant tenet for feminist theatre pedagogy by demonstrating the centrality of the teacher's voice in situating knowledge. Teachers and students strive for balance by honoring voices that will encourage both intellectual rigor and artistic innovation in classrooms and rehearsals.

WINNIE IN THE ATTIC
TOWARD A FEMINIST AWAKENING IN BECKETT'S *HAPPY DAYS*

Domnica Radulescu

More than two decades ago, when I was a student of English literature at
the University of Bucharest in Romania, I joined a student theatre which was
significantly influenced by the methods and philosophy of the Polish director
Jerzy Grotowski. In the 1960s and 70s Grotowski's Laboratory Theatre developed a highly experimental method of performance which focused on the interaction between actors and audience and utilized intensely physical acting
techniques.[1] Later in life, as a political émigré to the United States and a university teacher of French literature, these techniques and my experience of the
Grotwskian Romanian theatre proved to be extremely valuable, not only in my
directorial endeavors with undergraduate students but also as a catalyst for my
own feminist awakening. The purpose of this essay is to explore how my experiences with the Attic Theatre in Romania have informed my current pedagogical practices in my teaching of languages and literature through theatre, and to
chronicle my commitment to both teaching and theatre, which developed
simultaneously. I discuss pedagogical and performance theories particularly in
terms of the experience of female actors and from a feminist perspective. As a
literature professor at an American university with two and a half centuries of
an all-male tradition, I have made, over the years, prolific use of my training in
the Romanian experimental theatre, and ended up creating theatrical events
and experiences with my students which were subversive of patriarchal modes
of directing, teaching, and thinking. This set of pedagogical tools has facilitated
a better understanding of the intersections between the pedagogical relevance
of performance and the raising of feminist consciousness through the practice
of theatre. Further, this essay will discuss a subversion of patriarchal structures
within this already politically subversive theatre in Romania, principally
through collaborative directing and the female solidarity that ensued from it.

BEING WINNIE IN THE ATTIC

The theatre I was involved with as a student was called The Attic and was
literally situated in the attic of an old building in Bucharest; ironically, the same
building which housed the communist youth organization during the 1980s.

The theatre proudly considered itself a Grotowskian "poor theatre," technical sophistication being regarded as an impediment to the actor's work and performance. Costumes and sets were of utmost simplicity and were all re-usable. Although most shows and training took place in the theatre space itself, the troupe also traveled and gave shows in non-theatrical spaces such as restaurants, mental asylums, and school gyms, attempting to achieve a sense of flux and continuation "between theatre event and life event" (Wiles 114). We never rehearsed until we had done an hour of exercises to enhance our concentration, focus our emotional and physical energies, and make us look inward.[2]

One of the most exciting and revolutionary aspects of our "Attic" theatre was precisely the fact that we often performed outside our "attic" theatre space. In fact each one of our shows was meant to have the freedom to be performed in any kind of space and to be taken on the road. While the theatre of Grotowski was not an "activist" theatre in the sense that many feminist theatres are, neither was our Romanian experimental theatre. However, in an oppressive communist dictatorship, the lack of a foregrounded political ideology of this theatre was, in fact, a form of political dissidence.[3] Since we were expected to be the "communist youth" of the country, the fact that we were engaging day and night in a theatre which had little to do with communism was in itself a political stance. Performing Shakespeare or Japanese Kabuki theatre or Samuel Beckett's existentialist play *Happy Days* was, in that context, an act of political subversion. The Attic offered us some sort of relief from the falsity and oppression of the propaganda and ideology of the everyday. This was a place where we were spared hearing about the activities of the Communist Party and the "heroic" deeds of a tyrannical illiterate president and where we could be relieved of our everyday fears. The Attic was a space devoid of all associations with the outside world, cleanly black and neutral—in fact, one of the very few spaces we encountered in our lives which did not have the president's portrait hanging above our heads.

The artistic director of our theatre directed all the shows, about three or four a year. He made all the major decisions in the theatre and arranged tours and performances outside the theatre. Most of the actors were university students, some from theatre departments but also from disciplines as remote to theatre as geology or engineering. Our artistic director ran the theatre with something of an "iron hand," often losing his temper in rehearsals when directions were not carried out the way he wanted them to be. Yet the actors, even the few who were not students and were closer in age to him, greatly respected him and willingly took any amount of bad temper and harsh criticism in order to be in a show.

As the rising young intelligentsia in the capital of one of the most oppressively communist countries in the Eastern Bloc, we lived in passionate hatred of the regime and had unbridled greed for cutting-edge culture, existentialist philosophy, and American rock. What we most wanted and strived for was freedom of expression, freedom of speech, and recognition of our uniqueness as individuals. We would easily put up with the whims of a temperamental director who led us through the magic paths of theatre and with whom we could rehearse *Hamlet* until 3 a.m. and talk about the best actors and actresses of all times, or about the meaning of life and human nature as revealed in theatre. We could even utter words such as "spiritual" or "metaphysical," which were part of a vocabulary that was banned from public speech as "retrograde" and reflective of the dangerous "bourgeois mentality." Our general education had been sandwiched in between obligatory classes of Marxist economy, Russian language, and special meetings and/or classes of intense indoctrination about the role of the Communist Party in our overall "happiness." If ever a perfect example of what I would like to call the "pedagogy of tyranny" were to be found, then certainly such classes and meetings would be precisely that. Not only was the material of these subjects practically force-fed to us, but the classes and/or meetings never allowed discussion, questioning, or self-expression. Luckily, and paradoxically, the Romanian educational system had kept some of its rigorous study of the liberal arts and humanities from the pre-communist era, and numerous theatres which experimented with traditional forms of expression or, like our Attic theatre, subverted the very foundation of that "pedagogy of tyranny," still existed.

Bucharest, once called "the little Paris of the Balkans," was singing its swan song before sliding rapidly into the black hole of despair and horror that preceded the 1989 Revolution. The secret police were everywhere, watching and listening to us from every dark corner with diabolic perseverance; yet in our rebellious youth, we still filled Bucharest's cafés and spent hours over beers, smoking unfiltered cigarettes, discussing Heidegger, Nietzche, and Plato, or telling jokes about our leader and the Party in hushed tones. By some kind of fluke, and largely due to the ignorance of the communist leaders, the Bucharest theatres were still staging plays like Bulgakov's *The Master and Marguerita,* or Beckett's *Waiting for Godot,* or the cutting edge, politically charged production of Shakespeare's *The Tempest,* directed by the famous Liviu Ciulei, in which every intelligent Romanian citizen identified the monster Caliban with the "beloved leader" Ceausescu. Theatres were packed and we, the students of the University of Bucharest, would get our feet frostbitten on cold November nights, waiting in line for tickets. It was also students like us who, on some cold December nights in 1989, were going to take over the university square and give their lives so that words could be uttered freely, life lived to its fullest, and theatre played without fear. A conspicuous aspect of the Romanian Revolution was that most of its leaders were poets, actors, and theatre directors who took to the streets reclaiming freedom.

In the spring of 1981, a female actor in our theatre (who aspired to be a director) found a translation of a play by Samuel Beckett entitled *O ce zile fericite!* ("*Happy Days*"). It was a play about a woman buried first halfway, and then all the way up to her neck, inside a mound of dry earth who carries on through her torrid days under a merciless sun with amazing fortitude and grace, and at times with effervescent humor, reciting bits of love letters and half-forgotten lines of famous poetry, and reminiscing about the frightful and happy moments of her childhood and youth. The play intrigued our aspiring director enormously and she shared it with a group of four women, myself included. We immediately became entranced by the character and decided to stage the play. Winnie's line, "I am the one, I say the one, then the other. Now the one, then the other" (Beckett 51), prompted us each to play "one" of the Winnies, thus sharing the role. This was a revolutionary step within the hierarchical and largely male-dominated work system of the Attic theatre, a step which lead to a profound experience of artistic, emotional, and intellectual collaboration for the four of us.

The period of preparation for the part was maybe one of the most emotionally and artistically intense periods of my life, a time of true soul searching. I started to intuit with more intensity than I had ever before that there was something amiss in the gender politics of my country, and even in the theatre where I looked for refuge from the wrongs of the everyday. This was partly due to the strong female subjectivity of Winnie's character and partly due to the fact that as we started developing our show it became apparent that we did things differently than the male director of the theatre. There was no ordering around, no yelling or harsh criticism in our rehearsals; instead there was a lot of camaraderie, a lot of warmth, and lots of laughs. It was hard work, yet it also seemed effortless.

During this period, we watched several films showing Grotowski's actors rehearsing, playing, training, and working out. We tried to emulate them and earnestly did the special breathing exercises, the various acrobatics, and the voice and body movements that they were doing, in a process that was intended to develop a way of life for us rather than just a role or a set of exercises. More than two decades later, as I find myself closer to Winnie's age than I was then, the experience of the Attic and of that Winnie has not lost its attraction and intensity. On the contrary, it seems that I have been processing and living with it all of these years. I understand now why the actresses who have performed Beckett's characters talk with reverence about their experiences while also admitting the excruciating quality of pushing and testing their bodies and souls to their limits.[4]

The intense emotional bonds we established among ourselves and between ourselves and the character manifested in a fluid movement between gesture and language, emotion, thought and the body, and the self and the other. Much like Luce Irigaray's concept of "mimesis-mimickry," our process revealed that "patriarchal mimesis" could be subverted when women assume "the feminine role deliberately" and blur the boundaries "between inner and outer, depth and surface, truth and falsehood" (Diamond 373-76).[5] Looking back at working on

Happy Days I realize that the kind of collaborative direction we had at the Attic was very close to the type that takes place in feminist theatres and experimental groups, although probably none of us at the Attic Theatre had ever pronounced the word "feminist" in our lives. Instead, the process of engaging mimesis with mimicry brought forth a feminist consciousness.

The repetitive, slightly hypnotic nature of our practice–with its stress on gestures and the use of objects and of a neutral, timeless space–resembled the ritualistic nature of early feminist theatres, like those created by Maro Green and Caroline Griffin, which produced shows such as *More*, a production that has been seen as a feminist response to Beckett's *Waiting for Godot*.[6] Like *Waiting for Godot*, the text of *Happy Days* is replete with highly ritualistic gestures and repetitive formulae, such as the way Winnie starts each day by saying a prayer or the way she displays her objects around her in the morning and picks them up at night. To the ritualistic aspects of the text we added our own. One of the Winnies repeatedly put on and took off make-up during the show. Such gestures could be construed, in light of feminist theory, as destabilizing, time and again, the female presence as either "a consumable object" or a "commodified presence" (Love 276). As I re-live and re-discover the experience of "Winnie in the Attic," I find myself discovering feminist theory in practice.[7]

I was a college student, three decades younger than the character I was playing, yet Winnie was everywhere inside my mind and my soul and I was everywhere inside Winnie. Talking to the other "Winnies," it was evident we all shared the feeling that working on that part was a singular experience in the sense that it both took us very deeply inside and very far outside ourselves. The combination of Beckett's text and Grotowski's methods seemed to harmoniously work together and to bring out the deepest of both the character and the actor. However, we also made our own rules, which departed from Grotowski's methods, from Beckett's authorial authority and, as I found out much later, from his directorial practices. The most important departure was the refusal of a hierarchical distribution of power among ourselves. We as actors were not subordinated to the will of the director as in Grotowski's theatre and in our own Attic Theatre. While actresses who worked with Beckett, such as Billie Whitelaw or Madelaine Renaud, express awe and respect for his directorial choices and authority, it is clear that there was a certain level of tyranny in Beckett's manipulation and exertion of the actresses' psyches, as well as their bodies. For example, Whitelaw admits she developed chronic spine problems as a result of acting in Beckett's plays and that she would be depressed for weeks on end after playing one of his characters (Kalb 242-44). Brenda Bynum said that Beckett puts his actors in straight jackets, as he does with the text, cutting off their bodies and their senses (BenZvi, *Women in Beckett* 53).

In our production of Beckett's *Happy Days*, we took possession of both the text and the methods we had learned and made them our own. We thus performed a multi-layered subversion of patriarchal authority: we subverted the very text we performed by dividing the role into four parts, multiplying Winnie's tragic role as a trapped female but also, inevitably, multiplying the means by which she transcends her predicament time and again. More specifically, if her agony was multiplied by four, so were her ironic smiles, comments, and gestures. If four Winnies complained about the torrid heat, it was also four pairs of eyes who glared ironically at the audience or at Willie, the semi-human husband crawling in the shade. At the same time, and in a powerful way, we stressed and enhanced the parts of the text which give voice to Winnie's subjectivity. As Linda BenZvi has justly noted, "What makes the play so riveting, despite its one constant voice, is Beckett's ability to divide the voice into voices, each with slightly different nuances" (*Samuel Beckett* 158).

Against Beckett's indications in the text, we also broke Winnie out of her physical imprisonment several times. In some of the crucial moments of the play when Winnie reaches certain emotional heights, only one of the Winnies remained immobile, while the others moved or danced around, suggesting in a concrete, literal manner Winnie's desire to free herself from her prison. Something told us instinctively that, oppressed as we already were living under a dictatorship, we did not need an added dose of significant physical discomfort in what we perceived to be a liberating experience.

A level of female solidarity, unmatched in that theatre before our show, had developed throughout our rehearsals. As we were getting closer to the opening night, all the men in the theatre were referring to our show as the "women's show," and we ended up spending more time in each other's company, practicing, talking about Winnie, and relating most of her lines to our own lives and experiences. We each found in Winnie something that was relevant to our own life experiences and realized more and more through contact with the character and with each other that, besides our overall oppression by the communist system of power, we were further oppressed as women, either as a result of the abundance of sexist attitudes and jokes or, as it became more obvious within our own experimental theatre, by hierarchical systems of power in which men gave the orders and women carried them out. We found great solace in Winnie's bitter jokes about the insensitive men in her life and we acted with great pathos. We dramatized, in a way which went beyond Beckett's stage directions, Winnie's reminiscence of a possible rape or sexual abuse in her childhood. Most importantly, we derived great satisfaction in breaking Winnie's immobility and lack of freedom. We interpreted Winnie's imprisonment as a horrifying reminder of our own imprisonment within a multi-layered system of oppression and thus derived a true sense of liberation by liberating our character. Furthermore, by establishing a profound sense of unity among ourselves via the different voices of the character, we discovered that solidarity *can* be a way to freedom, even if precarious in our situations. I remember one young woman coming to us after the opening show with her eyes filled with tears and saying to us, "There was so much yelling, yet it was so comforting and disturbing at once." Although we did have several scenes in which we became rowdy and loud, particularly when Winnie relives her childhood traumas or when she loses her patience with Willie, we also very carefully and deliberately orchestrated our silences and synchronized our movements in something that at times looked almost like a ballet.

With regard to the actual physical production, improvisation and creating something from scratch was the key. The set requires the creation of a large hard mound to entrap the actress playing Winnie. We did not have the means to make a mound for Winnie so we used stools, the only things available to us, to suggest her entrapment. We also took turns being the Winnie in Winnie's mind, moving around while the main Winnie talked, restrained in her fixed position under a threatening yet fragile mound of wooden and canvas stools skillfully entangled with each other. We synchronized our gestures and movements as closely as possible and froze in our places every time one of the Winnies spoke. The goal was to establish a unity of thought and purpose among ourselves. Collectively, we formed one person who unfolded into her many dimensions onstage. One of us was the dreamy, poetic Winnie; another was the bawdy, sensuous one; another was the ironic and mocking one; and another was the central, frightened Winnie who tells the story of possible rape and horror, and who prays and expresses her sorrows. We each ended up sharing, to some extent, the moods of the other three. We were all expected to know the entire text, whether we said it out loud or not, and to utter every word in our minds as each of the Winnies spoke. Thus we were at all times the same character, yet slightly different. Since we were all part of the same character, a bond was established between us that unified and synchronized our thoughts to an almost uncanny degree. We were often caught performing the same kinds of gestures or uttering the same lines even during the rehearsal breaks.

In *Speculum*, Irigaray notes that "one must assume the feminine role deliberately. Which means already to convert a form of subordination into an affirmation, and thus to begin to thwart it..." (Diamond 373). Though we lacked the theoretical knowledge or language to articulate our stance and our way of producing and acting, this is precisely what we did as we worked the ins and outs of this tragic female character. For instance, at one point in her monologue, oppressed by the merciless heat, Winnie starts fantasizing about the spontaneous combustions of things, including her own self. She says, "With the sun blazing so much fiercer, is it not natural things should go on fire never known to do so, in this way I mean, spontaneous like. Shall I myself not melt perhaps in the end, or burn..." (Beckett 38). At this point, the Winnies who were free from the mound started swirling around actually setting fire to pieces of paper which, we had decided, represented the burning of old love letters. Setting fire to remainders of lost relationships proved to be liberating and exhilarating. We danced, we laughed, we swirled around while effecting the combustion of love letters in a manner which became both spontaneous and perfectly synchro-nized. It was a scene that simply emerged and which had a different edge with each performance. Finally, what made this scene so authentic and theatrical at the same time was the fact that we freely brought to it our own experiences, even burning scraps of our own love letters.[8]

In many traditional and non-traditional ways, Winnie is a tragic character, a heroine whose physical suffering and gruesome entrapment form not only the center of the play's discourse but also the physical reality of the character onstage. Actresses who have played this role have noted its physically demand-ing aspect, especially the pain, discomfort, and panic of being entrapped; Charlotte White admits to starting every rehearsal in Carey Perloff's production with a good dose of crying (Perloff 166).[9] The idea of creating a metaphor which suggests the drama of female entrapment points to the various levels of the oppression of women in society. In our sharing of both the role and the directorial process, Winnie's suffering and discomfort, sadness and hopeless-ness, were made more poignant and more bearable. It also allowed us to show that Winnie takes control over her suffering and to a certain degree transcends it. We de-centered and shared the suffering, humiliation, and discomfort of the heroine and thus established a certain distance between the expression of suf-fering and the heroine who endures it. We had the intuition that the heroine's suffering would be diffused and dispersed if she were multiplied into several voices and bodies who each shared a little part of it.

In terms of our status as female students at the University of Bucharest in the early eighties, our Winnie experience rendered us more gutsy in dealing with the humiliations of the everyday. For instance, it was common for men in positions of power to make inappropriate sexual advances or comments to young women. I became much more vehemently resistant to such behavior after experiencing Winnie and thinking so much about what it was to be a woman in a man's world. The next time the editor of a student literary journal for which I was writing made a wildly inappropriate comment, accompanied by an even more inappropriate gesture, I ruthlessly put him in his place and never spoke to him again. One day a secret police officer approached me and sug-gested that I become a collaborator, which would have meant informing on the "irregular activities" of my fellow students at the university. In that moment, the defiant Winnie smile and the echoes of the screams of joy from my fellow actresses burning old love letters joined with the nausea and hatred rising in my throat at the suggestion and helped me find the courage to reject the abom-inable offer.

That theatrical experience also helped me learn how to be rebellious and subversive in productive and creative ways. For instance, as students of lan-guage and literature we were obligated to pass a one-year course on pedagogy. The articulation of a certain set of rules about teaching glossed over by commu-nist ideology was painfully banal and boring to us. After late nights spent rehearsing Winnie's role, I remember finding the pedagogy classes even more difficult to sit through. As I prepared to teach my first class a year later, I kept seeing the four Winnies swirl around the stage, tearing and burning old love letters. I decided I was not going to follow the model proposed to us, but follow my own instincts and make it my goal to get the students to talk and participate, to do something precisely the opposite of the "pedagogy of tyranny."

Since I had grown up among both teachers and artists, I always thought that teaching, poetry, theatre, and constant dialogue and questioning must all be inseparable in some profound way. But I also remember that as I plunged more deeply into the production of *Happy Days*, I became angrier at the director of the Attic Theatre and his authoritative ways. Somehow all of that was present in my mind as I was frantically preparing my lesson plan the night before my first class. That first class ended up being the epiphany of my vocation. All ideas of a "pedagogy" actually disappeared once I found myself in front of thirty high school boys and girls eager to learn English. I felt entirely at ease, yet overwhelmed by waves of affection for the students in front of me. The sense of giddiness and exhilaration I experienced from allowing those students to perform and to express and discover themselves convinced me that I had to devote the rest of my life to teaching. Two decades of teaching and theatre has confirmed for me time and again two important truths that were revealed to me the morning of my first class: that teaching and theatre are most authentic and genuine when they are focused toward facilitating a process of self-discovery, when students are, as bell hooks so beautifully puts it, engaged in "the practice of freedom" and teaching is done "in a manner that respects and cares for the souls of our students" (*Teaching to Transgress* 13).

bell hooks' discussion of the importance of awareness and respect for diversity within the academy is pertinent for my experience in communist Romania, though less from the standpoint of race and sexual orientation than of individuality and world view. Oppressive regimes all aim at preventing self-discovery and promoting uniformity of thought and action under a set of rigid rules. And all oppressive regimes can be seen as extreme forms of patriarchy because they all aim in their respectively violent ways toward a false "harmony" among individuals and toward an erasure of difference. Our communist leader was often called "the father of our nation." During Hitler's rule, Germany was called the "fatherland." In both regimes, uniformity of behavior, physical appearance, and ways of thinking were imposed through brutal means. In both regimes, women were often used and abused without justice ever being done. Ceausescu's son, Nicu, used to pick women he found attractive in bars or restaurants and make them his lovers by force. I still remember, with piercing sadness, the gaunt, pale, frozen expression on the face of our world-famous gymnast Nadia Comaneci, walking on the arm of this notorious "son of the nation" during an important sports event, when she was nineteen. I understand intellectually now what I instinctively understood then: that within the many levels of oppression

I was living under, women were at the very bottom and that our Winnie experience was something of a little feminist revolution.

Ultimately, both my experience of acting and teaching discussed here could be inscribed within Augusto Boal's theory of an "Aesthetics of the Oppressed." I mean this in the sense of developing what he calls an "Aesthetic Process" which ultimately leads to a "Product" through which individuals, by using the "capacity to metaphorize," end up doing what oppressive systems prevent them from doing: expressing themselves in an authentic way. This process subverts the uniformity of a false art created under the "guidance" of an oppressive ideology. One of the most laughable and embarrassing aspects of the Romanian state- or party-directed art, poetry, and theatre was their lack of elasticity, of subtlety, of individuality. They were simply uniform and trite. For instance, all poems written by those who were designated as "national" poets had the same ring and lack of metaphor, as they all did the same thing: falsely praised the glory and "nobility" of an illiterate, tyrannical leader. The pedagogy of tyranny did the same: it told us, without any room for questioning or dialogue, that our leader was the ultimate incarnation of human intelligence, generosity, and courage, when precisely the contrary was true. Thus, members of the Attic Theatre, by becoming immersed in a diverse theatrical repertoire, performed a radical subversion of communist ideology and the pedagogy of tyranny, developing an "Aesthetic of the Oppressed." What our collaborative direction of Beckett's *Happy Days* within that already subversive theatre did was to take this "Aesthetic of the Oppressed" a few steps further by breaking through the oppression of gender hierarchies. Even further, we exploded the canon of a male-created, male-directed aesthetic which was blind to gender differences and marginalized female subjectivity.

DIRECTING WINNIE

Years later, as a professor of literature and director of an annual theatre production in the U.S., Winnie still haunted me. I returned to her with my students in a university production performed in the original French. Partly for the practical reason of giving every woman in the class a speaking role, partly as a result of my own nostalgia for the theatrical experience of Winnie that I had in the Attic Theatre in Romania more than a decade earlier, I divided the part of Winnie into four different roles once again. I had the students perform similar, though much tamer and less time consuming, exercises—these American students being significantly less willing to put themselves on the line and push themselves to the limits of their endurance as we were in communist Romania.

However, other obstacles and reasons for subversion and resistance were present in my American experience of directing *Happy Days*. Washington and Lee University, the school where I have been teaching and directing plays for a decade, has been co-educational for only twenty years, as it used to be an all-male school educating "southern gentlemen." Eight years ago, when I directed

Happy Days, women were still something of a novelty and both men and women were still adjusting after only a little more than a decade of co-education. Most students at my university are from relatively conservative families, and feminism is still something of an exotic, if not a curse, word among many students. Sexual assault of women and alcohol-related sexual misconduct are significant problems, despite enhanced disciplinary regulations. Although it was the presence of female students that skyrocketed the academic ratings of the university and women enrolled on our campus arrive with and generally maintain higher GPAs, women's concerns and accomplishments are still secondary to those of men on campus. The Women's Studies Program, which I chair and helped found, is now only in its sixth year of existence and has encountered significant opposition from both students and some faculty since its inception. The women in my theatre class of eight years ago, even the more liberated ones, found Winnie "weird" at first. They felt very uncomfortable with a female character who is buried alive and who tries at all costs to survive each day with a certain amount of dignity and irony. The climactic point in the play, when Winnie recounts a childhood scene disturbingly reminiscent of a rape, increased their discomfort. It took me several years of teaching at Washington and Lee to understand that often women students carry within themselves similar, painful stories. It took some convincing and talking to get the actors to appear onstage in their camisoles and utter long monologues about broken love dreams, memories of rape, or insensitive men.

The more I relinquished my directorial power, the more successful I seemed to be as a director. After we had spent some time discussing Winnie's predicament, her thoughts, her wishes, her position onstage, her relationship to her half-wit husband, and the significance of her gestures, my students' acting started to flow, the words and gestures started to achieve a heightened level of coherence and fluidity. I let them divide and distribute Winnie's lines among themselves, knowing from my own experience in Romania that they would choose what felt closest to their personal experiences. In our production at the Attic Theatre, each one of the Winnies stood or walked around or danced at least once. However for this American production, I tried to move slightly closer to the original staging of Beckett's play, which calls for Winnie's entrapment while subverting this oppressive symbol in a different way. To do this, I created the suggestion of Winnie's entrapment by wrapping a piece of cloth around the actors, creating a scenic element that looked more like a mound than the stools in the Romanian production. I still felt I needed to resist the extreme level of discomfort that a solid mound of hard material would have entailed for them, as I felt it was oppressive, if not abusive, of the women's bodies. Beckett's notorious exigencies with his female actresses were, ironically, reenforcing what Beckett tried to represent symbolically through Winnie's entrapment. The same symbolism can be suggested with a mound or set which does not inflict physical pain onto the actress.

I watched my students experience the same process of merging with each other which had so conspicuously marked my Romanian experience of Winnie. Their faces started to twitch in the same manner, their eyes to blink at the same time, their hands to fidget in the same way and around the same lines. Instead of having the Winnies walk around and dance or freeze for periods of time while one of them talked, the way we had done in the Romanian production, we decided to have the four actresses hold the piece of cloth up to their waists in the first half of the play and up to their necks in the second half, with only minimal movement. They found the experience of sitting immobile and wrapped up in a heavy piece of cloth for the time of the rehearsals and of the show quite difficult. Mindful of the fine line between discomfort and real pain, I made sure that the most discomfort they would experience was that their limbs might get numb for a while or that they might get fidgety. More than anything, they found the act of sitting in one place for the duration of the play difficult from a psychological point of view. For us in Romania, freedom and the freedom of expression were of the essence and informed almost everything we did in the theatre. Just acting the classics in experimental ways during times when others were holding or participating in meetings of the communist youth was lived by us as a form of freedom of expression and a subversion of the regime. Creating and being part of different rigorous forms of artistic discipline than the one imposed on us by the Marxist regime was liberating. For my privileged American students, who have enjoyed the benefits of a free democratic society their entire lives, this is not really an issue. My American students were used to expressing themselves freely and manifesting their individuality; it was second nature to them, while for us, in Romania, it was something we had to struggle for every day. My American students, however, had issues with engaging in activities such as being trapped beneath a mound of cloth which forced them to push as far as possible the limits of their comfort and of accepted behaviors, the limits of their preconceived notions about the world, and the limits of their own consciousness. What was also an issue, in terms of a feminist pedagogy, was questioning the very notion of their freedom, discovering and coming to terms with the fact that everything was far from perfect in their worlds and in the society in which we live, democratic as it may be on the surface. In our case, the women in the cast discovered through their experience of Winnie and her entrapment that freedom, equality, and justice are still an issue when it comes to women, even in a democratic society. Through Winnie's experience, they became lucid about the manner in which patriarchy limits the freedom of women. In some way, the physical entrapment and discomfort they felt while being in Winnie's mound was the closest thing they had ever experienced to having a physical, literal experience of patriarchy as a structure. By being so close to each other physically their discomfort was intensified–intensified, but also, as they reported, somehow sublimated. Eventually, they said, their legs became so numb that they didn't know which were their own legs and which were the legs of their partners. That physical closeness ended up being a powerful experience and contributed to their psychological and emotional closeness to each other.

I urged the women playing Winnie, just as I had been urged during my Romanian experience, to bring as much as possible of themselves to the role, including physical objects to fill Winnie's bag. During one of the shows, one of the women took tampons out of her bag while another took out condoms. Ultimately, each of the Winnies became a unique individual and the students revealed themselves and their personal experiences in profound ways. Thus the actors achieved wholeness, a diversity among them and their experiences, and the variety of feminist positions they inhabited. They discovered their many differences while also realizing that they could feel an increased sense of solidarity not *despite*, but *because* of their differences. Of the group of four women, one was a neuroscience and French major; another an international studies in business and French major; another a ballet dancer, singer, and French major; and the fourth a French major who also sang and danced. One of the actors was Filipina and the other three were white. All were heterosexual and middle class. They were strikingly different, however, in temperament, life experiences, and in their understanding and approach to the play. In fact, these women argued with each other and had numerous clashes at the beginning of the rehearsal process. However, soon their acting started to flow and their words began to be better integrated with their gestures. Through the production process, these students transcended the stereotypical female rivalry and "cattiness" with which they began and transformed those negative energies into creative and emotional solidarity.

The fact that the students performed in French also enhanced their sense of freedom. The linguistic and cultural difference they experienced by acting in a different language allowed them to reveal aspects of themselves that they would not were they to perform in English. The experience of uprooting oneself, of detaching oneself from one's own language and culture, made it easier for these students to overcome their shyness, their inhibitions, and their insecurities because it gave them something like a protective cloak. In an even more profound, ontological way, this experience points to what humanist and cultural critics since Montaigne and Montesquieu, all the way to Edward Said, have been trying to tell us: that by acquiring a deep understanding of the Other, by actually completely putting oneself under the "skin" of the Other, one ends up better understanding oneself and actually becoming critical of the very process of "othering" those who are different. Via a non-native language, in which some were still struggling, my students connected with Winnie, who represented in so many ways someone very different from them: an older French woman with a heavy past, on the verge of a nervous breakdown. But interestingly, the moment when they managed to synchronize their speech to their gestures and use of objects was also the moment when they connected with Winnie at a gut level–and to like her, because they had become her, at least to a considerable degree. By the end of the course, the female students in my class had formed a sisterhood under Winnie's mound. Winnie's suffering, her sadness and often rage at her traumatic experiences, her irony and intelligence, and the meticulous way she cared for her personal hygiene with something of a poetic flair brought them to the understanding that their differences were to be cherished and that they still had so much to share.

Looking back at my directorial experience with *Happy Days* through the lens of both feminist theory and of my re-theorized experience of Winnie in Romania, one important conclusion I have to draw is that pedagogical concerns were almost inseparable from directorial concerns. That which made for a most genuine theatre experience also engendered an intense learning experience. The process of self-discovery, the accomplishment of a certain sense of solidarity among women, the celebration of difference, the increased awareness of the gruesome nature of the predicament of a woman who is "buried alive," the even more sobering realization that the image of a woman buried alive is disturbingly representative of the lives and status of so many women in society today, and, finally, the validation of anger and rebellion as legitimate feelings vis-à-vis such a predicament were all part of the students' learning and of their theatrical experience. What the audiences saw each night was equally the result of a pedagogy that refused to congeal itself into a set of rules and of a direction that refused to be directorial in the traditional sense. Instead, both the pedagogy and the direction that made the show an authentic and a moving experience derived from the concatenation of varied individual experiences which were very distinctively women's experiences, and which interrogated stereotypical views of women as well as traditional forms of the representation of women onstage. Many women in the audience told us how moving they thought the show was. When it came to the men, however, some of whom were colleagues, professors, or administrators, a few fell asleep, and others tried to avoid talking to the cast or to me after the show and left quickly. Maybe that was their way of being moved! Or not.

CONCLUSION

In light of my experience with theatre and my feminist performance research over the last decade, I am convinced that the two productions of Beckett's *Happy Days* were feminist productions in the best sense of the word. Both productions were the result of a significant subversion of authorial authority; both were the result of collaborative directing; both involved simultaneously exposing and valorizing the personal experiences of the actresses and involved and enhanced a sense of unity and solidarity among them; both simultaneously subverted or transcended the tragic dimension of the heroine through role-splitting, staging choices, and emphasizing the irony and the comedy of the text; and finally, both were achieved with very limited means of production. In addition, both productions engaged, in a more or less conscious manner, a ritualistic approach in which gestures and the use of objects acquired a particular relevance for both the actors involved and the audience. Ritualistic elements were also present both through the creation, in both productions, of a timeless, placeless space onstage that rendered each with an almost mythical quality. The distinctions between art and reality were blurred and the overall experience joined performers and audience in a "theatre" event.

The two productions were also drastically different. The Romanian production became central to the lives of the women involved even though our involvement in the Attic Theatre was entirely voluntary, with the shows as the only end result. The students involved in the American production were actually enrolled in a course with a grade and credit following the last performance, and yet they were less intensely involved with their production emotionally and psychologically. For us in Romania, the greatest recompense from the production was that it became an escape and liberation from political oppression. Working on *Happy Days* soothed our souls from the everyday "banality of evil." In addition, we, in communist Romania, felt less oppressed as *women* and much more as individuals. Ours was an "equal opportunity" oppression, so to speak, which men and women "enjoyed" almost equally. Because of our everyday resistance and hatred of a common enemy, as well as the fact that under the communist regime men and women formed equal parts of the national work force, we were more bold and confident as women than the American female students. The American experience involved awakening a feminist consciousness in the actors more so than the Romanian experience did. In fact, authoritarian as he often was when directing his own shows, the director of the Romanian theatre loved our show when he first saw it and gave us complete freedom to produce it in any way we wanted. We felt much freer to parody, mock, and subvert both the male presence of the author of the play and the male character in the play. The American women needed some coaching, some amount of discussion to realize Winnie's tragic predicament and to be able to identify with her. Once they did, however, they went farther in both representing and subverting her tragedy than we had in Romania. The joy with which they produced their own objects from Winnie's bag, the ease and confidence with which they ended up playing in front of a conservative audience while wearing camisoles or nightgowns that were not flattering in the conventional sense, the understanding of their differences and the solidarity they established as a result of that understanding, and the general sense of exhilaration they ultimately experienced by the end of the show, were, I believe, marks of their newly found feminist consciousness.

Through the experience of my students, I not only re-lived the experience of the Romanian Winnie, but I retroactively experienced the feminist awakening I probably should have experienced when acting in the Attic Theatre. I realized the autocratic manner in which the theatre was run. I realized that in some ways the Grotowski methods themselves were largely idealized and were based on a certain amount of blind submission to the will and whims of a father figure director. I realized that we were so willing to follow "our" theatrical father figure partly because it was much more exciting and spiritually uplifting to do so than to have stopped on the first floor of the building where the Attic Theatre was located and to have socialized with the Communist Youth who were under the spell of an Orwellian, spiritually empty father figure and ideology.

Finally, along with my students, my own feminist consciousness was significantly sharpened as I became more aware of the subtler, yet also noxious, forms of gender oppression and marginalization of professional women in a traditional academic environment. I understood that capitalist societies have just as many "traps" for women as Marxist societies, and that these traps can be veiled under various forms of consumerism and objectification, and for that reason, are easier to fall into, as they are disguised under colorful make-up and attractive clothes. I understood that if we in communist Romanian institutions of higher learning suffered from a "pedagogy of oppression," in American academic institutions we are often confronted with an "oppressive pedagogy," a pedagogy which reinforces the status quo of patriarchy through traditional power relations between teacher and students, or between director and actor-students. However, unlike our status under the dictatorship of Ceausescu, in the American academy we can still openly resist, undermine, and ultimately explode such pedagogies–unless of course we allow for initiatives such as the Patriot Act to acquire the terrifying power of a pedagogy of tyranny.

A comparative look at the two productions of Beckett's *Happy Days* illustrates the power of theatre as a form of resistance against oppression of many kinds. As Gay Gibson Cima eloquently put it, theatre "can help to make the revolutions in consciousness that lead to change" ("Strategies" 93). It also illustrates the fluid way in which feminist theory and practice are connected. My experience of twenty years ago was very much a feminist production, yet the women involved were not only unaware of it, but feminism was not even a concern for them. It was only in retrospect that I interpreted the experience as a feminist one and tried to view it in terms of some of the feminist theories I had become aware of since my days in the Romanian theatre. I was then able to apply both the experience and theory to the American production of the play, and in the process developed both a new understanding of the theory and performed a re-evaluation of the practice. Now, having both the theoretical and practical tools to resist oppression by means of theatrical expression and feminist pedagogy, I can continue to teach undergraduate men and women methods of resistance to and subversion of oppressions of all kinds. And from her earthy mound, Winnie winks at me approvingly.

NOTES

[1] According to Timothy Wiles, Grotowski's "poor theatre" is "stripped of any element not deemed essential to the theatre event," and is marked by "the minimalist tendency or reduction quality," similar to the theatre of Beckett, Pinter, or Handke (114).

[2] The idea of looking "inward" is a crucial one for Samuel Beckett's theatre. When, during a performance of *Happy Days*, actress Billie Whitelaw asked Beckett, who was directing the play, where to look, he answered simply "inward." The actress considers that to be one of "the most marvelous, succinct piece of direction I've ever been given" (Kalb 240). Grotowski's exercises also had a very profound impact on this process of inward looking. Most exercises and activities we engaged in made us focus on something "inward," be it a personal experience, our connection to the character, or simply finding silence in ourselves. I Wayan Lendra describes similar exercises and theatre practices as part of "The Objective Drama Project." Lendra mentions the exerting physical exercises and the long hours of practice extending well into the night, and comments that:

> [T]he work affected my perceptions on many levels simultaneously. There was a change of consciousness and awareness, a change of physical impulses and behavior, and an intensity which developed throughout the work. Generally I felt my body was awake even though I was working long hours almost every day. I was very much connected with myself and certainly with my native culture (139).

[3] Grotowski's theatre emerged as a form of resistance to the communist regime in Poland, and its stress on the spiritual, mystical, and mythic level of the theatre experience was at the core of its subversive quality (although, as Lendra remarks, Grotowski never used himself words such as "spiritual").

[4] Among these actresses, Billie Whitelaw and Madelaine Renaud are particularly important. They both acted as Winnie in *Happy Days* and appreciated the manner in which Beckett guided them to their role.

[5] Diamond discusses at length Irigaray's anti-mimetic practice and theory of theatre, in particular her notion of the "hystera theater" which "subverts the illusion of psychic coherence" (373-76).

[6] See the chapter called "Maro Green and Caroline Griffin" in Lizbeth Goodman's book *Contemporary Feminist Theaters*, which discusses the feminist performance strategies of Green and Griffin and their feminist play *More*. See also the comparison with Beckett's *Waiting for Godot* in Donkin and Clement's *Upstaging Big Daddy*.

[7] This connects to Gay Gibson Cima's ideas about subverting the canon and, in particular, about the ways in which practice turns into theory, which goes back into practice.

[8] As Sabrina Hamilton points out in a description of her experience with the feminist theatre collective Split Britches, "[T]he permission to include personal imagery that may feel somewhat obscure to the audience gives the piece a very particular aesthetic, unpolished by some dramatic standards but brimming with authenticity" (141).

[9] See Linda BenZvi's remarkable feminist study *Women in Beckett: Performance and Critical Perspectives* in which she interviews twelve of Beckett's actresses, who discuss their experiences of working with Beckett. See *Women in Beckett*, as well as Gay Gibson Cima's *Performing Women* for feminist interpretations of Winnie's symbolism.

WORKS CITED

Beckett, Samuel. *Happy Days*. New York: Grove Press, 1961.

Ben-Zvi, Linda. *Samuel Beckett*. Boston, MA: Twayne Publishers, 1986.

---. *Women in Beckett: Performance and Critical Perspectives*. Urbana: University of Illinois Press, 1990.

Boal, Augusto. *The Aesthetics of the Oppressed*. London and New York: Routledge, 2006.

Cima, Gay Gibson. *Performing Women: Female Characters, Male Playwrights, and the Modern Stage*. Ithaca: Cornell University Press, 1993.

---. "Strategies for Subverting the Canon." *Upstaging Big Daddy.* Ellen Donkin and Susan Clement, eds. Ann Arbor: University of Michigan Press, 1993. 91-106.

Diamond, Elin. "Mimesis, Mimicry and the 'true' Real." *Acting Out: Feminist Performances.* Lynda Hart and Peggy Phelan, eds. Ann Arbor: University of Michigan, 1993. 363-382.

Essif, Les. "Teaching Literary Dramatic Texts as Culture-in-Process in the Foreign Language Theater Practicum: the Strategy of Combining Texts." *ADFL Bulletin* 29. 3 (1998): 19-27.

Goodman, Lizbeth. *Contemporary Feminist Theatres: To Each Her Own.* New York: Routledge, 1993.

Grotowski, Jerzy. *Towards a Poor Theatre.* Trans. T.K. Wiewiorowski. New York: Bobbs-Merrill, 1969.

Hamilton, Sabrina. "Split Britiches and the Alcestis Lesson." *Upstaging Big Daddy: Directing Theatre as if Gender and Race Matter.* Ellen Donkin and Susan Clement, eds. Ann Arbor: the University of Michigan Press, 1993. 133-150.

hooks, bell. *Teaching to Transgress: Education as the Practice of Freedom.* New York: Routledge, 1994

---. Yearning: Race, Gender, and Cultural Politics. Boston: South End Press, 1990.

Irigaray, Luce. *An Ethics of Sexual Difference.* Trans. Carolyn Burke & Gillian C. Gill. Ithaca, New York: Cornell University Press, 1993.

Kalb, Jonathan. *Beckett in Performance.* New York: Cambridge University Press, 1989.

Lendra, I Wayan. "Bali and Grotowski: Some parallels in the training process." *Acting (Re)Considered.* Ed. Phillip B. Zarrilli. London and New York: Routledge, 1995. 137-154.

Love, Lauren. "Resisting the Organic: A feminist actor's approach." *Acting (Re)Considered: Theories and Practices.* Ed. Phillip Zarrilli. London and New York: Routledge, 1995. 275-289.

Perloff, Carey. "Three Women and a Mound: Directing Happy Days." *Directing Beckett.* Lois Oppenheim ed. Ann Arbor: University of Michigan Press, 1994. 161-170.

Wiles, J. Timothy. *The Theater Event. Modern Theories of Performance.* Chicago: University of Chicago Press, 1980.

AN IRREVOCABLE PROMISE
STAGING THE STORY XICANA*

Cherríe Moraga

THE WRITER'S HEART

The ceremony always begins for me in the same way…always the hungry woman. Always the place of disquiet (inquietud) moves the writing to become a kind of excavation, an earth-dig of the spirit found through the body. The impulse to write may begin in the dream, the déjà vu, a few words, which once uttered through my own mouth or the mouth of another, refuse to leave the body of the heart. Writing is an act prompted by intuition, a whispered voice, a tightening of the gut. It is an irrevocable promise to not forget what the body holds as memory.

Writing for the stage is the reenactment of this ceremony of remembering. Experience first generated through the body returns to the body in the flesh of the staged performance. In this sense, for me, it is as close to direct political activism as I can get as an artist, for theater requires the body to make testimony and requires other bodies to bear witness to it. The question remains: *bear witness to what?* It is a question all artists, the survivor-children of Amerikan genocide, must ask. And so I, too, ask myself most simply: what is the story Xicana?

As a teacher and maker of theater, I still consider the importance of Brazilian teatrista Augusto Boal's ideas on the ways in which mainstream theater is used as a tool for political and cultural domination. In his 1979 *Theatre of the Oppressed*, Boal calls for a theater practice welded and wielded as a weapon of political resistance. For me, his early writings assume even greater importance in the face of the growing collective amnesia in América aggravated by global capital.

I have always viewed my work as a writer in general, and a playwright in particular, within the context of an art of resistance or a literature *toward* libera-

---

* This essay was first presented at III Congreso internacional de literature chicana on May 21, 2002 in Málaga, Spain. On July 25 of the same year, it was presented in an expanded version as the keynote address for the Association for Theatre in Higher Education in San Diego, California.

tion. "Toward," I believe is the operative term here, as Xicana art and its forms are hardly free. In fact, if anything accurately describes the Xicana story, it would be the site of conflict and resistance, revolt but not revolution. Not yet. Or not ever, as at times it feels we are moving, with the growing commodification of Latinidad, further and further away from that requirement in our art. Still I have never questioned the revolutionary *potential* in bringing the Xicana experience full-bodied to the center of the stage (and page). What I do question are the forms, the shapes in which that staged story-telling might be rendered. What languages do we use? What physical action? What objects are called forth? What voices? Help me remember, I ask of my dioses, what I never read and may never have witnessed, but somehow know. This is the mantra of my own writing process. Help me believe I have the *right* to remember and know what at times only my troubled heart tells me to be true.

AGAINST AMNESIA

For over fifteen years now, I have wielded theater as part of my arsenal of cultural resistance as both an artist and teacher. It is not the single nor necessarily the most effective weapon I carry, but once lifted, it has impacted all the genres I endeavor, as well as my role as an educator. I came upon theater organically, out of the spoken voice of my first fictional character, which was in fact not me. To say my work emerged from the oral tradition of my meXicanismo is to tell you a simple truth that my voices have always had bodies and as such required the physical space of staging, if only spoken aloud through the body that is me behind this podium. The oral tradition is the only "literary legacy" I am completely sure about since books did not hold the first stories that held me. The rest of what I know as a playwright and a writer has been garnered, learned, appropriated. And all of this is what I bring to the art of teaching.

※ ※ ※

Cinco de Mayo Celebration, 2002
Sequoia Elementary, Oakland Unified School District

I am doing a children's play, or so I tell myself. "This is only a children's play," which I have authored in order to provide my eight-year-old son and his Oakland public school with some notion of Mechicano history and culture beyond the obligatory Ballet Folklórico performance, red, green and white crepe paper draped from the cafeteria ceiling, and tortilla chips with salsa. (My compadre and fellow playwright, Ricardo Bracho, affectionately referred to this three-month residency at Sequoia School as my unofficial TCG grant. What a country it would be if national granting programs actually paid for such work.)

The majority of the kids in my son's second-third grade class are African American, followed by Asian American and Latino; there is one white girl amongst them (who herself claims to be a quarter-breed Mexican. I don't doubt her). The project of our coming together is clear in my mind: the opportunity to re-(en)vision Mexican and Xicano history from a Xicana Indígena and feminist perspective onstage. I don't exactly articulate this to anyone, but was gratified to find that the teacher of my son's class, African American and a lesbian, was only too eager to yield the stage floor to me and my ideas.

In "The History and Future of the People of the Corn," as this play was called, human beings are created by Grandmother from the ground corn of her metate and the oil of her tortilla-making palms (true to the Quiché Maya Creation Story). The Spanish are not brave explorers, but foreign invaders. Columbus wears a suit and tie and carries a cell phone as he encounters the Arawak for the first time. As the play progresses, he will, in the tradition of Teatro Chicano, bear a sign that names him "Greed." Greed becomes the enemy and reappears in the body of the Spanish Conquistador, Hernán Cortez, and all subsequent historical enemies of the disenfranchised Indians of México. "Greed" battles Father Hidalgo, Benito Juárez, Emiliano Zapata, and Las Soldaderas of the Mexican Revolution. He goes on to encounter César Chávez, Dolores Huerta, and the contemporary Zapatistas of Chiapas. The four female four-feet-tall Zapatistas, their eyes peering from above their bandanas, surround "Greed" and he is forced to succumb to the righteous power of revolutionary resistance. They overtake "Greed" and remove his sign, replacing it with another. "Compartir," it reads, which means "Share." And, in this manner, one American history lesson is told to right the record, just a bit, and Oakland City Schools' kids of color (which are the vast majority) are just a little less deprived of themselves and their history.

The seven- and eight-year-old actors are having a good time with this interpretation. It is new material for them in terms of their schoolbooks, but it is not new to them intuitively. They giggle out of a subtle sense of the danger in this version. In one rehearsal, we "improvise" the story of the first encuentro (meeting) between Columbus and the Arawak, using gibberish. This is a standard theater game for adult actors, which teaches them about the function of subtext, how we understand the meaning of words by tone, gesture, body language, when we may not know the language at all. I first ask the kids, what language do you think Columbus spoke? Some agree, Spanish…some of the more astute ones even venture Italian. When I ask them what the Arawak spoke they respond, English. Which, of course, to them is the "American Language."

By way of illustration, I call two Cantonese-speaking kids to the center of the circle and ask them to speak their native tongue. They do so, at first shyly, then proudly that they have something special to contribute to this lesson. The rest of the kids–African American, Latino, Pilipino–respond that the words sound like nonsense to them. In short, it is gibberish. We begin to improvise. Five kids volunteer to be Columbus and his crew and another five an Arawak chief and his tribe. The two groups confront each other, speaking "gibberish"– gibberish that ends up meaning, "I came for gold and if you refuse to give me what I want, I will kill you," which is exactly where genocide and greed meet. Columbus and crew raise and shoot their rifles and the Arawak drop dead en masse. They had not been directed to do so. This was an improvisation. And thus ends our rehearsal for the day and begins our first lesson in colonization. And we, the kids and I, *have fallen in love with the power of theater to teach.* Truth. Or lies. You choose, as Boal reminds us.

Days later, in rehearsal again, we move onto the history of the slave trade. In the scene, two Black kids, a boy and a girl, are put on the slave auction block. They have their hands bound, their faces drop into their chests and, after being sold, they are led offstage to the tune of Billy Holiday's "Strange Fruit,"

Southern trees bear strange fruit,
Blood on the leaves and blood at the root,
Black bodies swinging in the southern breeze.
Strange fruit hanging from the poplar trees.

The Arawak chief symbolically stands alone centerstage and shakes his head in despair. The first time we rehearsed this, the entire troupe of twenty stop. We are speechless—maybe only for a few moments when the silence is broken by the nervous laughter of another child. An eight-year-old female snaps back at him, "It's not funny," and the kid stops laughing.

Of course, it's not funny. Black bodies. Real children's black bodies. I had asked the two kids to show in their bodies "great loss, great sadness." And somehow these children who are not actors, knew how to enact this story, for there was an agelessness, an old knowledge, in their bearing that indicated to all of us that they remembered slavery on a visceral (genetic?) level. Nicole and Dion are their ancestors incarnate. Nicole and Dion are slave children being separated from their mothers. And I know and they know we will never forget this lesson in remembering. This is the marvelous horror and promise of Teatro. Real bodies. This is what brings me back to theater again and again. The lesson of it. The promise of conscientización, coming to consciousness, through the physical act of art.

In my three-month "residency" at Sequoia Elementary School, I was honored to observe twenty seven- and eight-year-olds discover for themselves the infinite political and life-saving promise in the making of Teatro. Their bodies did it. They did not enact the "discovery" of Amerika, where the white male is always the agent of superior intellect and moral rectitude. They enacted a historical moment of murder and thievery that continues to shape their own twenty-first century place in this country, as African American, Xicano, salvadoreño, and the children of Asian immigrants. The theatre project brought home to them, *through their bodies,* the knowledge that their second-class status in the U.S. is not a natural-born fact: something I barely began to glimpse in my twenties.

THE BODY'S PROMISE

The violation of the collective body is re-membered in these staged enactments. Here the pieces of ourselves broken by racial and colonial incursions are re-collected and reconfigured through an art of social transformation. Historical oppression, however, is always experienced individually and intimately. This is what made the scene of the slave auction so compelling: the actors' *individual* embodiment of that trauma.

About twelve years ago, in working with a pre-teen Latina actor, I experienced the same visceral confrontation with oppression, but this time one which mandated a secret, private world, without public acknowledgement. In the premiere of my play, *Shadow of a Man*, director María Irene Fornes[1] cast an eleven-year-old girl to play an eleven-year-old girl, Lupe, who suffered from an intimacy with her father she did not want. Although not enacted sexually, his habitual drunken visits to her bed for an abrazo (embrace) after a night spent in the bar, evoked the same childhood burden of guilt and shame that incest inspires. I had written the scene, seen it enacted numerous times by actors sixteen years old and older in other rehearsals and staged readings, but never by a real live girl, whose body balanced itself precariously and quite beautifully on the verge of puberty. So, when that two-hundred-pound man playing the father, Manuel, drops his drunken head onto Lupe's blanketed eleven-year-old belly, I was not prepared for the holy terror of that moment. Although I had written the scene, I had not anticipated my own sense of revulsion, as I felt the audience gasp in the visceral experience of Lupe's vulnerability. It was exactly the effect I conjured in the words of my writings, but it took the Xicana stage to realize it. The conscienced enactment of the oppressed body of this girl-child proffers the possibility of an end to such clandestine violations. For women in the audience, such a visceral unromantic staging made public an oppression reliant on its secrecy for its power.

The revolutionary promise of a theater of liberation lies in the embodied rendering of our prisons and, in the act, our release from them. In this light, I think of my teatro student, Gabriel–Gabriel with the poet's heart, the delicate hands, the sharp wit of a cultural survivor. While rehearsing a performance piece he had written about the one-hundred-year legacy of machismo in his family–from Mexican miner, to revolutionary, to impassive laborer father– Gabriel is suddenly overcome with tears. He breaks down right there on the stage floor. A moment later, he has quickly recovered himself, laughing nervously, "I didn't know this was gonna be therapy." But it is not therapy. "Therapy" is a privatized gringo concept that our illness is somehow individual, as is our cure. Gabriel performs a history of the formation of masculinity in his meXicano family. He is its ambivalent inheritor, as are the majority of our young men. He is involved in the art of unraveling how we all got here in this mess–men estranged from women and themselves. His writing and its enactment, even beneath the shadow of Stanford's colonial archways, reflect a contemporary curanderismo. It emerges from an ancestral knowledge that a story told with the body can cure and create great warriors of heart on the cultural battlefield. "Word Warriors," author Denise Chavez calls them.[2]

The bodies of Teatro Maíz (those second and third graders), Lupe of *Shadow of a Man*, and Gabriel's "queer" portrait of masculinity occupy censored sites of knowing on the Amerikan stage. But it is more than institutionalized censorship exposed here; it is what Latino queer scholar Alberto Sandoval-Sánchez calls the "abject" body–the body of the enslaved, the violated, the queer–performing itself as an act of transgression against the master-class. "Performing abjection," Sandoval tells us, "has the potential to disrupt normality. The abject is dangerous.... It menaces hegemonic culture" (549). Although Sandoval uses the Latino queer man with AIDS as the paradigmatic embodiment of abjection, the performing bodies of these young people accomplish similar acts of disruption. The place of the "abject" as the ultimate site of state-sanctioned contempt and derision is also where the Xicana-identified body is staged. Sandoval goes on to describe disease (in this case AIDS) as a kind of internal alien. He asks, "Do women ever have a fear of giving birth to a monster?"[3] And I want to shout back, "Hermano, we *are* the monsters, we Chicanas!" I have written elsewhere of my heroic and disfigured monstruos: the bodiless Cerezita of *Heroes and Saints*, the infanticidal Mexican Medea from *The Hungry Woman*, the thoroughly unredeemable Yolanda Saldívar, that self-loathing, closeted queer killer of tejano music star Selena, characterized in my play-essay, "Who Killed Yolanda Saldívar?"[4] These characters represent those sites of abjection, which when given stage time and space, intend to "menace" the lie of colored queer invisibility, criminality, and "perversion." The honest "performance" of these "sites of abjection" declares to the dominant culture that we "others" have minds and bodies and ideas and history which, if critically rendered, hold the promise of revolt. Still, as Guillermo Gómez-Peña reminds us, "dominance is contextual" (13-14). And those same bodies/characters in revolt against mainstream/mainstage Amerika, might also find that they are censored and ostracized from sites where ethnicity and a history of ethnic oppression is shared, while gender and sexuality are not.

MEXICANA MENACE

I was reminded of how dangerous Xicana-identified writing can be within the framework of male-identified Chicano Teatro, when not one woman's play was selected to be part of a Chicano Classics Teatro Festival held at UCLA in June 2002. I decided to boycott the conference in protest against its decision to only feature plays that were written and/or developed by men or male-directed teatros.

In an "Open Letter" to conference organizers I wrote:
   ...there are reasons so few of us (Chicanas) were writing this kind of

work...during El Movimiento. Many women of my generation could speak to this, this history of real self-censorship imposed from male leadership and "collective" agreement. Ask the women of El Teatro Campesino during its "classic" period.... [W]hat remains taboo in Chicano Teatro [is]complex female desire portrayed by us women, gay and straight.

I return to Sandoval's argument. "Performing abjection...menaces hegemonic culture." In Mechicano terms, women's sexuality has occupied a fundamental site of abjection in our collective imagination since Malinztín Tenepal's fateful rape by conquistador Hernán Cortez.[5] Abjection: Debasement. Depravation. Abnormality. We are despised from within and without—our bodies, the conquered nation. The perverse irony is that we are further despised, especially within our own cultural ranks, when we refuse to be vanquished. Is it a secret we women pass on to one another, those remembered acts of resistance, those native rebellions against female enslavement? For Xicanas (and I must add all women of color who walk in a remembered history of colonial rape) the enactment of de-colonized female desire defines the parameters of abjection for majority populations.

We are despised when we speak up; we are despised when we act out. We are despised when we create honest depictions of female sexuality (and not some man-pleasing, minstrel-like, middle-class portraiture of women "wanting it"). Whether we are lesbian or heterosexual, as self-proclaimed desirers we become bodies of revolt, bodies in dissent against oblivion. I am reminded here of Alicia Gaspar de Alba's depiction of Malintzín in her short story "Los Derechos de Malinche." In it, an imprisoned Malinche, in anticipation of Cortez's arrival to her cell, places a nopal con espinas (a thorny prickly pear) inside her vagina. She awaits her rapist. She is a body in dissent against oblivion.

Against oblivion, our bodies refuse to forget our pre-conquest selves.

As a teatrista, I have thought often of the Stanislavski acting method based on the concept of using physical action to generate memory in the body. The process of physicalization in performance requires uncovering resistant, resilient, and living memory. If remembering counters oblivion, how does the Xicana artist draw upon memory she has been historically sanctioned to forget? How do I give my characters real bodies resurrected from the colony? Sandoval goes on to describe abjection in correspondence with the exiled, those who have been forcibly displaced from their homelands. "Death," of course, he tells us, as a daily survivor of AIDS, is the "ultimate exile."[6] Then genocide is also the ultimate site of collective abjection. This is the Xicana story: the story of displacement, amnesia, exile, orphanhood, rape, and genocide. This is the story of female desire forgotten.

Journal Entry. March 14, 2002

After my speaking engagement at a Jesuit college, the young Mexican Americans in

the audience were so quiet at my words: "Dyke," "Indian," "Nation," "Queer," "Death."
Their faces impassive, I could not read from them how they received me. In the q & a fol-
lowing, they did not speak. Had I frightened them so? I come home to dream I am among
Jews in a Second World War concentration camp. (It is not the first time I have dreamed
myself there imprisoned, awaiting extermination). In this dream, however, I lay naked in
a small hard bunk, a naked woman laying her full length on top of me. We hold each
other. We will be killed for this act.

When I awaken I realize I had fallen asleep afraid; for, although I was the
invited speaker by a small group of progressive faculty at this Catholic university, for the majority, my words were hard to hear. I felt this speaking. It is
impossible to ignore the feeling of being silently objectified, quietly made to be
the "other." "That dyke, that white-faced Mexican, that lady who talks Indian,
she ain't me. There is no 'we' in these words." I have no idea what, in fact,
those students felt; only my dreams showed me what I felt: that sense of utter
vulnerability in claiming all that we are at once–lesbian, Xicana, hungry for a
free nation when the americanworld around us tells us we are already free. I
am/we are those women who, as unrecognized and unreconciled aging artists
in a whiteman's world, are one day found scratching out ancient symbols on
cave walls "with shit and blood for pigment." We are the women on display,
the Mexican bearded-woman-circus-freak–the Julia Pastranas of the world,[7]
mocked and mummified by a culture plagued by the fear of difference.

"Hay que indianizar a los q'aras
The Q'ara (criollos and mestizos) must become Indianized." (Sanjinés 49)

Only a truly liberationist teatro could house an uncompromised story of
dissent, one where the axis upon which freedom is imagined spins freely from
an alternate world view, as El Mallku, the Amayra Leader of the Karismo
Movement, suggests above. It is a theater generated not from some neo-liberal
Latin American notion of mestisaje nor corporate-conspired definition of multiculturalism nor academic-inspired discourse on hybridity nor New Age fantasy
of indigeneity; but one conceived by those who have been erased by the official
narrative of colonization. It is *our* liberationist theory assuming flesh on the
América stage. It is *our* work of resistance. It is a *living* art, requiring tools of our
own making, our *own* objects, our sacred and profane practices; or maybe for us
lost mestizos, it is just some clumsy grasping at a pre-colonial language and a
history almost forgotten.

I have no nostalgia about some idealized original tongue we, the thousands
of tribes that make up the Xicano nation, once had. Still, I admit that as an
artist not borne from the educated classes, I am always protecting what *may* be
original in me, not me alone, but the "we" of me. I am suspect of Western
Thought, even as I stand here as its product. I do not naively confide in the
post-colonial theory created by the colonists or the liberation theory of my
oppressors. I am both the freed slave and the enslaved. I am talking out of both
sides of my mouth. I contradict and speak to you in their language, which is my

language. And is not. I am the mestiza: Indian and white, more white than Indian. I have forgotten almost everything. I pick and borrow what I can to try and find my way to a manner of expression that will, from the simple vantage of an eight year old, stop greed. I want to turn the sign around.

Sometimes, as a writer, I feel my task comes down to the simple fact of declaring, Sí existimos. We exist and have always been here. I remember the mother in my play, *Shadow of a Man*, trying to get her husband to respond to her. She cries, "Manuel existo. Existo yo." Maybe this is the same refrain in all of my work: an insistence on a presence where the world perceives absence. Maybe this is fundamentally the project of all Xicana work: to announce our presence to one another and the world, but in our own tongue, on our own ground, brandishing our own homegrown instruments of naming. This is where the project of revolutionary Teatro occurs–self-defined, self-determined, employing words and images before and beyond the colony.

THE XICANA STAGE: BEYOND THE COLONY

The language of the Xicana story–if it were to be real–is fragmented, it is the stutter, the garbled utterance caught in the silence between tongues, tongues literally ripped from mouths. It resides in the taboo languages of the body: the vulva pressed unashamedly against a bed of dirt or the body of another woman in the effort to remember what got lost somewhere. It is a paling Tepehuan descendant speaking in the tongue of Xicana performance.

❉ ❉ ❉

Oaxaca, Mexico. Día de los muertos 2001.

It is the last evening of a four-day encuentro between Mexican and Xicana visual artists. Celia Herrera Rodríguez[8] is to perform in the colonial courtyard of Santo Domingo, a massive cathedral-turned-cultural center. I was there among the audience beneath the moonlit, delicately clouded evening sky. I was there when that pearly disk slipped out from behind a cloud and showed herself in all her full moon wonder. I was there when Celia threw down a petate (a straw mat) the size of a beach towel, onto the cobblestoned ground and said to an overwhelming upper-middle-class Mexican audience, "This is what's left of my land."

Stunned silence all around. Me, too. I had seen this performance several times before, but suddenly, here among the Mexicans, it is different. Suddenly, we Xicanos, in one gesture of claiming, become bodies in our own right, a nation of people dispossessed and displaced. We are not caricatures of what could have been, malinchistas, wannabe gringos or vendido-mexicanos. We are a people, that petate said, in exile from a México Antiguo. We are people who made our presence known in the physical body of one MeXicana/Tepehuan woman and one damn "prop," I tell Celia later that day. She responds, "It isn't a prop," meaning the petate. And of course, it isn't. As her "perform-ance" is not a play. It is something else, not quite performance art, but art and perform-

ance at once. I don't know how she does it. I know it is not scripted, only thought about for many days in advance while washing dishes, hanging out laundry, spreading water-color onto a piece of amate paper. It is a ritual of remembering, a kind of prayer as in ceremony. It is the Xicana stage. A land and history reclaimed.

Sí, existo. Existo yo.

Always in my imagination, before I write, the stage is as empty as the page, always I wonder how to fill it. How to tell a story differently than what has been prescribed to us: something beyond progressive plot lines, the Euro-centric "arc" of a story, and the single protagonist. Something beyond a literature that entertains Euro-American audiences by describing who we are to them with them in mind. I think this is what moved me about Celia's performance that night—that the objects she utilized came from us, that a story could be told through a single Xicana gesture and a dozen words.

Seven months later, she will "perform" in Málaga, Spain. She will take the Patron Saint of Málaga (every city in Spain has a patron), and smash the Virgin Madonna in one fatal blow to the head. She will return the favor to Spain. Smash their gods as our gods were smashed. It is a brief visceral moment of historical reckoning. A truth told. Again. But how hard it is to find that truth and give it shape. Simple. Direct. Courageous.

I think here of the Cuban-American conceptual performance artist Ana Mendieta, spirit-sister to Celia Herrera Rodríguez, in her effort to re-member an almost premordial rupture from the mother-land. In her early 1980s series "Siluetas," Mendieta creates out of Cuban earth, gun powder and fire, the shape of her own figure in the ground. Lillian Manzor writes of the artist who died tragically in her mid-30s in 1985, "Her work was an obsessive act intended to reconnect herself with the earth, to reunite herself with the ancestral origins from which she was torn apart" (382).

"From which she was torn apart." How do we re-member genocide? I write. A pitiful and necessary gesture toward something unnamed, beyond what we have been schooled to imagine.

✳ ✳ ✳

"The Poet" begins to move her bare feet across the wood of the stage floor, which is covered with a thin layer of sand. Her movement is a kind of dance, which she invents in the spirit of the O'odham, from the land of her Sonoran ancestors. It is a silent un-dramatic gesture, accompanied by the sound of one hand beating on an overturned woven basket. When her beloved asks what the movement means, she responds, "I'm just trying to do something else other than theirs on this stage."

And that is all this writer's journey is to me: the effort to uncover what we don't remember, to use the body as a way to dig up the dirt. To find something of what is left of us.

I will tell you how hungry my body is to know something beyond the colony. I am she who puts her face in the dirt, my bare knees slipping beneath me. I lay belly down on the ground and press my vulva there. The hard earth is a pillow for my cheek, but I do not rest. I make rite (right) with dirt and fingernail, stone and fire. I eat dirt like sacrament. I tell you, I am just that hungry for just one whole story that feels true to me.

NOTES

[1] The world premier of the play took place in 1990 and was produced by the Eureka Theater and Brava Theater Center of San Francisco.

[2] "Warrior Words/Word Warriors" was the theme of the tenth annual Border Books Festival, which took place in Las Cruces, New Mexico in 2004. The name was coined by Denise Chavez, fiction writer and director of the festival.

[3] From a public address given at the conference "Crossing Borders '99: Latino/a and Latin American Lesbian and Gay Testimony, Autobiography, and Self-Figuration," Center for Lesbian and Gay Studies (CLAGS of CUNY), March 1999.

[4] Presented at the Lesbian Playwright's Festival at the Magic Theater, San Francisco, directed by Irma Mayorgas, January 2000.

[5] Malinztín (also known as Malinche) Tenepal was a young woman of the Aztec ruling class who was sold into slavery and presented as a gift to the Spaniard Hernán Cortez upon his arrival in Vera Cruz in 1519. As the translator, tactical advisor, and courtesan to Cortez, she served Cortez in his efforts to conquer indigenous Mexico. She is controversial figure in Mechicana history. By some, she is considered a kind of "Mexican Eve" for what is seen as her traitorous complicity in the conquest of ancient Mexico. By Chicana Feminists, she has been characterized as a woman who rose beyond her enslaved status to become a political leader in her own right, and whose actions were prompted by a deep spiritual mandate. See Moraga's "A Long Line of Vendidas" in *Loving in the War Years.* Boston: South End Press, 1983/2000. Also, Norma Alarcon's "Chicana's Feminist Literature: A Re-Vison through Malintzin…" in *This Bridge Called My Back: Writings by Radical Women of Color,* eds. Gloria Anzaldúa and Cherríe Moraga. NY: Kitchen Table Press, 1983; Aleida del Castillos's "Malintzin Tenepal: A Preliminary Look into a New Perspective" in *Essays on La Mujer,* eds. R. Sanchez and R. Martinez Cruz. UCLA: Chicano Studies Center Publication, 1977.

[6] See endnote 3.

[7] Julia Pastrana, who had hypertrichosis teminalis (her face and body were covered in black hair), was an indigenous Mexican woman of the mid-nineteenth century. She was bought for exhibition by a man who would later become her husband. After her death and the death of her three-day-old baby, also suffering from the same condition, the two were mummified and continued to be exhibited by the husband.

[8] Celia Herrera Rodríguez is a painter and installation artist who teaches in the Chicano Studies Program at UC Berkeley.

WORKS CITED

Boal, Augusto. *Theatre of the Oppressed.* New York: Theatre Communications Group, 1985.

Gaspar de Alba, Alicia. "Los Derechos de Malinche." *Mystery of Survival and Other Stories.* Tempe, AZ: Bilingual Review Press, 1993. 47-53.

Gómez-Peña, Guillermo. *The New World Border: Prophecies, Poems, and Loqueras for the End of the Century.* San Francisco, CA: City Light Books, 1996. 13-14.

Manzor, Lillian. "From Minimalism to Performative Excess: The Two Tropicanas." *Latinas On Stage.* Eds. Alicia Arrizón and Lillian Manzor. Berkeley, CA: Third Woman Press, 2000. 370-396.

Moraga, Cherríe. "Shadow of a Man" in *Heroes and Saints and Other Plays*. Alburquerque, NM: West End Press, 1986. 37-84.

---------"Who Killed Yolanda Saldivar?" Unpublished dramatized essay. January 2000.

Sandoval-Sanchez, Alberto. "Politicizing Abjection: In the Manner of a Prologue for the Articulation of AIDS Latino Queer Identities." *American Literary History.* 17.3 (2005): 542-49.

Sanjinés C. Javier. "Mestisaje Upside Down: Subaltern Knowledges and the Known." *Nepantla: Views from South.* 3.1 (2002): 49.

PLAYING OUT A PAST, RECOVERING AN EDUCATION
Ellen Margolis

SEPTEMBER 1992

I am one year into a doctoral program in Dramatic Art at the University of California, Santa Barbara. It is not at all what I hoped or expected, not at all what I need. I find it not just challenging but profoundly alienating, and I have from the first. Afternoon seminars find me vigorously wringing my hands and rubbing my arms beneath a weighty, glossy wooden table in an effort to stay present in my body while, above deck, I try to keep up with the deracinating conversation. I do, in a sense, keep up. My transcript from the previous year is peppered with As and A+s, so I must be doing some things right, but I am horribly lost. There is clearly no order or plan to the selection of seminars I find myself in; I am to take what is offered when it is offered. Very little that is said melds with anything I know of theatre or of life; worse, what I seem to be learning is that my experiences are not valid and that I don't know how to talk about them correctly. Almost nothing resonates with the interests that compelled me to return to school.

Over nearly a decade as an actor and acting teacher, I have grown increasingly curious about stories and how they serve communities, and less interested in simply being plugged into stories chosen by someone else. I want to consider theatre in a bigger context and with more complexity than has been available to me so far. But here in school, a conversation about theatre never seems to take hold. In fact, to be too interested in theatre practice—even to like theatre too much—undermines one's potential credibility as a scholar. There are certainly some passionate lovers of theatre among the faculty, some really good artists, some born teachers. But there seems to be an inverse correlation between a professor's desire to communicate with students and his stature in the department and academy.

The methods of academia baffle me as well. The rules seem to change from seminar to seminar. In some classes, we read plays and talk about them, in others we "unpack texts" (which looks a great deal like reading plays and talking about them, but is obviously a much worthier pursuit). In some classes, the personal adventures of the writers we study form the basis of all our conversation; in others this material is taboo. Clearly, there are different methodologies at work, but those methodologies are never named or explained. I am absorbing the sense that we revere the Derridean abime but that actual uncertainty is not to be tolerated, that ideas not delivered through the rhetoric of contemporary performance theory (which we are apparently supposed to have learned sometime between being accepted to the program and arriving on campus) should be dismissed out of hand, and that the most assured person wins. By the end of my second year of courses, I will have lost any sense of identification with my work. My intellectual life stays afloat mostly thanks to my teaching assignments, which are fortunately frequent. When I teach, my curiosity and drive spring back to life. But the ostensible purpose of my program is not to train teachers, it is to create scholars like the scholars leading my seminars.

Years later, I recognize that I arrived in graduate school in time to experience the tail end of a very old model of teaching, one in which students wallow in the overspray of their professors' current projects and then rise out of the mist with meaningful projects of our own. While the ideas in the air were the currency of postmodernism, their delivery could not have been more traditional. And while I believe that nearly everyone on the faculty was a committed feminist, I now recognize the pedagogy as exactly the sort that made a need for feminist pedagogy apparent to many of my generation—disembodied, isolating, and encouraging of competition rather than collaboration.

This program and I are not a good fit, but I am more stubborn than I am smart. One of the two other students who started with me has left at the end of the first year to deal with personal issues, and my envy for her choice is palpable, but, for me, to leave would feel like a failure. I'd rather stay and feel like a misfit and a fraud, especially for having other desires in life besides thinking and writing, and other things to take care of.

Sociologist Martha N. Beck has noted of the academic culture in the European tradition:

> When the Enlightenment philosophers outlined their ideal society...it was a society where every rational individual would do rational work (the kind of work philosophers did), and be equal to every other rational individual. *This model of society assumed, as a matter of course, that all rational individuals would have all their traditional work done for them, by people who did not work for money, but for the traditional rewards of protection and sustenance* (34, emphasis in original).

Rational people do rational work and only rational work, unencumbered by demands like cooking and changing diapers. Soon after my son is born (while I am writing my dissertation), I am told that it is a grave mistake to have a baby before one gets tenure. I don't need to be told this. I have entirely absorbed the academic vision of what a scholar looks like, the profile Beck describes. And I understand that if I can't be an unencumbered Enlightenment male, I should at least make every effort to look like one.

For the most part, the university's method of initiation into the academy is sink or swim, but there are a few buoys on the horizon. During my second year in the program, the department institutes a graduate colloquium that meets once a month (subject to frequent cancellation) to deal with the few practical matters deemed pertinent to academic life. This is clearly considered an unfortunate concession by several of the faculty, one of whom grumbles, at the end of our lone 90-minute gathering dedicated to the nuts and bolts of publishing, that "the way to get published is not to sit around talking about it, but to be in our offices writing." Apparently, anyone not born knowing how and when to submit to *The Drama Review* has no place in the profession.

I will, in fact, learn a great deal in my doctoral program, mostly by sitting in on undergraduate classes with a far greater interest and commitment at thirty than I had at twenty. A lifelong feminist, I will be introduced to feminist theorists and scholars whose thinking will liberate and reform both my work and my personal life. I will have a grand time investigating the career and writings of legendary American actress Laurette Taylor for my dissertation, under the guidance of a brilliant advisor. But I will never figure out how to learn in those seminars.

SEPTEMBER 1998

I have landed a job, my first out of graduate school. Armed with my doctorate, I am off to a tenure-track position at the University of Wisconsin-Stevens Point, a comprehensive university. The Department of Theatre and Dance is one of the largest and most distinguished on campus, boasting between 150 and 200 students. From this program, students go on to regional theatres and Broadway, to arts administration, to M.F.A. programs in design and technology, to doctoral programs in performance studies, and to teaching careers of their own. Some of them start theatre companies. For the most part, what they know about theatre history and dramatic literature is what I will manage to teach them in three or four semester-long classes, and literally only that, as I am the sole Ph.D. on the faculty, and the designated instructor for academic courses in a department strongly oriented toward practice. I feel a big responsibility every day, with every class, to live up to my training. At the very least, I should be introducing a variety of perspectives, engaging critical thinking, and encouraging respect for complexity. I sense that my students also expect a certain amount of reliable factual information about theatre architecture, acting companies, who wrote what, and who lived when. My teaching load—four preps a semester—creates each day a kind of crisis, bringing with it both a focusing pressure and a fatalistic recklessness. There is little space to reflect, no time to fret about past mistakes or be paralyzed by the inevitability of future ones. It is imperative, each day, to get going.

Within days it becomes clear that I am utterly lacking in the skills I need to stay afloat in this job. My graduate program has included zero guidance in ped-agogy. Nor are the materials I moved from Santa Barbara to Wisconsin any help. I have a four-drawer file cabinet crammed with unintelligible notes from those graduate seminars. Absent any formal tools to help me contextualize the methodologies of contemporary scholarship, I had tried to fill the void by writ-ing, verbatim, as much of what was said in class as possible. These pages of notes are perhaps most interesting for their marginalia. "Shhh" I wrote on more than one occasion, after volunteering a badly-received opinion. And frequently, for reasons I can only guess at, "HELP." Were my dissertation at all germane to any of the courses I now teach, I could fill forty minutes a year with a com-pelling précis of it, but I sense that it doesn't belong on any of my syllabuses, so I never do.

And while I want to help these students toward a kind of engagement, an agency in their own education that I have never felt, they don't seem to desire this. I am replacing a faculty member who taught in my position for more than twenty years. So complete is his identification with the history/lit sequence that some students and colleagues still refer to the courses as "Bob I" through "Bob IV." And Bob's method was to disseminate information through lectures and then evaluate the students' learning through massive, detailed, fact-based exams. My students appear to do the reading I've assigned them, but they sit passive and aloof in the large lecture halls where we meet, waiting for me to tell them what they need to know.

Still, through trial and error, I come to find a way to teach dramatic litera-ture and theatre history that promises to work for all of us. In desperation, I grab at a model distinctly unlike the bloodless academic one. Among the many part-time jobs in my past, I have put in two years teaching traffic school, a time-honored survival gig for California actors. Working for a company called Traffic Safety Taught with Humor, I have been responsible for keeping countless Saturdays' worth of unwilling students captive in eight-hour classes where the pedagogical goal was for every student to pass an exam at the end of the day with a high percentage of correct answers. In other words, the expectation was that every student could succeed. A good traffic school teacher used every pos-sible tactic (including personal anecdotes, visual aids, hands-on projects, role-playing, improvisation, and multiple opportunities during the day for students to restate new material and relate it to their own experiences) not only to keep the students' interest, but to ensure that the material was being learned and retained. To my relief, I find that this model works in my university classroom as well.

With an expectation that all of my students can develop a lively, confident, and useful grasp on the material and concepts of their history and literature courses, I begin to vary my approaches to the material every day and to break things up even within a one-hour class meeting so that these students, who believe acting is a lot more fun than ideas, will find a way in. It does not feel like pandering to the often-decried short attention span of our time. It feels like class is becoming a place where something happens, where we work actively with material and ideas. Students argue with each other and with me; they suggest questions that take us far beyond what I have presented or prepared; they bring their theatrical sensibilities to our studies, staging debates or creating puppet shows to help themselves and their classmates get a handle on difficult material. My teaching flourishes, and I gobble up information on learning styles (David A. Kolb, Howard Gardner) and critical thinking.

A second development emerges unconsciously but unmistakably: I find myself sharing a lot of stories from my undergraduate career. Strangely often, I begin a class meeting by mentioning how the day's material (or the nearest thing to it, which is sometimes a real stretch) was presented to me in the authoritative voices of the UC Berkeley theatre faculty in the late 1970s. I *could* simply begin by telling my students that the Attic political system had centers and margins like any other, rather than "when I was an undergraduate, I was told that fifth-century Athens was a perfect model of democracy." I *could* simply introduce Susan Glaspell, Eugene O'Neill, and other major players of the U.S. art theatre movement, and I do, but only (usually) *after* announcing that "when I was twenty years old, I was told that O'Neill was without question the only 'great' American playwright." ("One may feel *sorry* for a Blanche DuBois or a Willie Loman…" I can hear my professor intoning, invoking, I suppose, the only two other plausible contenders for greatness.) It is as if I need to set up an obsolete version of the story we are about to explore, a version of which my students would otherwise be innocent. When we read Gilbert and Gubar, my students learn that I was not raised on *The Madwoman in the Attic*, but on *Jane Eyre* and *Little Women*. Would it be more wholesome simply to present history, themes, problems according to my best current grasp of them rather than perhaps unnecessarily belaboring–relaboring–my process of revising? What does it mean to begin the way I do?

Certainly, some of this impulse to write my own history onto my students' minds is inevitable. I am nearly twice their age. In my body, in my memory, I hold the past for them, tenuously linking the history of the theatre with the future they will make. Telling them that *A Raisin in the Sun* was written the year I was born or describing Irene Worth's performance in *Happy Days* shares my holdings with them, allows them to extend their foundations. It is a sweet and useful function.

But why does this autobiographical telling feel so close to the heart of my highest aims as a teacher? Am I, in the spirit of a transgressive pedagogy, undermining my authority by making it clear that I had to learn this stuff too, that I was not born knowing it? (In contrast, my professors seemed to have no personal histories at all, not even academic ones.) Is the opposite true–am I slyly asserting my authority by letting it be known that I have been familiar with this material since about the time these students were born? Could it be both?

Is mine a strategy of containment? Is it that, when confronting a room full of keen young people who have been educated in a fine public school system in a fairly liberal–but also racially, culturally, and religiously homogenous– state, I am not sure what shape their resistance may take, so I want to provide my own? Am I creating a straw antagonist to unite "us" artificially? The only self-described feminist on the theatre faculty, I have already had a number of frustrating run-ins with the department chair (over season choices I find offensive, over his lecturing student actresses about their weight). As far as I can tell, the students are receptive to feminism in practice but innocent of how it may pertain in the classroom, and I find myself wanting to tread carefully, as if a sudden move might scare them off.

Am I short-circuiting investigation by writing a metanarrative of my own, a history of thought that implies forward motion, a narrative that in the end gains credibility from my own inaccuracies and hesitations on the way to immaculate knowledge? Am I covering my ass (I have no head for dates and often spell things wrong in the heat of the moment)? Or am I serving the students by guiding them through a brief version of my own history as a thinker, complete with resistance and resentment ("Artaud really pissed me off the first five or ten times I read him"), confusion and contemplation ("I might suggest that Julia Kristeva is best read at a rate of two or three sentences a night, preferably in the bathtub"), and a current (and growing) batch of questions, thus providing an immediate model? Whatever else it may be, is feminist historiography also at some level the writing of the history of a feminist, this feminist?

From what I hear in passing, every September sees an outbreak of disclaimers in humanities and social science classrooms as instructors are forthcoming about the materialist-feminist or otherwise politically informed position from which they read the world, all in the name of fairness and full disclosure. Perhaps my gesture is not so different, except that it happens in sticky little dribs and drabs rather than all at once and grandly. Perhaps all at once and grandly is better, braver, more inspiring, but for me it would be less authentic. At the level of my frankest self-examination, I think I am trying to highlight the very real possibility of error–not mistaken names or dates, but the much more significant kind of error that points people in the wrong direction, that tells them what's true or untrue, important or unimportant. Perhaps the best I can do is to suggest that, in case the voice of authority in the academy has not changed enough in twenty years, one may survive to repudiate one's teachers, and to do so in as public a place as a classroom.

Teaching, I have often thought, is a most generous way to make a living– not selfless, but generous. The exchange of gifts creates community. Giving my students the gifts of my history, I hope for the gifts of their experiments. What distinguishes a learning community from other sorts? What gifts has any teacher to offer but freedom from herself? Reminding myself and my students that I am a body and mind continually written upon and, now, attended by every doubt and fear, writing upon them, I hope to free them from me.

But am I serving myself as well? Am I, by writing the history of my education again and again, healing the trauma of dissociation that was my four years of undergraduate studies at UC Berkeley? I think I can answer this one: yes.

I had arrived in Berkeley in 1977 as poorly prepared for academic life on a campus of 25,000 as it is possible to be, and drifted from classes to rehearsals to the co-op where I lived secure only in the knowledge that no one seemed to know or care where I was at any time. Unlike most academics I know, I identify very little with my formal education. Other people remember the classes they took in college, their advisors, the papers they wrote, the books they read. What I remember from undergraduate life are apartments, roommates, part-time jobs, long walks—very little that happened in classrooms. So it seems more than a little odd that I, of all people, am always going on about things my teachers said and did.

In fact, it seems that the only moments I remember from classes are moments when something felt very wrong. Strong emotion cements certain events in the mind, and the moments I remember are those that made me feel at least unsettled, sometimes downright violated. I have no trouble accepting the Freirean insight that oppression can be a source of knowledge, and yet I am reluctant to acknowledge that my privileged schooling was a form of oppression. But in truth it did my young mind a kind of violence to hear that the misogyny of *Miss Julie* is beside the point and that to talk about it would be a waste of time. Perhaps my insistence on relating this memory to my students is nothing more than a repetition compulsion. In the classrooms where I at last determine the course of the conversation (to a large extent anyway), I can revisit this particular trauma until it is one day exorcised.

My near-perpetual state of vagueness in those undergraduate days was disrupted occasionally by the uppity voices of some extraordinary graduate students who said things, in and out of classes, that I had never imagined could be said. While most of the theatre professors were scholars with little interest in teaching, our teaching assistants were young men and women of unmistakable passions and in some cases trailblazing intelligence.

It may be worth repeating that I started college in 1977. Chronologically, my education bridges a gap between the early, consciousness-raising years of the second wave of feminism and the embracing of feminist scholarship by the academy. In memory I see Sue-Ellen Case in a stand-off with a faculty member who had just directed a floridly misogynist production of Ben Jonson's *Epicoene*. I did not understand much of the conversation, but I remember his complacency, and I remember her anger, and I remember the air shimmering in the grubby rehearsal room where she had convened a departmental postmortem of the production.

Her frustration billowed, climaxed. "Would you produce a minstrel show, Bill? 'Niggers' scraping and bowing and doing the cakewalk?"

"Yes."

I remember her throwing her hands up as you do when argument fails and your only hope is that your righteousness, and your adversary's short-sightedness, will not be lost to history.

Carolyn Heilbrun, whose *Writing a Woman's Life* identifies patterns and constructs in the biographies and autobiographies of women, asserts that "power consists to a large extent in deciding what stories will be told" (43). By the time I went on the academic job market in 1997, Heilbrun's book had a permanent place in my bedside bookshelf, and those words became the first line of the cover letter that accompanied my CV. Twenty years before, I'd had no language for what was happening at that postmortem. I came from a world where women did not express anger, even about the things that affected them most immediately, let alone how some fictional character is represented on some obscure university stage. But something in my gut told me that the stakes were very real, and that I should not look away.

This memory stands—or has stood for a long time—as something outside the bounds of my education, something not to pay too much attention to, perhaps because it didn't take place in a classroom. Or perhaps I don't trust myself to convey all that was packed into that moment; at any rate, I have not shared this particular memory with my students. But I have told them about watching Case seem to fight for her life at a time when feminist criticism appeared—at least to the men who held her career in their hands—irrelevant at best. Witnesses to battle must recount what they have witnessed, for everybody's sake.

DECEMBER 2005

Seven years have passed. A lot has changed in my life. A second baby has joined my family. Against all good advice, I've left the job in Wisconsin, the tenure-track job with the sweet, smart, motivated students. The party line is that my husband and I have decided we'd like to live in the west. It is true that Ryan missed the mountains. But there are other factors, somewhat more complicated. With the adoption of that new baby, subterranean anxieties and stresses in my life come to a head. With one young child, a two-career marriage, and a tenure-track job, I spent a great deal of time patrolling the borders between my sixty-hour-a-week professional life and my personal life, vigilant against any outward sign that having a family was affecting my job performance. With a second child on the scene, an infant, it became clear that something had to give. I couldn't play at being an unencumbered scholar anymore, and the pretense no longer interested me. So I walked away from what had been my dream job five years before, and headed to Oregon with no idea what would come next.

For a year, I took care of my kids and tried my hand at playwriting. I was lucky to pick up some adjunct work and keep my teaching energies flowing.

Then, bizarrely, I landed a terrific full-time job at a small liberal arts campus thirty minutes from our new home. My workload, if anything, is heavier than before; I am now chair and the only full-time faculty member in theatre. But I am less panicky about time and preparation, largely because I've developed some reliable skills and a body of useful notes. My students are positive, caring people who are willing to work hard for their education; the big difference between this school and my last is that students tend to be more appreciative of the liberal arts, and thus the history and theory in my classes, for their own sake. Also, a certain amount of energy has been freed up. In my previous job, a great deal of mental and physical energy went into resisting and/or navigating the patriarchal departmental culture. A reward for the heavy lifting of a one-person department is that I am the departmental culture, and the decisions, mistakes, and biases I live with are my own. Finally, having jumped off the academic tightrope and landed on my feet once, I'm less concerned about appearing to be good at my job.

In *No Angel in the Classroom: Teaching through Feminist Discourse*, Berenice Malka Fisher writes:

> How feminist academics and other teachers define and respond to the problems that arise in teaching is shaped in great part through the conjunction of a teacher's political and educational values, the models of teaching and learning she has encountered and adopted, and the institutional and social conditions under which she teaches. Moreover, an individual teacher may subscribe to conflicting values or models of teaching and learning. She may be subject to contradictory institutional and social conditions. She may modify or abandon some of her values and acquire new models of teaching as she changes institutions or the institutional and social conditions change around her. (25)

Fisher evokes a feminist teacher in an active, dialectical relationship with her daily work, continually refining and uncovering the most authentic, activist pedagogy she is capable of at a given moment. Certainly, a lot has changed in my teaching, whether from acquired wisdom, active examination, or sheer expediency. I seem to be watching the students more and watching myself less, and obsessing over the quality of their thinking and writing more than ever. By many standards, I am a better teacher than I was six or seven years ago.

But how has my effectiveness as a *feminist* teacher evolved? Is there a downside to not having colleagues to resist? Do my resistance muscles threaten to atrophy? I am less self-conscious in my introduction of feminist perspectives and issues in my history classes. I don't wait for each new batch of students to find their way to a definition of feminism that they can embrace. I still encourage different perspectives and still urge students to think of good arguments that might counter their own opinions, but I am less tolerant of the suggestion that all ideas are equally valid and less generous with discussion time. Perhaps as a result, my teaching style has edged closer to that of my former teachers.

Am I less interested in my students' freedom? Maybe. Or maybe I trust that freedom is only one of many things I have to offer.

My autobiographical tendency is still in evidence, but it has taken a different form. I still speak about my own experiences, but much less about my college years. My children, whom I never would have mentioned in class five years ago, are often part of my stories, especially when they've articulated a great idea or illustrated a particular way of thinking. At first, talking about my children to students or colleagues felt like the most transgressive talking of all, a gesture of personal aggression upon the academy. Now, it would feel artificial not to talk about these people who are so important to me. Perhaps this is proof that I have finally shaken off the model of the Enlightenment scholar, a model that may have been strongest in my own consciousness. As for the rehashing of my own education, I seem to have unconsciously let go of a number of stories and simply stopped telling them. Perhaps the impulse was almost entirely self-serving after all, and perhaps this shift is a sign that I'm mostly healed from the damaging aspects of my education.

Or has this shift occurred because I sense that a certain moment in history has passed? Are my students now so much more receptive to feminism that there is no longer a reason to restage the good fight of my youth? Have I capitulated to the notion that our times are "post-feminist?" This is the most troubling possibility of all. Eight years ago, I would begin a particular discussion by asking each student to write down his or her own definition of feminism. Comparison of our definitions would lead to an introduction to various kinds of feminism, discussion of how certain discourses in this country have been defined by ideologues and extremists, and lots and lots of questions. Today, because experience has taught me that most students are not (at least overtly) hostile to feminism, I short-circuit all of this potentially rich and useful conversation. I may be turning away from a set of difficulties that Fisher suggests are important to confront. "Often," she notes, "our values remain only loosely tied to our practices. But, loose as they may be, these ties have a crucial function. While institutional pressures strain the relation between values and practices, our willingness to reflect on that tension prevents us from slipping into a shallow pragmatism in which we seek only methods that 'work'" (25).

For an overextended professor juggling the conflicting, sometimes irreconcilable demands of the academy (let alone a personal life), "methods that 'work'" may be the greatest enemy of feminist pedagogy. While "willingness to reflect" is surely to be valued, *time* to reflect can be almost non-existent. In my case, the writing of this article has brought about an important recognition. I now realize how privileged I was to witness what I did in the 1970s, to matriculate in that awkward, angry, productive time, and how significant my position as witness can be to the next generation of thinkers and artists. And suddenly, my history—my confusion, my frustration, my years of missteps, my struggles to find an engaged intellectual life, my feeling like a fraud, my *being* a fraud—this personal history no longer feels beside the point. It feels, in fact, like part of a long and important story that is more than just my own, a story that needs to be treasured, recorded, and shared.

WORKS CITED

Beck, Martha N., *Breaking Point: Why Women Fall Apart and How They Can Re-Create Their Lives*. New York: Random House, 1997.

Fisher, Berenice Malka. *No Angel in the Classroom: Teaching Through Feminist Discourse*. Lanham, MD: Roman & Littlefield Publishers, Inc., 2001.

Gilbert, Sandra M. and Susan Gubar. *The Madwoman in the Attic: the Woman Writer and the Nineteenth-century Literary Imagination*. New Haven: Yale University Press, 1979.

Heilbrun, Carolyn G. *Writing a Woman's Life*. New York: Random House, 1988.

GOOD FEMALE PARTS
ANALYZING THE CULTURE OF INSTITUTIONALIZED THEATRE EDUCATION
Corinne Rusch-Drutz

In George Bernard Shaw's most famous play, *Pygmalion*, Eliza Doolittle, a Covent Garden flower girl, is metamorphosed from a lowly street urchin into a woman who speaks and behaves like an aristocrat by Professor Henry Higgins, a phonetician eager to test his theories of language by "elevating" the young woman's station in life. Sold to the great Professor by her father for a mere £5, Eliza is positioned as a site of transaction between the old generation and the new, divested of agency and defined only as an object to be used and ultimately transformed by male subjects (de Lauretis 113; Aston 39). Throughout her course of study Eliza is trained to function in a new social reality by acquiring another language, learning a series of gestures and other forms of symbolic social signs, until she is eventually able to pass as one of the upper classes, ready to be debuted as a "woman." "I said I'd make a woman of you: and I have," Higgins boasts to Eliza at the play's end, elucidating how she has come to constitute a social agent (Act IV).

A number of feminist readings of Shaw have established Eliza as a creation of patriarchal culture.[1] Molded by Higgins in his own image, supplied with his verbal skill and gesticular instruction, she is forced to, as Sue-Ellen Case contends, "enter the doors of discourse in male drag" ("Split Subject" 131).[2] But Higgins and Eliza offer more than fodder for the debate surrounding female subjectivity: they illustrate the practice of teaching and the concept of pedagogy from a patriarchal perspective, one that remains deeply entrenched in the academy even a century after Shaw's depiction. As Arnold Silver has noted, "Higgins as an artist most clearly resembles none other than a playwright-director. He creates a role for Eliza, supplies her with lines and polishes her delivery, plots for her a climactic scene, and then tests her out beforehand in a dress rehearsal at his mother's house" (874). Within this educational system, Eliza becomes the product of an institutionalized discourse that assimilates her but does not address her specific experience. "They might as well be blocks of wood," Higgins barks at the thought of adjusting his methodology to fit the particularity of his subject (Act II). As a student, Eliza is saturated with phallocentric knowledges, entering an educational structure ruled by a male professor and masculinist epistemology (Luke and Gore 2). Left to learn her role under this restrictive tutelage, Eliza represents the way many women learn to play "good female parts" within theatre education. Like Eliza, they enter a profession that in many ways is structured to contain and discriminate against them as they struggle to adapt to elitist assumptions within theatre education that are posited as neutral forms of artistic practice.

The mark of Shaw's fictionalized pedagogy continues to be reproduced in institutionalized theatre discourses in classrooms across North America. Using a series of personal interviews as an investigative methodology, this analysis will question what it means for women to enter university in order to study theatre. Based on a series of interviews of professional women theatre practitioners in Toronto, it will reflect on the interviewees' (and my own) everyday experiences as women studying theatre and drama in a formal, post-secondary setting.[3] It will look at the ways in which theatre education intersects with and shapes women's personal and professional lived experience, examine the "neutral" vocabulary of theatre, and explore how gendered hierarchies within educational institutions are then perpetuated in the professional world.

The methodology employed here looks at institutionalized theatre education through the lives of its participants, grounded in women's material realities (Stanley and Wise 25).[4] Based on the work of sociologist Dorothy Smith in her book, *The Everyday World As Problematic* (1987), this analysis sees women as active participants (i.e., interpreters) in the formation of the social process, not bystanders in the ruling society. Smith points out that social relations in most organizations are rationally organized, systematically interrelated, and claim universality, thereby creating a seemingly neutral ruling apparatus that conceals the male subtext beneath its form, excluding women from the practices of power (4).[5] In this essay, the language that interviewees use to describe their institutional experiences affords the feminist researcher a standpoint from which to observe and analyze women's work, while at the same time critiquing the discourse, categories, sub-disciplines, and taxonomies that institutional theatre discourse devises. Feminist theorist Anne Marie Goetz argues that such structures actually "embody a history of social choices by particular groups. A critical analysis of institutions can show how these choices are sometimes socially sub-optimal, not made with either equity or efficiency in mind, but rather made to preserve the power of particular groups" (6).

TEACHING THEATRE IN CANADA

Recent theories about the practice of teaching theatre have created an "uneasy" multilogue (Luke and Gore ix), allowing a series of diverse approaches to the current debates surrounding pedagogical practice in theatre education and training. In theatre and drama programmes across Canada, a key factor in these debates is, as theatre theorist Richard Paul Knowles notes, "the myth of objectivity that underlies so much of our educational theory, practice and administration" (4).[6]

In Canada, drama and theatre are studied in myriad ways, with each environment offering students something different. The primary approaches focus on education, conservatory, and professional training. Knowles makes some useful distinctions when he notes that the term "education" generally refers to two types of curricula: "theatre" programmes, focused on theory and practice in colleges and conservatories that generally involve intensive training in acting, directing, or technical theatre along with elective courses, and which usually lead to a B.F.A. and sometimes M.F.A. degree; or "drama" programmes, usually functioning under the auspices of a college of Arts, which include traditional studies in the humanities and related fields, and which require a range of courses outside of the area of concentration, leading towards a B.A., or sometimes an M.A. or Ph.D. degree (1). Conservatory training, like that offered at the National Theatre School (NTS) in Montreal, focuses less on academic studies and instead offers an intense programme of studio work in which students acquire a blend of skills, methods, and techniques that will guide them toward a professional career. Professional training generally refers to intensive private studio instruction and is beyond the scope of my inquiry here.

LOOKING AT EDUCATION IN PRACTICE: LEARNING INSTITUTIONAL IDEOLOGIES

Both the "university programme" and "conservatory" approaches to theatre education focus on training individuals to work in the professional theatre. Once enrolled, students are introduced to the established subdisciplines within theatre–directing, playwriting, design, acting, and technical production–each with its own gendered subtext and history. Moreover, the use of traditional theatrical discourse (like Stanislavski-based acting methodologies or heavy reliance on classical canonical texts in history courses) subsumes students as individual subjects, preparing them to recognize standardized sets of knowledge as they enter the professional field. In studying these theatrical principles, students learn how to replicate those ideologies that will allow them entry into the system. Learning these ideologies, as Althusser notes, interpellates individuals as subjects, transforming them into actors in the mise en scène. In this case, the mise en scène is the School, with students' respective roles embedded in the very structure of the universities (29-31; 44-51).

Thus, in looking at university programmes and conservatory theatre training, it is necessary to take into account the ways in which systems have preconditioned individuals as social agents, reconstituting gendered modes of organization that uphold the dominant culture. Professional theatre (with some exceptions) is highly dependent upon a social organization in which the actors, designers, and technicians are subordinate to management and artistic leadership. This historical hierarchy of theatrical production conceals a gender subtext within its structural order. Directing and playwriting, for example, are two areas of theatre practice that are in no way limited to, but are more readily associated with, the masculine. Acting and design both fall under the rubric of the director's "vision," while the less conspicuous forms of theatre practice like technical production, costume work, and front-of-house coordination, which take place offstage, can be seen as more "feminized" forms of support labour in relation to their power.[7] For this reason, this analysis will focus not on playwriting or directing but will instead concentrate on actors and designer/technicians—how their physical nature within the organizational structure serves the "vision" of the playwright and director. As the ensuing interviews reveal, institutional ideologies in theatre education teach students to recycle their experiences into recognizable forms so that the subject is brought into discourse through a system that limits choice and mobility within the profession. In these interviewees' experiences, pre-existing notions of class, race, and gender are interlaced with student expectations and institutional structures, serving to perpetuate theatrical hierarchies, gender stereotypes, and barriers, particularly for women and minority actors.

In the narrative that follows, Jo[8] describes her educational experiences in theatre early on in her undergraduate years. In response to the question of why she chose to go to a university programme in order to study theatre, Jo, a stage carpenter and a lighting designer and operator, talks about the importance of family in her decision and the planning stages post-high school:

> When I was in high school I was very good at shop and drama...and I wanted to go to university. I'm sort of expected to. My parents are both immigrants; neither one of them finished high school.... When the applications went out I filled out the forms.... I remember I was so surprised to get accepted completely.... [w]ith my little portfolio, with all my little shows that I had done, plays I'd taken to Sears [Drama Festival]...I wanted to know more. [My family] did not necessarily go to theatre. I knew that it was a rather safe course to go off to university. I graduated from high school [a semester early]. I had a term to start working in the world and I...knew even then that there was no way that I was going to survive in that environment and I was hoping through studying more about theatre that I would be able to.

In her narrative, Jo looks towards theatre education in a university setting as a stepping-stone toward a professional career in theatre, one she knows she cannot attain straight out of high school. Her language suggests that the choice to attend university is accomplished by both Jo and her parents; even though theatre itself is not a part of her family's cultural life, the family's attitude toward university is deeply ingrained in their working-class, immigrant roots. While neither Jo's father (a steel company factory worker) nor her mother (a homemaker) are university educated, they, like Eliza Doolittle, trust that education will grant Jo success in *any* field, even one they know relatively little about. The subtext to the decision is clear: the opportunities afforded by the university are a safe course of action--serving as a career guarantor, a degree in theatre will raise her profile in the theatre community; a good job will provide her with the means to maintain economic viability; and without a university degree there is "no way" that Jo will be able to survive in a professional environment. Indeed, Jo's decision assumes that a university education is a necessary course of action to gain access to the professional world, what Samuel Weber calls "the institutional expression and articulation of professionalism" (31). Like many students, Jo interpellates herself as a subject within both an educational and professional context.

Upon consideration ten years after graduation, Jo feels that attending university was a good choice to have made:

> In retrospect it certainly gave me both theory and practical, which I think you need to start with. And while at the time I was not entirely convinced that I needed to know everything about theatre from the Greeks onward, in retrospect, it's actually served me so well–in the sense of being able to see larger pictures, in the sense of being able to put things in context.... So I think in that sense it was the best place for me.

The language Jo uses preserves the institutional relations of the university setting, framing professional theatre's discourses, sub-disciplines, and taxonomies in micro form, and relating them back to the macro institution of the profession at large. Jo's recognition of the importance of "theatre from the Greeks onward" reflects the traditional nature of her schooling, as well as the patriarchal value system of the theatrical canon, which privileges Western male cultural production.[9] The canon posits itself as a neutral system, highlighting the "classic" periods in Western theatre history with plays that appeal to a "universal" spectator, one that Jill Dolan has argued is assumed to be "white, middle-class, heterosexual, and male" (*Feminist Spectator* 1). By reiterating the importance of this type of historical knowledge, Jo reinforces and preserves its significance. Like Eliza, she has becomed versed in an institutional discourse that allows her to operate within a pre-existing context, using language of the discipline and her knowledge of the "universal" canon of dramatic literature as her tools.

THEORIZING DIFFERENCE: UNEARTHING THE "NEUTRAL" VOCABULARY OF THEATRE

One of the best ways to explicate the inner workings of a social institution is via the language used by its participants to define, determine, and describe their daily activities. The nexus between individual practices, institutional ideologies, and the organization of social relations becomes apparent when analyzing the language used by its actors. Theatre education is particularly ripe for investigation, as language is both what is performed onstage and in the everyday world.

In the following passage, Jillian, an actor, playwright, and acting teacher, responds to a question about how she feels about her undergraduate institution:

> I went to York [University], which I think gave me a very *usable* education.

> And by that I mean that I got work pretty much after I graduated, which to me was the whole point of going to school in the first place.... In addition to the regular actor training and voice and movement classes there were constant rehearsals that required your full attention and crazy hours.... So it was a crazy time. I really enjoyed my undergrad years and I made some great friends. As far as my education is concerned I think that it was good insofar as it got me work pretty quickly.

Jillian's narrative lays bare the way her educational experience intersected with social relations that stretched beyond the institution itself. In addition to revealing the way in which she defines herself and her use-value post graduation, Jillian employs a number of language categories which seem "neutral" enough in their description but in actuality reveal the ways in which her education has shaped her thinking about professional theatre. For example, terms like "actor training," "voice," and "movement"—all essential aspects of theatre curricula—reside in the pedagogical coordination of countless institutions, but inherent in this vocabulary are ideologies that are not readily present in the terms themselves. For example, "voice" implies the training of actors in voice and speech, generally involving exercises in breathing, tone, articulation, pronunciation, interpretation, and expression. An essential part of any general actor training program, the voice class teaches actors how to use one of their most powerful instruments. As a stand-alone term, "voice" seems rather innocuous; it goes without saying that actors need to be vocally trained. But the ideology that is integrated into the term and its meaning locate it in specific social and institutional relations. Here, Kata, an NTS graduate and an actor, dancer, and movement instructor, offers her analysis of the social relations of voice training:

> But there were problems. Though, it's funny, at the time I never really thought about them as problems in the way I do now. NTS does really intensive voice and speech work with its ensemble. I had a slight Jamaican accent that was mixed with English from the years that my family lived outside London, though I could imitate both accents in pure form perfectly. NTS pretty much tried to get me to speak with a Canadian accent, which, as they see it, is a neutral way of speaking properly. Yeah, well you can imagine that the more I thought about it, particularly years afterwards, it became an issue for me. Of course, the flip side to that is that I worked, I still work and I can turn on accents like a switch.

Kata's training resulted in a self-described double-edged sword: on the one hand, the badge of honour for having survived the rigorous NTS actor-training program, and on the other, the enforced denial of race and ethnicity in the face of upholding dominant standards for the sake of finding work—in short, institutionalized whitewashing. Yet Kata's set of circumstances are hardly unique in that they take place in a larger ideological context, at the core of which lies the struggle over power relations that are (as we witness with Jo) rooted in the texts, embedded in the curricula (as Jillian reveals), and (as Kata makes clear) ingrained in the methodologies.

Kata's example illustrates a particular pedagogical practice of theatre education, obscuring the racial and cultural identity of its individual members.[10] Her experience begs many of the questions Stan Brown asks: "Why are actors of all races and cultures taught a standard that remains relatively uninfluenced by living multicultural impacts on the English language?" (18). Developing a "Canadian accent," according to NTS pedagogical practice, "is a neutral way of speaking *properly*." This is what Dudley Knight refers to (in the context of the American system) as he discusses McLean and Skinner's *Good American Speech*, a book that has shaped generations of American actors, but one that places "good" in a "self-serving and archaic notion of Euphony, and in a model of class, ethnic, and racial hierarchy" (46). Kata is expected to embody institutional discourse, blindly accept it as the standard necessary to enter the professional realm, and assimilate this rhetoric in order to become a successful actor—not unlike what Paulo Freire refers to as the "banking system of education," one in which oppressors teach oppressed to internalize their dominant values.[11] Judith Butler also points out, in reference to the work of Paul Gilroy, that terms such as "universal" (and to that I would add "neutral") are premised on the exclusion of women and people of colour, among others, and that they are wrought along class lines with strong colonial interests. She maintains that this type of linguistic terminology is tainted and reinvokes contexts of oppression (*Excitable Speech* 160). Like Eliza, Kata's training operates as a tool used to erase and oppress her personal history, while at the same time allowing her entrance into the dominant discourse and professional realm.

Kata's example also troubles the idyllic notion of Canadian multiculturalism within the NTS system. Though in recent years the school has made attempts to balance traditional canonical performances (such as Dekker and Middleton's *The Honest Whore* [2005], Wilder's *Our Town* [2004]) with more progressive plays and collaborations (Kushner's *Angels in America* [2005], Sarah Stanley and Nick Carpenter's collaboration with the graduating class on social contracts and etiquette, *In Flagrante* [2004]), its general reliance upon time-honoured, well-made plays that conform to the "universalist" standards of the canon and uphold its traditional values in programming and practices. This comes as no surprise since NTS sees itself as producing a body of performers, directors, and designers that are best suited to serve the national landscape.[12] In an article for the *Canadian Theatre Review* on English-Canadian acting at the NTS, Denis Salter sums up the intention of the actor-training program: "The school's sense that it exists to serve what it perceives to be the needs of the existing Canadian theatre means that despite its subversive ambitions…it is inevitably constrained by the preservative values inscribed within its founding blueprint" (8).

While NTS may indeed have inclusive ambitions at heart, it, like many other theatre schools and programmes across Canada, sees multiculturalism as a language and policy to which it must adhere by applying it to an existing system of training and performance that inherently "others" those who fall outside its practices and procedures. Playwright and artistic director of Cahoots Theatre Projects, Guillermo Verdecchia, analyzes cultural diversity and ethnicity in Canadian theatre this way: "Multiculturalism, or the official policy of promoting polyethnicity, remains, after thirty years, misunderstood as the promotion and celebration of folkloric, frozen-in-time, cultures of origin" (135). He maintains that:

> If "we" expect or believe that a good production of a play by Congreve or Chekhov or Williams has something to offer just about everybody, why doesn't the same hold true for a play by M.J. Kang or Jovanni Sy or Padma Viswanathan? Too often the label multicultural, instead of meaning inclusion and diversity, means exclusion–alien and incomprehensible otherness. (135-36)

Though the Ontario theatre community in particular has seen the benefit of a number of companies focused exclusively on the representation of cultural diversity (Native Earth, Obsidian Theatre, Loud Mouth Asian Babes, Canasian Theatre, Rasik Arts, Cahoots Theatre Projects, fu-Gen Asian Canadian Theatre Company, and Caliban Arts, along with the work of other companies like Nightwood Theatre, Theatre Passe Muraille, and Factory Theatre–to name only a few), English training at NTS continues to be regarded as a "universalist aesthetic phenomenon" which students are expected to adhere to without question (Salter 9). Yet the strong and influential presence of companies like those mentioned above exposes the fissures between education and practice. Ironically, while the dominant ideology may be pushed in universities, it is not necessarily what is produced in the theatre world. (Witness, for instance, the fact that there are far more alternative theatre companies in Ontario alone than there are mainstream commercial houses; the difference lies within their size, permanent location, and annual operating budget, laying bare the ways in which economics and cultural dominance are directly intertwined).

This type of cultural dominance in theatre can be seen on multiple levels in theatre education programs. In his introduction to the anthology *Acting (Re)considered*, Phillip Zarrilli argues, "How theatre is made–from scene work and exercises, to rehearsals, to productions–includes attention to issues of race, gender, class and ethnicity. Failing that, we abrogate our responsibility not only to train students' acting skills but also to educate them about what they are being trained to perform" (3). NTS, for example, in its attempt to provide a universal program of "all things to all people" (Salter 7) teaches students to reconstruct their experiences into recognizable forms that it sees as more marketable to the theatre profession at large. In doing so, the program discounts the needs of individuals in favour of a quasi- "liberal humanist approach to actor training" (Salter 7).

Joel Greenberg notes that during the first year of most university and/or conservatory training programmes in Canada, students are encouraged to "shed old habits, mannerisms, and other holdovers that have helped the fledgling actor, designer, etc. to find security and comfort; this notion of change is predicated on the philosophy that until one recognizes one's neutral self all is superficial" (39). He points out that often this move toward "neutrality" "goes unnoticed by the individuals themselves" (39).

Under this methodology, students arrive at their professions armed with an identity formed within a patriarchal system of knowledge, scholarship, and pedagogical relations that mediates the ways in which they will utilize their training in performative practice (Luke and Gore 3). Thus–just as Eliza perceives at the end of *Pygmalion*–education that is meant to be all-encompassing to the student body eventually becomes not enough for anybody, as students eventually become aware that their training was not created with their specific experiences in mind (Salter 7).

Part of the problem with institutional ideologies in theatre education is that they are slippery slopes, with institutions oftentimes not owning up to the fact that they even exist at all. Some post-secondary theatre institutions refuse to admit that they even have an ideological framework from which they work, as *The Black Report on Theatre Training in Canada* notes:

> This question [of ideology] is usually quite embarrassing to staff and students, and many of them reject it, going so far as to say that the ideology of the school is not to have one. One fails to see, however, how any set of teaching methods can be adopted without some basis, conscious or otherwise, in certain fundamental options. (as qtd. in Salter 4)

While often overlooked–if it is even addressed at all–understanding the role of ideology, or what feminist theorists Maher and Tetreault refer to as the "constructed" or "fashioned" nature of knowledge (197), is crucial, because it allows students to evaluate their experiences in relation to the dominant culture. For instance, a feminist reading of Kata's experience reveals the ways in which the power relations within theatre education can operate. Her voice training speaks to issues surrounding representation (in both how something is represented and who is authorized to represent it), language (in its utterance and in the ways it structures the interpretation of personal experience), and performance (revealing its boundaries and constructions both ideological and, as the example of Leslie will reveal in the next section, physical).

THE COMPLICITY BETWEEN THE CLASSROOM AND THE PROFESSION

By actively eschewing any educational ideological standpoint, many institutions have adopted an art-for-art's-sake philosophy of theatre education that produces gendered outcomes within the organization. Despite being conceived in terms of liberal discourse on equality, classroom practices that purport to be "neutral" are often applied unequally (Smith 163), as Leslie, a university acting program graduate, actor, and writer, describes:

> Well, it was all well and good for them to say that as women we would be

treated equally with the guys in the class, and for the most part that seemed true. I certainly wouldn't say that women worked any harder than the men did, or vice versa. But the real kicker was at the end of second year when we had our individual evals [evaluations]. Acting programs are a weird thing because they are all mostly Stanislavski-based and so you're asked to basically reveal your innermost psychic self to a group of people who become your "therapy" group for the next four years. And I remember really clearly at the end of second year there was one girl who had offered up in one of these 'therapy-like' sessions that she'd been battling with an eating disorder. Well, at the end of the year during her eval, they told her that she was this great, bright, talented young thing who could certainly make it to Broadway if she lost about fifteen to twenty pounds. That's a hell of a way to end your year. She about lost it. Of course, the next fall she came back a lot thinner. And that wasn't unusual. I know quite a few women who were told something or other about how they looked. You know, "you'd be a great actress if your thighs weren't so fat." *Well that's really responsible.* I mean, they knew she had this eating thing going on and they told her anyway.

Leslie's story is an example of the institution reaching far beyond its educational boundaries. While much has been written on the pursuit of beauty among female actors, particularly in the Hollywood context,[13] from Naomi Wolf's seminal treatise *The Beauty Myth* to articles in *Vogue, Chatelaine, People,* and supermarket tabloids, relatively little research has been devoted to how the perpetuation of this unrealizable aesthetic is played out in the acting classroom via discursive and performative practice. As Leslie describes above, the evaluation process at her university requires students to measure up to a particular physical ideal and, via the neutralizing discourse used to mediate the process, assess students' body weights and appearances rather than their artistic merit. This evaluation gives both faculty and students a sense that they are producing a "product" that is ultimately sellable to the market, using standards that can be either explicit or implicit.

I am not suggesting that the kinds of comments Leslie refers to are in any way the norm, but they are not unheard of in both the Canadian and U.S. systems. Indeed, Dolan has commented upon the practice of telling students "they need to diet, fix their teeth or have plastic surgery" in the American training system (*Geographies of Learning* 63). As the Hollywood/Broadway aesthetic becomes the quality indicator within the cultural imaginary, schools have shifted to a more corporate educational model in order to consistently produce students who will succeed in the professional world according to dominant cultural standards. Certainly classroom practices are also able to subvert these ideologies (a topic I address later), but here we see the ways in which institutional values can literally be inscribed on students' bodies.

In evaluation processes,[14] educators slot students into a recognizable ranking system that rates the performance of the individual against a standard that mirrors a highly gendered social hierarchy, one that is more often than not mediated by the Hollywood/Broadway context. With such narrow definitions of beauty in this system, the repertoire of signs must be restricted to the known, familiar, and the marketable. While university conservatory programmes may enhance a student's chances for survival once out in the professional world, their institutional authority over individuals can send unambiguous messages to women that can and do have serious and lasting harm. As a consequence, evaluative procedures, a common method of communicating such messages, can affect a student's social identity, feelings of self worth, and emotional and physical well-being.

In the following interview, Ellen, a performer and movement instructor in a conservatory program at a major Canadian university, responds to the issue:

> I'm fully aware that we work in this dichotomy. You think I want to tell my students that they won't get hired unless they look a certain way? No way! It's ludicrous. But the fact of the matter is that is what we do. And the truth is that very few of them will get hired if they don't look like that. I hate it. I just hate it.

Students are not initiated into the cult of beauty for the first time at university—this perception has been firmly psychologically anchored well before they arrive—but the university provides ideal conditions for the reproduction of its ideology. I am not making the argument that aesthetic notions of contemporary beauty originate or are propagated only in theatre departments (the existing perception of beauty is influenced to a far greater extent by advertising and is reinforced by the media), but rather that university theatre departments are sites of cultural production (and are arguably producing the next generation of cultural producers and consumers).[15] Moreover, although theatre departments operate within informed contexts that account for gender (such as affirmative action and employment equity policies), many aspects of their curricula continue to reinscribe dominant notions of femininity that will have "market value" upon graduation.

CONCLUSIONS: TOWARD A DECONSTRUCTION OF INSTITUTIONALIZED IDEOLOGIES

"You can't take away the knowledge you gave me," Liza roars at the end of *Pygmalion* (Act IV). Indeed, her realization is an important one: once she is "educated," she will always have that knowledge at her disposal. What Eliza does not grasp in her defiance is that her training, steeped in the dominant social ideology, has taught her to package herself into a recognizable form that will allow her to seek employment once she has been granted the status of a "good" and "proper" woman. Similarly, once we teach students we cannot take away that knowledge; indeed, we encourage them to bridge what they know with how they will act once they have left the university. As Canadian playwright and educator Judith Thompson has observed, "Much of our learning culture is a stale leftover of the British military model, and Canadians traditionally have always preferred the precise, hierarchical rule-centered approach to learning" (28).

Part of my purpose here has been to explicate the notion that "theatre," as Canadian theorist Natalie Rewa notes, "is not gender-neutral, but much of the teaching of theatre appears to be based on that assumption" (1). And while it is true that simply explicating the institutional relations and ideology of theatre and drama programmes in university settings will not in and of itself transform the nature of theatre education, it does serve an important function, as it lays bare the process of construction. The specific, elaborated instances referred to here are just that, but in a broader context they point to the means by which many institutions (in both Canada and the U.S.) function. Theatre education remains imbued with dominant cultural values so that there are few, if any, opportunities for challenging the "cornerstones" of pedagogic practice at the institutional level. This task is more often than not left up to the particular professor, practitioner, or educator to "work against the grain," as hooks notes (203), by forming an individualist approach to emancipation in post-secondary theatre education. While one educator in one classroom can make all the difference in students' lives, there is only so much an individual can do within these larger confines. Although many individuals work against traditional theatre pedagogy from feminist, radical, materialist, or other counter-discursive perspectives, such individual, independent practices may not have any great effect on the ideology of the institution. Structural change and collective action are the only hope for feminist pedagogy to evolve beyond the traps of liberal ideology.

Working toward more resistant pedagogies in theatre is not an undertaking that can be accomplished overnight. Having taught in one of the largest undergraduate theatre departments in Canada, I am painfully aware of how time-consuming and incremental it can be to make even minor changes in a curriculum, and I am equally sensitive to the demands that most educators have on their time in addition to their teaching loads. Various external forces affect educators as well. As former director of the Graduate Centre for Study of Drama at the University of Toronto, Domenico Peitropaolo, points out, in an age of massive budget cuts and financial crisis, market-conscious university policies have often threatened drama as a discipline, resulting in the "institutional diminishment" of university drama programmes in Ontario (57). With the focus on big issues such as stabilizing government funding, securing corporate donations and endowment funds, overcrowded classrooms, and departmental atrophy as students leave before completing their degrees, it would appear that many universities have more pressing concerns than the circulation of ideological values. And while theatre may not be the most efficient and organized location to circulate dominant forms of discourse, it plays nonetheless an important role in the circulation of cultural producers and consumers. Yet it is essential that we move beyond a liberal notion of pedagogical change in theatre, which focuses on the work of particular individuals who seek to change the system, and challenge ideologies at the institutional level.

A brief survey of literature reveals a number of practical suggestions aimed at effecting such change. Knowles proposes a number of changes that resist the "liberal-education model of separating the 'scientific,' technological and methodological from the realm of values" such as developing classes, courses, and curricula that do not proclaim neutrality in either theatrical techniques or the transhistorical meanings of dramatic texts; engaging students and educators as practitioners *and* academics in discussions of "how" and "in whose interests" meaning is produced; reconceptualizing the relationship between theatre studies and theatre practice; and undertaking these resistant methodologies in script analyses, workshops, rehearsal halls, studios, and classrooms (5). Working toward this mode of pedagogy confirms Judith Thompson's assertion that teaching and artistic practice are not mutually exclusive (29). One example of a theatre programme that has taken up the challenge to adopt a broader and arguably more comprehensive approach to theatre education can be found at York University, where students in the Theatre Studies stream can enroll in a series of courses called Creative Ensemble, which focuses on the devising of original theatre in a collaborative setting. Through classroom exercises and the creation, rehearsal, and presentation of devised and interpreted performance projects, participants explore the essential questions and investigative tools of the theatre practitioner alongside courses in history, dramaturgy, political theatre, playwriting, aesthetics, and criticism. In this way, practice is placed directly within the context of theatre studies, allowing students to experience theatre from myriad perspectives, as they should in any theatre or drama programme.

Such perspectives might include attention to the ways in which the discipline might more accurately reflect realities of the twenty-first century. For instance, dramatic theorist Margaret B. Wilkerson has noted that educational institutions are currently faced with the challenge of bringing more people of colour and women into the academy and preparing students for a world filled with technological developments that are likely to redefine theatre (241). Correspondingly, Rewa suggests that institutions examine and reformulate the ways in which specific teaching methods and evaluative standards privilege a particular definition theatre. She suggests that the profound movement of peoples globally within the last two decades be integrated into the teaching of drama and theatre so that students can understand the impact this has had on theatre practice internationally (1). But this kind of democratic participation, as Fine, Weis and Powell argue, needs to be fostered by the institution. Echoing the work of Freire, they maintain that,

> [if schools] are to produce engaged, critical citizens who are willing to imagine and build multiracial and multiethnic communities, then we presume schools must take as their task the fostering of group life that ensures equal status but within a context that takes community-building as its task. The

process of sustaining a community must include a critical interrogation of difference as the rich substance of community life and an invitation for engagement that is relentlessly democratic, diverse, participatory, and always attentive to equity and parity. (252)

The dramatic upsurge of new scholarship that focuses on intersecting issues of gender, race, sexuality, class, ability, and nationality (among other topics) challenges our traditional view of theatre's history and culture to include theatrical histories and cultural acts. Indeed, the academy is well suited to tackle some of these important issues; it remains, as Dolan notes, "perhaps the one large influential public forum left…in which debates can be staged productively, and in which those otherwise disenfranchised from the largest public discourses can find their concerns studied, researched, and examined as worthy and meaningful" (*Geographies of Learning* 14-15). And yet, as we witness with the examples above, university theatre programmes and conservatory training continue, however unwittingly, to foster difference, making it a "product of institutions, where it is the outcome of institutionalized patterns of distributing resources and social value, public and private power" (Goetz 6). For this reason it is necessary to continuously investigate and challenge institutional ideologies in theatre and drama education. This will allow us to move toward a more resistant pedagogy that eschews the "good female parts" women have been encouraged to play (in the classroom, as educators, on the stage, and in culture) in favour of roles that reflect the veracity of their lived experiences. But this discussion is only useful if these changes can be developed in tandem with the practical world of theatre-making, allowing academics, administrators, activists, and artists to work concurrently toward reconstructing ideological fractures within the institution.

Almost a century after Shaw's creation, Eliza still represents theatre's power to educate, in all of its complexities. But Eliza also reminds us that the past continues to inform the present, offering insights into places where feminist intervention can act as a fissure in the geography of theatre education and unearth gendered conditions and practices that can and must be eliminated for the future of cultural production.

NOTES

[1] See, among others, the work of Bower, "Tyranny, Telling, Learning: Teaching and the Female Student"; Gainor, *Shaw's Daughters: Dramatic and Narrative Constructions of Gender*; Kaufman, G.B. *Shaw: A Collection of Critical Essays*; Lorichs, *The Unwomanly Woman in Bernard Shaw's Drama and Her Social and Political Background*; Muggleston, "Shaw, Subjective Inequality, and the Social Meanings of Language in *Pygmalion*"; and Watson, *The Shavian Guide to the Intelligent Woman*.

[2] In her re-reading of Lacan, Case identifies the entrance into language (metaphorically represented by Lacan as the "mirror stage") as the entrance into discourse, the external order that forms identity. Because the subject of discourse or representation in Lacanian philosophy is gendered as male, women cannot inhabit the subject position in the same way, unless they do so as male-identified subjects. Case offers the following analysis:

> Yet, if I might expand Lacan's metaphor in order to include the possibility of the female

subject, "she" also sees in that mirror that she is a woman. At that moment she further fractures, split once as the male-identified subject and his subjectivity and split once more as
the woman who observes her own subject position as both male-identified and female. She
acts in the system in the male position, but she also marks that position with her own
female action. This produces a double split for the woman subject: she is split in the way
the Lacanian subject is split, but she is also split in discourse. She cannot appear as a single,
whole, continuous subject as the male can because she senses that his story is not her story.
("From Split Subject to Split Britches" 131)

[3] Though Canadian and U.S. systems are not so dissimilar, this essay will focus only on theatre education in Canada.

[4] See also the work of, among others, Haraway, "A Manifesto for Cyborgs: Science, Technology, and
Socialist Feminism in the 1980s"; Harding, *Feminism & Methodology*; Hennessy, *Materialist Feminism and
the Politics of Discourse*; and Hennessy and Ingraham, *Materialist Feminism: A Reader in Class, Difference,
and Women's Lives.*

[5] The ruling apparatus is a complex of organized practices within the state that ideologically interpene-
trate the multiple sites of power within society. In his work "Ideology and Ideological State
Apparatuses (Notes towards an Investigation)," Althusser locates the functioning of the ruling apparatus in a dominant ideology, the ideological state apparatus (ISA), which he sees as the primary means
by which capitalism is secured. Althusser identifies the following institutions as ISAs: religious, educational (both public and private), family, legal, the political system (including all political parties), trade
and unions, communication, and cultural. What unifies each of these apparatuses in their apparent
diversity is their connection to both the public and private domains and the ways in which they function "massively" and "predominantly" by ideology (20).

[6] Pagination for this source refers to the printed version of the online document.

[7] *Adding it Up: The Status of Women in Canadian Theater* reveals that
> While women are not found in the triumvirate of power [artistic directors, playwrights, and
> directors] in great numbers, they abound in industry support occupations that serve the
> (usually male) creative figures—for example, as assistant directors, dramaturgs, administra-
> tive staff and box office workers. Moreover, the distribution and division of labour in the
> theatre profession indicates that traditional conceptions of conventional gender roles are
> holding firm: women are still relegated to areas associated with domesticity and so-called
> feminine abilities in the organizational realm, as costume designer, stage managers and gen-
> eral managers. (Burton 23)

[8] Interviews for this article were obtained as part of research for my doctoral dissertation, *Interviewing
the Mothers of Invention: A Qualitative Analysis of Women Theatre Practitioners in Toronto*, and were taken in
the years between 1995-2000. All of the participants' names have been changed.

[9] See, among others, the work of Aston; Austin; Belsey; Butler; Case; de Lauretis; Diamond, *Unmaking
Mimesis*, "(In)Visible Bodies in Churchill's Theatre," "Refusing the Romanticism of Identity: Narrative
Interventions in Churchill, Benmussa, Duras," "Mimesis, Mimicry and the 'True-Real;'" Dolan; and
Phelan. See in particular the work of Case; Donkin and Clement, *Upstaging Big Daddy: Directing Theatre
as if Gender and Race Matter*; and especially Dolan's essay "Feminism and the Canon: Questions of
Universality" in her collection *The Feminist Spectator as Critic* in relation to questions of institutionaliz-
ing and canonizing plays by women.

[10] My example(s) comes from the professional English training programme. NTS is a fully bilingual
school in both its programming and its culture; its English training programme is separate, but certainly not subordinate to, the French programme.

[11] In *Pedagogy of the Oppressed*, Freire describes the traditional educational model as one in which students
are seen as passive consumers. He sees much of mainstream education as a banking system in which
students are taught that effective learning is accomplished by memorizing information and regurgitat-
ing it, effectively training students to "deposit" knowledge that can be used at a later date within dominant cultural contexts. In *Teaching to Transgress*, bell hooks responds to Freire, observing that, "Since so
many professors teach from that standpoint, it is difficult to create the kind of learning community that

can fully embrace multiculturalism" (40).

[12] Though NTS claims that the "[s]chool's evolution has reflected the social, political, and cultural changes that swirled beyond its walls," it has responded to a narrowly-defined notion of diversity within the scope of the national landscape (http://www.ent-nts.qc.ca/nts/facts&highlights.htm

[13] See, among others, the work of Browning, "The Cultural Voice"; Chancer, *Reconcilable Differences: Confronting Beauty, Pornography, and the Future of Feminism*; Cogan and Erickson, *Lesbians, Levis, and Lipstick: The Meaning of Beauty in Our Lives*; Friday, *The Power of Beauty*; Grimshaw, *Women's Bodies: Discipline and Transgression*; Meceda, "In Pursuit of an Illusion: Effects of the Mass Media Ideal of Beauty on women's Body Image."; Thesander, *The Feminine Ideal*; and Wolf.

[14] Evaluations are common in conservatory programmes in which students are assessed, generally by a panel, upon their entry into the programme and throughout the year, the most important of these taking place at the end of each academic year. As Greenberg notes: "The end of the year is often marked by a final personal evaluation between each student and a panel of teachers who will recommend either moving on...or terminating the programme. In effect, the year ends where the previous year began—with a lengthy audition process with winners and losers..." (39)

[15] Watkins has observed that English departments are not only sites of culture production, but also sites of cultural circulation (22). Surely the same may be argued about theatre departments, where cultural production takes place on multiple levels. What makes theatre so unique is that these dynamics are played out on the bodies of students.

WORKS CITED

Althusser, Louis. *Essays on Ideology*. London: Verso Editions, 1984.

Aston, Elaine. *An Introduction to Feminism and Theatre*. London and New York: Routledge, 1995.

_____. *Feminist Theatre Practice: A Handbook*. London and New York: Routledge, 1999.

Austin, Gayle. *Feminist Theories for Dramatic Criticism*. Ann Arbor: U of Michigan P, 1990.

Browning, L. Delana. "More Than Just Appearances: Cosmetic Practices and the Cultural Construction of Gender." Diss. U of Pennsylvania, 1997.

Burton, Rebecca, main researcher. Working Draft [Sept. 17, 2006]. *Equity in Canadian Theatre: The Women's Initiative, A report on the Phase One Findings of the Status of Women in Canada*, 2006.

Butler, Judith. *Excitable Speech: The Politics of the Performative*. London and New York: Routledge, 1997.

_____. "Performative Acts and Gender Constitution: An Essay in Phenomenology and Feminist Theory." Ed. Sue-Ellen Case. *Performing Feminisms: Feminist Critical Theory and Theatre*. Baltimore and London: Johns Hopkins U P, 1990. 270-282.

_____. *Gender Trouble: Feminism and the Subversion of Identity*. London and New York: Routledge, 1990.

Case, Sue-Ellen. "From Split Subject to Split Britches." *Feminine Focus: The New Women Playwrights*. Ed. Enoch Brater. Oxford: Oxford U P, 1989: 126-146

_____. "*Feminism and Theatre*. New York: Routledge, 1988.

_____. "Re-viewing Hrotsvit." *Theatre Journal*. 35.4 (Dec 1983) 533-542.

de Lauretis, Teresa, ed. *Alice Doesn't: Feminism, Semiotics, Cinema*. Bloomington: Indiana UP, 1984.

Dolan, Jill. *The Feminist Spectator as Critic*. Ann Arbor: University of Michigan Press, 1991.

_____. *Presence & Desire: Essays on Gender, Sexuality, Performance*. Ann Arbor: U of Michigan P, 1993.

Fine, M, L. Weis and L.C. Powell. "Communities of Difference: A Critical Look at Desegregated Spaces Created for and by Youth." *Harvard Educational Review* 67.2: 247-284.

Freire, Paulo. *Pedagogy of the Oppressed*. Trans. Myra Bergman Ramos. 30th anniversary ed. New York: Continuum, 2000.

_____. "G.B.S. and the New Woman." *New England Theatre Journal* 1.1 (1990): 1-17.

Goetz, Anne Marie, ed. *Getting Institutions Right for Women in Development.* London and New York: Zed Books Ltd., 1997.

Greenberg, Joel. "Rhythms of Learning: Expectations and Aspirations." *Canadian Theatre Review* 78 (Spring 1992): 38-41.

hooks, bell. *Teaching to Transgress: Education as the Practice of Freedom.* London and New York: Routledge, 1994.

Knight, Dudley. "Standard Speech: the Ongoing Debate." *Voice and Speech Review* (2000): 31-54.

Knowles, Richard Paul. "This Discipline Which is Not One." *Theatre Research in Canada/Recherches Théâtrales au Canada* 16.1,2 (1995). 21 November 2003 <http://www.lib.unb.ca/Texts/TRIC/homepage.html>.

Luke, Carmen and Jennifer Gore. *Feminisms and Critical Pedagogy.* London and New York: Routledge, 1992.

Maher, Frances A. and Mary Kay Thompson Tetreault. *The Feminist Classroom.* New York: Basic Books, 1994.

National Theatre School of Canada. "Facts and Highlights." National Theatre School website. "FACTS AND HIGHLIGHTS." 28 October 2006 <http://www.ent-nts.qc.ca/nts/facts&highlights.htm>

Phelan, Peggy. "Feminist Theory, Poststructuralism, and Performance." *TDR: The Drama Review.* 32.1 (Spring 1988): 107-127.

_____. *Unmarked: The Politics of Performance.* New York and London: Routledge, Chapman and Hall, Inc., 1993.

_____. "White Men and Pregnancy: Discovering the Body to be Rescued." In *Acting Out: Feminist Performances.* Ed. Lynda Hart and Peggy Phelan. Ann Arbor: University of Michigan Press, 1993. 383-401.

Pietropaolo, Domenico. "The Professional Theatre and the Teaching of Drama in Ontario Universities." *How Theatre Educates: Convergences & Counterpoints.* Kathleen Gallagher,and David Booth,eds. Toronto: U of Toronto P, 2003. 56-66.

Rewa, Natalie. "Cultural Realities of Teaching." *Theatre Research in Canada/Recherches Théâtrales au Canada* 16.1,2 (1995). 21 November 2003 <http://www.lib.unb.ca/Texts/TRIC/homepage.html>.

Salter, Denis. "Body Politics: English-Canadian Acting at National Theatre School." *Canadian Theatre Review* 71 (Summer 1992): 4- 14.

Shaw, Bernard. *Pygmalion and Candida.* Avon, CN: Limited Editions Club, 1974.

Silver, Arnold. "Higgins and Shaw." *The Bedford Introduction to Drama. Third Edition.* Ed. Lee A. Jacobus. Boston: Bedford Books, 1997. 874-875.

Smith, Dorothy. *The Everyday World As Problematic.* Toronto: University of Toronto Press, 1987.

Stanley, Liz and Sue Wise. "Method, methodology and epistemology in feminist research process." Ed. Liz Stanley. *Feminist Praxis: Research, Theory and Epistemology in Feminist Sociology.* London and New York: Routledge, 1990. 20-62.

Thompson, Judith. "'I Will Tear You to Pieces': The Classroom as Theatre." *How Theatre Educates: Convergences & Counterpoints.* Kathleen Gallagher,and David Booth,eds. Toronto: U of Toronto P, 2003. 25-34.

Verdecchia, Guillermo. "Seven Things About Cahoots Theatre Projects." *How Theatre Educates: Convergences & Counterpoints.* Kathleen Gallagher,and David Booth,eds. Toronto: Uof Toronto P, 2003. 133-143.

Watkins, Evan. *Work Time: English Departments and the Circulation of Cultural Value.* Stanford: Stanford U P, 1989.

Weber, Samuel. *Institution and Interpretation*. Minneapolis: U Minnesota P, 1987.

Wolf, Naomi. *The Beauty Myth*. Toronto: Vintage Books, 1990, 1991.

Zarrilli, Phillip B. "General Introduction: Between Theory and Practice." *Acting (Re)considered: Theories and practices*. Ed. Phillip B. Zarrilli. New York: Routledge, 1995. 1-22.

2 ACTIVATING PRACTICE

As performance processes have become models for dialogue, learning, and social change, the roles of theatre artists and teachers have merged in important ways. For this reason, this section represents the work of artists and practitioners who work in a variety of ways as either faculty members or visiting artists. The writers in this section have developed feminist teaching strategies that are dangerous, subversive, out-spoken, sometimes eschew safety, and are always non-traditional. Their work encourages students to question and explore categories of identity through their bodies, imaginations, and intellects. These teachers and artists push students beyond the boundaries of comfort, safety, and convention, to take risks, and to challenge naturalized modes of theatre practice. The previous section emphasized feminist teachers' voices in theatre classrooms, rehearsals, and institutions. This section focuses on ways teachers can facilitate student agency and collaborative knowledge production based on rigorous theory and embodied practice. Various forms of improvisation and creative teaching techniques connect the essays in this section, encouraging teachers to challenge students in ways that can both empower and terrify. Through these practices, authors reflect upon how relationships between creative freedom and political freedom can be activated.

Joni L. Jones/Omi Osun Olomo in "Making Language: The Jazz Aesthetic and Feminist Foundations" dismantles conventions of theatrical process by exploring a "polyrhythmic musically driven language" that becomes an African American "jazz aesthetic." Jones/Olomo calls for the "destruction of conventional dramatic structure [as] a necessary step toward self making" and thus invokes the dangerous power of jazz music that involves living "a complex Blackness" and can represent the destruction of systems of oppression. Through an interview with director and performer Laurie Carlos and through invoking the work of performance poet Sharon Bridgforth, Jones/Olomo contrasts an "ethic of care" with the dangerous and even coercive methods Carlos uses to create deeply honest performances that engage the core of a performer's being.

Deb Margolin, like Laurie Carlos, encourages students to explore writing and rehearsal processes that involve nurturing and care but ultimately lead to outrageous revelations of self. Lisa Jo Epstein's interview with Deb Margolin charts the dangerous waters of her pedagogy of desire. Margolin's methods instill a grave sense of the responsibilities of artists and encourage students to face the deepest, often most frightening, parts of themselves. Collapsing boundaries of identity, Margolin resists notions of writing as a solitary act and instead helps students draw upon the rich resources of everyday life and auto-biography in a slippery space of collaborative creation. Margolin encourages students, as does Carlos, to undertake the radical act of transforming the per-sonal into the political via the body.

In "Play Fair: Feminist Tools for Teaching Improv," Amy Seham shares feminist antidotes to sexism, racism, and homophobia in traditional improvi-sational comedy. Echoing Carlos and Margolin, she acknowledges the cre-ative potential of improvisation "to offer participants both...individual agency and [a] sense of supportive community." However, Seham's teaching and directing of comedy improv is situated precariously close to some of the dan-gerous pitfalls that can reinscribe dominant cultural values. Seham acknowl-edges this and offers concrete solutions, proactive strategies, and specific improvisation exercises that infiltrate improv comedy with a feminist con-sciousness that challenges stereotypes.

Kathleen Juhl in "Feminism in the Acting Classroom" also offers concrete solutions for helping students avoid reinscribing stereotypes. Juhl rejects the traditional "master-teacher" approach to acting pedagogy and instead encour-ages students to play fluidly and spontaneously back and forth between improvisation and text work that involves cross-gender play and engenders rich interactional details. Playing the helpful "trickster," Juhl facilitates a process in which students are simultaneously in a state of flow and imbalance. Like Carlos's and Margolin's methods, the process involves teacher and stu-dents inspiring each other's work in a space of danger and seduction that is informed by feminist political consciousness.

Stacy Wolf, in "On the Gender Continuum," engages stereotypes by ask-ing students to identify famous personalities from popular culture as more or less masculine or feminine on a continuum. Facing their own attitudes toward gender, this exercise challenges students through a simple yet contentious exercise. Like Juhl and Seham, Wolf admits that using stereotypes can rein-force them, but she also sees in this teaching strategy a way in which the many variables that constitute gender can be viewed and subverted. Wolf pushes her students to confront personal perimeters of comfort, safety, dan-ger, and desire as she challenges them to interrogate gender.

Like all of the writers in this section, Kate Bornstein and Barbara Carellas use creative processes to open students and performers to artistic freedom through radically reconsidered political realizations. Interviewed here by Kathleen Juhl, Bornstein and Carellas discuss how Bornstein's identity as an M to F transgender person and Carellas' identity as a sex positive activist guides their teaching as a queer couple who call themselves "too tall blondes." They don't just invoke stereotypes; they embody them with honesty and gusto. Their teaching combines interests in paradox, trantric sex, and new age philosophies. Bornstein strives to instill a sense of morality as she empowers young students to create "gender queer" performances both in hir workshops and in their lives. Carrellas captures rich experiences of embodied feelings in her teaching by pushing students beyond intellectual realms. She unapologetically invokes the spiritual, sensual, and, of course, sexual in her teaching.

"MAKING LANGUAGE"
THE JAZZ AESTHETIC AND FEMINIST FOUNDATIONS
INCLUDING AN INTERVIEW WITH LAURIE CARLOS AND EXCERPTS FROM WRITING
BY SHARON BRIDGFORTH

Joni L. Jones/Omi Osun Olomo

> *the man who thought i wrote with intentions of outdoing the white man in the acro-*
> *batic distortions of english waz absolutely correct. I cant count the number of times I*
> *have viscerally wanted to attack deform n maim the language that I waz taught to*
> *hate myself in/ the language that perpetuates the notions that cause pain to every*
> *black child as he/she learns to speak of the world & the "self." Yes/being an afro-*
> *american writer is something to be self-conscious abt/ & yes/ in order to think n com-*
> *municate the thoughts n feelings I want to think n communicate/ I haveta fix my tool*
> *to my needs/ I have to take it apart to the bone/ so that the malignancies/ fall away/*
> *leaving us space to literally create our own image.*

—Ntozake Shange, "unrecovered losses/black theatre traditions"

When Audre Lorde powerfully declared "The master's tools will never dismantle the master's house" (1984) she was speaking as much about the nature
of women's writing as she was about any other method of political resistance.
For playwright and poet Ntozake Shange, this destruction of written convention
is a necessary step toward self making, which, along with jazz and Black
Feminism, offers insurgent resistive strategies for naming and living a complex
Blackness.

Although jazz music has been discussed, debated, defined, and redefined
since its emergence on the U.S. landscape at the top of the twentieth century, it
still eludes concise definitions. Duke Ellington has variously described jazz as "a
good barometer of freedom…the music is so free that many people say it is the
only unhampered, unhindered expression of complete freedom yet produced in
this country" (qtd. in Ward and Burns vii) and, more simply, jazz is "freedom of
expression" (qtd. in Dance 2-22). A theatrical jazz aesthetic similarly rests on
both a freedom within the act of creation and a politically understood freedom
that requires the insertion of the individual self through structured improvisation. A theatrical jazz aesthetic is also a performance form which often relies on
the subjective experience of one character, a memory-laden sense of time and

place, a keen attention to the visual/physical/imagistic aspects of the writer's work, and multivocalic, polyrhythmic, musically-driven language. Just as musical jazz requires the courage to explore one's own virtuosity, a theatrical jazz aesthetic insists on a personal integrity and arresting honesty that allows for flights of improvised brilliance in performance.

A theatrical jazz aesthetic discards or bends the "master's tools" of conventional dramatic structure, casting, actor training, and performance to create work that is immediate, visceral, and life altering–once you dismantle oppressive conventions in your art, you inevitably/simultaneously dismantle the overt and latent structures in your everyday life. Jazz critic Albert Murray describes jazz as the "heroic moment…when you establish your identity" (112). Murray's comment aligns well with the manifesto created by the Combahee River Collective, which states "If Black women were free, it would mean that everyone else would have to be free since our freedom would necessitate the destruction of all the systems of oppression" (232). The very freedom imbedded in the Collective's definition of Black Feminism is the same freedom that undergirds jazz, as both freedoms seek to radically re-imagine systems of power so that people, on the one hand, and art on the other, can be forces for liberation.

Laurie Carlos, an elder and maverick in this performance mode, has worked closely with genre-defying writer Sharon Bridgforth. Their collaborative production history includes six productions: *Blood Pudding, Alaskan Heat Blue Dot, con flama, geechee crossing/marsha's overture,* and *The Pork Chop Wars.*[1] This artistic alliance has generated work that is squarely situated in a theatrical jazz aesthetic and which demonstrates the feminist/womanist principles that run alongside the tradition. The intertwined relationship between Black Feminist theory and key elements of a theatrical jazz aesthetic is demonstrated in the structure, voice, and content of an unpublished essay by Bridgforth:

i believe that we/wy'mn of Colour write to save ourselves/to breathe
to understand and celebrate our Ancestors
to honor our elders
to keep from going crazy/to make space for our lives in a world that denies the complexities of
our existence.
i believe that we/wy'mn of Colour have to deal with generations of voices that have
historically pounded lies in our heads/each time we imagine ourselves writing. lies like;
your story isn't important–you're not good enough–you don't deserve to make time for
art–no one wants to hear what you have to say–art isn't as important as "real" activism-
you can't make a living as a writer   etc.
…
i am interested in the musicality of language/creating word operas to explore the
personal/to articulate and examine the spaces between and connecting autobiography and
mythology/memory.
with poetry as the base/changing rhythms
making blues
my goal is to use the page as a canvas for sonic creation/in the tradition of jazz.

...
i do my work in the spaces made by wy'mn of Colour writers like
june jordan laurie carlos cherríe moraga jessica hagedorn robbie mccauley audre lorde
and so many others/who have dedicated their lives to
not only the work of craft but the
work of teaching/mentoring/bringing along new generations of wy'mn of
    Colour/voices. (2004)

This essay explores the artistic alliance between Carlos and Bridgforth
through interviews with both artists, excerpts from Bridgforth's work, and my
own experiences (interspersed in italics) as a dramaturg for Bridgforth and a
performer under Carlos's direction. This latter strategy I borrow from Kim
Benston's idea of autocritography, a methodology that is one part autoethnogra-
phy and one part critical analysis (284). My desire is to place three practitioners
of a jazz aesthetic—Carlos, Bridgforth, and myself—in conversation through the
juxtaposition of our distinctive voices.

Through their years of commitment to art and to one another, Bridgforth
and Carlos demonstrate the fundamentals of Black feminist theory as they—in
Carlos's words—"make language" together. Bridgforth acknowledges the significance of this mutually understood language when she describes her work and
her relationship with Carlos in a 2003 interview, which took place in Daniel
Alexander Jones's[2] New York apartment. We discussed our history of work in a
jazz aesthetic, and when asked to describe her artistic influences, Bridgforth
stated,

> ... the way [Carlos] approaches work is so validating...the other thing was
> knowing that I was working inside of a lineage, because before it was all
> intuitive and spirits.... So listening to her talk helped me to find some of
> that...to watch her work is to watch magic, is to watch a priestess, is to
> watch a way that the world can be a better place.... I write in these little pic-
> tures and then, what I watched her do was shape layers of the story that I
> had written with gestures, movement, and other things. So she layers the
> story, she pulled the story out.... So it helped me to see what I was writing.
> (Bridgforth 2003)

Black feminist scholar Joy James speaks of the need for warriors rather than
soldiers in the fight against racism and misogyny (1-2). For James, soldiers work
for the state and are therefore bound by state law—this is hardly a break with
the master's tools—while warriors are independent freedom fighters who are
bound to the rules they create together in their fight for the sanctity of their
identities. Carlos and Bridgforth are such warriors, as each has resisted the artistic institutionalization that so many artists must yield to in order to economically and critically survive. Their continued work with each other in various
cities around the country makes them artistic warriors who create nomadic,
transient "institutions" wherever their collaborations occur.

Carlos and Bridgforth's artistic choices must be examined through their
relationship to formal institutions. They have eschewed an extended affiliation

with academic institutions, though Carlos's friend and collaborator Robbie McCauley offers an example of how non-traditional work might function within a university theatre department. McCauley is an OBIE Award-winning playwright whose most recent works have been rooted in an examination of social issues. She has been an Associate Professor of Theatre at Emerson College since 2001, where she teaches African-American Theatre and Culture, and Theatre and Community, among other courses. This institutionalization affords her a professional visibility and an economic stability that are rarely granted to artists who do not have such affiliations.

In critiquing her own teaching Jane Tompkins argues, "I think that this essentially, and more than anything else, is what we teach our students: how to perform within an institutional academic setting in such a way that they will be thought highly of by their colleagues and instructors" (654). Institutions foster an environment in which being liked takes precedence over doing good work, in which gaining favor with the teacher or the director is more important than a full exploration of a dramatic moment. Institutions encourage the very polite and politically savvy masking that undermines Carlos's insistence on integrity to one's self and honesty in the moment of artistic creation. Although Carlos has not formally held a university teaching position, her rehearsals are an extraordinary site for a rigorous education. What she teaches through rehearsals, productions, and her rare performances exceeds the bounds of much academic theatre training precisely because she has not succumbed to the often stifling demands of institutions.

Like Carlos, Bridgforth has shunned institutional commitments and has doggedly pursued her own artistic path. While she has presented workshops and readings on the university lecture circuit, she has not held a university position that supports her writing or her productions. The result is that she has not enjoyed the same reputation as those artists who have been teachers or artists-in-residence at universities and colleges, yet through her commitment to RedBone Press (the independent press that has published her work), listening to the stories the ancestors tell, and her self-defined apprenticeship with Carlos, she has established herself in literary and avant-garde performance circles as an award-winning innovator. In this way, Bridgforth has participated in and created alternative institutional structures. Through her writing workshops she has developed a community of writers with whom she nurtures and grows long after the workshops have ended. She also works on the fringes of institutions— for example, serving as the Anchor Artist for The Austin Project, produced by the Center for African and African American Studies at the University of Texas at Austin; leading workshops for the YWCA; acting as Artistic Director for an Austin-based queer people of color organization; and being guest artist at several universities. Carlos has also participated in alternative institutional structures, such as curating Penumbra Theatre's Late Night Series, serving as guest artist to The Austin Project, and acting as guest director to university theatres around the country. These fringe positions allow Carlos and Bridgforth to reap some of the benefits of institutions–administrative expertise, regular salary, consistent communities–while enacting subversive strategies for art-making and social change.

Of course, as noted in the case of McCauley, institutions are capable of supporting some artists' non-traditional work. Indeed, Carlos has developed ongoing relationships with the Center for African and African American Studies at the University of Texas and the Department of Theatre at Arizona State University. Although she serves as an occasional guest artist rather than a full-time employee at these universities, these relatively recent academic alliances in her career help blunt the personal challenges of living as an independent artist.

In 2006, Laurie was in Austin working with the women of The Austin Project, sponsored by the Center for African and African American Studies (CAAAS) at the University of Texas at Austin. The Austin Project consists of women of color artists, scholars, activists, and their allies who learn to use writing as a tool for social change. Although CAAAS sponsors the group, most of the participants are not affiliated with the university. Laurie rehearsed intensely with the women in the evenings, and during the day she agreed to visit some classes in the Department of Theatre and Dance. I was teaching a course for the department's M.F.A. actors and was excited to have Laurie work with them. When Laurie came to the class, the students did not have time to curry favor with her. They were thrust into some of the most challenging work of the semester without any sense of how to win her over with smiles or wit. A student performed her work, and Laurie instantly had her start again. Laurie seemed to almost growl as she questioned the student about her choices in the performance. As the student started her work again, Laurie walked up to her, grabbed her buttocks, and said, "This is what you are afraid of! Now do it again—from here," as she firmly held the student's buttocks in her hands. The student was shocked into honesty and began to cry. "Now talk! Say the lines!" The student mumbled through her tears. "Now, do the gesture!" The student offered the gesture that was now transformed into a movement that came from her groin rather than her rehearsed plan. "THAT'S what you are working for! There's your story!"

When the student finished and sat in the performance space, Laurie joined her and grabbed her foot. "See, you hate your feet! That's where your story is." The student nodded in recognition. I sat there in distress. I knew Laurie was doing what was needed, I knew the student was instantly making strides that could have taken years to achieve. I had cringed in so many workshops and rehearsals when Laurie snarled a hidden truth at a performer who later recognized the importance of that humbling moment. I had been on the receiving end of Laurie's direction and knew well the horror of this public exposure, as well as the revelation that such exposure had given me. In spite of what I knew firsthand to be a critical moment of self-awareness, I worried if the students could see it for themselves. Would they be frightened and angry by Laurie's masterful exposure of performance lies? Had they—had I—become so accustomed to being nice in the classroom that we couldn't accept the ruptures necessary for finding our true work? Had I avoided such essential directness and clarity because I had internalized the need for student approval over twenty-plus years of teaching? Later, a few students told me how powerful and important it was to have Laurie work with them. She opened them to new possibilities in performance because she put the work before all else.

Nel Noddings' "ethic of care," the idea that caring about others should be the foundation for education and justice (23-4), has provided a useful frame for examining feminist pedagogy, yet this "ethic of care" might offer feminist pedagogy new strategies if considered through an African-American lens. African-American women have stereotypically been viewed as caregivers, so much so that the Mammy icon has stifled our ability to be respected as three-dimensional individuals. This is particularly true in academic settings, where some students expect African-American women professors to be nurturing counselors rather than incisive artists and intellectuals. Interestingly, in spite of the stereotype, some scholars have discovered that African-American women do indeed engage in an "ethic of care," at least in their interactions with other African-American women. Feminist scholars Patricia Hill Collins, Marsha Houston, and bell hooks speak of a "relationship of sisterhood among black women" (Collins 195), "expressions of empathy and support" (Houston 83), and "woman speech" (hooks 6) as distinctive features of African-American women's communication styles. On the surface, this might seem to be Mammy doling out pearls of wisdom, but this particular brand of an "ethic of care" is "not always concerned with agreeing or identifying with the narrative content, but with validating the storyteller's interpretation of her experience" (Houston 85). Indeed, among African-American women, a caring communication might actually sting. This is certainly true of the way Carlos works with performers.

I believe that by being free from institutional demands and philosophies (including the cumbersome and pedagogically dubious end-of-semester teacher evaluations), Laurie has been able to pursue the most dynamic and useful elements of a feminist pedagogy—an "ethic of caring" with a decidedly Black flavor, the rejection of a Cartesian mind/body duality, and a challenging method of collaboration that is neither condescending nor precious.

During the workshop that served as the foundation for Laurie's Alaskan Heat Blue Dot, *each participant was given a series of exercises that were later shared with the larger group. After one participant shared the monologue she was required to write, Laurie challenged her choices. Rather than the smooth evaluations of others' work, this commentary was full of barbs and landmines. The participant was near tears, and the rest of us turned away, embarrassed by the public exposure of the participant's artifice.*

This is not the supportive interaction that either Noddings or Collins discusses; this is support laced with sass.

In a workshop sponsored by the University of Texas Department of Communication Studies, Laurie declares "Kill the editor bitch!" Throughout the day, when the participants hesitated or relied on clichés, she shouted "Kill the editor bitch!"

Laurie insists on holding up often painful mirrors to performers and unflinchingly requires them to stand on their own without relying on her as the measure of their artistic success.

In 2006, during rehearsals with The Austin Project, Laurie was working with movement that had been created by three women to examine one woman's complex relationship with her mother and grandmother. The women showed the movement to Laurie, and Laurie began her critique. "So why do you turn away without looking at your mother? Why do you snatch the jacket from her? This piece is about you and your resentment of your mother. That's what you need to work on!" The woman was stunned, but she endured. Everyone knew how she had struggled to even begin an examination of her relationship with her mother, and now Laurie peeled back layers that the woman didn't know existed. The woman almost left the production, but she knew from previous work with Laurie that the very fact that she wanted to run away was evidence that she really needed to stay.

The performer's job is neither to be liked nor to feel good; it is to be honest and clear.

Rehearsal practices reveal Carlos's *counter*-institutional predisposition through which alternative traditions are developed.

Laurie enters the rehearsal space dressed in her characteristic layered linens. Laughing with other collaborators, bearing food to sustain us through the rehearsal, she immediately sets a mood of ease and comfort and seasoned professionalism. Over the past seven years, I have come to work with Laurie as her dramaturg, as an actor under her direction, and as co-performers in a production by Daniel Alexander Jones. During rehearsals for Sharon Bridgforth's con flama, I was an unpaid dramaturg and casual ethnographer charting Laurie's artistic work. Laurie, Sharon, the composers, and the performers talked and ate from the always sumptuous array of goodies—cranberry walnut cookies, pistachios, cherries, dark chocolate, occasionally Popeye's or Church's, tortilla chips and salsa, brie and sturdy bread. It was well after the scheduled start time for the rehearsal, and Laurie didn't seem to notice. She munched lime-flavored tortilla chips, exchanged gossip with some of the performers, then moved the rehearsal to its more obvious beginning. I realized that I was both anxious and relieved about how the time was handled. I seem to be late for almost everything, and was grateful to be in a space where my internal clock might have found an easy home; I also wondered how much work we would get done if we didn't start soon. The rehearsal had its own rhythm and flow, dictated by the needs of the moment rather than the presumed needs of the future perform-

ance. In fact, the rehearsal had started as everyone began the critical process of learning themselves in relation to one another.

Not starting "on time" means that everyone has the opportunity to begin the rehearsal relaxed and respected. There are no stage managers reminding the director about the importance of punctuality or admonishing the performers for not doing their personal warm-ups before rehearsal. Instead, these standard rehearsal expectations are replaced with new ones–luscious fruits, gourmet cookies, cheese and nuts to be eaten throughout the rehearsal, and an organic sense of time. In such a setting, performers are likely to feel less of the surveillance that characterizes institutions and cramps the freedom necessary for creative spontaneity in rehearsals. Feminist pedagogue Mimi Orner believes that the classroom can become the site where students "internalize systems of surveillance to the point that we become our own overseer" (83). Although the surveillance principle may be in effect during Laurie's rehearsals, because her rehearsals adhere to their own set of rules, actors spend more time discovering the conventions in her work rather than policing their responses in order to present a likeable self to the authority figure.

Laurie and I were a bit late to my M.F.A. acting class, and we got to work quickly. I did not introduce her properly, though I had prepared the students for her visit during the previous class session. With little transition or orienting commentary, one student did his work, and Laurie began hers. The student's piece was a moving tribute to his mother. Several students were crying when he finished, and Laurie brusquely told him to start again, sharply halted him, questioned him about props that he didn't use, asked him what he wanted for himself in the performance, exposed the places where he was not coming close to the goal he stated, then had him do it all again. Several of the students seemed angry by Laurie's brand of direction. One said, through tears, "But this means so much to him!" Laurie insisted on pushing the student to the most honest and deep work possible. She didn't care that the students were angry with her. Her job was to help them make art, not to make friends. The greatest gift she could offer was her years of experience and her demand for rigor. A student from a previous workshop calls this style "Laurie's Tough Love." Should I have prepared them better for it? What had happened to the safe space we had worked hard to create? Would I be vilified by the students for not "protecting" them? And why was I so concerned about myself in this moment in which I was a witness more than an active participant? To what invisible shackles was I binding myself?

Classroom surveillance can work in multiple directions that ensnare students as well as teachers.

Orner critiques the use of "talking circles" by feminist teachers as "an expression of disciplinary power" that requires "the regulation of the self through the internalization of the regulation of others" (83). The "talking circle" requires the student to share intimate feelings about the course and the subject while under the disciplining eye of the professor. Carlos opens each rehearsal with a process she calls "checking in." The entire company of performers, designers, and technicians sits on the floor in a circle and then describes where they are emotionally/physically/psychically as the rehearsal begins. This gives everyone a chance to assess the energy that is coming into the rehearsal and to initiate those invisible and tenuous bonds that are necessary for strong ensemble work. However, "check-ins" have the same potential for regulating behavior that "talking circles" have. Performers could try to figure out which comments are most rewarded during check-in and thereby shut down the very individual spontaneity that the practice is designed to foster. Carlos anticipates this problem by not allowing anyone to respond in any way to someone else's check-in. Because she creates counter-institutional structures during rehearsal, check-ins are less mired in implicit requirements for the company members to be admired by their colleagues.

Ten days before con flama opened, Laurie had only worked through half the play. In spite of this, she continued to begin rehearsals with the grounding practice of check-ins. She did not hurry the company through their comments nor did she anxiously remind everyone of how much time they had left before opening night. As much attention to process was given in this rehearsal as the very early rehearsals in which the scepter of time had not hovered menacingly over the work. Laurie sat on the floor in a circle with the company, her legs spread and feet wagging as she listened silently to each story about each company member's day.

Check-in time is sacred. The information shared during check-in will become a part of the rehearsal, a starting point through which the work moves. Performers are not asked to leave their problems at the door. They are invited to bring them in, to put them into the stew. The priority here is on the process of acquiring the jazz aesthetic in the bones, as a deep and abiding way of life and performance, rather than arriving at the production itself. With this process as the priority, time becomes a saturated present tense exploration instead of a linear drive toward the future. Growth and anger are sometimes necessary companions. A Yoruba proverb states, "Siblings that come out of a room smiling have deceived each other; the ones who come out of the room frowning were brutally honest." If feminist caring is more than saccharine support and extends to the challenging and frustrating development of integrity and honesty, anger can be a by-product of caring. As feminist pedagogue Margo Culley believes, "Anger is a challenging and necessary part of life in the feminist classroom" (216).

When I performed in Alaskan Heat Blue Dot under Laurie's direction, I was just lost. I had so few other tools to bring to the experience. I was working with four other performers, two of whom had worked with Laurie before and seemed at ease with the mapping of non-literal movements onto the words of the text. I, on the other hand, was floundering. And eventually, I became angry. How could this woman know so much about me and my performance tricks? Other directors had praised my work! What was wrong with her? My initial work in a jazz aesthetic uprooted my sense of myself as a good performer, and forced me to begin relinquishing my old methods for new and uncomfortable ones.

Anger can be the initial stage of yielding to Carlos's work. To those who are neophytes to feminist pedagogy and to Laurie's work in a jazz aesthetic, the rehearsals can be frustrating and disorienting, and may induce the anger that will open the performer to new forms. Both jazz and feminism draw from a rich period of maturation in which the *process* of creation, of exploration and discovery, are revered. During this time, the goal is a deepening of the performer's awareness and expression; the aim is to be present and pliable. The product— that which can be repeated and, usually, commodified—is placed in the background while people examine the now. It is clear that Bridgforth understands this requirement for presentness from the vantage point of a writer when she states:

i learned a long time ago that the process of writing/working/and living is as important as the outcome—a well written story/a great performance. i have seen artists give up/live bitter & burned out/driven to addiction and narcissism—because the writer's life is so hard/so very demanding/and not secure or even truly respected in this society. for me it has been critical to my sanity and long term growth that i consider each moment of the day/part of my writing process/part of the measure of my success. i do mothering/sistering/making home/i mentor artists/do my administrative work/travel/read/make theatre/teach/write/eat good food/go for long walks/take vitamins/drink strong coffee/Pray
Heal
cry
love myself
a little more
each day/in process
writing.
(2004)

This emphasis on what is happening right in this second puts much attention on the immediacy of the body. bell hooks notes "those of us who have been intimately engaged as students or teachers with feminist thinking have always recognized the legitimacy of a pedagogy that dares to subvert the mind/body split and allow us to be whole in the classroom, and as a consequence wholehearted" (193). For Carlos's work, it is as important to be body smart as it is to be a "thinking actor." Intelligence in Carlos's artistic domain consists of a physical and emotional honesty that is at once idiosyncratic and recognizable.

Before Ntozake Shange wrote "all theatre artists should work with dancers and musicians to make their work strong" (ii) and began several collaborations with her, Carlos understood how to mold the language of the body, the flexible sounds possible from the vocal folds, and a written text into a multi-layered theatrical experience. With body work, Carlos employs a provocative blend of vernacular movements, modern dance-inflected idioms, and everyday gestures to make a text vibrant. When what may appear to be random movements are woven into theatrical language, the result is an intriguing, compelling, and sometimes tantalizingly unsettling performance. Carlos' productions are as much about painting the space with bodies as they are about filling the air with words. The bodies create their own story that sometimes challenges, sometimes complements the spoken text. Carlos' theatre pieces are so full of movement that one critic, in reviewing the Penumbra Theatre production of Bridgforth's *con flama* (directed by Carlos), wrote "This isn't a linear play so much as a collection of tightly interlocking poetry, image, music and movement" (Papatola).

Carlos' characteristic circular breath work was being explored by several artists in the mid 1970s, including Dianne McIntyre in her Harlem Sounds in Motion Dance Studio. Shange introduced Carlos to McIntyre who was working with musicians and dancers to create a distinctive performance experience that blended breath, words, movement and music. Through Carlos' nascent explorations in a jazz aesthetic she became an original company member in Shange's for *colored girls who have considered suicide, when the rainbow is enuf,* artistic partners with Robbie McCauley and Jessica Hagedorn[3] on the groundbreaking *Teeny Town,* a founding member of Urban Bush Women, and the artistic guide to a host of other artists, including Daniel Alexander Jones, Djola Branner,[4] Grisha Coleman,[5] Sekou Sundiata[6] and Craig Harris,[7] Carl Hancock Rux,[8] and Bridgforth. Carlos and these artists are all creating new forms which require new approaches.

During rehearsals for the Austin, Texas, production of Sharon's con flama, Laurie often made time to discover the movement in her own body, and then passed that movement on to the company members. Once, she asked a performer to speak a monologue from the play. As Laurie listened, she began to move to the words, finding a pulse here or a flutter there. The performer repeated, Laurie "danced." When a movement seemed to strike her in a special way, she taught that movement to the performer. I watched the two bodies learn from each other, for although Laurie had a clear series of movements in mind, she was attentive to the way the performer's body wore those movements. Most times, Laurie would allow performers' everyday gestural vocabularies to inform the movement she created. In this way, she encouraged the performers to bring themselves fully to the rehearsals. Rather than a strategy of "erasing" the performer's self, Laurie looks for the distinctive fusion of what she envisions as the physicality of the text and the way performers inevitably modify that vision.

This honoring of personal choices seems central to a feminist pedagogy that seeks to examine varied viable options rather than a single teacher-driven answer. For Carlos, this does not mean a passive acceptance of everything the performer offers. She pushes the performer to closely watch her body and then strive to get the height of the elbow or the curve of a hip or the rhythm of a clap just so. So while she allows for individuality, it is a rigorous training that has her own physical vision as the necessary foundation.

Carlos explains this body-centered tradition best in her own words during the interviews I conducted in the summer of 2003. In those interviews, Carlos shared her understandings of a jazz aesthetic, and how her work fit into that tradition. As a way of establishing the background for her particular use and development of a theatrical jazz aesthetic, I asked Carlos to begin the interview by naming her artistic lineage:

LAURIE: …my grandmother's father was a guitar player with Johnny Smith, my father's a drummer, and my mom is a dancer. And then…we always had the music and all that stuff around us all the time. Then because of where I lived there were all these artists who lived there and so I think that music is always a big chunk of everything and dance is always a big chunk of everything. So between the jazz and the rock and roll…my grandmother on my mother's side was actually a pianist and a music teacher who hated jazz and ragtime, didn't allow it her sphere. She played gospel music and she played these old popular songs, but she didn't like jazz, she didn't like ragtime. I think growing up in the 50s, you know, like you're born into this thing where Billie Holiday already existed and the Duke already existed and Ma Rainey already existed and all of those people had already come and so there was this landscape already developed and you walk into Josephine Baker and Lavern Baker…so…the genealogy personally for me was already in place at the point that I was born…there were so many flavors to pick off of…

OMI: Where did the specific body idioms come from?

LAURIE: I think those were around. They were in everything. My great-grandmother would do the Ball and Jack in the kitchen, and the Black Bottom, and she liked to show you that in the kitchen. My grandmother on my mother's side didn't do dancing like that. All her stuff was up here this way [gestures with her hands and rotates her shoulders]. That's a very integral part of how I work in my body. There're all those dancers and stuff and you, you start to pick up what is rhythm and movement. But there were a lot of things brought to the kitchens and brought to the parties from a thousand different places, yeah, yeah.

OMI: So when you encounter a print text, can you describe at all what happens? I've seen some of what happens in rehearsals, you know, and…it's like a kind of alchemy that happens with the text when you find rhythm and music and movement with it. Can you describe any of that?

LAURIE: Uh...you know, I think we're all trying to seek at this point some kind of language that describes what that is. And it is so...so deep and integral that it's something that everyone else is going to have to put labels and stuff on, but when I hear, I hear a word or hear a series of words put together, I react to them. And I try to go to where the writer lives in that language physically. Now, the deal is that it's not magic, because it can be initiated and translated. So it ain't magic. And several other people can do it. It's a kind of method in the work. I think people have squelched the impetus for movement around text, because they could control it in a particular kind of way. But I think if when you start to talk about language, when language begins to happen, it affects the body. It affects memory. It affects what's in the bones and it affects music. When you start to speak, language becomes music based on how you use it or how you line it up on the page. And so, there's really no way to move away from movement when you are creating language. Because of the Eurocentricity of our culture you separate everything into these categories and then you strive to think through each category and discipline in order to do the work. And it is not a natural state to be in because when you hear the language, you automatically begin to move, if you really release all the categories. And...I think there's always been people for whom that was always true.

OMI: Such as?

LAURIE: Donald.[9] Ailey.[10] This is true. This is true in the Black church. This is true in the Pentecostal Church...for Latinos. This is true for the Planas. This is true for Hava Nagila. This is true in terms of the text, in how you deal with the text. There's really the only thing that could happen, someone moves into it and removes it. Because what originally exists is the movement... and I think whenever you write, you write movement, period.

OMI: Do you actually physically move as you write?

LAURIE: I think most people do.

OMI: So you move around the room.

LAURIE: Well sometimes you do. But I move and when I'm writing, you know, you sometimes can jump up, you can fall down, you can, you get up, you know, the action is in the hand and when you're connected, yeah, you breathe, you move, your foot goes up, you know, things happen when trying to create the language. So it happens anyway. So when you look at the language you go back to the initial place that the writer's coming from in the movement. The text ignites movement. Yeah.

OMI: Were you as clear, and I guess I know the answer to this, but it'd be good to hear you talk about it—were you as clear when you were working with Robbie or Jessica on *Teeny Town* about some of this?

LAURIE: Yes, we were very clear about it at that point. Very, very, very, very, very clear, so that every single thing in *Teeny Town* is choreographed. Everything is written for choreography. We're very clear about it. There was no doubt. Every line is written for gesture. Uh hm.

OMI: Thinking 'bout those two collaborators, I know they've been extremely important—what do you say you receive, you experience, when you work with Robbie? What are the sets of things that you can rely on when you work with her, or in what way does she feed you?

LAURIE: Yeah, when you work with Robbie you can depend on conflict and contradiction. It's the basis of her work. You can also depend on disagreement. The thing that you agree on with Robbie is that you're going to disagree respectfully. And so a lot of the improvisation work that Robbie and I have done has been about the disagreement respectfully. So that we're always talking about a conflict and we're always talking about the contradictions. A favorite word of hers is "contradictions."

OMI: What about with Jessica?

LAURIE: Same thing. I don't agree with anything Jessica writes, anything she does physically, or any of Jessica's opinions. And so she is with me. Jessica just doesn't agree with anything I write, any of my movements, or any of my opinions. And that is why we work well together, because we respect each other's—what she calls "blah blah." We respect the "blah blah." So when all three of us are in the room we are in such a state of contradiction, of dialogue, of conflict, of bending of aesthetics. There's a lot of chaos. Jessica's always trying to reach in and pull out the order of chaos; she's always trying to make that thing orderly. I work well with chaos and Robbie causes chaos. So that's the dynamic in the room and a lot of times we just look at each other and: "I don't," "I'm not doing that," or "I don't agree," "I can't"—and then we respect one another enough to make an attempt to always realize the other person's vision.

OMI: Is the chaos or the contradiction an element of the jazz aesthetic, as you see it?

LAURIE: Absolutely, absolutely. The jazz aesthetic is not about a set of agreements other than you agree to disagree and respect that. The jazz aesthetic is always about that, always, because it has to be. It's your very personal, deep spiritual journey through the experience. Three people move forward, somebody jumps, somebody else falls to the floor, somebody else stands still, three other people move in, two people play the melody line, somebody else only plays accents, somebody else just takes four beats, that's the way it has to move so that you get the full experience of what the text and the movement and the sound of the piece is. Yeah, yeah, yeah, and the text is like that melody line that…that happens, yeah.

OMI: What do you do when you work with people who resist this process, who see what you do as an imposition on their work?

LAURIE: I don't work with them. I mean why argue...the deal is to be...an instrument or a source that allows the writer to do what the writer wants to do...and when a writer...I don't do their work. Then that's not what they're interested in–they're trying to speak in a particular way and there are people who will be able to do their work that way. Everybody's concept of their work does not lend itself to my interpretation and they should have their interpretation. I didn't believe that five years ago...

OMI: What have been some of your most satisfying experiences in this aesthetic?

LAURIE: I don't know. I don't know. I haven't been able to do certain things where I walk away and I'm excited, but I don't think I've been totally satisfied with anything in maybe ten...in maybe twenty years. I think I've been asking...there are a lot of questions on top of it. But I've had very exciting, incredibly exciting and challenging works to do, be a part of, create over the past twenty-five, thirty years...I'm always still looking for something. Yeah, there's always something and part of it has to do with not having...part of it has to do with a lot of not having language.

OMI: Uh huh.

LAURIE: ...I don't have to deal with those people that ain't speaking my language anymore. I can choose not to do that, because there are people in this configuration of aesthetic and American theatre, American literature, we are all walking in the room together and there are things happening, really happening. They are not the same things, we are not all speaking the same language, we are not...I mean...we're not telling the same story is what I'm trying to say...And each one of the people in this space is telling the story their way. And so the idea is to be able to support one another in that and that has grown a lot. It's like you walk in the room now, it's like twenty people. That's very important, you know, that's very, very important. And they're good, the people who are doing the work are strong, they are literate, they are imaginative, they are daring, they are...fools. And we're all making an incredible examination of what it is we're doing. (Carlos 2003)

Bridgforth has been one such "literate imaginative fool" who has provided Carlos with an artistic and personal comradship that has fueled both of their work. Bridgforth reveals the power of daring to create a community of fools when she writes,

if we are to get down to the business of writing works that will save our lives/and Heal
for generations to come   we have to go to and examine the raw places

tell the stories that we have not wanted to tell/open/listen
work to be vulnerable and present/in our bodies/hearts/minds/Spirits.
this is very hard to do. it is dangerous/volatile/isolating/frightening
and is at some point/best done in community with other writers.
(2004)

Bridgforth knows the language of this aesthetic–deeply personal, bitingly honest, blues fed, and jazz bred. Her work exemplifies the use of a musically-inflected sound, memory, and transcendent time that has become the way in which many Black feminists must create emergent forms so as not to be erased or maimed. Her work in a theatrical jazz aesthetic took a momentous turn when Carlos directed *con flama*. Bridgforth recalls the experience with passion and detail in an email interview:

> My original idea for *con flama* was that it was to be a poetic journey through my Los Angeles (1960s-1980s). I used the bus ride to school that I took as a kid going from south central L.A. to Echo Park, riding through this segregated people of color populated city (cause for the most part the white folk had moved, no they fled to the suburbs. Except of course for the Jewish community which was in the heart of the city) as a vehicle to look at the cultural landscape of the city. I had received a TCG/NEA Playwright in Residence (at Frontera[Fest] @ Hyde Park Theatre [Austin, TX], Vicky Boone, Artistic Director) grant to write the piece. It was the first time I was able to write without having at least three jobs. So I was able to do a lot of dreaming, listening to music, researching. I pulled out about three small boxes of family slides that I had never looked at, that I had been carrying with me since my great aunt had passed some years previous. Those slides were priceless. Old family photos, including some of me at about the age of three.
>
> Well fast forward a long story short; myself, the composers Lourdes Perez and Annette D'Armata, and Laurie were meeting up for coffee before going into the first rehearsal. Or at least I thought we were having coffee, you know, a lil happy time before work. "Chile," Laurie came in, she looked at me, she held the script up in the air, and she threw it down on the floor. Lourdes and Annette backed up, my mouth dropped, Laurie said, "This is a piece of shit. Oh it's pretty, cause you're a good writer. But you have not said what you need to say, and until you do, you will be writing the same thing over and over for the rest of your life!" Laurie leaned in close, pointing at me, Lourdes and Annette were almost out the door, Laurie said, "You need to write about why that little girl was on the bus. Where was her mama? What did she want from her mama? What is that little girl's story? That's what this piece is about. Until you write THAT…"
> Well, at that I started crying. I was crying cause I knew she was right, cause deep down the little girl had already been talking to me, and I didn't want to deal with her. That little girl, me, had been waiting all her life for someone to pay attention. She wanted very much to tell her story. I cried, Lourdes and Annette cried, Laurie cried. Then we pulled ourselves together and went to rehearsal. That night I stayed up till I was done. I wrote in the

voice of the little girl. It took me a few years to really finish the piece cause that's just how it is. Writers need the opportunity to work the work over time. I was Blessed to be able to continue the work during a couple of staged readings (one directed by Dr. Joni Jones at the Esperanza Peace and Justice Center, San Antonio, TX) and another production. Penumbra produced *con flama* in St. Paul, MN, as a main stage production. Laurie directed, Lourdes, Annette and most of the original cast came back to work on that production. After that production is when I finished the piece. For me, *con flama* was a turning point. It is the most articulated performance piece that I have written. If not for *con flama* I would not have been able to write my performance/novel *love conjure/blues*. If not for Laurie Carlos I would not be as mature and happy an artist and mentor as I am today. That day in that coffee shop, Laurie took the time, the care, the risk, the Love, to help me. I will forever be grateful. She is my model for Living as an artist with Grace, compassion, joy and Mercy. Laurie Carlos. I Love you!! (2006)

It is difficult to imagine that the little girl Carlos unearthed from Bridgforth's hiding places didn't always exist as the guide in *con flama*. This little girl has the courage to love her wayward grandmother and forgive her emotionally absent mother—the very sort of raw sincerity that the jazz aesthetic requires. She tells the audience,

we got evicted cause grandmother drank up three months rent money and my mother didn't know/and that's how we ended up in los angeles cause right when we got on the street grandmother's sister came by on her way to los angeles and me and my mother got in the car/went with her.
grandmother stayed on the street waving
> bye babies
> i love you.
my mother is still angry about that   but i didn't care
cause i knew grandmother would join us when the next great-aunty car came by.

four years later my mother sent me south to stay at the home house until she finished night school   i didn't care
cause grandmother was back at the home house too and as soon as i saw her i loved her more again. more than ever.
(Bridgforth 2002)

When encountering the jazz aesthetic on the page, it can be useful to speak the work out loud. Know that the spaces, the periods and back slashes, the bold and the lower case are ways to give full and distinctive expression to the individuality of Black female identities and to the musically driven cadence of a jazz aesthetic.

Much of Carlos and Bridgforth's work begins with the premise that Black includes everything. June Jordan wrote that she was compelled to "abhor and defy definitions of Black heritage and Black experience that suggest we are anything less complicated, less unpredictable, than the whole world" (85). In

Carlos's work, Black is not essentialized or even color-coded. The inclusiveness of Blackness makes for a rich text, as with Bridgforth's *con flama*, which folds a Japanese internment camp survivor, African sugar laborers, Brown Berets, and Chumash ancestors in a Los Angeles tapestry that is Black, and then some. This inclusiveness also makes for powerful production choices. Carlos most often casts across race and gender so that one's very notion of Blackness and gendered identities are disrupted and expanded. In both the Austin, Texas, and St. Paul, Minnesota, productions of *con flama*, Laurie cast a Latina as one of the Black characters (i ask lil magwa why he had to go do' poppin on my good time), a Black man as a Japanese character (**my birth place was/ manzanar/ one of ten/ internment camps / that held 120,000 of my people/ 77,000 of us/ u.s. citizens/ no one had committed a crime**), and the racially diverse ensemble often made an echoed refrain of the many passages of overlapping Spanish and English:

La Republica Dominicana
                                 The Dominican Republic april 1965
More jobs more schools more food
mas trabajos mas escuelas mas comida
                                 bang bang/**the authorities turned on the people**
run lolo run   they're machine gunning from planes
                                                 confusion frustration and drama
run anabel run

                                                 they are dropping bombs in the streets
corre lolo corre   estan disparandonos desde los aviones
corre anabel corre   estan tirando bombas en las calles
                                                 bang   **police guns**
                                                                 con flama
(Bridgforth 2002)

In addition to seeing Black as "the whole world," these artists are creating new theatrical forms which challenge the notion of "straight" vs. musical theatre, call into question the distinction between dance and drama, and dare to muddy the boundaries between stylized and everyday movement. There is a great deal of music in *con flama* (my neck is hurtn/ my back is sho brokedown/ say/ my neck is hurtn/ my back is sho brokedown/ but gotdamnit wo'mn/ I do plans to stick around) but it is neither a book musical, nor a concept musical, nor a musical review. Carlos stages a great deal of movement into her work, but it does not follow the conventions of a dance performance, which generally does not include the spoken word or narratives, either linear or seriate. Anthropologist Mary Catherine Bateson sees this structural improvisational ability as particularly keen in women as she writes, "…our productivity depends on the discovery of new forms of flexibility…our very visions are products of growth and adaptation, not fixed but emergent" (235-37). These emergent forms and approaches develop through intimate and rigorous collaborations, collaborations that honor the individual contribution of each person within a specific set of aesthetic requirements.

Through years of intense, tough, tender artmaking, Bridgforth and Carlos have developed a personal and artistic language shaped by a call to freedom, by counter-institutional structures, by improvisatory survival, practices that are the hallmarks of both Black Feminist theory and jazz aesthetics. They have made a language that sustains them and can be passed on to others willing to make the commitment and take the necessary risks.

NOTES

[1] - *Blood Pudding:* written by Bridgforth and directed by Carlos, Frontera @ Hyde Park Theatre, Austin, TX, 1998

- *Alaskan Heat Blue Dot:* written by several authors, with excerpts of Bridgforth's work, directed by Carlos, Frontera @ Hyde Park Theatre, Austin, TX, 1999

- *con flama:* written by by Bridgforth, directed by Carlos, Fronter @ Hyde Park Theatre, Austin, TX, 2000-
geechee crossing/marsha's overture: written by Bridgforth, curated by Carlos, Penumbra Theatre Late Night Series, Minneapolis, MN, 2002

- *con flama:* written by Bridgforth, directed by Carlos, Penumbra Theatre, Minneapolis, MN, 2002

- *The Pork Chop Wars,* written by Carlos, dramaturged by Bridgforth, Center for African and African American Studies, University of Texas at Austin, TX, 2005

[2] Daniel Alexander Jones is another expert practitioner of a theatrical jazz aesthetic. He has worked with Carlos and Bridgforth on several projects, including his *Ambient Love Rites,* Carlos's *Marion's Terrible Time of Joy,* and Bridgforth's *love conjure/blues.* He received his M.A. in theatre at Brown University, and is the 2006 Alpert Award winner in theatre.

[3] Jessica Hagedorn is a poet, novelist, and performance artist who has also collaborated with Ntozake Shange and Thulani Davis. Her first play, *Mango Tango,* was produced by Joseph Papp in 1978.

[4] Djola Branner is a performance artist, dancer, actor, and writer. He is one of the founders of the highly influential Pomo Afro Homos (Post-Modern African American Homosexuals). Carlos directed Branner in *Mighty Real,* Branners's play about the legendary Sylvester.

[5] Grisha Coleman is a composer, cellist, dancer, and writer who founded the a cappella group Hot Mouth. She has danced with Urban Bush Women and worked with Carlos for several years. Most recently, she directed Carlos in "echo::system," a performance art exploration of ecological devastation, conceived by Coleman.

[6] Sekou Sundiata is a spoken word artist and long-time collaborator with Craig Harris. He was featured on the PBS series "The Language of Life," and has conceived and performed *51st (dream) state,* a contemplation on U.S. identity. He co-authored the 1994 theatre piece "Kick the Boot, Raise the Dust and Fly" with Laurie Carlos and Carl Hancock Rux.

[7] Craig Harris is a jazz trombonist who has collaborated with Sekou Sundiata, Jessica Hagedorn, Ntozake Shange, Amiri Baraka, Marlies Yearby, and Carlos, who served as dramaturg for his choreographed tribute to Muhammed Ali, *Brown Butterfly.*

[8] Carl Hancock Rux is a multi-disciplinary writer who was selected by the *Village Voice* as one of "Eight Writers on the Verge of (Impacting) the Literary Landscape." He was a featured performer in Robert Wilson's *The Temptation of St. Anthony.* Carlos has directed his plays *Smoke, Lilies, and Jade,* and *Geneva Cottrell, Waiting for the Dog to Die.*

[9] Donald Meissner is a composer and musician who created music for all of Carlos' work from 1985 to 1992.

[10] Alvin Ailey founded the internationally famous Alvin Ailey Dance Theater in 1965.

WORKS CITED

Bateson, Mary Catherine. *Composing a Life.* New York: Plume, 1990.

Benston, Kimberly W. *Performing Blackness: Enactments of African-American Modernism.* New York: Routledge. 2000.

Bridgforth, Sharon. Email Interview. Fall 2006. Austin, Texas.

Bridgforth, Sharon. Video Recorded Interview. Summer 2003. New York City.

Bridgforth, Sharon. *Con flama.* Unpublished. 2002.

Bridgforth, Sharon. "writing for my mother/my daughter   for me." Unpublished. 2004.

Carlos, Laurie. Video Recorded Interview. New York City. Summer 2003.

Collins, Patricia Hill. "The Social Construction of Black Feminist Thought." *The Black Feminist Reader.* Eds. Joy James and T. Deanean Sharpley-Whiting. Malden, Massachussetts: Blackwell Publishers. 2000. 183-207.

Combahee River Collective. "A Black Feminist Statement."*Words of Fire: An Anthology of African-American Feminist Thought,* Ed. Beverly Guy-Sheftall. New York: W. W. Norton, 1995. 231-240.

Culley, Margo. "Anger and Authority in the Introductory Women's Studies Classroom." *Gendered Subjects: The Dynamics of Feminist Teaching.* Ed. Margo Culley and Catherine Portuges. Boston: Routledge and Kegan Paul, 1985. 209-217.

Dance, Stanley. *The World of Duke Ellington.* Stanley Dance. NY: Scribner's, 1970.

Ellington, Duke. Quoted in *Jazz: A History of America's Music.* Eds. Geoffrey C. Ward and Ken Burns. New York: Alfred A. Knopf, 2000.

hooks, bell. *Talking Back: Thinking Feminist, Thinking Black.* Boston: South End Press. 1989.

Houston, Marsha. "Triumph Stories: Caring and Accountability in African American Women's Conversation Narratives." *Centering Ourselves: African American Feminist and Womanist Studies of Discourse.* Eds. Marsha Houston and Olga Idriss Davis. Cresskill, New Jersey: Hampton Press, Inc. 2002. 77-98.

James, Joy. *Shadowboxing: Representations of Black Feminist Politics.* NY: Palgrave Macmillan, 2002.

Jordan, June. *Civil Wars.* Boston: Beacon Press, 1981.

Lorde, Audre. "The Master's Tools Will Never Dismantle the Master's House." *Sister Outsider.* Freedom, CA: The Crossing Press, 1984. 110-113.

Murray, Albert. "Improvisation and the Creative Process." *The Jazz Cadence of American Culture.* Ed. Robert G. O'Meally. New York: Columbia University Press, 1998. 111-116.

Noddings, Nel. *The Challenge to Care in Schools: An Alternative Approach to Education.* New York: Teacher's College Press, 1992.

Orner, Mimi. "Interrupting the Calls for Student Voice in 'Liberatory' Education: A Feminist Poststructrualist Perspective." *Feminisms and Critical Pedagogy,* eds. Carmen Luke and Jennifer Gore. 74-89.

Papatola, Dominic P. "Tightly Wound 'Con Flama' Seethes with Kinetic Energy." *Pioneer Press* [St. Paul]: Feb 4, 2002: B3.

Shange, Ntozake. "forward/unrecovered losses/ black theater traditions" *Three Pieces.* New York: St. Martin's Press, 1981 ix-xvi.

Tompkins, Jane. "Pedagogy of the Distressed." *College English.* 52.6 (October 1990): 653-661.

COLLAPSIBLE BOUNDARIES
DEB MARGOLIN'S PEDAGOGY FOR A THEATRE OF DESIRE
AN INTERVIEW WITH DEB MARGOLIN

Lisa Jo Epstein

INTRODUCTION

Deb Margolin's writing, performances, and approach to teaching encourage students to step into the fire of emotional places they have not previously thought to touch in their work. Her language, combined with her genuine, selfless passion for teaching, has a force, a visceral quality that seems to permeate others at a cellular level. She beckons you to embody speech, and trusts your desires before you do. Imagine then, being her student over the course of a semester or two, and the journey you might take.

Deb began her pedagogical apprenticeship as a founding member of the Split Britches theatre company, teaching students their particular approach to creating theatre in their performances at schools and universities. Deb has taught at NYU's graduate Performance Studies Program, undergraduate Tisch School of the Arts, and Gallatin School for Independent Study. She is now an Associate Professor in the Theatre Studies Program at Yale University, touring her solo plays, and continuing to teach wherever she goes. Through these years and experiences, she has bridged the ages, teaching students the virtues of committing to one's desires as the "surest way to accomplish creative acts," as I have heard her say countless times in different workshop and class settings. It is this connection of desire to reality that gives her work its tremendous force. From her first experience witnessing Women's Experimental Theatre in the 1970s to working with Lois Weaver and Peggy Shaw in Split Britches during the 1980s and early 1990s to her most recent plays, Deb has developed her understanding of what happens when you dare to put your own desires onstage. I first interviewed her in 1997, when she was the Newcomb College/Tulane University Zale Writer-in-Residence. During the interview, she avowed that putting one's desires onstage "is a radical political act because it assumes the beauty and the importance of your personal experience." Thus, Deb has personalized a feminist pedagogy for a "theatre of desire" in order to "support others as they go to make that life-changing realization for themselves."[1]

In the first moment of a playwriting class or workshop, Deb squarely states that everyone is a desiring subject and that these desires beg to gain a useful materiality through writing. That students—and teachers—are desiring subjects is not normally or openly acknowledged in traditional playwriting classes, where mastering various forms and structures takes precedence over the productive mess of emotions and lived experience. Structure is the last thing Deb addresses, as she firmly believes that form comes out of one's passion for speech, and that this is where students must begin. She reminds students that "plays don't write themselves in a linear manner, because that is not how life gets lived." The simplicity of this statement is revelatory, a relief, but a challenge for students to embrace when they have been conditioned to think otherwise. Deb is prepared when good "ideas" about what to write buck and jostle deeper impulses out of place; her classes abound with writing exercises that function like tiny miraculous lassoes to harness desires as they elude capture or hide behind one's inner critic.

Deb teaches students to banish both internal and external voices of judgment. Autobiographical experiences are accessed through the sharing of images—spoken briefly but in great detail, a process which hones a writer's sense of what works. Her exercises demonstrate the power of letting an image just sit as if in silence, unexplained by its author, letting multiple meanings be available to others. Her writer's barre exercises guide students as they move from delving into the fabric of their lives to writing in the voices of the characters they are imagining through the texture of those experiences. Deb herself is a remarkable illustration of this notion. She has always written and performed about her obsessions and desires, investing time and energy into the most mundane things, which, in her plays, come to signify some larger, deeper humanity with which audiences can identify.

Deb's pedagogy transforms casual camaraderie into a tightly-knit citizenry of young, dynamic artists who hold each other up. Her students collapse the boundaries between themselves, lending images from their desires to one another, freely letting them make guest appearances, albeit in different guises, in each other's writing, as well as in their own. As they tap into their own images and begin to trade and exchange with others, Deb's students develop a unique communal social imagination that reflects who they are in a moment of time, and how they bear witness to each other's struggles to let their desires speak freely, to accept and honor their right to speak these desires.

After a class with Deb Margolin, students are empowered as theatre practitioners, moving fiercely forward into other classes, and into their lives, as knowing subjects. Deb's students have consistently secured slots in the annual high-profile Yale Playwrights Festival, have started their own theatre companies, and have been reviewed in the *New York Times*.

Throughout this interview, which took place in January 2006, Deb expands on the exercises she uses to invite students to speak from their bodies, and how she helps them collapse their boundaries and infuse their own experiences into those of their characters in ways that "signify beyond the experience itself." I end this beginning with words Lynda Hart chose to describe Deb in the introduction to the 1999 collection *Of All the Nerve: Deb Margolin Solo*: "Deb Margolin has carved out for herself a place in the theater that pays homage to her ancestors and her peers, while at the same time being richly original."[2] The same holds true for her work as a teacher.

INTERVIEW

LISA JO: What is the role of desire in your classroom? For example, at the end of the first day of class you give an assignment in which you ask students to write you a love letter that you also call a "user's manual," a written note that reveals how you can help and support them. You make this unlikely but fluid juxtaposition of "love letter" and "user's manual," which instantaneously redefines the nature of each of those forms of writing, giving a rightful place to eros in the utilitarian manual, and utility to the love note.

DEB: I like to introduce desire and love because of their agency and utility. I feel that in teaching any of the skills of theatre, or the skills of life or love, it is necessary to locate one's impulse and desire for speech, particularly in playwriting or acting. The thing about a new playwright, a young playwright, is that the desire for speech is the most certain compass for the correct direction in which to turn with one's writing. As a general rule, ideas do not get a playwright through the most grueling, impossible, and mystical aspects of writing a play. Writing a play is a useless and magnificent and impossible and perfect pursuit, and it's really impossible to get through those moments of obscurity which come, really, right on schedule, if you are not in love with the purpose beneath the endeavor.

I use love in a very clinical sense, in a very Shakespearean sense, like in Henry [IV], "Thou owest me a million," Falstaff says, "Thy love is worth a million and thou owest me thy love." It's that clinical brotherhood, sisterhood, to which I'm referring, that state of safety where your ideas, your passions—however bizarre—can be made available to you, and then you can make use of them. So, this idea of love, eros, and desire juxtaposed with utility—your question illuminates for me how purposeful that juxtaposition is.

LISA JO: How do you get students to fall in love with that purpose?

DEB: One of the things I consider my first obligation to these students of playwriting is to assist them in locating their deepest impulse for speech. People come to a playwriting class because they want to say what they see. They want to say something and they want to take that speech and place it in a human body. There are many beautiful forms of writing–you can write a poem, you can write a novel, you can write a short story–you can work on and perfect those forms, but nowhere is the embodied voice except in the theatre. That embodiment of language is the singular province and glory of the theater. And there is an inherent eros the minute you put the language into the body. It comes from the body, it returns to the body. It's really important to juxtapose utility and desire because that's what gets things done in a playwriting classroom and in a playwright's laboratory.

Additionally, and perhaps secondarily, comes the fact that love is a form of invention. What I mean by that is that the minute you fall in love with something, you have invented it. The only original source we have is our compulsion and passion for speech and for each other; that is the original thing about us. What is there original to say? There isn't. The desire to speak is where originality is resident and locatable. And thus I feel it's important for people to understand when they fall in love with–let's say a Car Cash commercial–they are experiencing an aspect of their vision that can be investigated and utilized artistically. There's this Car Cash commercial that was played on the radio. Every time it was played, I started sobbing. Now, it is a very plebian commercial, it's kind of stupid, with this young girl singing, "I'm feeling good all over, and here's the reason why, I just sold my car to Car Cash, I'm in love with those car cash guys," but every time it came on, I just started sobbing at the wheel of my car. I only ever heard it in my car, and would start sobbing, but why was I sobbing? I knew that if I took a look at why I was sobbing and why I felt such emotion, such love, that I would discover something about myself. Because theatre is about the revelation of humanity, that's why we go to the theatre. We go there to see ourselves, to see humanity revealed in ways that daily life sometimes makes obscure, impossible, or less clear. If I took a look at what it was about that commercial that made me cry, then I'd find something about my own humanity that was revelatory and artistically viable and indeed, I did. I encourage students to consider love and eros as forms of creativity and invention, insofar as if we love the way someone sits, if we feel moved by a picture, then we invented that posture, that picture. We invented that moment, and it belongs to us as writers and actors.

It has been my experience that ideas arise in service of a passion much more readily than passion will arise in service of an idea. Working from a state of desire is a surer way. Some people, particularly at the school where I teach, come with very definite ideas, such as, "I want to write a play about the struggle of the huh-huhs against the huh-huhs." That's a very good idea, perhaps a politically conscious idea, but if it comes from an idea as opposed to an aching, a passion, it becomes very hard to find the energy to get through what's obscure and difficult about it. When you're in love with what you're saying, ideas will come to serve you as you struggle to organize a transformative arc that honors dramatic form. But if you just come with an idea, you may find yourself watching Kojak episodes on TV instead of finishing your play.

LISA JO: And their responses to Kojak or one of the commercials might just wind their way into their plays if they're in your class! What are some of the steps students take towards identifying their passions and then channeling these impulses into their writing?

DEB: Acquainting students with their desires comes first, and then comes working towards the sense of prerogative for speech. Often, students being young, do not feel they have the right to talk about things. They feel they don't know enough, they're too young, they think they're too stupid, it's someone else's story, it's not my story, I want to honor my great aunt, she's lost both her legs but she has written a history of the Civil War, she speaks in a way that doesn't represent her, I know who she is and the way she speaks doesn't represent her. Do I have the right to reinvent her speech, to write about her? Yes! You can rearrange the way she speaks so that you DO represent her.

LISA JO: Your method allows a fusion of the playwright's memories and imagination. The students' plays become a lens to reflect their own desires, even if they haven't fully identified them yet. How do you lead them to trust themselves, to own their desire to write about something?

DEB: Finding the prerogative to honor your desire is a very hard thing. In teaching playwriting, you need to empower a student to put words in other people's mouths. There are various ways to help a student find that prerogative. Once you've found it, you can see that the discovery was almost accidental. It's an accident to discover how to write a play, but it's an accident that can be caused—that sounds like an oxymoron, but it's true. I have an exercise where I ask students to take a bunch of characters, all of whom are writing about them, and how they want out of the scene that they are in. The characters speak of nothing but the playwright and how annoying, bad, and silly she is, how her hair looks, her grammar—for a student in a state of paralysis, when it comes to putting words in other people's mouths, that's often a really good trick, because words flow easily when it comes to the doubt and struggle the playwright is having, and they put those words in someone else's mouth. There will be assignments to write a dream scene, a scene based on a dream. That is also a very liberating thing because the student discovers that the normal rules of daily life do not need to appertain, that we can—as Lawrence Durrell said—rearrange daily life to show its significant side. That's what dreams do and that's the playwright's prerogative. I often ask students to read *Angels in America* because Tony Kushner so brilliantly took people from different people's dreams and placed them at a table, yelling at each other. This is our prerogative: we are the god of that particular universe and often, if we have humility and haven't written a play before, that divine role is hard for us. Conversations with God, yelling at God, denying the existence of God, these are also very provocative and helpful exercises for discovering the prerogative because they engage directly in the conflict itself of whether or not we have the right to put words into other people's mouths. When you turn into the skid, you discover how much fun it is.

LISA JO: Believing in, and actually writing about, that to which you are passionately drawn seem like two different things. Will you share some of the exercises you use to facilitate students' discovery of this prerogative?

DEB: There are many tricks, like automatic writing, where students write and write and write and write and write and in the middle, discover some voice they didn't know was there. We do fill-in-the-blanks. Fill-in-the-blanks are when I give you a sentence and you fill in the blank in the end. And, you can fill in the blanks for your characters. We go all around the circle; it has a very hypnotic, generative quality. Fill-ins are sentences with blanks at the end; they call for an image, not a story, and are generative of a larger image life. Some examples might be:

I've never been the same since _____;

My oldest anger has to do with _____;

I want to fall into _____;

I remember _____;

My father _____;

I want to dance with _____;

My relationship with God is like my relationship with _____.

Everything changes when you ask, "How would your character fill in the blank?" or "What would your character say?" When you allow your character to fill in the blank, your character doesn't have to invent the sentence or the predication from which that sentence came. When you hear your character fill in the blank, suddenly there is a color to the screen on which that character appears. You get a sense, and you can write from that place.

LISA JO: I'm reminded of what you told me the first time I interviewed you at Tulane University in 1997, that "as writers, as human beings, we have collapsible boundaries, that we are not made of the kinds of steel and solidity that we think we are, that our experiences can go effortlessly into the mouths of characters, that things we see in the world can come into our bodies and out onto the stage" (see note 1).

DEB: Yes, I sneak you into the mind of your character by asking you to fill in the blank, then fill in the blank as your character. Prerogative is a funny thing, and it is discovered anew by every playwright. It's a shock to realize that you CAN do that, that you can remember, that you can amalgamate, trace from four different people and place them in this one character who embodies your obsession with whatever. There is the theory that characters are embodied obsessions. If that's true—and it's a good way to start—then when you discover an obsession, you find a character who might embody that for you, and figure out what trajectory, what transformative arc that obsession in the form of this embodied person might have. These are tricks; these are accidents. It is like learning to wiggle your ears—you discover it accidentally when you're swallowing funny.

We also work on techniques for eavesdropping. I really feel the playwright does best when he or she hears the voice of the character rather than masterminds the voice of the character. You just listen. You don't move until you see it. There's that beautiful movie *Searching for Bobby Fischer* that I love so much, where at the end, this child is trying to win this chess tournament and his teacher is thinking, sending him this message, "Don't move until you see it." This is the thing: you wait until you hear the voice of the character and then you write down what that person says. Eavesdropping in a coffee shop is a really good way to perfect this technique. You don't make up what a person says, you listen to what these two ladies are talking about, and you write it down as fast as you possibly can. The actual technique of eavesdropping on "real" people is a prelude and a practice and a rehearsal for writing down what real characters in your play say. Eavesdropping is a great technique because the literal, physical, kinetic act of writing down what people say is another way of finding your prerogative to transcribe the voices of your characters.

LISA JO: Your exercises seem designed to activate students' innermost selves, to bring them to consciousness of how they can deliberately use their lived knowledge, what shapes them and their imaginations; your assignments restore value in how they define themselves.

DEB: Yes and it's a hard thing to do. Often students can write monologues before they can write dialogues because with a monologue, you can stay very still and you don't have to realize quite the magnificence and multiplicity of what it is you are doing when you write from another character's perspective. Then when it comes to dialogue, all of a sudden it's like you're a deer in headlights, sometimes. But I will not let a student leave my classroom until she feels confident that she can write dialogue. That's part of my obligation. It's very important that we get comfortable with this. We do come to terms with the fact that it's a radical act to stage a piece of theatre. It's a radical act, it's a beautiful dream, and with that dream comes very grave responsibilities. But we focus first on what precedes the political responsibility of the artist.

LISA JO: As students enter this process, it seems that they must be accessing and negotiating the inherited narratives of themselves that they've been unconsciously performing all their lives. Rather than asking students to develop an idea they may have for a play–to, in a way, install themselves in a single subject matter and demonstrate their ability to pursue it–it seems you have your students start with their many selves and build outwards so they discover that identity is a process, that making theatre also means to work relentlessly with an ever-developing self, and that they need to filter their experiences into dialogue precisely because that act can reveal whatever chaos and clarity about the human condition lingers inside them.

DEB: It's really interesting to see the students struggling with these narratives. I have some students in my performance class who were very engaged by a famous poet teaching on our campus, who would insult the students every time they came to class. He would say "although you submitted poetry and got into class, don't think any of you are writers–your writing is garbage." And they were delighted by him. He flattered some sense of, you know, the way medicine has to taste bad, and of course we have to suffer these degrading insults at the hand of a Pulitzer Prize-winning poet. That's the way these women were used to being insulted. They felt like to study at the feet of the master should be a bruising experience; it was kneeling on salt, to study at his feet.

LISA JO: Clearly, there is no such thing as a neutral educational process. Who we are, as students and teachers, our autobiographies if you will, are tangled up in the classroom and only variably are recognized as valuable.

DEB: Students bring various relationships to the intimacy of the classroom. Sorry, I just think that teaching creative writing, playwriting, acting–we have no other source but the deepest aspects of the self from which to work. I really think that it is a truism that all fiction is the redistribution of autobiography; that's what it is, that's what it has to be. We have nothing but ourselves from which to work–we have nothing but our own images, memories, ideas, imaginations, observations, and passions, that's what we work from. It's solipsistic, I think, to think otherwise. Encouraging students to become acquainted with themselves on the deepest level is part of what I have to do in order to teach playwriting. It's not that I'm interested in getting involved in the personal lives of my students, but I feel obliged in a sacred way to acquaint the students with themselves in that particular way, and for each student that process has more or less valence, more or less terror, more or less joy. Students bring all sorts of self-images, eating disorders, repressed sexualities–people bring themselves to this work, and when they acquaint themselves with the deepest aspects of their inner lives and passions for speech, there is a re-envisioning of the self and the uses of self in the classroom.

LISA JO: Relearning to trust one's desires is a delicate process, especially if you've developed an unconscious sense of chronic distress and patterns of response from years of kneeling on salt.

DEB: Absolutely. If you think of a poetry class where you're told your writing is garbage, and the only reason you're in the class is because he had to pick somebody, that's a whole other thing, a different approach. Now sure, if you're going to write poetry, perhaps you'll find a way to write it, and perhaps find a way to hand it in to such person, and it may even excite you if you have the sort of sadomasochistic relationship that women have often been kept in, in regards to their aspirations either academically or professionally. You may even feel aroused by that, or invited by that, or excited or incited to acts of violence through great achievement that such an approach to pedagogy offers. I'm not saying that it's an either/or situation—either you're insulted or you're invited into the deepest levels of your own passion for speech—there are many places in between. However, I've found, through many years of experience, that inviting students to love and respect themselves creates a very productive space, in which risk-taking and an extraordinarily deep kind of honesty can enter the process freely.

LISA JO: This poetry teacher's pedagogy demands that the students conform to his expectations or fail—essentially he is asking them to be like him. Your feminist approach to teaching playwriting rejects the kind of false charity of more traditional top-down pedagogy that purports to support open exploration. When I've watched you teach, I've seen how your methods welcome the contradictions and joys that comprise each person's way of living, thinking, and imagining. To be honest, even after decades of feminist movement, it's amazing and sad that it remains a radical act to have students engage with their own realities in the way that you do in a theatre class. Unlike traditional teaching arrangements where students are validated by the professor's singular authority, you have your students share and borrow each other's images while they're sitting in a circle on the floor, then integrate those images into their own writing, which inevitably transforms them. It seems to me that this technique engages a circular, collective-based approach to writing that validates everyone's imagination.

DEB: In my classroom, it's very intimate. It's an intimate place you're invited to, and your relationship with that intimacy at a very young age can vary. I feel that in terms of the circularity of the vision of self, there are two aspects to hearing your own comments reflected back by other people in the room. Firstly, it is extremely flattering in the deepest sense, that something you said and felt was noted by another student. It validates your experience in a very gentle way. Secondly, it reminds the students that as playwrights and artists, we're working all the time, that the work is not just going on when we're talking or when you're writing or at home at your computer. In the world, our sources are infinite. Our lives are littered with beauty and littered with difficulties and humanity, and when we raise our consciousness to that fact, we have so much more material to work with and so many more hours in the day to harvest. The work is constant. It is going on when you're walking down the street, it's going on when you walk into Starbucks to buy your coffee. The work is constant and you can always overhear, notice, see the way the light is coming through, the way the stalks of the hyacinths have been broken by a cat–your work is constant. Therefore, you have so much more material and sources to draw from than you presume if you only consider your memory or your interactions in the classroom.

LISA JO: The feminist pedagogy you practice in your classroom activates an eros of the everyday as the foundation from which to work, letting what we love serve as a stimulus for what we create.

DEB: I feel that the feminist theatre movement was really about acknowledging that the personal is political and, correlative to that, that the personal is artistically viable. There is something inherently feminist, I think, about this approach to teaching. You don't just bring a scene and analyze the conflict between two characters. We acknowledge the conflict of even creating a character! We acknowledge that, given our mortality, conflict and resolution are inherent in the simplest human gesture, and that's where our theatre comes from. To me, it just makes sense. I understand from a wide-angle perspective that I inherit a feminist prerogative in introducing this way of studying playwriting into a classroom. I know that it's not a commonly accepted way of teaching playwriting. To me, it's just the only way to teach playwriting.

LISA JO: Can you elaborate upon that?

DEB: You don't have to know what you're talking about in class, but you are responsible for an articulate desire to speak, that's your responsibility. You don't have to understand where that passion comes from immediately, and you don't have to organize that passion right away. You need to be responsible for an articulate desire to speak, as opposed to an organized speech. I really feel like the great works came from a great passion. The permission to work from that aspect of the self is, I think, something that is inherently feminist theatre. Look back at Women's Experimental Theatre and their feelings and need to reinvent the vocabulary that was used in the theatre because, as Roberta Sklar says, the form of the Open Theatre was very exciting to her, but the content had nothing to do with her. She needed to go back and figure out a way to speak, a new vocabulary, a lexicon for self-representation, a way to, as she says, externalize internal experience. When you go even before that, you find that the very idea that internal experience is worth externalizing in the theatre–and is artistic, is viable, is important–is inherently feminist. I think it leads to great work, and it always has been what led to great work, but it has not been characterized as such, and it is usually not taught as such.

LISA JO: Prior to teaching in the academy, you were a writer and performer for many years. Do you think your experience has freed you to teach as you desire, without the need to meet any traditional academic expectations or definitions, to teach in the way that you learned to create theatre when you were part of Split Britches and then continued to develop as a solo performer and professor?

DEB: I try to teach the way I learned. I notice certain things about the ways in which plays get written and the way performance gets made, certain very intimate, personal things about the nature of these creative acts, which I try to bring into the classroom. I'd rather save students the time, if I can. It took me thirty years to realize that certain aspects of my responses were artistic in their nature and artistically viable in their use. And so, it takes a while. No one tells you that, no one lets you know that. If no one tells you that you're working all the time and that the way the light comes through the tan curtains and looks like weak coffee and makes you laugh and reminds you of a Hershey Bar commercial and that commercial reminds you of someone's touch on your shoulder when you were at the beach many years ago is actually important artistic material, it takes a long time to realize that on your own. If nobody teaches you about the way the mind works, and the uses and senses and cleanliness and poetry of the way your mind is organized, you just don't know. It takes years to figure it out. Since I notice the way I write and the ways plays get written, since I've paid attention to these processes, it has made a big difference in my feeling free to support students in this particular way.

LISA JO: You say it took you thirty years to understand the playwriting process. How do you get young students to take that journey in a semester?

DEB: When it comes to getting creative work done, I think the most efficient way is to encourage students, and to bring them to a consciousness of their own beauty, of their own ideation, of their own processes, of their own agency. I definitely think your remark is true, that if I hadn't been in some absurd situation where I was given the opportunity, quite accidentally, to notice these things, i.e., suddenly I was called in to help these women write a play about these other women that I knew nothing about, then I accidentally might not have discovered the ways in which my experience could be placed effortlessly and with tremendous grace into the mouths of characters who had on the surface nothing in common with me—timewise, religiously, culturally, physically—except for our shared humanity and our shared femininity, and suddenly when I made that discovery, I was like, "Oh, that's how this happens, that's how this gets done."

I'm trying to bring that experience into the classroom and it really works, really works. I can facilitate that accident and students go "ahh," and they get a sense of how this works. So I do feel liberated from certain strictures, and feel a tremendous sense of urgency. We have fourteen meetings, and in those meetings, I want to bring you to consciousness of your own beauty, your own passion and prerogative for speech, and offer various techniques by which you can take these things and make use of them to honor dramatic form. Fourteen encounters in which to support you, to encourage you to recognize the things that you have to work with, and to learn how to work with them. Insofar as I can remind them that the things they notice about themselves because I did not insult them, because they sat there on the floor, adjusting their butts on the floor—we always sit on the floor because you can't forget your body; when you sit in a chair you can sort of go deaf from the neck down, but when you sit on the floor, it's really annoying, you're shifting, you're always reminded of the length of your legs, the thickness of them, and the way your knees feel and your feet—insofar as I can support them in maintaining their belief in the power of these personal impulses, I will always continue to do so.

LISA JO: Your work, then, as a teacher is a living theory that is ever-responsive to your own life and to that of your students.

DEB: That's the interesting thing about being a practitioner as opposed to a scholar in the academy. I think it's very lovely, very lush, very healthy, like a flower with fresh rain on it. I like the fact that although I will attempt to apprehend theory when it crosses my path on the sidewalk, like a tree branch that's fallen in a storm, I work from experience as opposed to from theory. I teach feminist theatre but not from a scholarly perspective. It's interesting to not really have a strong wide angle about where I fit into the landscape of American theatre, feminist theatre, or any other continuum. I always refer to Shakespeare's Sonnet #94 that I sent Richard Nixon, which he didn't write back to and I'm still upset about, and it has that beautiful couplet that I thought about for ten years, "The summer's flower is to the summer sweet though to itself it only live and die." I'm just a flower that was to the summer sweet; to the second wave of feminism I was one flower in the field of thousands of flowers and I enjoyed myself and the summer appreciated me in its limited way, but that's it. To myself, I only lived and died, and now, I live on. I was raised in the lesbian feminist theatre. I was raised to have a very broad spectrum of what constitutes feminine identity, and what constitutes identity at all. I was raised in a theatre of desire, in a theatre of political consciousness and I came to realize within that education—which was an education through practice—that good theatre, good art, is pre-political in its essence. It does not take place on a political continuum in its initial, tender budding impulses; it is profoundly personal, it is profoundly of the sentiment and the spirit, and then as it grows, develops, it is perforce political in its nature. And as it steps forward and presents itself to a group of people, it has a political valence that can be embraced, that is radical in its personal-ness, particularly when it is done by women and people of color. I was raised in a certain way and, beautifully enough for me, as a teacher, those precepts seem very sound as pedagogical principles. It's not just that I feel they are politically correct or right or just or fair, although they definitely do keep judgment, racism, sexism, and homophobia out of the discourse by their very nature, but that is not what makes them most beautiful to me. What makes them most beautiful to me in the classroom is that they work, that these feminist precepts by which I was raised in the theatre are effective pedagogically.

LISA JO: What do you think makes these precepts so effective in the classroom?

DEB: The theatre of desire is the right theatre. I think that Shakespeare had a theatre of desire, I think he wrote from his desperate passion to look at the ways in which these men behaved and everything else; he was not bored by these human impulses and he was not merely moved by commercial instincts. This man couldn't wait to talk about the ways the king was really just as naked under his clothes as anyone else. Great art comes from passion, from a need to expose human spirit in the face of mortality, the small cruelties and heroisms that make up daily life—that's where great work comes from, and if you enable students in this way to discover those impulses and observations in themselves, those heroisms and cruelties in themselves, you create an atmosphere in which art can emerge. These techniques work. You tap into something else when you insult people, but I don't think that's what gets results. It may get a certain kind of result, but the precepts by which I was raised in the theatre make excellent pedagogical tools. That's what got results from me. I was raised in this other place, in the academy, went to NYU, studied at the feet of the masters, such as they were, but what got me really writing plays were these two wild Spiderwoman refugees who encouraged me to just start laughing at this record of Mother Goddam from the *Shanghai Gesture* or whatever compelled me—I wanted to sing "I Want to Be in America" in Yiddish, and when we did that, you could see the layers of the diaspora that we were looking at. We felt so marginal that we were singing a song about marginalized people in a marginalized language in a marginalized outfit. This is meaningful. I learned how meaning aggregates around desire. I learned it firsthand and then I bring it into the classroom and it works. Although I can see, in my non-scholarly way, see how these are fundamentally feminist and feminine precepts from which I'm working, I like them because they get results. I also like the energy in the classroom, the warmth, the sense of community.

LISA JO: Just as theatre is a communal act.

DEB: Yes, and it's a physical act, it is an erotic act. Nothing will replace it. The blackberries, blueberries, whatever those machines are, I don't care, computers and the Internet and the instant message… I find email very sexy, I like saying things for which I don't have to take physical responsibility–it's very titillating. On the other hand, there is nothing so sexy as the body, really. The reason that the computer is sexy is that we are alone with our bodies. I am in love with the theatre because it is of the body, and I also love the theatre and feel most relaxed teaching language for the theatre because language fails. Let's face it–language is a failure. It's the most magnificent failure we have, and the theatre is about the failure of language, so there's a lot of margin for error.

LISA JO: Can you talk more about that in relation to your students?

DEB: Students freeze in the face of needing to get everything right. The thing about theatre is that it is subtextual, it's metatextual. It's not what you say, it's what was unspeakable, it's what you wanted to say but instead you said something else. If language worked, there would be no theatre, no drama, no tension. There would be no drama without the failure of language and that's why it is perfectly insensible, so sexy-insensible, so erotic-insensible, and so perfect to use language. Language is never more appropriate in all its failings and beauty than in the theatre. With all of this history, I find no greater purpose for my pedagogy than in teaching theatre and no greater tools for teaching theatre than those I learned in the feminist theatre as an actor, as a practitioner, as a writer–all of that gets brought to bear most sensibly. In doing, I learned how to teach theatre.

LISA JO: Let's return to the formative impact that Roberta Sklar and the Women's Experimental Theatre had on you, particularly because it seems to me that you have developed a feminist playwriting pedagogy that bridges and weaves ages together, that holds onto feminist precepts which characterized women's theatre companies that flourished particularly in the late 1960s and 1970s, less in the 1980s, but certainly with Split Britches, all the while allowing students to pursue what propels them forward today, in their own lives, through their own currency. Can you elaborate upon WET's connection to your pedagogy?

DEB: Roberta Sklar and Sondra Segal recently came to my Feminist Theatre class. They had changed my life years ago, seeing them work, seeing their interstitial performance that came from inside their lives, from deep within their bodies and their experiences as women. In class, Sondra said that they realized that what one does not say becomes unsayable, what one does not speak becomes unspeakable. Their rediscovery of a vocabulary for representation of women's experience and the insistence that such a thing was even artistic and worthy of the stage was a radical act in and of itself.

LISA JO: Wasn't [WET's] *Electra Speaks* particularly important to you?

DEB: We had read *Electra Speaks* in my Early Feminist Theater Class, which is written in a very primary language in terms of representing feminine experience. It is a look at the events of the House of Atreus from the women's point of view, which was never really focused on by any of the great writers. The material is written in a repetitive, circular motion, circling around and around and around. All my students were very moved by it. After Roberta and Sondra spoke at length, one of the students said, "You know, here we are, women, allowed into this Ivy League institution, allowed to study at this institution, and we get jobs, we have around us the artifice of equality, and it is that artifice that keeps us from achieving anything anymore. Can you help us? Won't you return? Why have you stopped? Will you help us? Are you ready?" And Sondra looked at her and said, "Are you?" And they looked at each other, and in that moment, I felt this bridge between the past and the present, the theatre of the past, the matriarchs that had created a rubric of looking, a way for us to consider what was wrong—it's hard to even say what's wrong when you're in so much pain as women were and have been for so many years. They created a vocabulary, a safe space, and a way of looking at these matters and now, here, the results of their work are somewhat evident. But the artifice of equality, such a beautiful phrase—these two women looked at each other, and suddenly, okay, we need to get back to work, we need you to come back and help us. And now they are, and next semester we are going to stage *Electra Speaks*.

LISA JO: This young woman points to the necessity of feminist pedagogy such as yours in the academy, in the theatre. In your classroom, where you invite students who have varying aesthetic and social values to see the usefulness of their deepest desires, your process leads to a product. What happens when they move from reading their fill-in-the-blanks and source exercises to actual scenes and plays?

DEB: First, ground rules are laid for the way work is talked about. This is not a group critique or an American Idol-style, free-for-all opportunity to tell people what's right and wrong with their work, or to rewrite the work. It is, rather, a collective investigation of the way a scene or series of scenes signifies. There is never an acceptable time or way to say: That stunk, was no good, failed, etc. Language is reflective, inquisitive; a fellow student who acts as a dramaturg can say what she has seen, can ask questions about what she did not understand, can mention something she found implicit rather than explicit, can refer to past work and inquire about its relationship to the scenes just read. In class, the playwright assigns parts to fellow students from his work, and then addresses the class regarding who the characters are, and then any particular way in which he wants us to listen to the scene, or any particular way in which our focus might be helpful to him following the reading. If he has no specific idea of what kind of reflective focus he'd like us to have, that's perfect also. Then the scene or scenes are read. Always, after the reading, the first person to speak is the playwright, in her most vulnerable and confused moment. She may say, "I had no idea how funny that was, that part when_____," or "I didn't understand how bizarre that moment was until I heard it read," or "I'm embarrassed by how personal that felt," or "I enjoyed that and I don't know what else to say," or whatever. Then we open the floor to others for observations, comments, questions. Comments might begin with "I liked the way _____," "I felt confused by _____," "Where in the play does this fall?" "I loved the recurring image of _____," "Did you consciously decide to make _____say or do _____, or was that something that just happened as you heard the voice of the character?"

LISA JO: The kinds of questions you just shared reveal that you model certain ways of responding–and I'll say feminist ways–to another's work that leads students to bear witness and take responsibility for listening to each other. They must develop active listening and question-making skills in order to open pathways for each other as playwrights in non-competitive ways so that each re-hears their own words and can see new meaning there. This is in keeping with your emphasis that your class is a room without a critic. And since you emphasize that students are seeking "the aching place from which to speak," as I have heard you say, there is no space for a teacher to hand down the "truth" about a student's play from a position of authority, like that poet, nor for students to critique each other in terms of getting things "right," which indicates that there is a standard to live up to, or in comparison to their respective work. How do you facilitate the responses that follow the playwright's own comments?

DEB: As the leader of the discussion, I am always interested in asking the questions: one, what kind of cog is this scene in the machine of the entire play? What work does this scene do to advance the transformative arc of your play? And, two, good plays tend to have some aspect of their dominant thematic content present in every scene; where in this scene should we look for the guiding conceits of your play? Students make notes during discussion, and usually come away feeling positive about the conversation, and in the best case, clearer and more excited about how their work signifies and about where they'd like to take the work from that point. Sometimes, after a scene is read, I will ask for it to be reread by different "actors," perhaps re-gendering the reading, or rearranging the voices in another way that may liberate the playwright from one particular way of hearing the work. This has sometimes had very moving consequences; asking a woman to read a man's part or a man to read a woman's; having a sex scene read by two men instead of a man and a woman. Things get shaken loose in terms of underlying meanings, and can be viewed independent of certain conventions by which the playwright did not know herself to be bound.

LISA JO: Speaking of underlying meanings, and coming to understand the elements that define someone as a playwright, that shape us as thinkers, I was wondering if you might address the way in which teaching as a Jewish woman informs your pedagogy and performing.

DEB: In terms of performing, I'm just so Jewish. In preparation for my trip to Israel last May to perform in and co-direct *Critical Mass* in Hebrew, Linda Ben-Zvi, this wonderful Beckett scholar who teaches at the University of Tel Aviv, said that my play had the "Jewish complement." When I asked what that meant, she said that what she meant was that it had a very Jewish sensibility. I loved having my work recognized as Jewish; even though that play doesn't talk about Jewish matters, it argues in a Jewish way. There's a Jewish insistence, willingness, and all points in between, to turn an issue around and look at it from every possible angle and still not be content that there is an absolute. And I love that about Jewish literature, I love that about Jewish text, and I love that in the whole Jewish way of life–like waiting for the Messiah, you never know, it's not definite. Is the Messiah this or is the Messiah that, there's no telling. There's that willingness to argue, by which I mean look at something from every possible angle and still not feel like you've finished the conversation. In that sense, I do feel that I have this desperately Jewish quality, which I love in my own ideation, and in my own life. In terms of my pedagogy, I think my insistence on a non-judgmental classroom means that any idea can be entertained, that you cannot tell anybody that they cannot talk about this or cannot be this or that, and at the same time, it evinces in general a profound and abiding unspoken tolerance of every race, religion, sexual orientation; there is an insistence on cleanliness of permission, there is a clean permission for any attitude.

LISA JO: Does this open approach ever backfire?

DEB: I recently had a very jarring experience with a student in my class. She is generally very contrary–we all, as teachers, get contrary students, students who when you ask them for this they bring that, when you call for the fireman, they bring the arsonist, something that all teachers have to encounter– and I have a young woman like that and I welcome the challenge of that as we all do. This student in class recently said, "Well in my automatic writing, I surprised myself with this diatribe against Jews that was interesting." Not having read this text, I took a deep breath and said, "Well, you know, it's important to acknowledge these feelings. We are all raised with certain racist ideas and you cannot transcend what you will not acknowledge." One of the symptoms of racism is that it does not acknowledge itself. True racism never acknowledges itself, racism never says "I am racist" or "I am sexist." Racism vogues as observation. And so, I said, "It's beautiful to acknowledge this, as you can't transcend what you won't acknowledge. That's the first point I want to make to you, dear one, and the second point I'd like to make is that you do not have the freedom to put onstage those things that we are free to discuss in class or in a coffee shop. When something is onstage, it defies rebuttal, a, and b, it is in a frame you have chosen of all possible things; the fact that you have chosen this means that you have given it a meta-significance, a universality that you must be prepared to take responsibility for." And we talked about the way in which work onstage signifies politically in a way that a conversation in a coffee shop may not.

Then, I actually read the text in question and it was a very painful diatribe in which the student wrote something like, "I used to think Jews were innocent and I felt sorry for them in the Holocaust but they're not innocent. When you turn your back on a Jew and then turn back to them, your wallet is gone. They control all the money, should be wiped off the map." These are some pretty dramatic comments and qualify possibly as hate speech if they were presented in a forum other than in the safety of our class, which doesn't mean I wasn't profoundly hurt by them. I was profoundly hurt by them and couldn't respond for a number of hours after I read this text. It's just so unoriginal. It's so interesting the way stereotypes are redundant over the years despite change, despite effort, despite forward and progressive motion; the things we say about one another are the same again and again and again. The idea of your wallet being missing? What wallet? What Jew? Someone suggested jokingly that I should come to class and say "Listen, missy, this is off the record and has nothing to do with class, I just need to ask you something. Which pocket is your wallet in?" That was a healing joke that I shared with a fellow teacher. Then, the assignment I gave her was to write, was to imagine that that character–I accredited it with being a character as opposed to her feelings–and I gave her the assignment to read *O Wholly Night*, which is this comical solo piece I wrote about the sexiness of waiting for the Messiah, in which I talk about the stereotypes Jews are placed in and that's definitely one of them, the money thing, money lenders, and I gave her the assignment to imagine that character saying those things on stage and imagine Dr. Martin Luther King Jr.'s rebuttal to that character. So now we have a dialogue, and she needs to find inside of herself a rejection of the call to wipe Jews off the map, or of any violent act–not just Jews–much less the higher calling to a deeper morality, a commitment to the acceptance of humanity. So she's going to have to look for that voice, she's going to have to find it, or not. I feel like when you create a classroom where all images and ideas are permissible and you get a contrary student within that context, she or he may confront you with, "Okay, you asked for honesty, here's honesty." She threw that at me and I tossed these other ideas back to her as gently as I could.

LISA JO: As your pedagogy allows students to unearth the unexpected, you are also responsible for guiding them to consciously negotiate these surprising elements in their playwriting. Do you think being Jewish affects what you focus on in their work and how you shape your responses to them?

DEB: Yes. Being a Jewish woman in a pedagogical circumstance, I really feel greatly lifted up and informed by the willingness to look at everything, the refusal to stop and settle on any one answer, and the absurdity and sense of humor of all that, the mumuloschen, the joy, the maternal. The maternal question is also very interesting. Reading Roberta Sklar's interview with Cornelia Brunner, which is a beautiful and revelatory interview she gave many years ago about the failure of the Open Theatre to gratify her as a feminist and as a woman, as a person, no matter how radical and political Chaikin's ideas, she said, "When I direct, I'm not your mother. I'm just a woman here, a person here, looking at this text. Don't ask me to mother you." And I felt deeply indebted to her in her refusal to mother people. She earned for me the freedom to mother. She did the work, and now I'm in the academy, in this Ivy League without a Ph.D., without a Master's degree, mothering the hell out of my kids. I got that right on her tuchus, on her back, I got that right. I wept when I read that. She refused to do that, and I just feel such a sense of pride. Now, as a teacher, I'm all over your life, you have a problem, I want to hear about it because it directly affects your work and your ability to work, and it affects the content of your work.

LISA JO: Feminists have debated and parsed the meaning of maternal for decades. What strikes me at this moment is the passage of time from Roberta's comment in 1980 to your relocation of mothering within the academy in the twenty-first century. With the *Daughters Cycle* trilogy [1977-81], WET challenged audiences to recognize the objectification of mothers, as well as the complexity of the mother's role in society, particularly in relation to daughters and vice versa. Roberta's refusal seems like it was a plea not to be reduced to mothering as the only means for her to relate to another. Now, in 2006, where a visiting poet can "father" students in ways that silence them into action, I can only imagine the response to your kind of attentive mothering...

DEB: I have very clear boundaries: no one thinks I'm going to date them or make out with them, nobody thinks I'm going to come to their house and live with them and cook them dinner or take them to the doctor, but we work as we live. There's no such thing as writer's block, there's living block. Our lives directly overlap with our work, and so I mother my students in a certain way. They know I am available to them on many different levels. Roberta Sklar earned the validity of my approach to teaching, this matriarch of feminist theatre who I had the honor of bringing to my class. Her remark about mothering was so profound. It allowed me to see where the architecture for my feminist praxis in the classroom came from. I teach my playwriting class and I see the foundations of my own work in the work of these women from the 60s and the 70s. And these are Jewish women too, although that's not something we talked about.

LISA JO: You encourage your students to take the risk of lending themselves in vulnerable ways to their characters just as the feminist theatre matriarchs did for themselves–and they had to, and it was urgent for them to find their own forms and language to represent their experiences, to respond artistically to being continually silenced. You successfully do that for yourself in your own work. Creating plays in this way in the professional world is fraught with and heightened by so many uncertainties; and as you said earlier, it took you many years to recognize the viability of your impulses. It seems like your choice to "mother" in the classroom is a result of your own experiences and your commitment to utilizing this knowledge to enable your students to develop original, vibrant, effective new plays. How do your students shape their desires into a play?

DEB: We talk about the definition of plot, the one that I have come up with–like in science, you find the theory that works in every instance, then you'll go with that theory, and when you apply it to different instances it works. When I think what is plot, you have Aristotelian definitions of plot and story–when I go to define plot for my students who are so intimidated by the idea of creating plot, just as they are intimidated by putting words into other people's mouths, plot is transformation. That is the definition I have come up with over the years that fits every instance. It's transformation. There are many different ways to honor the form, to honor dramatic form. A poem is one thing, short story is another, and a play is another, and you have to figure out how to honor those different art forms. A short story is going to be constructed differently than a play or poem. In a play, language signifies differently. What is dramatic form and how can we honor it? It's by describing a transformative arc; a person or a group of people transform. Who are these people, we need to find out, and what transformation will they go through?

When I was writing *Three Seconds in the Key*, a play about a woman with Hodgkin's disease, I knew that she had Hodgkin's disease and knew that she loved basketball and I knew that she was living in exile from her body. So, what was going to happen to change this woman? Something was going to reincorporate her, put her back in her body. Once I realized that the woman, whether she lived or died, needed to live in her body again, I was able to pull out certain circumstances and actions.

LISA JO: How do you lead students to find their characters' transformations?

DEB: We have different exercises, for example, the unwanted revelation: what brings about transformation? Age, falling in love, unwanted revelation, i.e., the finding out of something one didn't want to find out, the unraveling of a lie that a character tells him or herself; we all tell ourselves lies to get through the day. We have a bunch of exercises that are transformative in their nature and I offer students opportunities to apply these techniques to characters in whom they have already invested.

So, if we define plot as transformation–which, after discussion and exercise, works–I ask students to say what the transformation is, who is transforming, what is the transformative arc and what tools can we use in dialogue and dramatic form to bring about that transformation. Eventually, that accident that is the discovery of oneself as a playwright happens. There gets a point in class where I say "You bring me this scene or something better. Write a scene in which somebody reveals something to your protagonist that she or he does not want to know; bring me that or something better." You do that exercise. I put these tools into scene assignments and then you do that assignment and you discover something else and then you write another scene. A character discovers she or he is in love with someone of the same sex; a character discovers that his father was married before and loved the previous wife; a character discovers that his son is sexually active even though that child is only thirteen. Discovery, perspective-altering events, sudden change in circumstances, and other exercises designed to have the student explore who is transforming and by what means. Once we discover that, we can figure out the means of their transformation, and that means calls forth many different forces, and textures, and characters to bear in service of that transformation.

LISA JO: Can you discuss one of these exercises that facilitates the accident?

DEB: There are certain pragmatic things that spark the great conflagration that is a passionate play and that's how I work. We have exercises in class such as "the power of the irrelevant remark" in a scene. Irrelevant remarks, when somebody says something radically irrelevant in the middle of a scene–first of all, it is immediately humorous, it's instant comedy, it instantly creates a poetry between the relevant and irrelevant subject. If you're in the middle of talking about how Papa is dying and I start talking about Carefree gum and how irritating it is that they won't use a real rhyme, they say, "Carefree gum is sugarless, and it comes in full-sized sticks no less," see, you were in the middle of talking about somebody dying and you bring that up? There's an immediate poetry that gets created. First of all, I'm in denial, I'm clearly having an issue with the relevant subject. Second of all, I'm talking about less, and everything is less, and less, and less. It's magical, the power of an irrelevant remark in a scene. This is a very practical assignment. I ask everyone to read aloud from texts–I ask everyone to go around the circle, ask you to tell us something that you think about often that really doesn't fit into any category of thought. It is irrelevant to almost any school of thought, like the Carefree gum commercial and how annoyed I get that they pay these advertising executives a lot of money and they couldn't even rhyme, there's no school of thought into which that would fit. We go around the circle and everyone has something like that, like, why are the milk bottles in this particular shape? It doesn't serve the pouring. Once everybody has come up with an irrelevant thought, we begin an exercise where somebody reads out loud from an automatic writing and at the appropriate moment or at an impulsive moment, the person on your left starts up about the milk bottle or the Carefree gum and you stop what you're saying and listen to this and everybody starts laughing because of course it's either poetic or ridiculous or whatever it is, and then we finish reading from the automatic writing. Then we go on to the next person who begins to read and the person on their left interrupts with whatever it is. Then you see the power that this could have in a scene to illuminate. A student wrote this beautiful scene: these people, a mother and son, were trying to pick a gravestone for the father and this hysterical conversation ensued that illuminated the void created by the death of the father in a way that no direct monologue could have done. Another student wrote a beautiful scene that was just read as part of the Yale Playwrights Festival about these two kids playing; suddenly they were talking about a noose they had found that looked like a puppet, then one of them, she draped it around her neck and the other child said, "you look very pretty, Molly." This exercise is a practical tool that has resonant repercussions when you assign it to a student so they accidentally discover how to write their scene. Finally, it's the fulfillment of a transformative arc.

LISA JO: How do you get the students to complete the scenes with which they are experimenting and move towards creating a play?

DEB: There's a whole panoply of scene assignments. Once you get on a roll with your play, if you don't want to do the scene assignments that's okay, then bringing in something better or more relevant to what you're doing is okay. In the beginning though, you do all the assignments as I tell you. I assign students: I've got to write a play about _____, and I'm in love with and obsessed by _____. Then I ask, what would this thing you're in love with and obsessed by be doing in a play about what you said you've got to write a play about? Think about that, then write a set description of a play in which the thing you are in love with and obsessed by is in a play that you've got to write about. You put those two together and write a set description, which is really generative. I'll ask you to write a scene that's nothing but stage directions, not one word is spoken. I will ask you to write a scene based on the power of an irrelevant remark. I will ask you to write a dream scene, a sex scene, a scene based on the power of an unwanted revelation. I will ask students about a moment of unwanted revelation in their own lives so we can examine the texture of experience. Very often the scene assignment is preceded by classwork in which I ask you to describe something like that in your own life, and I emphasize that we are interested in the textures of your experience—in the experience, of course—but if we can fully incorporate the texture of experience, we can then give it to our characters. When they go to give their characters such experiences, they are informed by the texture of their own experience. I will ask students to describe a stunning moment on the telephone and then ask them to give their characters such a moment. I will ask students to describe a moment of unexpected sexual feeling, then I will ask them to give their character such a moment. What brings about transformation? What leads them to plot? A change in perspective. I will ask students to describe a moment when they saw something completely differently than when they had seen it in the past due to age or after they broke up with someone or they came back after their mother died. Tell us about a time when you saw something completely differently than you'd seen it in the past, and what did it feel like to see it so differently. You look at your experience and its texture, then when you come to these exercises, you have examined and listened to other people examining the texture of that particular experience. You cannot, really cannot, write about what you have no experience with, either in your imagination or your life. Since we're dealing with young people, it is very helpful to talk about such experiences in their own lives. Having acquainted themselves—even in passing—with experience like that in their own lives, it is easier then, to lend such experiences to characters.

LISA JO: All that you've said brings to mind some questions that Andrew Parker and Eve Sedgwick talk about in their book *Performativity and Performance*. They ask, "When is saying something doing something? And how is saying something doing something?" In your classes, through the act of saying something, students do something for their characters upon which they can expand in their plays; they also do something for themselves and gain an understanding of the power of their imagery, and each other's. As they succeed, they give back to you.

DEB: When my students take these humble practitioner's lessons into the world and cobble together a life in the theatre, I am just filled with exultation. They might not be making feminist theatre as it has been defined in a scholarly way, but I do feel that it is feminist at its source because it comes from a place of desire, and the accreditation of personal desire and impulses and images as artistically viable, and I do feel that is the direct heritage of the feminist matriarchs in the theatre and the feminist movement; I definitely feel that connection. Teaching morally underwrites the profound pleasures of performance. I arrogate the right to myself to do this beautiful thing; I also offer to help you should you wish to do it. It's like sharing a certain kind of wealth. If I just wrote plays and didn't help others who wished to write plays, it would feel as if I opened up a huge meal in a homeless shelter and didn't offer food to anyone else. I can't do that. This way, I do and you do too.

NOTES

[1] "Meet Deb Margolin!: The text of her public interview with Lisa Jo Epstein, Zale Writer in Residence Program at Newcomb College Center for Research on Women. http://www.tulane.edu/~wc/zale/margolin/margolin.html

[2] Lynda Hart, *Of All the Nerve: Deb Margolin SOLO.* (New York: Cassell, 1999).

[3] In her plays, Deb frequently integrates television commercials, radio ads, and other pop culture arti-facts in uncanny ways that simultaneously offer high humor and incisive cultural critique. She effort-lessly re-situates fragments of omnipresent consumerism, as well as her personal responses to them, as viable theatrical–and decidedly contemporary–metaphors for individual and societal exploration. In terms of her revelations about her own humanity that were accidentally purveyed through the CarCash commercial, Deb looked at the lyrics of it as text:

> I'm feeling good all over
> And here's the reason why:
> I just sold my car to CarCash
> I'm in love with those CarCash guys!

Deb says she realized that she not only heard words and melody when the song was sung, but also envisioned a protagonist: a young, susceptible woman who, by sheer dint of the sale of her vehicle, was feeling good all over, not just relieved mentally, but ALL OVER her whole BODY, and now was in love with the people who had given her this good feeling, but these people had no such feel-ings for her, as why should they when they're in the middle of buying and selling cars; and the very act of selling the car now ended her entire reason for having anything further to do with these peo-ple, and now she's just STANDING in a PARKING LOT without even a ride home. A realization of Deb's personal identification with the loneliness of this woman's position, about Deb's personal imag-ination of this woman who engaged in a finite transaction that led to an infinite, unrequited love, was the payoff of Deb's investigation of her own response to these lyrics. She mined them for their sur-face comedy, and their underlying resonance. To read Deb's solo work, see Lynda Hart, ed., *Of All the Nerve: Deb Margolin SOLO.*

[4] See Wendy S. Hesford, Framing Identities: Autobiography and the Politics of Pedagogy, (Minneapolis: University of Minnesota Press, 1999).

[5] For more information about the Women's Experimental Theater, see Roberta Sklar, "Sisters,' or Never Trust Anyone Outside the Family, " *Women & Performance Journal*, Vol. 1., No. 1 (1983); also Clare Coss, Sondra Segal and Roberta Sklar, "Why Do We Need a Feminist Theatre?" *Women & Performance Journal* 1.1 (1983); Clare Coss, Sondra Segal and Roberta Sklar, "Separation and Survival: Mothers, Daughters, Sisters–The Women's Experimental Theater" in Hester Eisenstein and Alice Jardine, eds., *The Future of Difference* (Boston: G.K.Hall, 1980); Sondra Segal and Roberta Sklar, "The Women's Experimental Theater," *The Drama Review: TDR*, Vol. 27, no. 4 (Winter 1983); Cornelia Brunner, "Roberta Sklar: Toward Creating a Women's Theater," *TDR* Vol. 24, No. 2, Women & Performance Issue (June 1980); Charlotte Canning, *Feminist Theaters in the USA* (New York: Routledge, 1996); Julie Malnig and Judy C. Rosenthal, "The Women's Experimental Theatre: Transforming Family Stories into Feminist Questions," in Lynda Hart & Peggy Phelan, eds., *Acting Out: Feminist Performances*, (Ann Arbor: University of Michigan Press, 1996); Karen Malpede "Notes on the Women's Experimental Theatre" in Malpede ed., *Women and Theatre: Compassion and Hope* (New York: Drama Book Publishers, 1983); Helen Krich Chinoy and Linda Walsh Jenkins, *Women In American Theatre*, 3rd edi-tion (NY: TCG, 2006).

[6] Andrew Parker and Eve Kosofsky Sedgwick eds., *Performativity and Performance* (New York: Routledge, 1995).

PLAY FAIR
FEMINIST TOOLS FOR TEACHING IMPROV
Amy Seham

Scenario: Your acting students are playing Freeze-Tag, a popular improv game designed to strengthen skills of spontaneity and cooperative creativity. As you watch, you notice that many of the young women in the class spend most of their time cheering from the sidelines, hesitant to jump into this fast-paced, quick-witted game. Still, everyone seems to be enjoying the exercise. There is great energy and laughter, especially when the students make pop culture references that everyone recognizes. The stereotypes connected to race, gender, sexuality, class–differences of all kinds–grow broader and broader, encouraged by audience response. No one seems bothered by the content or by the unbalanced participation but you. What do you do?

The scenario described above is only one example of the ways that improv often takes shape in the classroom or on the stage. Rare is the acting teacher who has not drawn heavily on Viola Spolin's improvisational games and exercises (including "Mirror" and "Who, Where"), or popular adaptations of her work (such as Freeze-Tag) to build basic performance skills. These games are clearly a valuable way for students to work through self-consciousness and activate their imaginations. For many feminist directors, educators, and performers, improvisation has great potential as a tool for creating theatre. Iconoclastic movements from Dada and Surrealism to the collective feminist theatres of the 1970s to Augusto Boal's Theatre of the Oppressed have used improvisation as a vital means of subverting the prescriptive rules of conventional theatre and society. But for feminists, improvisation may also involve more risks than advantages for creating theatre.

As educators themselves, important pioneers of improv Spolin and Keith Johnstone, describe goals and values largely consistent with feminist pedagogy. Like feminist educators, they strive to create through improv a "liberatory environment…a model of ways for people to work together to accomplish mutual or shared goals, and to help each other reach individual goals" (Shrewsbury 8-9). Spolin's improvisational games are designed to produce the kind of spontaneity that "creates an explosion that for the moment frees us from handed-down frames of reference, memory choked with old facts and information...[it] is the moment of personal freedom" (Spolin 4).

Improvisation is used in a variety of contexts and for a variety of purposes. Directors may use improvisation to help actors explore character or develop deeper understanding of the text in a scripted play. Playwrights or facilitators may use improvisation to develop material based on the experiences and imaginations of a community of performers. Educators use improvisation not only in acting classes, but also in role-playing exercises and scenarios. Social justice activists use improv as a way to enable spectators to imagine alternatives and even rehearse resistance to oppression. Entertainers use many forms of improvisation, including improv-comedy, which most often depends on game structures to elicit humorous characters, scenes, and situations for an audience. Despite the differences in primary purpose, actors experience similar challenges in all of these contexts. A structure, text, or set of rules provides the outline, and performers must spontaneously collaborate to invent each specific relationship or situation. Improvisation foregrounds the very process of creation, and the product (or performance) is ephemeral and unrepeatable. This focus on process recalls a Brechtian approach to performance—and a feminist interest in making narrative choices and means of production more visible.[1] It would appear that, far more than scripted work, improvisation could be what feminist theatre theorist Jill Dolan describes as "a place to experiment with the production of cultural meanings, on bodies willing to try a range of different significations for spectators willing to read them" (432).

Indeed, improv often looks quite like a feminist model of group creation. Its open spontaneity seems to offer participants both the individual agency and the sense of supportive community so important to feminist pedagogy. Improvisational performance appears to realize the power of tangible transformation. It holds out the promise that everyone can play, that everyone's story can be told, that every possibility can be imagined and embodied. Yet, as my research into improv has revealed, improvisation, particularly when combined with comedy, is more likely to reinscribe stereotypes, reinforce hierarchies, and naturalize conservative values than it is to challenge them. As Gay Gibson Cima warns feminist directors, "If you build your directorial work upon actors' improvisations, plan carefully, because improvisations can inadvertently reproduce the dominant ideological structures that you are trying to critique. Actors may spontaneously voice their own unrecognized biases or they may move in stereotypical ways, ways that reinforce rather than redirect the traditional values promoted in the canon" (100).

The feminist educator working with improvisation must find ways to help students resist the tendency merely to repeat mainstream power relations and to regurgitate the popular culture they have been fed, from fairy tales to beer commercials. As Carolyn Shrewsbury argues, feminist pedagogy "recognizes the genderedness of all social relations and consequently of all societal institutions and structures...it requires continuous questioning and making assumptions explicit." (8). The challenge is to find ways to balance the benefits of spontaneity in improv with the need for critical engagement with emerging content and power relations. The exercises and examples below are designed to begin such a process.

In practice, however, there is often a radical difference between the expressed ideals of improvisation and the reality of improv in popular performance.[2] Building on Spolin's teachings, virtually every school of improv teaches the fundamental rule of "agreement," the concept of creating scenes, characters, and situations by saying "yes...and." For example, if two people are playing an improvisational game, one player accepts the other player's offer (yes) and then adds to it by exploring or heightening the given idea (and). This model assumes an equal give and take between scene partners as they build a scene together. It is often the case, however, that the first person who speaks in a scene, or the person who speaks most aggressively, controls the premise of the scene and even defines the roles that others will play in it.

For a number of reasons having to do with upbringing and socialization, many women improvisers tend to be less assertive in taking initiative and focus onstage than male players. Women often find themselves "agreeing" to play the supportive, backseat position in scenes that express the male perspective, allowing men to define (or, in improv terms, to "endow") them exclusively as stereotypical wives, girlfriends, and mothers. Some women even feel more comfortable in these support roles and may consistently abdicate the responsibility of driving the scene toward "the funny" outcome.

Agreement is crucial to improv not only at the level of the two-person scene, but for the entire performance troupe as well. Spolin wrote, "The game is a natural group form providing the involvement and personal freedom necessary for experiencing...There must be group agreement on the rules of the game and group interaction moving toward the objective if the game is to be played" (5). Most improvisers highly value "groupthink" or "groupmind," as they call the group agreement that allows the company to work together toward the same goals, often with seemingly miraculous intuition. According to Halpern, Close, and Howard's *Truth in Comedy*, a guidebook for long-form improv, when improvisers achieve "groupmind" they are linked to "a universal intelligence, enabling them to perform fantastic, sometimes unbelievable feats" (93). While many players and teachers take great pleasure in the seemingly natural consensus of the improvisers, many social scientists consider "groupthink" a means of forcible conformity and assimilation (Janis quoted in Brown 158).

For example, women who resist or "deny" conventional gender roles may be criticized for imposing the inappropriate "political agenda" of feminism on a scene, or may simply be accused of being bad team players. Similarly, improvisers of color often find that their references, allusions, and perceptions of incongruity are not immediately grasped by white players. Thus, as improviser Frances Callier has said, players may feel that they must "whitewash [their] humor" in order to participate fully in the group (personal interview quoted in Seham, 189). Groupmind, so valued in improv, is for the most part simply the heterosexual white male mind. As improviser Stephanie Weir put it, "the white male lifestyle and experience is so on the forefront of everyone's mind, TV, everything in our lives, that everyone has that common experience. We all know how to support that, 'Oh, that's familiar, I can heighten that'" (personal interview quoted in Seham 70).

Many educators approached me over the course of my study of Chicago improv, expressing genuine concerns about the practical task of teaching or directing improvisation. How, they wonder, can their students reap the benefits of working in such a spontaneous, expressive, and entertaining mode without succumbing to the worst excesses of stereotyping, power plays, and conformity? How can teachers help to balance the gender inequities that prevail in many, if not all, young companies? Is it even possible to have a multicultural troupe that does not completely assimilate every form of difference or revert to mainstream ideologies?

In seeking answers to these questions, I have designed workshops for the Funny Woman Festival, the touring companies of Second City Toronto, Laughing Matters workshops with Fringe Benefits of Los Angeles, the Visthar Outreach Program in Bangalore, India, and with my students at Gustavus Adolphus College. These workshops explore the dynamics of improv when questions of gender, race, sexuality, and power are consciously addressed. The material from these workshops, along with my earlier research, interviews, and experience, have enabled me to create a broad set of guidelines and specific exercises that I believe will help directors and educators deal with many of the issues that improv raises. And yes, for all its pitfalls, I believe strongly that improv is a valuable tool for teaching acting, encouraging spontaneity, creating scripts, and exploring alternative versions of reality. Yes, there is such a thing as feminist improv.

I have organized my approach into five interconnected categories: Philosophy; Casting; Stereotypes and References; Status and Sharing the Stage; and (as a last resort) Defensive Tactics. It is my hope that the following ideas and exercises will benefit educators, troupe leaders, and others striving to shape a positive improv experience for all participants.

PHILOSOPHY

Don't be afraid to have one. Some improvisers might resist the notion of feminist improv. Many sincere, experienced players argue passionately that improv is a spiritual, and therefore an apolitical, practice. According to traditional improv doctrine, players must not be too much "in their heads," but rather, must improvise from a state of "no-mindedness" that allows them to bypass all societal inhibitions and thus to reach a greater "truth." Real improv, they insist, must have no agenda to distract the player from his or her purely spontaneous response to each stimulus. These improvisers vehemently resist the notion that their "neutral" stance is, in fact, a passive support for the status quo, and that *everything* is political. Like "common sense," this notion of neutral spontaneity is a cultural construction. Explain to your students or company of performers that spontaneous improvisation does not produce a deeper, more cosmic "truth." Rather, improvisation is most likely to rearrange and recombine the fragments of mainstream culture that we already recognize. Improvisation is based on our shared set of references, and taps into what we have been taught to believe. This realization may threaten to disillusion eager improvisers at first. But this greater "political" awareness need not spell the end of improv as an intensely bonding experience, nor the demise of its spirit, energy, or entertainment value. Perhaps paradoxically, greater awareness of the often unmarked hierarchies of society increases the improvisers' arsenal of comedy to include critiques of "things as they are." So, even as you point to the pitfalls and misuses of improvisation, you can encourage student performers to recognize its genuine potential as a strategy for imagining transformation, a means to "create new cultures and new futures" (Ropers-Huilman 19).

Using some of the strategies I outline below, you may draw attention to the stereotypes and assumptions that reinforce society's power structures. To address concerns that "awareness" is contrary to improv's insistence on spontaneity, you may need to make a clear distinction between improv in the workshop or rehearsal process and improv in performance or in a "just play" mode. The greater understanding, inclusiveness, and openness you foster in your workshops can slowly but surely help the troupe create a new set of shared references. Eventually, these alternative references will begin to be available for spontaneous access in "play mode" or performance–without the self-consciousness or sense of pre-planning that improvisers strive to avoid. Overcoming self-consciousness is still a crucial goal for improvisers at every level, and with this foundation even improv-comedy has the potential to be what Augusto Boal has described as "a rehearsal for revolution" (155).

Improvisational performance, even the broadest improv-comedy, is not a free-for-all. It is created within a set of goals and guidelines–sometimes with lofty ideals, sometimes with more commercial aspirations. Most often, a vision for troupe or classroom work is put forward and modeled by a troupe leader or teacher. It is crucial that everyone involved understands and feels included in the mission of the work. As a group, is it your primary purpose to create marketable entertainment? Ask yourselves what kind of laughs you want and what you're willing to do to get them. Are you focused on actor education? Decide what kinds of skills you're teaching, and emphasize the value of sharing the stage with other players. Does the company want to create social commentary? Acknowledge the work and the research it takes to create informed satire. Do you see the group as an ensemble or as a group of individual stars and support players? *Most young improvisers will say they prefer an ensemble. Strive to hold them to it.* Do you want to create humor that degrades women, gays, or people of color? Most will say no. You may need to remind them of that decision. Don't get bogged down in endless discussions, but do talk about these questions, and invite participants to collaborate in creating a short manifesto or mission statement for the group. If group members participate in creating their own policies about power dynamics in their work and their own standards for the quality of their material, they will feel far more invested in them. Players will then be able, quite literally, to be on the "same page" as their teammates. Simply by increasing the shared awareness of the issues, a manifesto will allow the feminist coach or troupe leader to de-center her authority and avoid the appearance of censoring or imposing "politically correct" rules on the company.

"But it's improvisation…I can't help what comes out of my mouth, it's spontaneous." This is the excuse many young improvisers give for tasteless humor, stereotypes, or for railroading fellow players. *Explain that the notion of pure spontaneity in improvisation is a myth.* Players always maintain a double consciousness in order to remember the rules of the game being played and to respond to audience reaction. Professional improvisers are always working within a set of rules. For example, Chicago's Second City, the most influential improv theatre in the United States, maintains a rule against four-letter words, yet the performers are able to be highly spontaneous in their improv sets. In the same way, student improvisers can learn to find a balance between unthinking spontaneity and an awareness of their actions onstage.

Think about the form as well as the content of the improvisation. Workshop or rehearsal improvisations can be very loosely structured, based on the needs of the project at hand. They are usually focused on the development of material for an original piece or the exploration of themes and characters in a scripted work. This mode of improv serves best as fodder for discussion, and the feminist educator can take an active role in shaping students' experience of the process by encouraging thoughtful analysis of these spontaneously created scenarios. Performance improv can be a more pressured mode because the improvisation itself is the final product, and is expected to be entertaining. Most performance improv is structured in one of two formats: short form and long form. Short form improv is based on game structures and lends itself to broad humor and stereotypes, although it can certainly accommodate serious content. Long form improv tends to be more personal and more surreal, but can also rely on unexamined stereotypes and truisms. To help young improvisers navigate the pitfalls and pressures of performance improv, the feminist teacher can guide the development of foundational skills, and help raise students' awareness of power and difference as an integral part of their training process.

Improvisation is a key element in many aspects of Boal's Theatre of the Oppressed (TO). If the students in your group are interested in using improv to develop performances about social issues, you may wish to explore Boal's techniques, including Forum Theatre, Image Theatre, and Invisible Theatre. According to Deborah Thomson and Julia T. Wood, Forum Theatre in particular "contributes to feminist pedagogy's transformative power by empowering students to be agents" (202) and its improvisational quality "provides participants a space to explore scenarios of their own creation while developing creative problem-solving skills that can later be applied to real life" (209). Be aware, however, that this valuable mode of improvisation may also foster stereotypical characterizations and situations. As Berenice Fisher writes,

> The tremendous vitality of TO lies in its power to uncover and support spontaneous expression about political issues. But spontaneous expression often includes oppressive and sometimes self-oppressive, elements. Making good political sense out of spontaneous responses requires political experience and political discussion. It requires a growing and evolving wisdom about the nature of our political values and commitments (196).

No troupe leader or teacher wants to censor or engender self-consciousness in improv. But the feminist educator can show that if we learn to respect others, to be aware of our use of stereotypes, and to strive for equity on stage, it is not in order to do safe, inoffensive improv, but rather to create a better, funnier and more rewarding kind of improv for everyone to enjoy.

CASTING

It's clear from observing the improv troupes on campuses, television, and in theatres that white men far outnumber white women and people of color. If your improvisers are the students in a class, you will have little control over the make-up of the group. But, when and if you are casting a troupe, *choose your players with attention to the dynamics of difference.* Work to create as much balance as possible, both in terms of gender and race. My research clearly shows that women and people of color improvise more freely when they are not the lone representative of their identity position (Seham passim). The "only" woman or the "only" person of color in a group often feels constrained to represent his or her identity in a positive light, or may find her or himself relegated to token characters in scene after scene.

Although some improv manuals suggest that a troupe should be cast for compatibility and similarity of approach, thereby facilitating "groupmind," I would argue that a variety of cultural backgrounds and a good gender balance will allow for the richest kind of humor. It is up to the leader of the group, then, to help the performers find a common ground that is not dependent on "groupmind," but rather, on mutual respect. *Keep an eye out for anyone who may feel outnumbered and therefore may be tacitly pressured to conform or assimilate.* Pay close attention as well, when possible, to the backstage dynamics of the company. *Try not to allow players' personal friendships and social alliances to freeze others out onstage.* Mix up the pairings and groupings in games and scenes. You may find it beneficial to use some class time or rehearsal time for discussion and informal games that help students get to know one another outside the pressure of performance.

An example from Second City history demonstrates the significance of casting practices. Since its first season in 1959, Second City had a long-standing casting tradition regarding women. Anne Libera, artistic director of the Second City Training Center, points out, "If you look at photos of Second City casts over the years you can see the pattern. In every company you see four or five men and two women—the pretty one and the funny one" (quoted in Seham 19). For the most part, women in these troupes played roles as needed in scenes by, for, and about men. Need a girlfriend? Use the pretty one. Mother-in-law? Cast the funny one. Women were trapped in an age-old, false duality. But when, in the early 1990s, Second City experimented with a cast of three men and three women for one of its touring companies, the gender dynamic shifted dramatically. Because touring companies perform recreations of "classic" Second City scenes, which originated from their traditionally configured troupes, the third woman often found herself playing larger and more interesting roles previously played by men. In fact, the female dichotomy of pretty one/funny one was forcefully interrupted by this wild card in the form of the third female player. In their post-show improv sets, all three women in this troupe found that they were suddenly freer to shift among a number of identities, and felt more supported when initiating scenes. In recent years, even the mainstage troupes at Second City occasionally use an equal gender split.

However your group is configured, help the players learn to value the different styles and approaches to comedy that each improviser brings with her or him, and teach them to take turns supporting one another on a scene-by-scene (or even a moment-by-moment) basis. *Inculcate in your players a sense of the value of each individual voice, as well as of the troupe identity.*

STEREOTYPES AND REFERENCES

Use the stereotype, but don't let the stereotype use you. Stereotypes, archetypes, and pop culture references are an inevitable part of improvised performance and have been since the first days of *commedia dell'arte.* In fact, the recognition of character types and familiar images is part of improv's delight for an audience. Nevertheless, improvisers can learn to reduce their level of reliance on shallow clichés. The trick is not to eliminate these elements, but to choose them, shape them, and deepen them to create a richer form of comedy. Mark the stereotypes that arise in improv play and acknowledge them for what they are. *Don't allow young improvisers to confuse those stereotypes with true observation or intrinsic reality.* Terrified of having nothing to say, young improvisers often grab for an easy stereotype or pop culture reference when they are under the pressure of the performance moment. As a leader, you can provide them with some other alternatives. As an educator, you can help add to the mix of images and facts that the improvisers draw upon.

Assign "homework thinking." Encourage young improvisers to read and discuss current issues and events both at home and in the improv workshop. The improv games that follow will be influenced by these new stimuli. In general, it works best to insist that your improvisers be well-informed, caught up on current events, and familiar with classic genres of movies, books, plays, and music. If they've never heard of film noir, can't identify Virginia Woolf or tell you who's the present Secretary of State, you might need to spend some workshop time getting them in shape. The more they know, the deeper their pool of references. The deeper the pool, the better and the less stereotyped the improv will be.

Assign a physical or motivational objective to the scene. Improviser and instructor Susan Messing from Chicago's Annoyance Theatre believes that improvisers go to stereotype when they have no other focus to guide their work (Seham 155-158). If they concentrate on a physicalization, such as leading with a particular body part, or on expressing a particular emotion, they are less likely to rely purely on types.

Don't be afraid of silence. Practice some deliberately slow improvs in which the pressure to be instantaneously clever is vastly reduced. You may be able to speed up again with similar results.

If you have to, impose habit-breaking rules. The best rules prescribe a consequence rather than an outright prohibition. For example, director Anne Libera established the "honey rule" to subvert the tendency of a male player's first line to immediately define his female scene partner in relationship to him as his "honey." "If a man walks out onstage and calls 'Honey,' says Libera, "I directed that only another man—or no one—was allowed to respond. After a series of gay scenes, the male players started to get the picture and come up with more creative alternatives"(Seham 229 n.5).

Similarly, if your troupe tends to play gay stereotypes and homophobic scenes, you might create a rule that every gay or lesbian character must be embraced by the other players onstage. If you have inexperienced and/or homophobic improvisers who immediately reject or automatically run away from gay characters, this rule can help.[4] You may choose to enforce these rules only in rehearsals and workshops, or you may feel it necessary to keep them in place during performances as well.

Beginning improvisers may ask, "But if I play someone who is a different race, gender, or sexuality from me, is that automatically bad?" Indeed, quite a few players feel paralyzed by (and thus resentful of) half-understood notions of "political correctness." What they believe is always "bad" in the sense of "incorrect" is more likely to be "bad" in the sense of unimaginative, clichéd improv. Play someone unlike yourself? The professional improvisers I've interviewed say, "go ahead"—with the following admonitions that you as the leader can share with your company. *Ask yourself where the joke is.* Are you playing a character who's laughable simply because he is gay, or are you playing a funny gay character? Is your joke at the character's expense, using degrading stereotypes to put him or her down, or are you allowing the character to generate the humor? If you play someone gay, of a different race or ethnicity, or across gender, give the person humanity and self-respect. This is important for any characterization; you can be just as funny laughing *with* the character as you can by laughing *at* him or her. Take responsibility to know what you're talking about. Shaun Landry, of the African American improv troupe Oui Be Negroes, says, "If you want to be a white guy who's playing a black person or a straight who wants to do gay, you better know the history behind it. Because you're going to look like a damn fool doing it" (qtd. in Seham 191).

Share references. If players from a variety of cultural backgrounds and gendered experiences are working in the same troupe, create some time for them to exchange ideas offstage as well as on. If improvised initiations are dropped because of a scene partner's ignorance, create an opportunity for the players to explain what was meant. Don't chastise the player who rode over or missed a reference–but do create a learning opportunity so that teammates can increase their ability to support one another. (See "What's That About?" exercise below.)

In her discussion of feminist pedagogy and Theatre of the Oppressed improvisations, Berenice Fisher asserts, "Not letting stereotyped portrayals go unchallenged, and holding students accountable for the images they project, creates room for reflection" (195). The following exercises can be an enjoyable, educational way to provoke discussion and reflection for your group.

EXERCISES FOR STEREOTYPES AND REFERENCES

Secrets and Dreams. Choose a stereotype that seems particularly prevalent in your troupe's work. Ask the players to list each clichéd action, posture, attitude, vocal quality, or gesture that goes into the portrayal of that stereotype. Have an actor go through an improv scene relying solely on those superficial elements to create the character. Note the shallowness and lack of originality in the scene. Then try the scene again, this time giving the stereotyped character a specific comical (or even a serious) subtext.

In their improvised parodies of Tennessee Williams, the Chicago improv group The Free Associates created absurd yet nuanced characters by taking audience suggestions for their characters' not-quite-hidden issues. You might select a "painful secret" (pretends to be a Southern belle, but was actually raised in Brooklyn) or an "unrealized dream" (she'd give anything to be an astronaut) or other hidden desire (he's obsessed with Barbie dolls). Challenge the players to use these suggestions to give an extra layer of detail, even depth to the character. (Based on the performance techniques of The Free Associates.)

First Lines. Ask your players to wander the room until they hear you call out a first line of dialogue. Then, they must confront the nearest player and begin a dialogue that starts with that line. Openers may include, but are not limited to the following: Just a trim today; How 'bout that game?; What's for dinner?; Grab me a beer; You know how *those* people are; You'll never get a boyfriend that way; Crying again?; Do I look fat in this?; Honey, I'm home!; One dollar is too much for that; Spare change?; Where's my money?; Don't forget to dust under the bed.

Do NOT explain ahead of time that these lines are designed to elicit stereotypical characters in response. After the exercise is over, discuss the responses with the players. Questions might include: Did you fall into a stereotype? Did the gender of your partner matter? Did you assume the line was yours, or your partner's? Why?[5] Did any lines take on racial overtones? Did issues of class arise? Were you uncomfortable with lines that opened the possibility of gay or lesbian relationships? Can you subvert that stereotype within the scene? By making an opposite choice? By making the obvious choice in an unexpected way? By making a physical choice? By commenting on the stereotype from an outsider's perspective? Discuss the humor that can be created by thwarting the spectators' assumptions and expectations.[6] (Developed in a workshop with the touring companies of Second City Toronto and with Laughing Matters workshops in California.)

What's That About? Give two players a location or relationship to begin a scene. One player makes references to cultural elements that he or she thinks the other player may not know. The second player must not ignore or override the unfamiliar reference, but must ask loudly, "What's that about?" The first player will then explain the reference, and turn the scene into a teaching scenario in which the second player must become involved in the cultural activity. A third player may then enter the scene, observe the activity, and ask, "What's that about?" The second player must then explain what he has learned. For example, a woman mentions Judy Blume to a male player. "What's that about?" elicits a teaching scene in which the first player teaches important facts about her favorite book. The second player must then teach the material to the third player. This knowledge exchange develops all-important listening skills, and increases the whole troupe's ability to move past stereotypes based on ignorance.

STATUS AND SHARING THE STAGE

Many experienced players insist that power imbalances onstage are simply a result of poor improv technique. After all, everyone knows that "yes…and" is the cardinal rule. Everyone is taught to initiate and support, to "give and take" in improvisation. So why do the same players seem to dominate in scene after scene? Why are players so often considered good (strong) or bad (weak) according to the perceived power dynamic onstage? The issues are complex, but the bottom line is this: it is not enough merely to explain the concepts of agreement and sharing the creative moment. To break through the set patterns of power—you have to rehearse alternative possibilities. To enable students to experience transformation—you have to drill openness. Sharing the stage does not come naturally. You have to practice.

Watch for a balance of initiation and support. A player is bulldozing when he or she ignores the initiations of a fellow player and insists on pursuing his or her preconceived idea. Many players, particularly women who don't feel supported in a troupe or classroom exercise, will simply let go of their initiations and move to support the stronger player's idea. As the educator/leader of the activity, you can point out moments of bulldozing, which may be caused by ignorance as often as by egocentrism. Coach shy players to make stronger, clearer initiations and insist that more aggressive players practice listening, observing, and reading the initiations of others. (See the "Steadfast" exercise below.)

Assign games and exercises that take players out of their comfort zones. Force bold players into supporting roles and shyer players into leading ones. Remind young women that it is not selfish or wrong to take the lead in a scene. Several of the women from Chicago's all-woman troupe, Jane, laughingly remember the scenes between two women where each was trying so hard to support the other that no one would make an assertive move (Seham 71). Those scenes go nowhere! It can be just as generous to make a strong offer as it is to practice agreement.

Most improvisers are familiar with Keith Johnstone's important discussion of the concept of *status* as a key element of improv (and all theatre). In his seminal work, *Impro*, Johnstone writes that human beings are "pecking order animals" and that all human interaction can be seen in terms of status negotiations (74). Oddly enough, though Johnstone talks about class and power dynamics (using the metaphor of the servant/master relationship), he does not discuss gender as a factor of status. Yet offstage status almost always recapitulates onstage status in improv, and male improvisers almost always take higher status onstage—both as characters and as players. Inexperienced improvisers tend to get in a rut of playing the same level of status in every game. While some players simply play their own "felt" status, others may play "high" defensively, to protect themselves against more powerful improvisers. Some can be so worried about being undercut onstage that they cannot be open to the comic potential in choosing to play a low status character. The late Don DePollo, beloved Second City improv teacher and director, often exhorted aggressive players to "give the gift of status" to others and to experiment with a range of characters. *Support players may also be urged to give the gift of status to themselves.*

Status manifests itself in a number of ways, including the centrality, importance, or aggressiveness of the character, and the *balance* of initiation versus support in the performance. High status characters/performers also tend to be in control of the *space* onstage. Finally, status is also reflected in the *pacing* of each scene, often making a crucial difference in the perceived "success" of each performance.

Encourage low-status players to TAKE UP SPACE. One element of status that I have found directly linked to gender is the notion of the ownership and use of space. Johnstone again discusses this issue in terms of the master/servant relationship: "A servant's primary function is to elevate the status of the master. Footmen can't lean against the wall, because it's the master's wall. Servants must make no unnecessary noise or movement because it's the master's air they're breathing. [He] has to be quiet, to move neatly, and not to let his arms or legs intrude into the space around him" (63-64). Yet these are the same terms Sandra Bartky might use to describe the way society disciplines women through, "a regulation of the body's size and contours, its appetite, posture, gestures and general comportment in space, and the appearance of each of its visible parts....Feminine movement, gesture and posture must exhibit not only constriction, but grace and a certain eroticism restrained by modesty: all three. (67)"

Many women's discomfort with their own bodies, along with their self-consciousness about taking up space and time, has undermined their ability to go for the funny physical gag or grab the punchline. Jane improviser Tami Sagher, for example, notes that she felt more comfortable taking the initiative and being aggressive when she played a male character in her all-woman troupe. She also felt more comfortable being physically imposing–big, heavy, or powerful–when she was in a male persona (Seham 72-73). For Sagher, as for many women improvisers, male characters are automatically higher status than female ones, and women may experience the sensation of having more personal status when they play male roles (see the "Gender Switch" exercise below). While this status imbalance has somewhat subsided in recent years in adult improv groups (both professional and non-professional), it is still a very real issue, especially for young women and girls. Improv can either reinforce conventional gender roles or it can help girls break out of their perceived subordinate status by allowing them to "rehearse" a greater sense of confidence and a freer use of physical space.

Faster improv does not mean better improv. High status characters or players also control the pacing of a scene. According to a number of Chicago improvisers, men tend to be intent on finding the punchline, joke, or game of a scene, while most women tend to be content to let relationships and character unfold through improvisation (of course some men love leisurely improv and some women are whizzes at the quick and dirty stuff) (Seham 66). Point out these differences to your players, and explain that both approaches are important and valuable to good, three-dimensional, entertaining improv.

If many of the women in your class or troupe are particularly shy, try holding a workshop or class without the men present. The women of Jane found that improvising together empowered them to be more confident and assertive in later coed groups.

EXERCISES FOR STATUS AND SHARING THE STAGE

Advertising. This is a fun, high-energy game that gives every actor in the troupe an exhilarating sense of total support. Divide the company into small groups of four to six players. Take a suggestion from the company for a consumer product that doesn't yet exist, but should (suggestions might range from an automatic lint-picker to a nose-bra). One player must then introduce the product to the small group as their newest advertising account. The group must then brainstorm *onstage* to create every aspect of their ad campaign on the spot. They must include a catchy name for the new product, a slogan, a special concept for packaging, a target market (children, young mothers, senior citizens), the best venue for marketing (television, radio, magazines), a celebrity spokesperson, a description of the television commercial or glossy magazine ad, and should end with the full group's rendition of the musical jingle. NO IDEA MAY BE REJECTED. In fact, every suggestion made by any member of the group *must* be greeted with a chorus of enthusiastic shouts of "Yes!!" Don't let members of the team shout yes and then change the idea. They must accept, *with enthusiasm*, any and every idea expressed and then build those ideas into the campaign. Be sure that everyone participates and puts her two cents in. Keep them cheering and clapping for *each* suggestion. It's a lot of fun, and it also serves to embolden previously shy players and to force aggressive ones to support and make good use of ideas they might not otherwise think are "good enough." (Adapted from Spolin and Johnstone.)

Status Switch/Gender Switch. Set up a situation in which two characters are at opposite ends of the status spectrum. Give the players a location or relationship, and then assign them to play the scene such that the characters slowly exchange status levels. Insist that the relative status goes through several phases, so that the actors may explore subtle status shifts and the experience of being just a bit higher or lower than their scene partner. The scene ends when the high status character is utterly low, and the low status character is at her highest point. Use this exercise particularly with players who tend to be stuck in a particular position.

Follow Status Switch immediately with *Gender Switch*. Players begin by playing any gender (they may begin or end with their own gender). Slowly, through the action of the scene, the characters must switch to the opposite gender role (the role in which their scene partner began). Almost invariably, players will use high status body language, gestures, voice, and attitude while playing a male character, and low status while playing a female character. Invite students to compare the exercises, and to discuss the embodied relationship of status and gender. Why did the players make the choices they made? What does that tell us about our own gender roles? Point out the interesting characters, relationships, and situations that emerged when the players moved through the middle range between the extremes of gender performance. Encourage students to continue exploring alternatives to the classic gender stereotypes.

Not a Bitch/Not a Nerd. Challenge your improvisers to play a male/female scene in which the woman is higher status than the man, but is NOT a "bitch." It is surprisingly difficult, especially for younger players, to find positive ways to give status to the female character without the standard "ball-busting" stereotype. Follow this exercise with "Not a Nerd," in which the male player must have lower status than the female player, but is NOT a nerd or a patsy. Continue the exercise with different pairings. Be sure to discuss the implications of the scenes with the players, and encourage them to use these more complex characterizations onstage. (Developed in a workshop with the touring companies of Second City Toronto.)

Steadfast/Anti-Bulldozing. In this exercise, ask one player in each scene to initiate an obvious activity, such as digging a hole. Then invite a second player to try deliberately to "bulldoze" his or her partner by aggressively beginning a different scene in which digging a hole is incongruous–perhaps asking for breakfast to be served. For this game, the first player is *not allowed* to drop her first activity. Instead, she must be steadfast in her action of digging a hole, while working to find a way to blend her choice with the new information. (In this case, perhaps she is in a kitchen with a dirt floor, and she is digging up the potatoes she plans to cook.) This exercise may produce odd, eccentric scenes, but it is good practice for performers who might otherwise feel powerless on stage. Saying "Yes–and" to your partner's offers does *not* have to mean dropping your own ideas. (Developed at the Funny Woman Festival; based on Susan Messing's work at the Annoyance Theatre.)

DEFENSIVE TACTICS

Ideally, your students will be so well trained in equitable improv that no one will need to resort to defensive tactics onstage. Nevertheless, there are a few effective ways of holding one's own even with a selfish or ignorant scene partner. The "Steadfast" exercise above is drawn from what Susan Messing calls "Defenses and Escapes," a number of strategies she has developed for survival in the boisterous world of Chicago improv. Messing takes a very tough stance, and has little patience for women who "whine and complain" about bulldozing or power plays (Seham 155). She believes that anyone can make good improvisation out of bad. For example, Messing once established a scene in which she was sunbathing in Acapulco. Her scene partner ignored that initiation, and began a completely different scenario. From that point on, Messing portrayed a woman who, mistreated by a bullying husband, had frequent vivid fantasies of escaping to a beach in Acapulco.

Call attention to power abuses in performance. Another defensive tactic is known as "calling it onstage." In recalling her own experience, Dee Ryan, a member of the Second City mainstage company in the 1990s, says that because complaining backstage proved ineffective, women began to mark or "call" actor-to-actor power abuses right in front of the audience (Seham 118). For example, in a scene where the female player feels bulldozed or silenced, she might say, in character, "Gee, I can't seem to get a word in edgewise here." Thus, she makes her experienced reality part of the scene—an idea much praised in improv teaching. She also puts her scene partner on the spot—and on notice.

Messing and Ryan stay within the system by manipulating the established rules. Other players have formed their own alternative troupes in which they feel freer and better supported in their work. For example, Shaun Landry founded Oui Be Negroes, an African American troupe, to give black players a place to explore their own shared references and experiences through improvisation. Other troupes, such as Stir Friday Night, *iSalsation!*, and GayCo, have also opted out of mainstream improv to form identity-based troupes in which they are no longer tokens of diversity. As it was for the women of Jane, the opportunity to work in a group where "groupmind" has a distinctly different quality has given players of color and gays and lesbians a chance to find and develop their own voices. As feminist educators training a new generation of improvisers, we can urge players to practice what pedagogical theorist Henry Giroux calls "listening in," respectfully learning about identities different from our own, and learning "to look at difference in a way that doesn't require that it become us or that we become it" (440).

Within a feminist pedagogical framework, improvisation has the capacity to be a strategy for empowerment, a way to "practice visions of a feminist world, confronting difference to enrich all of us rather than to belittle some of us" (Shrewsbury 11). Redesigned for inclusivity, unscripted improvisation provides perhaps the greatest opportunity for what Jill Dolan hopes for theater studies overall, that "it becomes a material location...a pedagogically inflected field of play at which culture is liminal or liminoid and available for intervention" (432).

Students have had a lifetime to rehearse conventional roles and hierarchies. Give them the space, the time, and the education to explore, and real alternatives may then spring spontaneously from them—both onstage and in their daily lives. This is the great potential and hope of the tactical art of improvisation.

NOTES

[1] See Elin Diamond, "Brechtian Theory/Feminist Theory: Toward a Gestic Feminist Criticism" on potential feminist uses of Brecht's theatre techniques.

2 See Seham 2001 for an in-depth study of the ways this disjuncture reveals itself in Chicago improv.

[3] It may seem counterproductive to use players' fear of playing gay characters as a means of getting them to reevaluate their tendency to stereotype women. When using this technique, the feminist coach can draw attention to issues of homophobia as well as sexism, and encourage the positive portrayal of gay and lesbian couples as well as less stereotypical heterosexual couples.

[4] At Second City Toronto, improvisers said that the gay or "fag" stereotype was the most prevalent in audience suggestions, and thus was the image they wanted to work on subverting.

[5] At a Laughing Matters workshop in California, a woman, attending with her teen-age daughter, confessed with chagrin that she had assumed the "Do I look fat in this?" line was hers, just as she had felt obligated to wait for the male improviser to announce, "Honey, I'm home!" Her recognition of being "trapped" by these automatic self-stereotypes was a revelation to the entire workshop.

[6] There is a wonderful scene in Mel Brooks' *Blazing Saddles* that illustrates this reversal of expectation. When the white foremen on a railroad insist their black workers sing a "Negro spiritual," Cleavon Little and friends sing "I Get a Kick Out of You" with sophisticated style and grace. Frustrated, the bosses demonstrate what they want to see, soon taking on every negative stereotype of Jim Crow performance style as they shuck and jive to "Camptown Races."

[7] For a more complete (and invaluable) discussion of status, see Johnstone's *Impro*, and the various collections of games that have emerged from his Loose Moose theatre company.

WORKS CITED

Boal, Augusto. *Theatre of the Oppressed.* Trans. Charles A. and Maria-Odilia Leal McBride. London: Pluto Press, 1993.

Cima, Gay Gibson. "Strategies for Subverting the Canon." *Upstaging Big Daddy: Directing Theatre as if Gender and Race Matter.* Ellen Donkin and Susan Clement, eds. Ann Arbor: University of Michigan Press, 1993: 91-107.

Diamond, Elin. "Brechtian Theory/Feminist Theory: Toward a Gestic Feminist Criticism." *TDR: The Drama Review.* 32.1 (1988): 82-93.

Halpern, Charna, Del Close and Kim Howard. *Truth in Comedy.* Colorado Springs, CO: Meriwether Publishing, 1994.

Johnstone, Keith. *Impro: Improvisation and the Theatre.* London: Methuen, 1981.

Maher, Frances A. and Mary Kay Thompson Tetreault. *The Feminist Classroom: Dynamics of Gender, Race and Privilege.* Lanham, MD: Rowman and Littlefield Publishers, 2001.

Ropers-Huilman, Becky. *Feminist Teaching in Theory and Practice.* New York: Teachers College Press, 1998.

Seham, Amy. *Whose Improv Is It Anyway? Beyond Second City.* Jackson: University of Mississippi Press, 2001.

Shrewsbury, Carolyn. "What is Feminist Pedagogy?" *Women's Studies Quarterly* 21.3-4 (1993): 8-16

Spolin, Viola. *Improvisation for the Theatre.* 1963. Reprint, Evanston, IL: Northwestern University Press, 1983.

Thomson, Deborah M. and Julia T. Wood. "Rewriting Gendered Scripts: Using Forum Theatre to Teach Feminist Agency. " *The Feminist Teacher.* 13.3 (2001): 202-212.

FEMINISM IN THE ACTING CLASSROOM
PLAYFUL PRACTICE AS PROCESS
Kathleen Juhl

Several authors have argued the problems and advantages of Stanislavsky/Method-based approaches to feminist acting. Sue-Ellen Case has critiqued the Method's reconstruction of the hysterical woman as framed by the narrative devices of realism (1998). Lauren Love has created a hybrid approach between Brechtian and Stanslavskian methods (1995). Still others, like Rhonda Blair (2002) and Ellen Gainor (2002), emphasizing the historical context of the actor's work, have noted the complexity of the body-mind nexus that makes it difficult to critique Stanislavsky's system from a politicized point of view. Yet Stanislavsky's system is clearly an important practice and should not be discarded; however, it must be approached critically in terms of both practice and application. The feminist theatre company Split Britches is an example of one such critical approach. Deb Margolin, founding member of Split Britches, says that she, Lois Weaver, and Peggy Shaw "were just Method actors who didn't bother to clean up." Margolin cites the company's use of autobiography as their connection to the Method: "The jagged juncture between actor and character was the metaphysical site of our performances, and it felt dangerous to some critics, as if we ourselves might burst forth out of the play at any moment and infest them with life, with tragedy, with sex" (132). In my teaching of a beginning acting class to theatre majors, I utilized feminist pedagogy to inspire a playful practice, one that opened up a messy process and exposed the "jagged juncture" between actor and character as a foundation upon which to build a realistic performance. In this essay, I will discuss this intersection between feminist pedagogy and approaches to teaching acting as I describe the exercises and class protocol my students and I created.

Stanislavsky/Method-based approaches to acting privilege the connection between the actor's self and the character's, with the actor's self serving as the basis for developing the character. A Brechtian rehearsal process, by contrast, emphasizes the multiple choices of a character within a historical moment. Janelle Reinelt explains why Brecht consistently speaks to a feminist aesthetic: "Both Brecht and feminism emphasize the possibility of change, that things might be other, that history is not an inevitable narrative" (99). Rhonda Blair, in her discussion of acting processes, feminism, cognitive neuroscience, and their relation to mind/body connections, writes that "Constructing narratives [is] a core element of the actor's work." However, Blair goes beyond the traditional "psychologically and culturally conditioned" notions of everyday life and scripted narrative to hypothesize an ongoing "proto-narrative" that involves "sensing oneself in relationship to an object and sensing that one needs to do something about it." Blair is interested in the way the actor "connects her body with the physical environment of the studio or stage, and equally importantly, with her imagination…. Imagination, a result of our brain's evolutionary development, [is an] essential…fact of our physicality, not just our psyches" (183-84).

Influenced by these feminist approaches to acting, it struck me that the playful exploration of choices that occurs through improvisation could allow actors to challenge historically patriarchal narratives, as Reinelt suggests (or at least push the range of choices available within those narratives). With this in mind, I wanted to develop a process in the acting studio in which actors could engage creative choices for characterizations based on environment and imagination, as Blair posits. Narrative has the potential to foreclose choices and motivation, and, by empowering actors to go beyond narrative strictures, it can help them discover a fuller range of character choices. I was interested in finding a way to keep improvisation playfully open to inspirations from the actors' own lives and physical surroundings without having them constrained by the narrative structures in their scripted texts. Furthermore, I wanted to move actors beyond the constraints of their own identities by experimenting with the gendered behaviors of their characters to increase the range of possibilities and experiences they portrayed. This would not only help actors enhance their physical, emotional, and psychological vocabularies for approaching characters, but, as Elizabeth Stroppel posits, "The Method, which encourages the use of the self above the role, [would] help students envision ways in which they [could] subvert the gendered stereotypes in classical realism"(116-17).

Blending improvisational exercises with work on texts in both acting classes and theatre rehearsals is common practice. I was taught acting in very traditional classrooms led by "master teachers." In this approach, students are led through Stanislavsky/Method-based acting exercises and various improvisations during class. Outside of class, they rehearse scenes and then "show" them in class for the master teacher's critique. Sometimes students are also involved in the critique. After these sessions, students go away, rehearse some more, and "show" their scenes again for more critique. I found this pedagogy not only ineffective for developing my acting skills but also intimidating and disconnected from the work we were doing with exercises and improvisations in class. This approach is product-oriented, leads to objectification, and focuses on pleasing an authority figure. The "master teacher" approach not only disempowers actors but is a recipe for beginning acting students to develop bad habits because they are struggling to create product-oriented "performances" which they prepare for the master teacher's critique with no facilitation from a teacher who can lead them through exercises and improvisations connected directly to their work.

Instead, I wanted to experiment with blending exercises and improvisations that featured everyday, lifelike interactions with work on texts and, as much as possible, to downplay my own hierarchical power position in the classroom. By providing a working protocol that would emphasize students making choices about the work, while at the same time facilitating exercises that help them explore ways toward effective acting work, I am no longer the single authority in the classroom. I thought that by alternating improvisation and text work students could create nuance and detail for their character and, through playing with vocal and physical gender behaviors in both improvisation and text work modes, they could develop interesting non-stereotypical gender performances. Such a protocol could form the basis for a feminist acting pedagogy in a traditional acting classroom.

To provide some context, my Stanislavsky/Method-based acting class is part of a B.F.A. program in a conservative theatre department at a small, selective liberal arts university that has an active, highly respected feminist studies program. My academic life, as are the lives of many academic feminists, is rife with paradox. In order to deal with the paradox of teaching within a conservative theatre department and my own active commitment to feminism and the feminist studies program, I wanted to develop a feminist pedagogy for this acting class. I wanted to do this on two levels: first, I wanted to develop a playful and improvisational class protocol that would thwart the hierarchy of traditional master teacher approaches to acting pedagogy, and second, I wanted to inspire students to present gender in less stereotypical ways in scenes from realistic plays. Stroppel explains:

> Whether inadvertently or not, acting choices remain by and large aligned with the prevailing power structure. Acting methods as political choices, however, are generally not addressed within the average acting classroom. The focus in classrooms generally remains on developing a product rather than on investigating the politics of a process. (111-12)

The idea of developing "the politics of a process" informed by feminism through a politically aware improvisational class protocol was exactly what I had in mind.

IMPROVISATION, INTERACTION, AND FEMINIST THEORY

Viola Spolin wrote the important and now standard text on improvisation, *Improvisation for the Theatre* in 1963. Though not a professed feminist, Spolin had some interesting things to say about hierarchy and everyday interaction in the acting classroom. In her book and classes, Spolin provided theatre practitioners with a plethora of improvisational games and activities for developing improvised performance pieces and for working out problems *through process* in the theatre classrooms and rehearsals. Her process is not a master teacher approach. Her goal is to create a dialectical relationship with students, to create exchange between teacher and student rather than impose authority. In fact, one of Spolin's primary concerns is to "clear the air of authoritarianism" (9):

> True personal freedom and self-expression can flower only in an atmosphere where attitudes permit equality between student and teacher and the dependencies of teacher for student and student for teacher are done away with. The problems within the subject matter will teach both of them. (8)

Spolin's pedagogy, implicit in her theory of improvisation, depends on playful processes which can spin out only when teacher/student hierarchies are not the basis for relationships in the performance classroom or rehearsal process: "Do not teach," says Spolin. "*Expose* students to the theatrical environment through playing, and they will find their own way" (42). bell hooks talks in a similar way about engaging students, even saying that "Teaching is a performative act." As such, "it offers a space for change, invention, spontaneous shifts…. To embrace the performative aspect of teaching we are compelled to engage 'audiences,' to consider issues of reciprocity…it is meant to serve as a catalyst that calls everyone to become more and more engaged, to become active participants in learning" (11). I thought that if I could develop a pedagogy in which students "find their own way" into characters and I became an actor in my own acting classes, the anti-hierarchy of feminist processes could be engaged because we would all become *participants* in the learning. The whole process could evolve like a scene in which teacher and student work together toward that learning.

In Spolin's classrooms, improvisation is framed as a problem-solving device, defined and initiated based on the problem it is created to solve. Spolin says that "The problem-solving technique gives mutual objective focus to teacher and student. In its simplest terms it is *giving problems to solve problems*" (20). But I was convinced that, no matter how formal and structured the set-up, the way improvisational activities unfold in the classroom environment could be seen as analogous to the way interaction unfolds in everyday life, though framed in less formal ways than improvisational methods that, like Spolin's, are designed for solving problems in acting classrooms and rehearsals. Lesa Lockford and Ron Pelias, in "Bodily Poeticizing in Theatrical Improvisation: A Typology of Performative Knowledge," are concerned with the communicative aspects of improvisation. They say that "no matter the form or aim of the improv, the performer's work requires a communicative connection" (434). In fact, they describe improvisation as if it were, on one level, simple interaction:

> Improvisational moments are engaged through an ongoing process of negotiation and coordination, through a positioning and repositioning of performers and their characters, which is done in an instant. Adapting to emergent circumstances, these performers are called to be aware communicators who can draw upon their cognitive, affective, and intuitive abilities—

sometimes with great urgency–in order to absorb interactional details, create characters, and establish characters (434).

While Spolin's improvisers must do what Lockford and Pelias describe, the emphasis of her improvisational activities is on the rules of the game and "players," as she calls them, follow the rules to discover "emergent circumstances" and solve a creative problem. Spolin's method can be connected to feminist practices: she puts actors on an equal footing with one another to solve problems and make knowledges without prescriptive guidance from a teacher or director.

Embedded in all of these activities, including formal improvisational activities, is *interactional improvisation*–the spontaneous non-scripted negotiation of what will be spoken, and who will speak when, how, and where. In the activity I have developed, participants incorporate the scripted materials they are working on into improvised interactions based on those that occur in their everyday lives. Spontaneously negotiated interaction defines everyday human activity; here, only the context changes. Spolin recognizes and points to the importance of the connection between lived and theatrical interaction: "Everyone ad-libs every waking hour of the day and responds to the world through his senses. It is the enriching, restructuring, and integration of all of these daily life responses for use in the art form that makes up the training of the actor for scene improvisation and formal theatre" (43-44). For me, Spolin's work inspires ways to circumvent hierarchy and empower students to learn through activity and engagement, philosophies which seem remarkably connected to feminist pedagogy.

As Lockford and Pelias describe, improvisation is accomplished by engaging with circumstances designed to create theatrically interesting, pedagogically or artistically useful performance. This pertains to any kind of performativity or performance in time or space that has a social meaning or consequence. Many feminist theories of gender focus on the intersections between performance and everyday life and performativity. Feminist theorists Teresa de Lauretis and Judith Butler, for example, focus on the realm of "micropolitical practices" (de Lauretis 26) and "repetitions of acts" (Butler "Performative" 270) when they discuss the ways gender is culturally constituted, constructed, and "performed" in everyday life by social subjects interacting. Butler, in denying the existence of an "original" gendered subject, suggests that the "illusion" of gender as an inner psychic core is produced performatively on and with the surface of the "public body" moment-to-moment "on the skin, through the gesture, the move, the gait (that array of corporeal theatrics understood as gender presentation)" ("Imitation" 28). De Lauretis's and Butler's theories have provided important theoretical inspiration for my experiments with students to develop a feminist acting classroom. Gendered identity and, in the case of my pedagogy, a whole array of character behaviors are created performatively from the details of everyday behavior and interaction as they are constituted in time and space through repetitions of student actors' *acts.*

Butler and de Lauretis's theories are useful for informing my classroom processes by helping to create a feminist subtext through which the students begin to understand the fluidity of identity and the possibility of using this fluidity for exploring characters in myriad ways. I wanted to create an environment in which gesture and physicality, tone of voice, and other details of character would become creatively and potentially politically charged through corporeal enactment and process—a space of micro-political containment where possibilities for new visions that went beyond gender stereotypes were possible.

THE PROTOCOL FOR A FEMINIST ACTING CLASSROOM BASED ON PLAYFUL IMPROVISATION

In order to create an improvisational classroom protocol that offers students alternative ways of performing gender, emphasizing physicality in performance is crucial. Lockford and Pelius say that improvisers must be "artists with expressive bodies who can open creative possibilities for each other" (434). In improvisational activities developed by theorist practitioners from Viola Spolin to Augusto Boal, the physicality of the actor's body is critical for creating successful improvised characters. The actors' physicalizations can also inspire coordination and collaboration among actors as well as open possibilities for alternative gender performances. I am interested in creating an environment where actors learn to read and use the dynamics of power as played out on bodies in the classroom and then consciously explore them as they improvise and work on texts.

Similar to well-known improvisation games like "freeze tag," the pedagogy my students and I developed emphasized the exploration of power through a focus on physical characterization. Stimulated by the actor's presence in physical space, we explored the idea of the environment's potential to frame and facilitate playful, freely flowing interactional improvisation. One of our objectives for using this environmental approach was to provide a grounded and interesting space where actors were encouraged to include their personal experiences for building characters inspired by their relationship to the environment. In addition, I hoped the students would develop unique physicalities (including non-traditionally gendered physicalities) by working in a multi-layered space composed of the many surfaces, levels, and angles we created with rehearsal furniture that would help them make clear, bold, and non-stereotypical character choices. Students would be inspired by triggers and associations they discovered through the physical environment (as Blair suggests) and collaborative process rather than through the critiques inherent in a master teacher approach. In other words, to reiterate Margolin's phrase, we were using improv to explore the "jagged junctures," this time among actors, characters, and the environment. I also envisioned working as both teacher and performer within this environment in a non-traditional, non-hierarchical way.

In the activity we developed, pairs of actors create and then arrange themselves on rehearsal furniture and set pieces configured in a rather messy, chaotic–"jagged"–and complex circular formation so everyone has a good view. In this way, we create a practical space for improvisational and text work. Such an environment works best if a variety of levels is devised with objects such as pylons, platforms, and step units, along with chairs, tables, and other furniture in ways which allow the actors to discover complex physical configurations in relation to each other. The actors then arrange themselves within the space in close proximity to at least one other actor. I established a place for myself within the circle where I could easily get out and move around the outside of the circle but also facilitate as well as act as a participant in the activities.

We then begin improvising characters and scenarios two actors at a time. Importantly, characters and scenarios are developed based on the body positions, postures, and relationships that are implied by the way the students have arranged themselves. For example, if one person is sitting in a strong and open posture on a higher level than her partner, and the partner's physical posture on the lower level is closed and withdrawn, characters, a relationship, and a topic for an improvised conversation is implied in their physical relationship. The actor on the higher level may be berating the one on the lower level, for example.

After the first couple begins, subsequent couples, one after another, begin a new scenario or add to the previous one (with characters and relationships continuing to be defined by the environment and body positions) when a transition seems appropriate. As the exercise moves along, couples drop out of the exercise, paving the way for new or continued scenarios as other students become involved. Sometimes the transitions are smooth–a new improvisation continues or completes a previous interaction. Sometimes transitions are abrupt–a new couple simply jumps in and interrupts with a new conversation. Other times, interactions get stuck, don't go anywhere, and another couple jumps in to save it or I gently encourage another couple to do that by tapping them on the shoulders. Sometimes I start a new improvisation with a student sitting near me or I move to sit next to a student who hasn't been participating and start an improvisation with him. The important thing here is that continuous engagement is sustained. I tell the actors very explicitly that I want continuous flow, and they catch on very quickly when I start participating in order to maintain it.

The exercise works in a way similar to feminist director and acting teacher Lois Weaver's "multiple-choice" approach to acting. Weaver uses the metaphor of a pie–you stand in the middle of it and have many choices. Choices can be inspired by intentions, actions, physical impulses, or in the case of the improvisational activity my students and I engage, the environment we create. These choices allow actors to work "moment-to-moment" from a variety of stimuli that come from association: "You use the body as a resource, so that you can work through impulse to find a character" (Stroppel 17). Concerning Weaver's approach, Ann Elizabeth Armstrong points to the "creative agency" actors have as they are given the freedom to choose from all the stimuli in the improvisational situation. "Such forms of improvisation," says Armstrong, "draw upon the body and the environment as resources and eschew narrative structures that can create conditioned cause-and-effect responses" (205).

Working against ingrained (and stereotypical) physical configurations, the use of the environment and an emphasis on flow de-emphasizes the "critic" or authority figure of the teacher. Inspiring and pushing students beyond their familiar habits and safe choices leads to the development of free-flowing, environmentally-based improvisations that draw on personal concerns and interests. I strongly encourage students to play with gender behaviors during these improvisations, which allows students to discover a wider and deeper range of physicalized character details and possibilities. Because exploring gender is part of the protocol and because students are influenced by what their peers are doing, they build distinct and detailed physicalized characters that interact in rapidly evolving scenarios which feature intriguing relationships and eschew stereotypes. The rapid flow of activity allows students to lose self-consciousness and to have a deeper level of engagement with the work because they are responding primarily with their bodies. This improvised protocol helps actors understand the importance of nuanced physicalization for character development in a way similar to Weaver's "multiple-choice" approach that engages the body "as a resource" in spontaneous ways.

While I was developing this improvisational work with my students in acting classes, I had been studying the ways in which everyday interaction during pauses and breaks in the flow of production rehearsals affected the creative work of rehearsal. In rehearsal, alternating from work on the script to discussions about that work to improvisational activities designed to explore a variety of creative issues produced playful banter that seemed an inevitable part of the process. Such interactions enhanced the creativity of rehearsals, generating new ideas for performance choices and engendering ensemble through comraderie among participants. I wondered if I could simulate the same kinds of productive interactions in the acting classroom. Thinking back to feminist theories of gender behavior developed by de Lauretis and Butler, I wondered if the "micropolitics" and "repetitions of acts" that are connected to gendered behaviors could be exploited in the acting classroom to help students resist rather than reinforce stereotypical gendered representations in scripted material. I wanted to see what would happen if improvised and scripted materials were combined, as in rehearsals, and whether challenging gender stereotypes in the improvisation would help students successfully explore their improvised and scripted characters, as it had in earlier phases of our work.

Once the actors became adept at the free-flowing improvisation protocol, we modified it by incorporating short excerpts from monologues and scenes the students were preparing outside of class. Instead of showing their scripted materials in class for a master-teacher critique, the idea was that texts would be folded into the flow of the improvisational activities so that improvisation and texts would interact and blend with one another. When we first began working on scripted materials in this way, students were often hesitant to interrupt their classmates' scenes or monologues with their own scenes or monologues or with improvisations. Because of this, early performances of texts were often stilted and lacked detail and depth of characterization.

As we practiced this new protocol and students got used to the idea that interrupting a scripted performance with improvised or other scripted material was acceptable and productive, the exercises began to flow smoothly and continuously. The students began to incorporate performances from texts when the details of the improvised material seemed to create a natural transition or introduction or emotional or attitudinal ambiance which accommodated their material. Sometimes transitions were "jagged" in the sense that the content of new materials did not always flow in a logical way, and students seemed to be interrupting through counterpoint, or working in opposition to one another. Yet these contrapuntal transitions often incorporated gender play or surprising connections or physicalized innovations that deepened the work.

For example, an improvised conversation might be on the same subject matter as a scripted scene, which would create an easy transition. Or, an improvised conversation would become funny and someone who was working on a comic monologue would tap into this comic energy as an opening to introduce her monologue into the flow, whether the subject matter of the monologue was in sync with the improvisation or not. Perhaps anger was exuding from an improvisation which matched the attitude of a scene two students were working on: the students would pick up on that attitude and start their scene. But beyond emotion, attitude, or content, physical choices create important opportunities for students to explore new dimensions of their scripted work.

For instance, two students begin an improvisation in which one (a woman) is standing, knees apart, feet planted firmly on the ground in a stereotypically "male" stance. The other, a man, is standing in a similar manner but seems to be cringing a bit, his upper body pulled back from his partner. His gender performance is ambiguous. An improvised argument about lies and deception ensues. The woman has caught the man doing drugs. The partners are listening to one another and making well-reasoned arguments. They are moving physically in relationship to one another, the woman moving in on the man as she makes a particularly strong argument. The man is alternately cringing and moving toward his partner when he wants to make a strong point. Detailed, nuanced physical and vocal characterization follows the flow of the improvisation.

Another couple across the room is working on Scene 3 from *The Glass*

Menagerie, in which Tom and Amanda are fighting about where Tom goes at night. The scene climaxes when Tom calls Amanda "an ugly babbling old witch." In previous rehearsals of this scene, these actors had been stuck in stereotypically gendered, stiff physicalizations and had simply yelled at one another with little attention to the content of the dialogue. Their work had been stilted and disconnected. Tom had dominated the argument with little emotional nuance and Amanda had shied away from the argument in a traditionally feminine way. As he watches the improvisation about lies and deception, the actor playing Tom finds an opening in the improvised conversation, interrupts, and begins the dialogue from his scene with Amanda, imitating the recalcitrant physicalization of the improviser he had just observed. Amanda, who has planted her feet on the floor like the woman in the previous scene, plays the fight with strength and conviction. She and Tom are standing on either side of a table. She moves toward him in an intimidating manner when she says, "What is the matter with you, you big–big–IDIOT!" Tom backs away. They circle the table, and with each move the actions, intentions, and obstacles embedded in Williams's writing become clear and pointed. Tom transforms, moving toward Amanda when he says, "Listen! You think I'm crazy about the *warehouse?*" Amanda does not back down, advancing on him as he continues the rather long speech this line begins. She stands her ground until he starts attacking her with the speech beginning with "I'm going to opium dens…" which culminates in the climax when Tom throws his coat at the glass menagerie and calls Amanda a witch. Even then, she does not pull in physically or give into a stereotypically feminine self-deprecating posture. She remains upright in her stance and maintains her dignity. Tom also plays with more nuance. He is out of control, but after he speaks his nasty and demeaning lines, he pulls back physically as if he regrets what he has said. Acting technique, emotional ambiance, and physical nuance are enhanced as the scene is played in a surprising way. What had been stiff posturing and stereotypical gender behaviors become animated and ambiguous. The actors focus on the content of the scene and experiment with non-stereotypical ways of playing and physicalizing the characters. The improvised scene has influenced the scripted one.

For these transitions between improvisation and text, students must look and listen carefully for openings to introduce new material, improvised or scripted, as the focus shifts from one couple or individual to another. This develops actors' listening skills. The goal of the exercise is to keep the movement of improvisation and scripted materials flowing, improvisation to text, text to text, and text to improvisation, so that all of the material actors are circulating inspires and supports the others. Actors must pay close attention to one another in a complex environment where anyone could shift gears at any moment. Students begin to move around the space, sitting or standing next to their scene partners for the scripted materials or creating new relationships for improvised scenes. Students also reconfigure the rehearsal furniture to accommodate their scenes, monologues, and improvisations.

I participate in these exercises, continuing to create characters in improvised scenes or performing my own monologues in order to preserve the flow of the exercise. As before, if the action is lagging, I sit next to someone, configure my body in the environment in a way that suggests a character, and start an improvised interaction. For the same reason, I might begin to perform a monologue. I continue to encourage shy or reluctant students by gently tapping them on the shoulder to indicate that I'd like them to participate. In these cases, my interventions are cues to the students that the flow is breaking down and that someone needs to preserve it. But these kinds of interventions also allow me to avoid the master teacher approach and to model or remind quietly rather than direct or critique. If improvisations are becoming silly and non-productive or if scripted performance work is stilted or lacks detail and depth, I simply teach by engaging in the acting work rather than directing. I harness the flow of the improvisational space with my own interruptions, during which I am acting with the students until they regain their footing and go on to improvise or enact scenes on their own. If I have concrete ideas about how an improvisation or monologue or scene might go better, I offer props, cups and glasses of water, food, or costume pieces, or I add in lighting and sound effects in order to communicate these ideas without words. These kinds of interventions circumvent traditional authoritarian relationships. I am in the game with the students.

Other times, I take on more authority and use what Viola Spolin calls "side-coaching," directly encouraging actors to try new behaviors and performance strategies (28). I do this primarily during class days when I am introducing concepts from acting theory. For the sake of subsequent acting classes in the curriculum of the theatre department, my foundational acting class must introduce these concepts, and authoritative involvement from my position as "expert" is necessary. For example, I might remind a student to identify the specific objective of a moment in a scripted scene and to play the action that fulfills that objective more pointedly. I always do this quietly from the sidelines and attempt to fit my comments in with the flow of the performance work. I crouch down next to students to offer suggestions in as unobtrusive a way as possible. I choose moments carefully and speak in a way that emulates the emotional ambiance of what the actors are doing so they can continue on as if my comments were lines in their improvisations or scenes and monologues.

As a result, students move from a tendency to show off, "ACT" self-consciously, and create stereotypical representations to performing with sensitivity toward the text and audience. They naturally adapt their performance behaviors to and from the details of the classroom environment and are able to experiment with a wide variety of physical and emotional qualities. Within this micro-political environment that capitalizes on the details of physicalized acting behavior, repetition (to use Butler's terms), imitation, and inspiration from peer to peer, possibilities for building nuance of character (including interesting and unusual gender behaviors) is created. By interjecting improvised conversations into the flow of the exercise in conjunction with material from monologues and scenes, students are able to use their own complex responses to the class proto-col and their personal lives as material for character and scene analysis and development. I simply intervene as they develop their performances through an embodied process which encourages them to experiment in a wide variety of surprising and productive ways.

Interactional improvisation encouraged by this classroom protocol models the rhythm and ease of physicalization and physical relationships that realistic dramatic material calls for. When students perform scene or monologue materi-als right after they have observed or participated in an improvised conversa-tion, their acting tends to be more focused and spontaneous. By encouraging a range of gender behaviors in improvised conversations and assigning cross-gen-dered scenes and monologues, students begin to see that nuance and detail of physicalized character is much more effective than gender stereotyping. Such work also increases students' physical and vocal vocabularies. They tend to see that stereotyped gender behaviors restrict possibilities for unique and interest-ing characterizations that add surprising detail and nuance to their work, such as a strong stance for an ingénue female or a shy or reticent physicalization for a masculine male character. In addition, instead of stopping and starting the class to comment on playing actions or obstacles or subtext, which I do only occasionally, the improvisations seem to model those concepts so I don't need to interrupt as often. I don't need to stop and give notes to actors after they per-form a scene. They learn to solve acting problems on their own through inter-action with their peers and subtle interventions from me. bell hooks says that "In my classrooms, I do not expect students to take any risks that I would not take, to share in any way I would not share" (21). By engaging with my students as both actor participant and facilitator of learning, I model a way of being in the classroom in which the students teach each other but don't critique each other, in which we play out support for one another's work moment to moment.

The flow, however, does not move completely seamlessly; instead, imbal-ance is one of its key features. Often, students interrupt a scene because it is fal-tering, or because laughter or some other interruption threatens to break the flow. In describing her experience of theatre rehearsal process, director Anne Bogart says that a sense of instability is absolutely necessary to the creative process of making theatre: "In imbalance and falling lie the potential for cre-ation. When things start to fall apart in rehearsal, the possibility of creation exists" (10). Indeed, when things begin to fall apart in my classrooms, some-thing else has to happen to preserve the flow of activity. And when that "some-thing else" happens, new ideas for character and scene interaction emerge with very little coaching from me. My interruptions providing food, drink, props, and costumes contribute to this imbalance and can help actors discover nuances of vocal rhythm as they play, eat or drink, fiddle with an object, or put on a jacket or shoes as they deliver their lines.

Most striking for me is how little "authoritative" involvement is required of me. Spolin is right. The fluidity of alternating improvisation and text work initiated and sustained through the details of the classroom environment, including personal concerns, creates situations in which actors take agency in their creative work. I don't need to teach or direct in the conventional sense. I facilitate. Power, authority, and hierarchy are displaced and temporarily reframed as playful work spins out of a space of improvisation. But there is another sense in which all this playful activity is not simply spinning out magically: I do control the process–and so does Spolin. I make sure the work keeps moving ahead smoothly, as does Spolin with her "side-coaching." And I make it entertaining, fun. I am the joker in my classrooms.

Mady Schutzman, in her article "Guru Clown, or Pedgogy of the Carnivalesque," talks about her ambivalence about entertaining in the classroom: "To share my passion for intellectual rigor I found I had to make theory dance, sing and perform; to keep students' attention I had to 'entertain'....to keep education amusing at all costs" (64). Perhaps in my own passion for acting, I have discovered a way to play the actor in my own acting classes. I maintain a relatively egalitarian relationship to my students, in keeping with feminist pedagogy and, in that, there is a certain finesse to what I do. I facilitate, but keep that facilitation complex and collaborative. I perform my own monologues to keep the process going, I engage in improvised scenes, I provide appropriate comments, props, costumes, food, drink, lighting, and sound effects at opportune times. Like the joker in Augusto Boal's original "Joker System,"[1] I "...upset or destabilize the singular reality of the world as it is represented in the dramatic text (and as it is conventionally reproduced in performance) in order to explore alternate ways of representing and interpreting that world," as Ruth Laurion Bowman describes (140). I create a feminist atmosphere where alternative, more fluid representations of character, gender, and interaction are possible. Boal says that the Joker System "consists in the presentation within the same performance, both of the play and its analysis" (174). Clearly, in the context of an acting classroom, my aim is not to reinterpret dramatic texts for an audience, my job is to help students experience a variety of interpretations of the texts they are working on so they can explore them thoroughly and come up with effective performances. In the pedagogy my students and I have developed, this happens as the actors model each other's performance behaviors, both successes and failures, as the playfulness of the work flows. It is important to remember, however, that while I have found that these playful processes keep work on texts moving forward, I instigate that playfulness and maintain it just as the joker in Boal's "Joker System" and Forum Theatre does with reinterpretations of societal problems. There is an authoritative aspect to this work– feminist pedagogy is not simply about giving up authority. It is, rather, a pedagogy of empowerment, of exchange. In playing the joker, I can trick and manipulate my students toward effective exploratory work in the playful environments we create, but the real trick is to do so while at the same time giving them agency in their own learning.

Eventually, improvised scenarios fall away from our activities and the focus moves to monologues and scenes. Interruption to begin a new scene or monologue remains a part of the playing, but as the date for more formal performances approaches, rehearsals of full scenes and monologues gain more and more importance. When this happens, actors begin to more purposefully arrange rehearsal furniture and bring in their own props and costume pieces to accommodate their text work. I do more side-coaching that focuses on Stanislavsky's theories. My presence as teacher-joker intensifies as the time for grading nears, but the students always retain agency in the grading process. A critical part of my pedagogy is that students choose when their monologues and scenes will be graded. In fact, if there are any complaints from students about the process, it is that we rehearse so much they get tired of their texts and want to move on. The syllabus indicates a date by which all the scripted performances should be graded, but I start taking note of the quality of students' engagement process and the quality of the scenes or monologues before that date. The final graded performance of a monologue or scene could happen at any time. The students simply tell me, "That's it. Grade that one." Or they ask their peers if they think the performance needs more work. I always honor the students' assessment of when their scenes and monologues are ready to be graded.

Students also have choices about how they will perform. They almost always choose to perform within environments like the ones that were set up for class work, although once in a while they want to perform monologues proscenium style so they can practice for traditional cattle-call audition situations. The students seem to prefer the messy "jagged" environment of rehearsal furniture. In these acting classes, performance is always a part of the process. We have gotten rid of the binary constructed by the proscenium, which can stifle approaches to realism, and have instead created a space in which multiple dynamics can contribute to a fuller exploration of character and interactional choices. Furthermore, students can choose when and how they perform in both the exploratory and evaluative phases of the process.

CONCLUSION

My experience with students who take the acting classes utilizing this pedagogical practice is that they learn to work with me and my colleagues as active collaborators in the rehearsal process rather than expecting the director to take a hierarchical position.[2] These students also tend to develop ensemble work more readily. One student, Carrie Ponder Ameling, who went on to receive her

Ph.D. in theatre at Bowling Green University in Ohio and is now teaching, using her own version of this pedagogy with her students, said,

> The process created a sense of equality and ensemble among students who had different levels of experience and ability. It encapsulated what Stanislavsky was trying to achieve in terms of undermining the "star system." The creation of a production after you had been taught acting in this way became a group effort. Everyone had a voice in what we were creating and a stake in making the production successful. That kind of freedom can be scary if you're not used to it. You had to learn to trust your instincts just like in the classroom where we engaged in improvisations or worked on our texts when the spirit moved us. (Ameling)

Ameling also liked doing parts of scenes and monologues a little at a time in class³ and knowing she was going to participate in every class, as compared to a master teacher approach she once experienced in which she was expected to watch other people work, listen to the teacher's critique, and somehow learn from that. She liked doing and participating in every class. She also said the kind of acting pedagogy we developed

> [t]aught students to be in the moment and ready for anything. You just could not be passive when at any moment in class you might find yourself performing because someone engaged you in an improvisation or your scene partner started your scene or you decided to try out your monologue. Just like in rehearsal or performance, you had to be in a state of readiness all the time because we as students were responsible for our own learning through doing. We knew you weren't going to do it for us or tell us how to do it beyond teaching us basic acting theory and encouraging the flow of the process. (Ameling)

My perception, which has been echoed by my colleagues, is that students are simply more comfortable in the rehearsal process after experiencing this acting class protocol. They come into rehearsals having empowered themselves with ideas of their own. They ask questions and challenge the director's ideas. They are also willing to take more risks physically and vocally, embrace cross-gendered roles with enthusiasm and come up with less stereotypical gender behaviors by drawing on cross-gender work to find more interesting physicalized details for their characters. Women, for example, are more willing to take stronger physical stances and to take up more space. Men are more willing to use greater pitch variety in their voices or move to the side of the stage to let a woman take focus. They think about power relationships in the text, in their relationships with other actors, and with the director as they collaborate in the rehearsal process.

Improvisation seems to depend on "breaks in the surface" of interaction. Through these breaks, the artistry of playful poetics leaks to the surface, bubbling up in laughter and moments of interactional improvisation. Possibilities for subverting order, hierarchy, and authority present themselves. Once improvisation is the pedagogical protocol, perspectives shift and new possibilities for creative productivity emerge. The subversion of hierarchy in the structure of the classroom implies a critical feminist theory that subverts traditional acting class protocol in which the teacher is the ultimate authority. When students become the agents of their own work on improvisation and texts, and when playful interaction between improvisation and text materials dominate the classroom process, they also gain positive "political" power in the creative process and have the opportunity to explore characters that emulate a fluidity of identity, especially when attention to gender stereotypes is part of the equation. That fluidity of identity is made possible by the complexity of the game my students and I have invented, where we can play in the micro-political accoutrements of gesture, movement, vocal production, and power relationships connected to the gendered subtext of theatrical character-making. By allowing interactional improvisation to spin freely, the acting class becomes a space, a site where students can explore text and character from a creative position which can lead them to agency in the rehearsal process, in performance, in other classes, in their relationships, and everyday interactions. This kind of feminist acting pedagogy models a way for students to empower themselves in all aspects of their lives.

NOTES

[1] In his book *Theatre of the Oppressed*, Boal describes what he calls a "Joker System," developed by the Arena Theatre in San Paulo, Brazil. This system involved the presentation of conventional plays with an added character called the "Joker," who communicated the author's and director's analyses and intentions for the play directly to the audience as the play was being performed. In addition, actors often traded characters so that a separation between actor and character could be accomplished. Later, the joker character was modified for use in Forum Theatre, in which audience members can take the place of protagonists in order to explore solutions to social problems. The joker in Forum Theatre mediates between audience and actors in order to get "spect-actors" involved in the play and to interpret actions and scenarios.

[2] I often watch my colleagues' rehearsals because I work with them as the departmental voice, movement, dialect, and Alexander teacher, as well as dialect coach.

[3] Since improvisations, scenes, and monologues are always being interrupted during classroom work, students build performances of texts slowly, a section at a time.

WORKS CITED

Ameling, Carrie Ponder. Telephone Interview. 7 Oct. 2006.

Armstrong, Ann Elizabeth. "Building Coalitional Spaces in Lois Weaver's Performance Pedagogy." *Theatre Topics.* 15:2 (2005): 201-220.

Blair, Rhonda. "Reconsidering Stanislavsky: Feeling, Feminism, and the Actor." *Theatre Topics.* 12:2 (2002): 177-190.

Boal, Augusto. *Theatre of the Oppressed.* New York: Theatre Communications Group, 1985.

Bogart, Anne. "Terror, Disorientation and Difficulty." *Anne Bogart: Viewpoints.* Eds. Michael Bigelow Dixon and Joel A. Smith. Lyme, NH: Smith and Kraus, Inc. (1995). 3-12.

Bowman, Ruth Laurion. "'Joking' with the Classics: Using Boal's Joker System in the Performance Classroom." *Theatre Topics.* 7:2 (1997): 139-152

Butler, Judith. "Imitation and Gender Insubordination." *Inside/Out: Lesbian Theories, Gay Theories.* Ed. Diane Fuss. New York: Routledge, 1991: 13-31.

Case, Sue-Ellen. *Feminism and Performance.* New York: Metheun, 1988.

De Lauretis, Teresa. *Technologies of Gender.* Bloomington: Indiana University Press, 1987.

Gainor, J. Ellen. "Rethinking Feminism, Stanislavsky, and Performance." *Theatre Topics.* 12:2 (2002): 163-176.

hooks, bell. *Teaching to Transgress: Education as the Practice of Freedom.* New York: Routledge, 1994.

Lockford, Lesa and Ronald J. Pelias. "Bodily Poeticizing in Theatrical Improvisation: A Typology of Performative Knowledge." *Theatre Topics.* 14:2 (2004): 431-443

Love, Lauren. "Resisting the Organic: A Feminist Actor's Approach." *Acting (Re)Considered: Theories and Practices.* Ed. Phillip Zarrilli. London and New York: Routledge, 1995. 275-288.

Margolin, Deb. "Mining My Own Business: Paths between Text and Self." *Method Acting Reconsidered: Theory, Practice, Future.* Ed. David Krasner. New York: St. Martin's Press, 2000. 127-134.

Reinelt, Janelle. "Rethinking Brecht: Deconstruction, Feminism, and the Politics of Form." *Brecht Yearbook* 15 (1990): 99-109.

Schutzman, Mady. "Guru Clown, or Pedagogy of the Carnivalesque." *Theatre Topics.* 12:2 (2002): 63-84.

Spolin, Viola. *Improvisation for the Theatre.* Evanston, IL: Northwestern University Press, 1987.

Stroppel, Elizabeth C. "Reconciling the Past and the Present: Feminist Perspectives on the Method in the Classroom and on the Stage." *Method Acting Reconsidered: Theatre Practice, Future.* Ed. David Krasner. New York: St. Martin's Press, 2000. 111-126.

Williams, Tennessee. *The Glass Menagerie.* New York: New Directions Book, 1999.

ON THE GENDER CONTINUUM
Stacy Wolf

What does it mean to teach students that gender is performative? How do we go about it? What is the use-value of denaturalizing habitual gendered performances onstage and in everyday life? Why should we re-think commonsense assumptions about the gendered body? And why might this project be especially useful in a "postfeminist" moment?

It has become by now almost commonplace to say that everyday life is performative and that gender functions as a key, extremely visible, and significant element of that performance. Current undergraduates, for a variety of complex socio-historical reasons, seem particularly adept at understanding that we perform gender and that our performances are, even within the constraints of the physically-sexed body, mutable. They understand that the roles they play as women and men–how they dress, walk, carry themselves, and even how they gesture and speak–depend on the setting: the context, the situation, and the other people with whom they interact. "Being a woman" in a theatre history class differs from "being a woman" at a frat party and differs from "being a woman" at the opera. Yet however willing students are to accept intellectually the notion that gender is performative, and however easily they apply the term to themselves and find examples in their daily styles, I have found that they understand it differently when they practice it bodily and purposefully.

In what follows, I will describe an exercise called "The Gender Continuum," which seeks simultaneously to capitalize on what students already intuit and know and to complicate that knowledge. The exercise links gender and bodies to performance and ideology. It asks students to engage with questions of engendered bodies intellectually, emotionally, and physically.

The gender continuum can be used in a variety of courses in the arts or humanities. I have introduced it in rehearsals (whether or not the play is "about" gender), in acting workshops, and in dramatic literature, performance theory, and feminist and queer theory classes on both the undergraduate and graduate level. This exercise can enhance discussion in almost any course that asks questions about gender and representation, and it encourages students to re-think their daily, often unself-conscious performances of gender. And although the continuum is explicitly built around performances of gender, conversations move quickly to performances of sexuality, race, and class. The gender continuum provides an excellent way to assess how different aspects of one's performed identity are dependent on one another; for instance, there is no such thing as a "woman"–she must be a Latina, a Chinese-American woman, a white woman.

While some students may be hesitant at first to get up and move around and put their bodies on the line, they tend to become curious, enthusiastic, and energized about the various ways that they and their colleagues can perform masculinity and femininity. Because this kind of performance activity, while rigorous, challenging, and thought-provoking, is also funny and fun, students often surprise themselves with bold and sharp observations about how bodily performances wield power in culture. An exercise like the gender continuum necessarily breaks down the mind/body split so common in humanities courses, even in those that focus on performance. It makes theory practical and practice theoretical.

The gender continuum was developed by Jill Dolan, Phillip Zarrilli, Michael Peterson, and myself during rehearsals for *A Midsummer Night's Dream* at the University of Wisconsin-Madison in 1990 (Dolan 151-158). We came up with the idea for the continuum model because in this production many actors were cast across gender, but we wanted all of the actors to play at gender, including those whose gender corresponded to the gender of their character. In other words, we wanted the women actors who played Helena and Hermia to foreground their performances of femininity as aggressively as the woman who played Bottom underlined her performance of masculinity. In a fantastic theatrical world where things turn upside down and back again, we wanted the production to disrupt the correlation of bodies to gender and to mark all gendered performances as performance. We needed to find a quick and clear way to communicate these ideas to the student cast.

The gender continuum exercise basically works like this: I draw a long horizontal line on the board and mark numbers from 1 to 10. I ask the students which end is "masculine" (they invariably say "1") and mark the other end "feminine" ("10"). Explaining that this is a relative scale (that is, a continuum), I stress that its purpose is to become a working, shorthand vocabulary for the class, and so it necessarily relies entirely on stereotypes. We start by putting names of famous people on the scale at each end. We begin with the men, who tend to be easy. Students typically name Arnold Schwarzenegger in *The Terminator*, Vin Diesel, or Viggo Mortensen in *Lord of the Rings*. Naming women who are a "10" soon reveals how stereotypes of women are structured in binary oppositions, and so we often list both Marilyn Monroe and June Cleaver, and both Nicollette Sheridan of *Desperate Housewives* and Jennifer Aniston. We ask and discuss: Is the image of absolute femininity a mother? a whore? a virgin? To whom do we assign higher numbers, Sharon Stone or Reese Witherspoon? We then talk about what "5" means. Is it androgynous? neutral? multi-gendered? doubly-gendered? Is "5" the position of utmost strength or undefined weakness? Can either a man or a woman be a "5"? Is Michael Jackson a "5"? Ellen DeGeneres? Annie Lennox? The Scissor Sisters? Angelina Jolie (who might be named as a "5" or "10" or perhaps a "1")?[1] Our discussion of the complications of the "5" position soon leads to questions about sexuality, demonstrating how tied together are our ideas about gender and sexuality. Is a "5" bisexual? asexual? It also becomes readily apparent that ideas about gender are racialized. So, for example, can the most macho Asian-American man ever be as close to a "1" as, say, Samuel L. Jackson? What about Jackie Chan? Can Halle Berry, as an African-American woman, be a "10"?

During this first segment of the exercise, I write names continuously. The point is to have a lot of names listed as referents and for inspiration, even though many of the names may suggest contradictory meanings of the number on the scale. The students call out names, and I only moderate the discussion to confirm where they want me to put a name on the scale. When they disagree (and they often do, vociferously), I make a quick decision about where to list someone, without judging any students' opinions. As a supplement to students' recalling famous people (especially if they are shy or reticent about listing people), I might also use photographs from magazines to spur conversation about the physical and stylistic attributes that motivate our choices.[2] As I list names or show pictures, I tend not to ask the students why someone belongs someplace on the scale, although they frequently argue those points as I am writing. I reiterate (constantly) that we are dealing with stereotypes and assumptions about representations and not describing facts or reality. I also remind the group that this continuum is particular to our discussion and that every group will create its own. It's important that students see that the scale inevitably will be very conservative (and downright scary) in terms of representation. Rather than trying to dismantle, deconstruct, or ignore stereotypes, we will deal with them head-on.

Once we have at least one or two names listed for each number (or when I feel the group losing patience or getting distracted) we move away from the list, although as the workshop proceeds, if I find that students are losing focus I may refer to the names listed or remind them to "look at the people we listed as '6.'" My hope is that they have begun to internalize the scale and have gained a sense of the range of possible gendered performances available to them. If I am working with non-theatre students, I am especially careful to stress that this is a classroom exercise, and that virtuosic performances are neither expected nor desired.[3] If we are rehearsing for a play, I may remind the actors to mark for themselves locations along the gender continuum that resonate with their ideas about their characters (or other characters in the play). Similarly, I may ask acting students to note if their performances at specific places along the gender continuum remind them of characters they have played.

When we move into the action part of the exercise, I ask everyone to get up, and I instruct them to walk around the room. I ask them to try to drop all of their habitual, "natural," gendered ways of moving and get themselves to a "5." Then I ask them to walk like a "1," urging them to "act more masculine." At this step of the process, I don't yet ask what "masculine" means, but leave them to rely on their own stereotypical ideas about gender (and the names on the board) to figure out how to walk, sit, and stand. I call out numbers up and down the scale, sometimes in order and sometimes not, so they can get the feeling of how their different notions about gender feel on their bodies. I also coach them to do simple activities at a specific number on the continuum; for example, "Tie your shoe as a '4;'" "Butter a piece of bread as a '7;'" "Pick up and read a book as a '10.'" These actions can be pantomimed or students can use actual objects that are in the room. This can take anywhere from five minutes to an hour or more, depending on the energy, concentration, and interest of the instructor and the group.

After this movement segment, we analyze the students' specific performance choices. We consider, for example, the physical space that a "1" takes up as compared to a "10." We talk about where the students carry their weight at various points along the continuum (hips? thighs? feet? shoulders?) and how they demonstrate heaviness or lightness. We point to which body part–head, chest, or pelvis–leads the rest of the body with specific numbers. We note particular gestures or ways of sitting that seem to typify certain numbers. We observe the rhythm, pace, or speed of movement at different numbers, and compare numerical values of sharp, angular movements versus smooth and liquid ones. Because this part of the exercise stresses external, physical choices, we don't talk about how students feel, but focus on what they do. This is also an appropriate time for encouragement and side-coaching: students demonstrate their performances for one another and we talk about what we see. Both students and the instructor can offer ideas and suggestions for making a "2" seem more "2"-like. Again, there are no absolute answers to what the numbers mean or how they should be performed, but once a student or an actor understands what a "7" looks and feels like, that number can be a reference for future class discussions, workshops, or rehearsals.

We also spend some time exploring gradations of numbers. Each student walks around the room, and I call out numbers from 1 to 10 in order, giving them time to respond to each number, and then return from 10 to 1. Next the students take a position, either sitting or standing. The third part of this activity involves, again, repeating a very simple movement (drink from a glass; button a shirt, write your name) at each number up and down the scale. Although the activities are the same as in the first part of the workshop, the repetition of the gestures allows for distinct shifts at the various gradations of masculine or feminine, requiring additional focus and self-awareness of the nuances of movement and the body. After this section, we stop to talk about the small physical choices that differentiate a "1" from a "2," a "2" from a "3," and so on.

Once everyone is comfortable with walking, sitting, and performing simple activities at different places along the gender continuum, we do an exercise called "magazine covers." In this section, students imagine that they are "posing" for the cover of a magazine. First, I call out numbers and the students "pose" for the camera. I have them move up and down the scale, again coaching them to create the "essence" of the number. As they envision themselves on the cover of a magazine, they form a relationship with an imagined viewer, which immediately brings up questions of power and the gaze. During the discussion that follows this section, I ask, "At which number(s) do you look down or away from the camera?" "At which numbers do you look back?" "At which numbers do you feel you have power over the viewer?" "Do you feel possessed by the viewer or disempowered at any point on the continuum?" Again, there are no right answers, as this part of the exercise is designed for students to note how gender, power, and the gaze are interconnected, and emphasizes how gender is relational and social: someone looks and someone is looked at.[4]

This exercise can be extended to a larger social and political framework by calling out the title of a specific magazine; for example, "You are an '8' and on the cover of *Glamour*," "You are a '2' and on *Sports Illustrated*." Or, I give them less information: "You are on the cover of *Vogue*. Think about which number you are." "You are on *Runner's World*. Concentrate and embody a number." The activity moves the gender continuum from the body of the solo performer and requires the student to imagine gender within a situation and a context. Moreover, naming a magazine title stresses how gender is a commodity: gender, or more precisely, a certain performance of gender, sells. In the magazine cover situation, students suddenly look at gendered images as part of an entire ideological system. This provides opportunities to complicate the analysis and see how certain manifestations of gender support, enable, or represent particular "lifestyles." Although we don't necessarily discuss what each magazine means—we keep the focus on gender and its performance—students immediately see how this exercise allows them to appear to package a certain lifestyle. At the same time, they make connections with their own desires as viewers and as consumers, as the "magazine cover" locates them simultaneously as object (on the cover) and as subject (the viewer who wants to have or wants to be the model). Students begin to understand how, as social actors, they are always implicated in gendered performances.

There are endless variations on these basic exercises, as the gender continuum can be applied to virtually any acting exercise. For example, students can "meet and greet" each other at different numbers, which places gender in a relation to another (of the same or different number). How does a "5" look at another "5"? How do "9s" shake hands? How does a "9" shake hands with a "3"? How do "2s" approach each other? How does a "1" say hello to a "4"? By moving to interactions within the scale, students can begin to explore how such interactions work to mutually construct gender, and how any interaction can become an exchange of power. What each student's performance of gender means depends on how it is read and responded to by another student. Like any performance, gender is not only enacted and embodied, it is also observed, received, and interpreted. Numbers on the scale accrue value and status, although, interestingly, which numbers have more or less power varies with each class or group. I can never predict which interactions will be easy and which more difficult.

While I think the exercises are useful in themselves (even in a single workshop session of an hour or less, they always lead to excellent discussions about the performance of gender), the gender continuum seems to become more useful as a class or rehearsals go on. Once a class, group, or cast has a common vocabulary for talking about or embodying gender, it can aid in the analyses of other performances or texts. For example, students can work on any kind of improvisation with a specific location on the gender continuum as one of the rules of the exercise. Or, when studying a play, we may discuss where we imagine a particular character on the gender continuum, or we may place all the characters in the play on the scale: "Where do you imagine Linda Loman in *Death of a Salesman*?" "Are there other ways to play her so that her place on the continuum moves?" "What happens to our interpretation of the play if we imagine Linda as a '10' or a '6'?" "What choices might an actor make to place her at a '10' or a '6'?" "How does placing Linda at a '10' or a '6' inform the gendered choices of the actors playing Willy, Biff, and Happy?" These questions can lead to complex discussions of a gendered world within a play.

From the spectator's perspective, the gender continuum can be used to describe an actor's physical and gestural choices in a performance, whether live or on tape. One particularly useful side effect of the language of the gender continuum is that it forces students' observations to remain external and performative. Rather than judging if a character is "realistic" or "believable," which is often the default language of performance analysis, especially for undergraduates and less experienced theatre-goers, the gender continuum necessitates observations about choices and the body. We might explore the implications, meaning, and significance of an actor playing Lena in *A Raisin in the Sun* as a "4" versus a "7," and we might even discuss whether or not hers is an effective choice, but our conversation stays within the realm of physicalization. Because students often naturalize psychological or realistic vocabularies of performance analysis, a framework that eschews interiority and psychological motivations serves as an extremely useful counterbalance.

In the context of rehearsals for a play or for an acting workshop, the gender continuum prepares students/actors/participants in advance to re-form their bodies and bodily gestures and practices, since they are making active choices rather than relying on habits. From the start, the exercise does not ask them to play their own place on the continuum, but instead encourages an outside orientation to a character, thereby facilitating an imaginative relationship between the actor and the character, rather than an identificatory one. Because Method-based acting techniques are so ubiquitous, and in some settings thoroughly naturalized, the gender continuum offers an alternative and a supplementary tool. A director can use the gender continuum as a shorthand to ask the actor to try out different physicalities for a character: "Let's work on this scene tonight with you at a '7;'" "Try that monologue twice, once at a '2' and once at '8;'" "To me that looks like you're playing it at '3.' Can you try it at '1'?" For students, both actors and non-actors, the exercise demonstrates the range of physical choices available without relying on a character's psychology.

In acting classes or rehearsals, the gender continuum becomes a tool for performance; in other classes (both theatre and non-theatre), a tool for analysis. In fact, the gender continuum is equally effective as an analytical tool or as an acting technique. It works especially well in a non-theatre classroom to get students on their feet and to pull them out of the textual orientation presumed by many humanities departments. While I certainly don't value the kinesthetic over the intellectual in and of itself, I find it useful when teaching gender and performance to take a few moments to feel and think of our bodies as gendered, as sexualized, as raced, as performed and performative. In some situations, students move tentatively or express anxiety about moving in a classroom. Such resistance to performance in a non-performance-based class is almost always short-lived but, at the same time, resistance can be productive and informative when it opens a discussion about embodiment and the value of kinesthetic knowledges. I always find the gender continuum a productive exercise, as inevitably it becomes a point of reference during the rest of the class term. As Henry Giroux writes, the university is "a place that produces a particular selection and ordering of narratives and subjectivities. It is a place that is deeply political and unarguably normative" (qtd. in Malinowitz 101). The gender continuum wrests identity from the normative, psychological subjectivities to which Giroux refers, allowing the temporary embodiment of non-coincident subjectivities; whether or not a student "is" masculine, she is invited to perform masculinity in the extreme. However a student perceives himself and his gendered self-performance, he can try on different physicalities with the gender continuum as a tool. The gender continuum uses the body to push us beyond identity and identification.

Yet I also see (and have experienced in the classroom) the continuum's attendant risks. First, the gender continuum reinforces the idea of gender as a binary field and so is just the first step in deconstructing gender's enactment. How can we move past the gender continuum to re-think and re-perform gender, and to sidestep or reimagine its relentless binary configuration? Second, what are the potential dangers of possibly reinforcing many undergraduates' already overdeveloped sense of individual agency? While it's valuable for students to feel freedom and choice to perform gender in what feels like an infinite

number of ways, we should also stress that the very values of the gender continuum are socially and historically constructed, and in the scheme of how bodies
might move, severely limited.

The gender continuum is a useful step in one direction—that of noticing,
embodying, and exploiting stereotypes. In what might be described as a "post-
feminist" moment, privileging a "humanist" perspective that foregrounds all
genders as performative is a profoundly feminist act. That is, rather than stress-
ing how *women* are hampered by gendered stereotypes, we can explore how all
people are gendered, and extend the questions from there: how all genders are
at once binding and potentially freeing, how all genders are historically and
socially contingent, how all performances of gender take place within a social
and cultural context, how all performances of gender involve a social actor and
an audience that interprets gender and its meanings, and how all gendered
practices are political and do ideological work. The gender continuum is a pedagogical structure to enter into these conversations, and it provides an embodied framework that supports feminist theory. By facilitating students'
physicalized experimentations with gender, we can imagine, practice, and perform gender in ways that are enabling and empowering as well as critical and
socially responsible.

NOTES

[1] Thanks to Chase Bringardner for helping me with these examples and for pointing me to
http://uniorb.com/RCHECK/RAndrogyny.htm as a reference.

[2] Whether or not to use actual images is up to the instructor. In some situations, I think, seeing pictures
hobbles the students' creativity and their willingness to try out gender. For other students, real images
may clarify their opinions and/or motivate them.

[3] If it is an extraordinarily shy group that is reticent to move around, I will ask one student to model the
exercise by demonstrating a pose or a gesture while the other students side-coach directions. Still, this
attitude is rare; even non-theatre students are almost always eager to play and to try out gender performance.

[4] In a Women's Studies, film theory, or feminist theory class, this exercise might be contextualized with
readings on the "male gaze," the theory that mainstream films are constructed by presuming that the
central character, the camera, and the viewer are male. See, for example, Kaplan. Even though theories of the male gaze have been critiqued and discounted by some feminist scholars, such essays can
serve as productive intellectual, theoretical, and historical sources for these issues. Other useful readings include Bordo, Burt, Diamond, and Grosz.

WORKS CITED

Butler, Judith. "Performative Acts and Gender Constitution: An Essay in Phenomenology and
Feminist Theory." *Theatre Journal.* 40.4 (1988): 519-31.

Bordo, Susan. "Reading the Male Body." *The Male Body: Features, Destinies, Exposures.* Ed. Laurence
Goldstein. Ann Arbor: University of Michigan Press, 1994. 265-306.

Burt, Ramsey. "Looking at the Male." *The Male Dancer: Bodies, Spectacle, Sexualities.* New York:
Routledge, 1995. 49-73.

Diamond, Elin. "Brechtian Theory/Feminist Theory." *TDR: The Drama Review.* 32.1 (1988): 82-94.

Reprinted in *HBJ Anthology of Drama*, 2nd Edition. Ed. W.B. Worthen. Ft Worth, TX: HBJ Press, 1997. 1284-1292.

Dolan, Jill. "Peeling Away the Tropes of Visibility: Lesbian Sexuality and Materialist Performance Practice." *Presence and Desire: Essays on Gender, Sexuality, Performance.* Ann Arbor: University of Michigan Press, 1993. 151-158.

Grosz, Elizabeth. "Bodies and Pleasures in Queer Theory." *Who Can Speak?: Authority and Critical Identity.* Ed. Judith Roof and Robyn Wiegman. Urbana: University of Illinois Press, 1995. 221-230.

Kaplan, E. Ann, ed. *Feminism and Film.* New York: Oxford University Press, 2000.

Malinowitz, Harriet. *Textual Orientations: Lesbian and Gay Students and the Making of Discourse Communities.* Portsmouth, NH: Boynton/Cook, 1995.

NO GENDER IN THE CLASSROOM
AN INTERVIEW WITH KATE BORNSTEIN AND BARBARA CARRELLAS
Kathleen Juhl

INTRODUCTION

Kate Bornstein and Barbara Carrellas offer a unique location through which to view feminist values in teaching and performing, provoking us to think about gender and sexuality in ways that challenge feminist politics. Bornstein, a male to female transsexual, has an established career as an author, performer, playwright, and educator/activist. Hir published work, plays, and performance pieces are widely taught on college campuses all over the United States. These include *Gender Outlaw: On Men, Women, and the Rest of Us* (1994); *My Gender Workbook* (1998); *The Opposite Sex Is Neither* (1991); *Virtually Yours* (1994); and *Hello Cruel World: 101 Alternatives to Suicide for Teens Freaks and Other Outlaws* (2006). Hir current pedagogical explorations have been with groups of queer youth working on what ze calls "the language of paradox."

Barbara Carrellas, Bornstein's professional and personal partner, is a theatre artist, author, sex educator, motivational speaker, and workshop facilitator. Carrellas frequently works with Bornstein in the queer and transgender communities, but she also teaches independently, exploring sexual healing and sex as an avenue for personal and spiritual transformation. Inspired by New Age approaches, Bornstein and Carrellas practice a unique kind of teaching that locates a spiritual source through embodied practice. They direct these techniques with a range of students, including special interest populations, theatre students, and general university and community groups.

Bornstein evokes a "language of paradox" to describe hir approach to teaching and gender. Drawing on hir personal experiences as a transsexual, ze encourages students to embrace and live within their paradoxical identities. This interview also highlights many of the paradoxes with which feminist teachers struggle; for example, Bornstein describes one of hir teaching personas as that of a "crone," explaining that some (particularly transgender) youth don't have the "luxury" of self-questioning or personal discovery, practices usually associated with feminist pedagogy. Instead, ze notes that some students need a supportive but authoritarian voice—the crone. Yet in other situations, Bornstein and Carellas utilize a pedagogical strategy of "edutainment," becoming provocateurs through their "too tall blonde" personas. In these paradoxes, Bornstein and Carellas highlight both the variety and the context-specific nature of feminist teaching strategies, as well as their faith in the power of the body. Reacting against the dominance of the "mind" in Western culture, they seek to reclaim body and spirit in ways that challenge many of us who reside in the academy.

In March of 2004, Bornstein and Carrellas came to Southwestern University in Georgetown, Texas, where I teach theatre and was at that time Chair of the Feminist Studies Program. Their two-day residency was sponsored by the Feminist Studies Program's Jessie Daniel Ames Lecture series. At Southwestern, Bornstein and Carrellas gave what they called a "performative lecture" entitled "Too Tall Blondes Do Sex, Death and Gender" for a packed house of undergraduates, faculty, and administrators. They also led two workshops.

The first was called "The No-Gender Zen Walk" and was facilitated for an acting class to which non-theatre students were also invited. Students were asked to walk slowly across a fairly narrow rehearsal hall/classroom space, imaginatively and physically shedding their current gender and trading it for a new gender. They walked, let go of, and transformed their genders for an hour. The second workshop, open to the interested members of the campus community, was called "The Gender-Free Orgasm." It involved several minutes of conscious breathing and relaxation, after which participants were asked to tense all of their muscles and then let go. Bodies started shaking, participants found themselves giggling and wiggling, crying and laughing, and in general experiencing safe and hilarious embodied ecstasy. No touching or genitals were involved, just, as Carrellas calls it, "blissful breathing" and muscle holding and letting go to induce physiological release.

INTERVIEW

Note: Barbara Carrellas was called away before we began, and joined us about an hour into the interview.

JUHL: I have only experienced the workshops you did at Southwestern. Are there a range of workshops and classes and exercises that you use in other settings? Do you do other workshops with the transgender community?

KATE: Wow. Yes to it all. I'm kind of in the process of switching stuff over. I do the gender stuff right now and mostly it's with acting students. They're doing a cross-gender production, obviously, of *Cloud Nine* at Towson University, and I'm going to go down there and work with them for a week. That'll be fun, but what I really wanted to be getting into and what I'm toying around with now is this thing called the "language of paradox." I've done it for a

couple of years with a group of queer kids out in Portland. When I say kids–
fifteen to twenty-two, in that range. Of all genders. My golly. The exercise
was to take a week and find out the paradox in your life. The thing that gives
you the greatest joy that also is the most trouble for you in your life, and
name that, reconcile it, do a performance piece based on it. Sew it all
together and at the end of the week you've got a play that's like ten or fifteen
amazing performance pieces all about paradox. Not all of it about gender.
There was this one kid who was female-to-male but kind of going back to
female but that wasn't the problem at all, the real problem was that he was
too country for his punk friends and too punk for his country friends. Both of
those things gave him so much joy but he couldn't fully participate in either
so he had to perform that. So I'm working with that kind of stuff. I still do
the gender workshops, and Barbara and I do the gender-free orgasm stuff.

JUHL: Would you describe the pedagogy you use as feminist pedagogy? What I
mean by that is an approach to teaching that deals with gender injustice and
gets students to participate in their own learning.

KATE: I would hope so, yes. Hmm, now this is a thorny one, 'cause, yes, I have
been, up to this time, in all my work on gender, tried to present it in that
way. But I've got this new book that I'm working on, *Hello Cruel World: 101
Alternatives to Teen Suicide*, and I find that the voice I need to be using is much
more the voice of the elder, the crone, the parent, the "look, do this." Just do
this. It makes sense and here's what'll happen if you do. Because I'm not
talking...sadly, I'm not talking to people who have the luxury of any more
self-questioning at that point in their lives. And I've tried to embrace a loving
parent. Does *that* qualify as feminist pedagogy? I don't know.

JUHL: But you're encouraging people to come up with their own answers and
knowledge about themselves, right?

KATE: Yeah.

JUHL: So it's not so much that you're feeding them answers, but you're facilitating and you're giving them information that will hopefully help them discover lifesaving strategies for themselves, with your help as an older person
with experiences around the issue of suicide.

KATE: And I'm very clear that I'm taking on that "parent" kind of persona.

JUHL: And actually, feminist pedagogy is moving in that direction. For a while
it was kind of a free-for-all, and students talking about their personal experiences became very prominent in the classroom. Now there's been some
modification of that and realizations by teachers that they do have to intervene and lead the students toward important information.

KATE: Feminism to me has always been linked with goddess culture. If you've
got maiden, mother, and crone, then maybe feminist pedagogy is entering its

crone phase. I know I am.

JUHL: Yes, that's interesting. Another part of feminist pedagogy is acknowledging that we learn from our students, that the classroom is a place for mutual learning–collaborating to create knowledge. You must learn some amazing things from the kids in the language of paradox intensives.

KATE: Yes. There's this whole new era in trans subculture that hasn't been written about outside of…I think Ricki Wilchins has written about it and a lot of 'zines have written about it, it's "genderqueer." And that one isn't really on the mainstream cultural radar. And that's what I'm learning from these kids. I had this one young person. In Portland. And I knew her over the course of a year in which she changed her gender four times, each to a different gender–very conscious, very named, had different names, different look. I didn't recognize her any of the four times. And it's like "oh my god, they're fucking doing it." Damn! You know? I'm an old fart. I'm into transgender. I'm not a genderqueer. I am theoretically, but hell, I'm almost sixty years old. That's not my generation. But it sure tickles the hell out of me. It's so cute. It's sexy. It's beautiful. These young people are using their genders consciously to express their desire.

JUHL: If they're using their genders to express their desire, is the gender-switching always empowering? Was the person who switched four times always switching to empowering gender behaviors or representations?

KATE: No, it wasn't always empowering. There were some times when she was giving into things or he was giving into things. Collapsing into an old destructive behavior or two but taking the whole road, just going for it 100%. It wasn't always an empowering journey, but that's part of journeys, none of them are.

JUHL: And so we have the paradox of gender.

KATE: Yeah. 'Cause the other side of gender is its use in a power structure. Gender is, you know, it's…in this new book I've kind of figured it out. I've narrowed gender down in this culture. It's used for desire and power–to communicate those two things. I think this notion of empowerment is also a paradoxical one, because as soon as you grab for power, you're disempowered, or someone will try to disempower you, or you're a target. But it's when you can kind of let go of your need to have power, or be willing to share it, and adopting a gender which for you proclaims that. There's a side of pedagogy, and feminist pedagogy at that, that I never hear talked about– and that's spirituality, and it gets back to the whole goddess thing. And you know in this case it's not so much goddess stuff as it is Zen stuff. And where are we allowed to talk about that? If people are starting to talk about intelligent design and that should be in the schools, I say so should Zen Buddhism. There.

JUHL: Can you talk about the kinds of gender behaviors, the kinds of gendering that you see as empowering and disempowering?

KATE: Okay, well, what's empowering gender is taking on the gender that would give you the most power in that particular moment and not holding on to it to the next moment when you're in another situation and the gender you're being then totally disempowers you. I try to do my talks as girly-girly as I can get. Blonde. Girly girl. Cute. Everything that's not taken seriously. And so I mix things up. But that's a performance. If you try to do that in the world, you won't be taken seriously. And sometimes it's worth not being taken seriously, to explore a side of yourself that needs to be explored. And I don't think there's anything wrong with that if that's what's going to keep you alive.

JUHL: A big part of what you do on college campuses is performances. Do you think there is a way in which those performances could fit into this realm of feminist pedagogy that we've been talking about?

KATE: But sometimes I'm up there just to entertain. During that time I don't want them to do anything but laugh, or get affected by it, or experience the emotion of it, or the feeling of it, or get caught up in it as a theatre piece. That's more what I'm interested in.

JUHL: Okay, so there is a sense in which you stand away from the students and give them things.

KATE: Oh golly, sure. I give 'em a good time. Hey, big spender. You know, I do what I'm hired to do. And as an entertainer, you know, you find a delicate balance of the both. Do I stand apart? Well, yes and no. I build a whole lot of stuff. You know. It's manipulative. Art is downright manipulative. So I manipulate audience participation in all my stuff. I'm up there topping the audience. They trust me, and I have to top them lovingly. That's how I see it. And at the same time, when I get into the heavier stuff, I'm totally bottoming them…I'm saying "Here, rip me open." See?

JUHL: So in that sense you're provoking–you're being provocative and provoking questions from them.

KATE: No. Well, maybe. Maybe some of the content may provoke questions. But there's a very definite sense that it's entertainment. I think you can slide both in at the same time. I call it edu-tainment.

JUHL: In the shows you're doing right now, you and Barbara have created the "too tall blondes" personas. Why do you do the tall blonde thing? What is it about it that's attractive to you? Is it the irony of it?

KATE: Well, I mean, the irony is that here I am talking theory and that was never my intention when I went through my gender change. All I ever wanted to be was pretty. Okay. Really. I get an excuse to be pretty. Lots of people telling me I am. Looking at me like I am. That's great. It's a very selfish thing.

JUHL: And for you it's empowering?

KATE: Yeah, on one level. And when I'm up on the stage...well golly, I've just been introduced by their professor and they're kind of willing to give me something, a little bit of credit, and by the end of the evening, they give me a lot more credit. There was the shooing in of a paradox if you will...manipulatively.

JUHL: How about another paradox? What about issues of race and blonde?

KATE: Race is tricky in my case. Where I'm sitting, here in New York, I'm a white person. If I were to go over to England, I'd no longer be white, I'd be a Jew. And pretty much every place else in the world. And that would be my race. So race is relative. I went blonde because isn't that what the culture wanted me to do? Is this what they wanted me to want to be? So what's wrong with it? You know, I did it and still have a large measure of my integrity. So what's the problem? That's not serious? That's oppressive? No! It's pretty. It's paradoxical. I'm letting myself do that as consciously as I possibly can, and does it trap me? Yes. Do I fall down? Yes. But I'm learning. So that's what I'm talking about when I'm saying I go into "disempowering situations," if you will.

JUHL: Do you get in trouble doing it?

KATE: Sure. I've been raped, I've been date raped. I've been mugged. This happens.

JUHL: In your blonde persona?

KATE: Yeah. No, the rape was when I was a boy. But all the rest was, you know, girly-girl. And you go, okay, all right, all right, all right, all right.

JUHL: So you're taking on a dangerous persona?

KATE: For me it is. I'm not saying it is for everyone.

JUHL: In *My Gender Workbook*, some of the sections that I love are when you say, "Okay, we're going to do some theory now." Can you talk, in more explicit terms than we have been talking, about how you theorize your pedagogy?

KATE: You're walking on dangerous ground here. My inner theorist is quite closeted. So, repeat the question in a not-so-theory way so I understand it and can communicate it to my inner theorist.

JUHL: Mmmm....on what theoretical basis do you spin out your pedagogy? Is that better?

KATE: Better. I'm trying to do less and less of a theoretical base. Or what I'm getting out there and I'm trying to do, and I think that this is also part of crone stuff. I think there's a scale of principles, let's call them. At the very top of the scale is values, let's say. The value I think I'm working on the hardest right now is "Don't be mean." Okay. It's a simple value. When people can't simply do that, then you develop an ethical system, the next step down. And an ethical system might be "Do unto others as you would have them do unto to you." Okay, that's an ethical principle. Okay. Cool. Should work. Doesn't. So if ethics kind of falls apart then you've got morals. And it would be "The Ten Commandments or the Beatitudes will help us get that ethical principle," and meanwhile we've already forgotten about the value of "Don't be mean." Really, concerned with what does "coveting your neighbor's wife" mean anyway? And then if that falls apart, you've got law–crime and punishment. Right? Theory is somewhere around morals. And I think that unless we start aligning theory with a principle of "Don't be mean," what's the value of it? And I think if we, at our age, don't start setting that kind of an honest standard for what's important in our lives, then who is? We're going to continue on at a moral level or a theoretical level and the two will have it out in the great new debate between intelligent design and evolution.

JUHL: Can you expand a little bit for me, because I'm not quite clear about theory aligning with morals?

KATE: What is the purpose of theory? I think it's the same as the purpose for morals, which is to implement an ethical way of getting along in life. Theory would be, hopefully, a way to approach, analyze, implement higher standards of living. And so it's around the same level. If someone just isn't getting it, so let's theorize about it. And it's needed, just like morals are needed.

JUHL: What are some specific reactions that people have had to your pedagogy, particularly the "edutainment" pieces?

KATE: One I'll never forget. I was out in Wisconsin at a small college that will remain unnamed, and I was pretty early on in my touring, I guess, but I had a good act. I think it was called "Cut and Paste" or something like that. It was a series of different monologues and slam poems and performance pieces and theoretical texts, and usually followed by a Q&A. Well, I was brought into this one college. The total student body was maybe six hundred people and all six hundred people were in this auditorium with all the teachers and all the administration from the dean on down. Every student. I didn't know this was going to be mandatory, you know? They wanted to learn about trans stuff…okay. So off I went and I did my thing. And at the end, this one kid stood up and he said, "All right, if you're not a man and you're not a woman, what are you?" I said, "Well I'm a not man, not woman." "No, you have to be something–if you're not a man and you're not a woman, what are you?" "I'm a not man and not woman. I'm neither of those. Sometimes saying you're not either is enough." "No, it's not." He just…he would not accept that. He wrote letters to my agent for months afterwards.

Interestingly enough, none of the faculty or administration stopped the lad, which I would have hoped they would have done. You know, it was darned uncomfortable, and finally I had to speak to him firmly and say, "Young man, there are some things you simply must accept that you disagree with."

JUHL: He just wasn't going to accept who you are.

KATE: No.

JUHL: That must have been painful.

KATE: Well...yeah, it was. For the most part, I love college students. They're hungry for an adult to give them permission to be a little more wacky than they've been. They like knowing that you can still get taken seriously in the world if you're gonna have a little fun and step out.

JUHL: You just gave me a wonderful story about resistance to what you do, and I remember the first conversation that we had, and you said you were going to do a workshop called "No-Gender Orgasm," and I knew you must have just watched, in your mind's eye, this woman going, "Ahhhh...what?" and you immediately said, "They don't take their clothes off, they don't take their clothes off. And it's okay. And it's okay." Do you get other kinds of resistance from folks?

KATE: Honestly, no! People trust me. People who ask me to do that workshop by and large trust me. I've got a good reputation of being gentle. And not stepping on people's toes. I'm trading on that a lot with this new book. I'm asking people to forgive me a lot of stuff in this book. I'm telling kids to take drugs. I'm telling them to, you know, starve themselves. I'm telling them to do whatever they have to do to not kill themselves. Some of it's better than other stuff. But if it's gonna keep you alive, do it. So I'm trusting that people will respect the kindness of my motives, and when I present something called a workshop on gender-free orgasms, it's always in the context of gender theory.

JUHL: How do people respond to your workshops and exercises while you're doing them–the gender walk, or the no-gender orgasm, or anything else that you do? I mean it seemed to me that the no-gender orgasm workshop at Southwestern was enormously successful. I mean, it was just a riot. And do you get that in most places?

KATE: Yeah. And generally what I'll talk about afterwards, and what Barbara will talk about afterwards, is, "All right so get together a group." Do it, you know, do the real thing now. Find out about other kinds of orgasms. Get yourself twenty massage tables in a hall off campus and bring someone in to teach you this stuff.

JUHL: The students at Southwestern were really pumped up for more after the no-gender orgasm workshop. I didn't do it, but I think I could have gotten a group together to do it again. Barbara gave me instructions. I need to do that. It was so valuable. So tell me more specifics about some of the other workshops that you do.

KATE: Okay. A lot of them I'll take from *My Gender Workbook*. I do the one of getting people to just visualize arriving in their bodies. That old Viola Spolin stuff, and giving them a visual meditation and then have them wake up in these bodies as if they're aliens who are coming to do a fact-finding mission on earth. That's really kinda cool. Then there's actual scene work using lines from Tim Burton's *Batman*, or actually I think it was the Penguin, yeah, the second *Batman*, where the Penguin says, "You're just jealous because I'm a real freak and you have to wear a mask." And Batman responds, "You may just be right." Giving those as two lines to two people to work out in different genders, and have those lines make sense, and that's kinda cool. And then you do that and they pick a gender and the rest of the class has to guess what their gender is and they keep adding cues until the class knows for sure what gender they are. And you know you have cues—physical cues, contextual cues, movement cues, posture cues, accessory—all these different kinds of cues, and familiarizing the actor with what's it gonna take to get across the gender they'd like to get across.

JUHL: What are some of those genders are named?

KATE: Boy, girl, man, woman, lady, gentleman are some. Drag king, drag queen.

JUHL: Any beyond those?

KATE: No, no, no, because…the reason is that most of these classes are not taught to people whose passion is gender exploration. These are acting students. Who came to study Chekhov. Then there's this transsexual person urging them to fuck with their genders, and they have to do this in front of the girl they want to impress and it's really really scary…so, the fact that those are genders that they usually claim is actually quite…quite impressive. I have an exercise called "The Gender Identity Graphic Equilizer Tool." "GIGET" for short. GIGET is a series of maybe eight columns, eight binary pairs—fluid/solid, gallant/gracious, dark/light, these different kinds of pairs and you get to plot yourself, where you are now, where you'd like to be, and then you figure out how to get yourself there, and you start fine-tuning your gender. Rather than calling it "man" or "woman," you don't call it anything. You just say, "All right, if this is the nature of my desire, and when I'm experiencing my sexual fantasy, where would I be on this chart? Okay, now, how can I get to that point?" So I'm walking through my life like I'm walking through my sexual fantasy and that's kinda fun.

JUHL: Do you find when you do this work that the students have responses that are uncomfortable for them?

KATE: Very rarely. Very rarely. Like in the gender walk, I'm very careful to say "Don't pick qualities that are too far of a stretch. We're just gonna get the idea of how to do this." And I think that's important.

JUHL: Okay, so it becomes about the process.

KATE: Yeah.

JUHL: What about the personal and the political in this process? I mean, if the personal side of things invades the political, then it would seem that the body becomes a nexus, the meeting place of these forces of the personal, the political, and the practice. Have you seen this kind of nexus operating in your work? Does that make sense?

KATE: I saw it at Oglethorpe a few years back, where the LGBT group wanted to do something big and splashy and queer and proud and so we started getting them on to a drag show, and the feminist group wanted to do *The Vagina Monologues*, and the theatre group wanted to do a cross-gendered *As You Like It.* And that was thrilling. You had all these groups working to help each other. Kind of cross-pollinating. That was a thrill! That was great. They did good work. Every one of them. They got the drag show up. They got *The Vagina Monologues* up. The cross-gendered Shakespeare up. And they did it by working together. The trouble of course is that most of those students have graduated now, and how do things get passed down in colleges? That's a mystery. So, how lasting is it? I don't know.

JUHL: Perhaps how long-lasting it is has to do with how embodied it is. Sounds like these students were intensively engaged in embodying gender.

KATE: Yeah and I would imagine those students who left there are still carrying that around with them. I would hope so.

JUHL: At the beginning, when we were first talking, you described this person that ended up with four genders. Did that person come out of the workshop doing that or was that person doing this on their own before your workshop?

KATE: Oh, totally on their own. This is a truly free-thinkin', postmodern person. I mean, it was just cool to watch and be in their presence.

JUHL: The younger generation seems to be really exploring gender. Even at Southwestern they're fucking with it. I think every day I encounter somebody who's playing with gender. Which is always a delight to me.

KATE: It is. I think so too.

JUHL: When you do workshops on gender, is the experience like watching gender float around people's bodies like crazy?

KATE: Yeah. It's kind of like in the movie *The Matrix*, the way you can see the matrix? More like that.

JUHL: So is it like making operations of power visible on the bodies of your students? Do you think the students reclaim and reconstruct their identities through performance?

KATE: Yes. That describes my "Language of Paradox" intensive to a T. That's exactly what I hope it does.

JUHL: So the workshop participants reconstruct their identities and then build a community based on that?

KATE: Well, they build a community with each other. Everybody in the project. It's an intense learning experience. Like any theatre piece, you have this THING...my god, what is it? And then the show's over.

JUHL: Right. And then we all go away.

KATE: Well, in Portland some of them are still in touch with each other and working with each other, so that's kinda cool.

JUHL: Are they in touch with you?

KATE: Yeah. Every now and then.

JUHL: What does embodiment do for theory?

KATE: What does it do for morality?

JUHL: How does it change people?

KATE: You asked me how embodiment impacts theory. It hopefully would teach or give people the experience of living without theory, without morality, beyond those two things.

JUHL: Can you expand on that?

KATE: My experience has been, once I've been able to get something in my body, I don't need theory anymore. I needed the theory to kind of get to the point where I was willing to take the risk to embody it. That's where theory helped me. So I'm a big fan of theory. I'm a big fan of morality–not all morality. But I think you know, thank god. There'd be a lot more violence and murder and blah blah blah without the Ten Commandments [*laughter*]. You know? So cool. Go Ten Commandments. Go morality. But the people I wanna hang out with live beyond that and are willing to do more dangerous things in their lives and with their lives.

JUHL: Do you mean more dangerous things with gender? Or does it expand out to other to things that are not attached to gender?

KATE: Someone does something big, and it affects the way they do everything else. That just seems to be how it works. You know, once you've had a peak experience in one arena, you want another peak experience. It doesn't matter the arena. What matters is that it's a peak thing, you know? Sort of like that.

[*Barbara arrives.*]

KATE: Barbara, we're trying to get the notion of when you get people to embody theory.

BARBARA: Southwestern is a very academic school. Students are self-motivated and take on a lot of serious pressure to succeed. There's so much energy up in their heads. If you were to scan them energetically, their bodies would be cool but their heads would be white-hot. So when we did gender-free orgasms, it was delightful for me to see the dramatic difference in the students before and after the exercise. Most people who come to my workshops live in their heads, multitask, and live ninety-nine lives, but they tend to be a bit more balanced than the students who go to university and take it so seriously. Your students are so conscientious! The gender-free orgasm is a blissful breathing technique. We breathe for some twenty minutes in a conscious, alert way and then clench all our muscles—especially the pelvic floor muscles—for about fifteen seconds. Then we let go. It's real simple, but the effect is either like being imploded or exploded, depending on the individual. It's a very freeing experience and when your students did it, it was like [*laughter*] this big old plug blew out of the top of their collective head. All the accumulated tension went flying out and they giggled and looked so blissful. Later, you could watch them come back into their bodies as feeling came back into their legs and arms. One of the common after effects of this technique is the sensation of tingly fingers; you could see them gesturing as if playing with imaginary fairy dust. It was so rewarding because it so obviously brought them a balance between body and mind.

JUHL: So you got us embodied in a big way. It was fabulous. But what's the goal, and can you connect it to gender theory?

BARBARA: My whole mission is to get people to feel—to get people to step into their bodies and feel. When people are cut off from their bodies, their heads don't work. They produce intellectual spins without any grounding. When I have a discussion with someone I can always tell if they are really embodying what they think or if it's only a theory. If it's only a theory to them, I get bored and sleepy. But if they're embodying a theory that has gone into the body and become a belief—well, that's what we mean when we say someone is walking their talk. No matter how big or academic the words they use, you're absolutely riveted by what they're saying because it's become an embodied belief. It's no longer a theory.

JUHL: What do you observe about gender in those situations?

BARBARA: In the energy work that I do in universities, it disappears. It's why I called it "gender-free" orgasm. Gender is so pervasive, right? It has its specific place in sex, in school, in activities, in the workplace, in how you behave, and how you don't behave. But when we're all reduced to just breath and life force energy, gender disappears. So men have the same reaction women do, and women have the same reaction men do. When people finish the gender-free orgasm, they move differently, they treat each other differently. The men get softer and the women get stronger. Everybody winds up in essentially the same gender-free space. Hopefully the exercise helps them to drop their social and sexual barriers around what they're supposed to be as men and women.

JUHL: Does it happen differently in different groups?

BARBARA: There is a remarkable similarity when anyone drops into their body more deeply. I think everybody is asking the same question: I know there's something more out there; how do I let go and find it? How do I let go and find god? How do I let go and find orgasms? How do I let go and find wisdom? Creativity? Love?

JUHL: Since I participated in the gender-free orgasm workshop, I didn't see all the reactions people had while they were in the midst of it. Can you describe what happens?

BARBARA: Some people laugh and some people cry. Sometimes they get a flash of a sad experience. Other times fairies come to visit them and they giggle. Many people have a rolling experience of giggles, then tears, giggles, then tears. Often people are crying and laughing at the same time. The gender-free orgasm introduces people to the "totality of possibilities." That's a Science of Mind term. I just love the phrase. In the intense, augmented, heightened feeling state of a gender-free orgasm, you can dip your toe into the ocean of the totality of possibilities. Suddenly more things become possible. People open up and think thoughts they haven't thought before. Or make art that they couldn't conceive of before. Or make love in a way they could not conceive of before. It's all creative.

JUHL: It did seem creative and all about possibilities. It was an amazing embodying experience. Can you describe other workshops you do, and is the goal about embodiment the same?

BARBARA: The work I do in universities with Kate is usually performative entertainment pieces that get people to think about feeling. I want to encourage people to think about the possibilities of feeling differently, or feeling more, or even just to consider that feeling is important. Whether those feelings are of a psychic, intuitive, or sexual nature, any kind of feeling is important. Allowing students access to their emotions and their intuitive knowing really unleashes their true brilliance. Nothing I learned in college has been one ounce of use to me, but I remember specific cases in which my inner spirit—my intuitive knowing—was sparked by a particular professor on a particular subject, and that's what's still with me. I have never retained anything that some professor told me I must learn because it was important.

JUHL: The garbage in, garbage out stuff. The banking system of education.

BARBARA: Yes. The only good reason to be a student is to learn how your brain works and find some fun ways you might want to use it in your lifetime. I try to introduce people to their own intuitive, powerful, feel-good self. When we do something that feels good, we want to do more of it. It's those choices that make our lives all that they can be.

JUHL: Right. And someone could get really jazzed about really complex theory in a philosophy class. Do you think they get jazzed about it because they get it in their bodies as well?

BARBARA: Yes. They feel the truth and the logic of theory in their bodies. It's like a zing or a tingle or a yummy feeling in the pit of the stomach. Everyone has their own physical "Oh, yes!" signal.

JUHL: I'm interested in feminist pedagogy. Ways of teaching that deal with gender and justice and being non-hierarchical in the classroom and helping students come to conclusions on their own. In getting students to feel the logic or sense of intellectual issues, you're doing that, aren't you?

BARBARA: Yes. I try to do exactly that. I try to give people experiences that let them come to their own conclusions. I also encourage them not to get attached to the system I used to get them there. I really make a point–a career even–of fucking with the standard order of whatever I'm teaching. If I teach a breath orgasm one way, I'm going to be sure to encourage people to play around with it. Experiment. See what else you can do. I don't want people to walk out having grabbed onto yet another belief that there is only one right way to do something. Because it's that kind of thinking that causes intolerance and hierarchy and fundamentalism.

JUHL: What have you learned from your students about gender? You talked a little bit about that and I'm interested in the embodiment of power, in that you can actually see it on the body. Do you see anything more complex in terms of gender?

BARBARA: No. I try not to see gender as complex at all. I see gender as a rushing river–you can't dip your toe in the same place in the river twice. Gender, as we usually think of it, is a very narrow concept largely created by society. Gender is actually very fluid and much broader than that. In terms of conscious sexuality, it makes no difference whether someone is male, female, transgender, dual-gender, homosexual, heterosexual, or multi-sexual. The more work I do, the less important these differences are.

JUHL: What kinds of reactions have you had from individuals after a workshop? In my experience of doing the no-gender orgasm, it seemed while it was happening that a community was being created.

BARBARA: Yes. In that room in your school, it was.

JUHL: And we were really close together because it was a small room.

BARBARA: Yes, and it's also a reasonably small college, it's not a huge university where people who've never seen each other before gathered together to try the exercise. Although sometimes that's a good thing. Sometimes it's really freeing when nobody knows anybody. But usually it's good when there's some sense of community like this. I know there was a mix of students, including lots of feminist studies students, but there were also theatre students. Students of the arts are often more willing to embrace emotional or experimental exercises.

JUHL: What about when you do the No-Gender Walk? Did you think that was effective at Southwestern? I participated, so I wasn't watching.

BARBARA: Katie?

KATE: I thought the Gender Walk worked. When we did it at Southwestern, did we line them up around the room, most masculine to most feminine? I ask that everyone line up around the room so that a more masculine person is on their left, and a more feminine person is on their right. They do that. Then we go through the walk and then I have them line up again in their new genders, and of course positions have changed.[1] And then I say, okay, now get back to the gender you began with...there's always ten to fifteen percent of people who've really changed. They preferred the gender they became to the gender they began with.

JUHL: No you didn't do that, but I'm gonna try it!

NOTES

[1] Directions for the Gender Walk exercise are in Bornstein, Kate. *My Gender Workbook,* New York: Routledge, 1998: 233-237.

3 ENGAGING COMMUNITY

In this final section, authors address the ways in which the relationships and structures of community inform teaching practices. Engaging communities is, for feminist teachers, often a difficult process because feminism itself is fundamentally committed to recognizing and respecting differences. On one hand, that concern for gender and justice in teaching can lead students and teachers alike to enter the process with utopian ideas about compassion and care and an expectation of finding in that feminist classroom a safe place. On the other hand, that very openness to difference can increase the likelihood of conflict, and the attempt to create "safe space" for productive work must become a process of dealing with that conflict. In this kind of environment, teaching practices must take into account that difference must be dealt with through active listening that honors individual and collective voices from a variety of locations and identity positions.

In her essay "In Search of Beloved Community," Ann Elizabeth Armstrong describes a collaborative performance project she created with students at Miami University of Ohio entitled "Walk With Me: Freedom Summer Training at Western College Campus." Situated at an original site where activists trained for the Mississippi Summer Project of 1964, also known as Freedom Summer, the tour invites participants to witness a retelling of these events, moving them toward deep reflection that disrupts personal, historical, contextual, and institutional assumptions and bonding them in a temporary community of engaged witnesses. The tour explores how participants are implicated within local and national history and asks them to assume the role of ally in the fight for social justice.

Paul Jackson, in collaboration with Joan McCarty, in "Performing Spelman: Theatre, Warrior Women, and a Dramaturgy of Liberation" similarly engages with history by examining the development of an academic theatre department at the historically Black Spelman College for women in Atlanta, Georgia. Jackson writes what he calls a "talking essay," which constitutes a conversation among the voices of various community members—administrators, teachers, students, alumnae, and audience members—all involved in the development of theatre at Spelman. Through these voices, he also points out the ways the department "weathered and fostered change" and the ways it "mirrored, to a large extent, connections to the roles of African American women in society in general and in theatre in particular" (226). Through these histories, we see how the connections and relationships are generated by educational performance projects.

Rebecca Schneider in "Playing it Street" walks her readers through a "palimpsest" of her experiences as a teacher who makes the streets her classroom. Echoing Armstrong and Jackson's reflections on activism and historical perspective, Schneider imagines the site of teaching as "the space between the stage, the page, and the street." She invokes Elizabeth Freeman's notion of "temporal drag" as she narrates the evolution of her teaching practices that frequently provoked controversy. By "playing it street," Schneider takes her students into communities to incite rebellion but winds up examining her own and her students' connection to phenomena as diverse as sexual harassment, racism, religious ritual, ethnicity and whiteness, and transgender identity. Such teaching strategies upset the comfort level of assumed frameworks of knowledge and expose the differences among her students as they engage in street performance and classroom discussion.

Actual Lives is a theatre company that focuses on the performance of personal narratives of people with disabilities. The group claims disability in radical ways, refusing to portray disabled people as "good crips," relegated to the private sphere where asexual, modest, apologetic behavior is expected. In "The Actual Lives Performance Project," Chris Strickling describes the intersection of diversity, accommodation, and collaboration as a pedagogy in her work with the company. She explores the complicated layers of differences that include both visible and invisible disability, racial diversity, and class differences among members of the company. Collaboration and community building exists on multiple levels: from the work of the group facilitators, to performers helping each other develop and rehearse their pieces, to the involvement of non-disabled volunteers. Confronting the material constraints that prevent communication and collaboration, the artistic, social and political are joined together in a pedagogy of accommodation that literally reconfigures the physical site of theatre making. By making their presence known through theatre, Actual Lives has created activism within the Austin, Texas theatre community.

Jo Beth Gonzalez engages feminist pedagogies in her high school theatre classes, facilitating community-building among her students, within her institution, and with audience members that include parents. Using autobiographical writing, Gonzalez's students create performances that often transgress high school policies and curricular boundaries, dealing with topics such as teen incarceration, suicide, agnosticism, stereotypes, and death. Through group collaboration, Gonzalez downplays her own authority, allowing students to make their own choices and self-censor if censorship is necessary. She compares her classroom to a "fragile bubble" where bonding among students about the difficult issues of teen-age life flourishes dangerously and precariously in the context of forming crucial and necessary coalition among students, parents, teachers, and administrators who make this space possible.

Norma Bowles is the Artistic Director of Fringe Benefits, a Los Angeles-based theatre company dedicated to working with youth to create theatre that allows them to articulate their own needs and concerns. The company's process, in ways similar to Gonzalez's, involves a well-developed balance between flexibility and structure that makes writing plays with groups of youth, parents, administrators, counselors, and other community members possible, and politically efficacious. The company engages a complex dance between creating work narrowly focused on particular activist goals, identity issues or work that takes a comprehensive view of all "isms" and the relationships between them. In this interview with Ann Elizabeth Armstrong, Bowles says that she is often overwhelmed by the high risks and high stakes participants are willing to take on and the ways in which process opens up important avenues for social change.

Feminist theatre pedagogy used to create theatre for social change engages many levels of community. When dealing with differences among individuals in communities, learning happens in multiple directions–from teachers to students, students to teachers, artists to students, community members to students and community members to artists. Coalitions are possible when participants are empowered through their experience of empathy, by participating in the development of theatre, by innovating projects in the streets of their communities, and writing, improvising, and performing together. However, as all the writers in this section demonstrate, engaging community does not always mean engendering change. Most of the time, groups who engage theatre through community structures learn that they must be vigilant about a rigorous commitment to building relationships before that work in community is viable. The possibilities for successful activism with groups of diverse individuals are always fraught, never comfortable, and inevitably involve a lot of painstaking work and carefully crafted pedagogies.

IN SEARCH OF THE BELOVED COMMUNITY
ENGAGING AGENTS OF CHANGE THROUGH FREEDOM SUMMER 1964
Ann Elizabeth Armstrong

Does my pedagogy come from a place of connectedness in me so it can evoke in my students those connections that make learning possible?

−Parker Palmer[1]

Power-over is linked to domination and control; power-from-within is linked to the mysteries that awaken our deepest abilities and potential. Power-with is social power, the influence we wield among equals.

−Starhawk[2]

Any time you continue to carry on the same kind of organization that you say you are fighting against, you can't prove to me that you have made any change in your thinking.

−Ella Baker[3]

Anti-racist feminist educators continue to wrestle with the deep effects of white supremacy on their students and the institutionalized structures that perpetuate it. bell hooks plainly states the urgency: "All people of color who suffer racial exploitation and oppression know that white supremacy will not end until racist white people change" (57). Despite the efforts of anti-racist individuals, institutional structures that emanate from a history of racism seem to be resistant or unbearably slow to change. As tuitions have risen and affirmative action policies have been eroded, multicultural curricula have had a limited impact on the quest to create communities of learning that possess and acknowledge deep levels of diversity.[4] In looking at our individual classroom pedagogies and our isolated artistic endeavors, we must broaden the frame of analysis to consider historical, contextual and institutional assumptions. This means a constant awareness of how the micro-practices of interpersonal dialogue and embodied ways of knowing each other can provide an impetus for structural change. Could it be possible to create a movement in which our students participate in a process that influences structural changes within our universities? By thinking about a grassroots strategy that puts our pedagogy and our art in dialogue with history and institutional structures, the effort to address white privilege and to create allies in the struggle for social justice demands that we maintain an expanded consciousness that sees individual interactions as embedded within the larger context of a broad movement.

In June of 1964, the Mississippi Summer Project (now known as "Freedom Summer") brought both black and white college student volunteers to Western College for Women in Oxford, Ohio. Students came from all over the country for training before going to Mississippi to participate in various actions there. "Walk With Me: Freedom Summer Training at Western College Campus" is a 45-minute interactive presentation that takes place on a part of Miami University's campus that was once Western College. Small groups of 5-25 students, professors, or community members are led by two student guides on a site-specific, interactive tour that re-tells stories, re-traces the campus landscape, and re-enacts moments of conflict that occurred there in June 1964.

This essay will look at how the theatrical experience of the walking tour can transport students outside of their comfortable frameworks, challenge their assumptions, and deploy a radical empathy that connects them to the larger canvas of history, specifically, the events of Freedom Summer. Since the tour represents only a micro-practice and attempt at individual change, I broaden and complicate this analysis by relying upon methods within the field of community-based theatre, which have assisted me in placing the individual interactions of the walking tour within a larger, historical context. The impulse to re-enact, re-enter, and re-interpret this local connection to civil rights history is guided by an arts-based pedagogy that connects past to present. In short, theatre becomes the vehicle that transports students to other times and locations, all the while making an urgent connection to our present moment.[5]

These methods have also allowed me to consider the walking tour as part of a much larger, interdisciplinary project that seeks to transform an entire institution. Only by seeing theatrical work in relationship to its community will activist theatre educators be able to sustain the vitality of our art and measure the efficacy of our work. Scholars like Jill Dolan have noted that too often those in other disciplines expect theatre to work in service to their intellectual endeavors (Dolan, "Rehearsing" 1). At Miami University, however, there is an institution-wide project, "Finding Freedom Summer," that frames the walking tour, (which is centered in the Department of Theatre) in collaboration with other disciplines.

Because I come from the Department of Theatre, principles of collaboration and community organizing (as they are uniquely developed in theatre practices) drive the walking tour and "Finding Freedom Summer" project. Educational activist Parker Palmer calls for educators to see themselves as "community organizers" ("The New Professional"). Palmer says that in order to confront the "sicknesses" of our institutions, which creates "deformations of the spirit" we need to construct "truth telling" spaces that will build a "circle of trust" and allow individuals to gather around a vision to create a "cadre of

change agents." Palmer is specifically referring to alienating practices such as
the tenure process and other administrative and structural procedures that foreclose the possibilities for maintaining communication, feedback, and full ownership or engagement within multiple levels of the campus community. Palmer
self-consciously draws his rhetoric from his own experiences as a white man
involved in the civil rights movement ("truth telling" echoes James Forman's
famous statement that SNCC fostered a "band of brothers and sisters in a circle
of trust").

Palmer's "truth telling" spaces are exactly what community-based theatre
artists construct through story circles, participatory rituals, local mythologizing,
and spaces for dialogic interaction. John O'Neal, co-founder of Free Southern
Theatre, member of the Student Nonviolent Coordinating Committee (SNCC),
and staff member for the Mississippi Summer Project, is a significant figure who
developed such "truth telling" methodologies during the civil rights movement
using theatre as a means for dialogue to empower the grassroots activists
involved.[6] Indeed, the feminist movement and feminist pedagogy owe much of
their genealogy to the civil rights movement's tradition of both community
organizing and storytelling. Barbara Ransby explains in her biography of Ella
Baker, a founder of SNCC and mentor to its leaders, that Baker's non-hierarchical approach, which valued reciprocal learning and self-knowledge within a
collective process, prefigured both critical pedagogy and feminist pedagogy
(357-375).[7] Recent scholarship on second wave feminism further explores how
the methodologies of consciousness-raising were specifically influenced by the
strategies of the Mississippi Summer Project in 1964.[8]

With this genealogy in mind, Freedom Summer becomes an important historical moment for both second wave feminism and American grassroots theatre. I draw my inspiration from the pedagogical models and methods forged
during Freedom Summer, allowing it to guide the content, form, and philosophical values of my own project. Like the multifaceted strategy of Freedom
Summer, the walking tour is only one among many sustained and engaged conversations at the university that strive to empower a "cadre of change agents"
and work to confront all levels of structural organization, one that includes students, faculty, and administration in working for community change.

Freedom Summer is a particularly important historical inspiration for anti-
racist feminist educators for many reasons. A collaborative movement between
members of SNCC and other civil rights organizations, it was a complex
endeavor, led by college students, to bring national attention to the extreme
effects of white supremacy in Mississippi. During the summer of 1964, between
800 and 1000 students who were mostly white and privileged came to
Mississippi to register blacks to vote, teach black youth in "freedom schools,"
and engage in other forms of community development. A controversial strategy
that was critiqued by many both inside and outside the movement, Freedom
Summer was deemed a failure in its immediate aftermath. Though Lyndon B.

Johnson signed the Civil Rights Act later that summer, few blacks were regis-
tered to vote in Mississippi as a result of students' efforts, and events at the
August 1964 Democratic Convention, in which the integrated Mississippi
Freedom Democratic Party was denied admission, seemed to suggest that the
white power structure would not change. Despite the enormous publicity from
the brutal deaths of three Freedom Summer activists, Michael Schwerner,
James Chaney, and Andrew Goodman,[9] the American political system refused
to acknowledge the depth of institutionalized white supremacy. SNCC activists
had held out the hope that if only the nation knew the extent of the problem,
"the system would listen, the system would respond" (Lewis qtd. in hooks, 51-
52). But, as John Lewis explains, "Now, for the first time, we had made our way
to the center of the system. We had played by the rules, done everything we
were supposed to do...had arrived at the doorstep and found the door
slammed in our face." (qtd. in hooks, 51-52). The dream of the "beloved community," the non-violent transformation into a community of justice and equality, seemed lost.

As critical distance from the events have broadened the frame, the truly
radical aspects of Freedom Summer emerge. While the ideals of a "beloved
community" seemed lost in the short term, in the long term, individuals of privilege were transformed into allies who went on to fight for social justice and
lead other movements.[10] Historical accounts of events that summer also reveal
the tremendous tension generated at the intersection of not just race, but also
sexuality, gender, and class. The passionate emotional undercurrents that produced a "freedom high" simultaneously produced a deeper, revealing look at
the depths and structures of American racism. When one imagines the social
conditions of 1964 and then imagines white students from Yale and Stanford
living with, learning from, and supporting poor rural African Americans in
Mississippi, one only begins to glimpse how this radical collision of worlds challenged fundamental assumptions and transformed students and community
members into agents.[11]

The temporary enactment of a kind of "beloved community," despite its
being fraught with many tensions, conflicts, and anxieties, left an important
imprint on the Freedom Summer volunteers. It is important to acknowledge the
very real pain and dislocation white Freedom Summer volunteers experienced
when confronting (and being confronted with) their white guilt, their tendencies
toward paternalism, and their own implication within oppressive systems.[12]
Though many lacked networks to channel this tremendous emotional energy
generated by the conflicts they experienced that summer, history traces the
reverberations caused by the collision of worlds that took place in Mississippi
in 1964. Antonio Gramsci writes, "The starting point of critical elaboration is
'knowing thyself' as a product of the historical process...[w]hich has deposited
in you an infinity of traces, without leaving an inventory" (qtd. in Fishman and
McCarthy, 347). Through the Freedom Summer walking tour, I hope to make

an inventory of such traces visible to students, with the possibility of creating a collision of worlds that might make some reverberations of its own.

Freedom Summer is an important historical narrative and pedagogical inspiration to me for other reasons too. First, it has a direct connection to my local campus at Miami University, where I currently teach theatre. The training of all the summer volunteers actually took place at Western College for Women in Oxford, Ohio, which was later purchased by Miami University in 1974.[13] Though Miami University avoided all associations with Freedom Summer at the time, since 2000, it has been motivated to reclaim the history belonging to Western College for Women as it struggles to truly diversify its campus and curriculum. While this appropriation of a historical narrative is clearly problematic, the immediacy of the local connection to civil rights history creates a palpable means of consciousness-raising for the mostly white and privileged students at Miami, who lack an urgent and immediate sense of the need for social change. Second, the multifaceted strategy of Freedom Summer engaged many aspects of social life, including the arts. Black activists consciously created "truth telling" spaces through theatre, storytelling, and freedom songs that allowed a space for white students to enter into the movement, and these art forms reveal the spiritual dimensions of the movement.[14] The spiritual energy channeled by the artistic communion of these mostly white volunteers and black activist leaders reflects a burning desire to be a part of a visionary, interracial coalition.

Creating opportunities for bonding, radical empathy, and spaces for genuine dialogue, the emotional energy of the Freedom Summer volunteers drove a collective vision, daring students to see themselves within a broad framework. In theorizing the conditions necessary to engage cross-racial dialogue, Mark McPhail and Karen Dace use the term "implicature." Implicature demonstrates how empathy and bonding work as a bridge to expose that "our separateness [is an] illusion, and that *in reality*, we are all essentially implicated in each other" (440). Connecting politics, activism, spirituality, mind, and body, Starhawk describes a similar relationship, which she terms "power-with," which is "...more subtle, more fluid and fragile than authority. It is dependent on personal responsibility, on our own creativity and daring and on the willingness of others to respond" (8-9). While remaining critical of the potential traps in confronting white privilege, I am exploring how a theatrical experience can summon strong inner forces such as those Starhawk evokes, while balancing them with a critical understanding of one's position within the power structure and one's relation to others.

"WALK WITH ME": FREEDOM SUMMER TRAINING AT WESTERN COLLEGE CAMPUS

Miami University is a public liberal arts university in Southwestern Ohio, designated as one of the "public ivies." With only 8.9% ethnic minorities (3.8% African American), the university is overwhelmingly white ("Diversity Facts").

In the late 1990s, the campus began to aggressively address questions of diversity and multiculturalism by establishing various offices, programming, and curricula. Despite these efforts, the student body remains homogenous and the campus struggles with several issues related to diversity: the geographical location of the institution within a rural white community, a student body drawn primarily from Ohio's suburbs, and an alumni base without diversity, among others. With an average household income above $200,000 per year, this student body, sometimes pejoratively described as "J.Crew U," suffers from economic as well as racial homogeneity. Thus, programmatic changes have occurred at the institutional level without any corresponding "real life" connection for students. My impression, from talking to students and from participating in various workshops on diversity, is that most students, while not necessarily "opposed" to multiculturalism, feel that it is "rammed down their throats" and sense no urgent need for such a focus. This has created an enormous gulf between students, who have little context for valuing diversity, and faculty, who are (in most areas) striving to diversify curricula. Dialogue about these difficult issues has been stymied by this division between students and the faculty and administration, forcing the institution to consider new pedagogies and strategies that create a deeper sense of dialogue.

The "Walk with Me" tour is one potential strategy. The tour, which I created collaboratively with six Miami University students,[15] debuted in September 2004, just before a fortieth reunion of the historic Freedom Summer training on the Miami campus that hosted SNCC members, Mississippi residents, Freedom Summer volunteers, and other participants. The tour was originally created as an effort to introduce this history to students in preparation for their interaction with conference attendees, but it has continued since then, offered on request mostly to professors who bring their classes.[16] Much of the Western College campus where the 1964 training took place remains intact, so the tour begins in a dormitory where participants stayed, moves to the auditorium where training took place, and concludes at the Freedom Summer Memorial, an amphitheatre made of stones inscribed with headlines from events that summer. Much of the text for the tour script comes directly from the letters, journals, and oral histories of the college students who participated in Freedom Summer.

The tour begins with two tour guides addressing participants as if they have just arrived for orientation to the Mississippi Summer Project. They explain the purpose and urgency of the project, provide everyone with the actual pamphlet that was used for recruiting, and explain, "Don't forget, we need contact information for your next of kin, your congressional representatives, and any newspapers or media outlets in your hometown. We also need $150 bail money up front" ("Walk with Me" 4). After participants are oriented to the facilities and schedule, they move to a porch where guides note the racial tension that existed among the Summer Project staff and volunteers. Tour participants are invited to read notecards that reveal personal information about the volunteers. Each card begins with, "I come from..." and reveals various marks of identity for each of those volunteers: "I come from Sunday brunch, new cars, white linen and china...the brilliant hallways of Berkeley," "I come from generations of immigrants starting on the Lower East Side, Brooklyn Bridges, Jewelry Shops," "I come from pig's feet eatin' folks walkin' to corner stores with no shoes on" ("Walk with Me" 1, 7).[17] Participants are then moved across a field as they are barraged by the tour guide/trainers with the details of non-violent training: "If you're caught from behind, go limp.... Watch for cars without plates...and cops without badges" (8). These lines reiterate the different physical positions and physical responses that volunteers rehearsed on the lawn in order to prepare for confrontations with Mississippi police.

Once tour participants arrive at a stone bridge, the guides lead them through a trust exercise. Tour participants are asked to form a line with their eyes closed and their hands on each other's shoulders as they cross the bridge while the guides recount the volunteers' struggles with their internalized racism and ethical commitment to the project: "I was raised to distrust, raised to hate.... My family had a maid; she called me 'miss,' even when I was a child" ("Walk with Me" 10). After the group reaches the end of the bridge, tour participants form a circle in the grass and, after a moment of silence, open their eyes while the tour guides tell stories of specific experiences that created trust among the 1964 volunteers and staff. Guides recount the story of a film clip that was shown depicting a "slovenly fat white southern man" ("Walk with Me" 11) who blocked the courthouse door so that blacks could not register to vote. When the clip was shown, white volunteers began to laugh in disbelief, disrupting the training session. Several black SNCC staff, who were also Mississippi residents, stormed out, thinking, "These kids...laughing just proved how much education the volunteers really needed" (11). Later, when explaining why they had left, the SNCC staff revealed the extent of such violent realities in their everyday lives, and white volunteers were forced to confront their guilt and begin to be more honest about their fears: "The tension diffused, and everything came out into the open" (11). When volunteers understood what was at stake and internalized the gravity of the project, "The trust had been built. A bridge had been crossed" (11). By symbolizing this episode from the Freedom Summer training, the "bridge exercise" of the tour both *dis*orients and builds trust among tour participants.

Tour participants next move to the auditorium where trainees learned about conditions in Mississippi, legal issues, and prepared to teach Freedom Schools. One episode re-enacts the students' dismay when John Doar, deputy chief of the Department of Justice's Civil Rights division, explained that they would receive no federal protection while in Mississippi that summer. During the second week of training, Bob Moses, SNCC field secretary and leader of the project, announced, in the same auditorium, that their fellow workers, Schwerner, Chaney, and Goodman, who had left Western College two days earlier, were missing and presumed dead. Volunteers were left with the decision of whether to go to Mississippi or not. At this point, tour guides provide a coda to the narrative by bringing the discussion back to the present day, reminding participants of a cross burning that took place in Southwest Ohio in 2004 and the 2005 conviction of Edgar Ray Killen, an accomplice to Schwerner, Chaney, and Goodman's murders. Accompanied by a recording of the song "Freedom Is a Constant Struggle," the tour continues to a Freedom Summer memorial that commemorates the lives of the three men (and others) who lost their lives in the struggle for civil rights. After a brief reading of names of those lost in the struggle and moments of silence, tour guides begin a discussion with tour participants. Among the questions they ask participants are: Did you know about Freedom Summer before you took the tour? What are the important civil rights issues we're dealing with today? Do you think something like Freedom Summer could happen today? Would you have gone if you had been in their position? How do you think your parents would have reacted? Have you ever had to struggle to uphold a personal belief or ideal through your actions?

THE IMPORTANCE OF HISTORY AND PROBLEMS IN CONFRONTING WHITE PRIVILEGE

Teachers face many potential problems when confronting white privilege in the classroom. Often, students' strong emotional reactions and resistances make such work seem counterproductive. The walking tour is my attempt to find an effective way of evoking and reading these responses and to discover a means to translate them into active dialogue and student empowerment. I have drawn on the work of various scholars and educators from critical race studies, feminist theory, dialogue studies, and community-based theatre, as well as historians of the civil rights movement, in order to delineate and analyze the following issues, which I see as the major barriers to creating meaningful anti-racist curricula aimed primarily at white students: (1) white guilt that results in paralysis and lack of agency; (2) superficial empathy that leads to paternalism and a colonial mentality; (3) pleas of "color blindness" and a lack of historical context that stifles dialogue; (4) an abstract, theoretical notion of race that doesn't translate into embodied practices and social relations; (5) the fetishization and appropriation of the experiences and/or cultures of people of color; (6) lack of consciousness of white teachers or authority figures who inadvertently leave biases unexamined; and (7) students' resistance to conflict and contradiction, particularly at the idea of intersecting, multiple identities.[18]

An embodied, participatory performance like the Freedom Summer walking tour addresses these issues, utilizing pedagogical strategies that validate the role of personal experience while at the same time produce a structural analysis of systems of oppression and create relationships and networks. One key factor in this performative strategy is an analysis of identification and empathy that allows students to see themselves within the power structure and connect to a visceral sense of urgency. Performance is an ideal strategy for moving students from passive feelings of guilt into an active anti-racist role. Not only does a performance such as the walking tour define and identify this role and its boundaries, it also calls for emotional and spiritual engagement on the part of participants. In their article "Subverting Whiteness: Pedagogy at the Crossroads of Performance, Culture, and Politics," John Warren and Deanna Fassett point out that the "discomfort and vulnerability" that white students experience during these kinds of performative explorations is a crucial step toward self-realization and action, and should be "embrace[d] and celebrate[d]" (426). Warren and Fassett believe that performative exercises can allow "the residue of performance [to] stain [students'] bodies; it will remain long after they have walked out of these workshops" (426). Indeed, "Walk with Me" "stains" the bodies of its participants, imprinting them with both the social space of the campus landscape and the narratives of Freedom Summer. It is my hope that re-experiencing and re-enacting the stories of white students who have gone before them will trigger a similar commitment to social justice.[19] Certainly a 45-minute walking tour can't create a full transformation of each and every participant, but, through the tour and the discussions with faculty and peers that follow it, students are given the opportunity to repeat, echo, or integrate the experience into their own lives.

By performatively inserting students into history, the tour strives to blur boundaries between past and present, allowing students to see connections between them. Many tour participants begin with a lack of historical connection. (This lack of context speaks to why so many of them claim that we live in a "color blind" society. In other words, they claim that despite a history of racism, laws and systems have been "fixed" and now the problem, if it exists at all, is limited to backwards individuals who need to change). These students, who resist a sense of personal responsibility within the system and within history, frequently lack both an historical perspective and a sense of history's connection to the present moment. Though the distance of historical narrative should provide us with space for reflection and analysis, white students often use complex strategies of denial that limit its impact. As Mark McPhail notes, white students can't productively enter into cross-racial dialogue unless they reflect on their role within the historical narrative (212). Acknowledging a common history means acknowledging common assumptions, and, without a sense of the shared "reality" of that history of oppression, white students are poised to make naïve statements that exacerbate racial tensions. Although the Freedom Summer Walking Tour can potentially be interpreted as "merely" history, the immediacy of its historical location and identification with the Freedom Summer students who share the same age and background as participants frequently provides a jolt that forces students to recognize the violent realities of history.

As a participatory performance, the Freedom Summer walking tour offers participants the opportunity to embody the role of the anti-racist ally, potentially circumventing the paralysis resulting from white guilt or the dangerous potential for a paternalistic interpretation of the role of the anti-racist ally. While the performative dimensions of gender and whiteness have been thoroughly analyzed,[20] harnassing the performative power of allied behaviors in the struggle for social justice has tremendous potential for an anti-racist pedagogy. In her article "Interrupting the Cycle of Oppression: The Role of Allies as Agents of Change," Andrea Ayvazian provides a positive description of the role of the ally, one that is modeled by the story of Freedom Summer and evokes the performative dimensions of allied behavior. Ayvazian describes allied behavior as "...overt, consistent activity that challenges prevailing patterns of oppression, makes privileges that are so often invisible visible, and facilitates the empowerment of persons targeted by oppression.... These change agents or allies have such a powerful impact because their actions embody the values they profess: their behavior and beliefs are congruent" (598). Ayvazian also points out that allies need a community network and practice in identifying and claiming their role as ally (598); activities such as the walking tour are an ideal way to practice identifying this role in preparation for becoming one.

Once students have embraced the role of ally, other problems often emerge in their struggle to find their identity and place within an anti-racist framework. One such problem is an abstract, theoretical notion of race that doesn't translate into embodied practices and real social relations. However, the narratives of the civil rights movement and Freedom Summer themselves provide insight into this problem, and can be utilized in an anti-racist pedagogy. Like today's student who pleads that we are "color blind," many Freedom Summer volunteers had to radically revise their theoretical abstractions of race and oppression once they arrived in the South and had real-life interactions with the African Americans there. Sharing physical realities with Mississippi residents translated into a deeper social and political awareness for most Freedom Summer volunteers. Real social relationships with African Americans were also important. Many Freedom Summer volunteers who were from the northern states encountered blacks as equals and peers for the first time when they arrived, and began to ask themselves why they did not have such relationships in their own communities (a response shared by many contemporary students taking the tour). Friendships between blacks and whites during Freedom Summer usually emerged through struggles: struggles to communicate, to listen to each other, to understand one another's accents, to understand each other's values and sense of humor.[21] As Cornell West notes: "Dialogue is a form of struggle; it's not chitchat" (qtd. in McPhail 224), and these struggles, many of which are described in the walking tour, gave the abstraction of race an important sense of concreteness and embodied reality for Freedom Summer participants.

As students on the walking tour begin to internalize their connections with the people and events of the past, one of the goals of the "performance" of the

tour is that these connections will create a sense of empathy among participants. Yet in creating performances that draw upon empathy, it is important to
be wary of the dangers that are possible. The empathetic connections that arise
through identification can potentially lead to fetishizing and appropriating
African American experiences, a significant trap in confronting white racial
consciousness. Reflecting on the rocky attempts at cross-racial dialogue in feminist movements, Jean Wyatt notes the problems of appropriation, and she asks
a question those of us in feminist theatre repeatedly confront: "could identification be modulated so that one could identify with the other's perspective without usurping or distorting it?" (881).[22] Minnie Bruce Pratt explores this issue
when she describes her experience as a white woman singing in a black church:

> Sometimes we don't pretend to be the other, but we take something made
> by the other and use it for our own.... Then I understood that I was using
> Black people to weep for me, to express my sorrow at my responsibility,
> and that of my people, for their oppression; and I was mourning because I
> felt they had something I didn't, a closeness, a hope.... Finally I understood
> that I could feel sorrow during their music, and yet not confuse their sorrow
> with mine. (41)

In my previous experiences of creating performance from stories of the civil
rights movement with mostly white students, I found that they, like Pratt, fell
into this trap of appropriating the perspectives of African Americans rather
than expressing their own (Armstrong 2000). Inadvertently, the performances
we created seemed to suggest that black people had "soul" or a "community,"
while white characters were merely depicted as two-dimensional stereotypes.
The goal of my reconstruction of the narratives of Freedom Summer, however, is to explore both white *and* black experiences while keeping the complexity, context, and boundaries of identity foregrounded. As Pratt suggests,
empathy should both assist in the commitment to take on the perspective of
the "other," and acknowledge the boundaries of one's skin. Environmental
performance serves in this capacity, as viewers have to participate in their
environment as they move through the space without losing their sense of self
in the dark auditorium.

Several scholars have analyzed the role of white professors in addressing
white privilege, particularly in terms of how they might help with an analysis of
the context of oppression, and many have also written about coming to terms
with their own biases as teachers (Fishman and McCarthy; Maher and
Tetreault). Without diminishing the significant role of the professor in the classroom, I return to my problem at a university where the gulf between students'
and professors' perceptions of diversity limits professors' ability to broach the
topic. It's important to note that a "truth telling" space such as the one Parker
Palmer refers to must be a facilitated one, in which teachers are conscious of
the power dynamics in the room as they make attempts to equalize those hierarchies. The facilitator's own acknowledged biases, along with the group

dynamics, factor into a pedagogical strategy that make truth telling possible. The instructor also plays an important role in addressing conflicts, contradictions, and differences that students might otherwise gloss over. As a student-led performance, the Freedom Summer walking tour was designed to decentralize the professor, but at the same time, it was designed so that a professor could take the dialogue generated from the experience and sustain the discussion in the classroom. In examining how the micropractices of an embodied performance might translate into an opportunity to reflect upon the relationship between individuals and social structures, this becomes a particular pedagogical strategy and artistic choice. Unlike other kinds of theatrical experiences, my hope is that with this performance, professors play a role in bridging this gap between individual experience and a structural analysis of its context.

According to Megan Boler in *Feeling Power*, emotional responses are important sites through which resistance occurs. Creating spaces for students to experience their emotions (especially anger and frustration) also means that we aren't afraid to enter into emotional territory, but we must carefully consider strategies for connecting, channeling, and directing such emotion. In addressing a pedagogical strategy that confronts white privilege, I borrow explicitly from Augusto Boal's notion of the "spectactor," who is at once spectator and actor, not just voyeur but also participant. The spectactor is also fundamental to understanding how active emotional engagement as a participant is balanced by an analytical opportunity to reflect upon contexts and systems. Many educators have used Boal's techniques to achieve these goals. Lib Spry describes the potential of using Theatre of the Oppressed to work with agents of social change, particularly those with privilege, allowing them to find a vantage point from which to understand their position within the power structure (171-184).[24] Similarly, Warren and Fassett deploy Theatre of the Oppressed techniques as a way of getting students to embrace the fluidity of power, rather than being overwhelmed by static oppressive systems (421).

Performance offers not only a concrete embodied emotional experience but also an opportunity to see one's self in the context of others. Boler calls for an active form of collective witnessing as we avoid the binary traps of assigning guilt and instead take responsibility for change and re-imagine our relationship to history (168). Augusto Boal has similarly noted that the public confrontation with and enunciation of truth requires that the community take action (18-28).[25] One of the most important goals of an anti-racist performance project is that the sustained dialogue that occurs through the emotional energy of performance moves beyond merely placating white guilt to inspiring allies in social change. When this occurs, how can we then position stakeholders within our institutions that will channel this emotional energy? The walking tour reiterates the importance of a community of allies and role models, the complexity of history and its material effects, awareness of self within history, the material embodiment of race, the danger of empathy and appropriation, and the value of facilitated spaces for dialogue, all towards connecting the personal with the political. In the next section, I will offer a close reading of student responses to the tour as a way of analyzing the efficacy of these strategies.

RAISING CONSCIOUSNESS

Classes from varied disciplines such as anthropology, architecture, education, philosophy, gerontology, English, American studies and history have taken the Freedom Summer walking tour. Several professors have shared their students' informal written responses, which have provided a means of analyzing how students process the tour. I am interested in learning how the tour encourages reflections that acknowledge the emotional responses of identification and empathy, as well as reflections on students' role within the power structure. Despite the range of political consciousnesses around race and other identity issues, and various levels of knowledge about Freedom Summer, there is an interesting way in which all of the student responses I have seen vacillate between viewing the history of Freedom Summer as both close to them ("It was only 40 years ago," "It happened in my dorm") and far from them ("I can't imagine these circumstances"). While some responses reveal avoidance tactics and a clichéd gloss of the issue of race in the present, others reveal a deeper questioning of assumptions about their own actions and identities. I will look at how the tour challenged students' assumptions about history, created an embodied and visceral shock, provoked thinking about interpersonal relationships, pushed them towards analyzing the contradictions presented to them, and allowed them to see themselves as fully implicated within systems of power.[26] With further, long-term studies, I hope to learn if it did contribute to white students' understanding of themselves as agents of change.

When challenging or deepening their previous interpretations of history, students frequently express shock at new information, and sometimes this shock leads to questioning. In a small example, one student acknowledges the labor of organizing: "I was totally shocked that each student needed a will, bail money...I also did not even know there was a training process. I simply could not believe how much work and time was involved in the process." In other examples, students are shocked to learn of the degree of violence that was described in the South. However, some students begin to revise their knowledge of North/South relations, such as the student who states, "Many of the participating students were basically blacklisted because they were involved with the project. Although I feel naïve, the fact that this happened never really occurred to me. Although I did not think the North was perfect, I thought the northerners would support the effort." Similarly, another student recognizes that "The northerners may have felt the need to stand up against the students participating in Freedom Summer because they feared that the status quo in their areas might be challenged if the Freedom Summer movement gave rise to other movements." Such statements do reveal a kind of naïveté, but they also signal an important willingness to revise their conceptions of history, even gesturing to the interrelatedness of South and North in striving for a broader perspective.

While these responses reflect new ways of thinking about history, the emotional responses to the tour indicate that there is a powerful energy that initiates such reflections. Students repeatedly use the word "feel" in contexts such as, "[the tour] allowed me to get a better feel for what took place," "It's hard to explain how you feel when you realize you're in the exact place people were not that many years ago when they started changing history," "It makes me feel like I actually have a chance to make a difference in the world too." The bridge crossing and the discussion of the movie viewing, in particular, elicit strong feelings and emotional reactions: "It really took me out of my element. This forced me to feel the way that most of those college students in the Mississippi Summer Freedom Project must have felt, even if it was on a lesser scale." With these emotional responses, students move closer to the questions of "Would I have gone that summer?" and "Do I believe in anything this strongly?"

Another facet of Freedom Summer, and an objective of the tour, is the development of interpersonal connections. Creating "social capital" through these face-to-face interactions strengthens networks for activism, and further extends students' symbolic construction of community.[27] One student ponders the importance of these bonds to Freedom Summer trainees: "I think the longer they were together, the more they wanted to fight for their freedom, knowing it was also the freedom of their new friends." The following response gestures to the value of sharing the experience with classmates and how classroom community can be deepened: "One of my favorite parts of the field trip was when we walked across the bridge holding on to each other.... The fact that it was with my class, that I really do not know anyone in, also allowed me to connect with the volunteers. Many of them did not know each other, just like the students in the class, which meant they had to find a lot of trust for each other."

Responses also demonstrate an ability to analyze the contradictions surrounding messages about race and, furthermore, to see themselves as fully implicated within these systems of power. The most significant contradiction in the responses includes reconciling this local history of civil rights with the present state of diversity at the university. While several students note this relationship as incongruous (and many conflate the history of Miami with the history of Western college), one student connects both institutional responsibility and the student body's position in the lack of diversity at Miami:

> While an outsider would view the Freedom Summer Project as interesting...an insider can fully understand the bizarreness and irony of such an important part of the civil rights movement happening at this university. Miami University could be described as having the diversity of a white

> wall.... I have not encountered anyone on campus that is against integration
> and diversity, but I will say that I found most people apathetic to the whole
> concept.

This apathy is perhaps one of the more important issues the walking tour
aims to address through the emotional medium of the arts.

The walking tour creates a radical sense of empathy that causes students to
literally put themselves in the shoes of volunteers and ask, according to these
student papers, "Would I have really spent the summer this way if given the
opportunity?" "What would my parents have thought?" "It made me think
about what I'm doing with my time and whether or not the activities I am
involved in are as worthwhile as the Freedom Summer program." While such
personal self-scrutiny is important, it is also interesting how such statements
reveal students' relationship to others and to structures of power. Do they
develop a sense of "implicature" that links to an ethical vision? Do they begin
to see themselves as agents within the power structure?

The following response reveals a dawning awareness of the ways in which
white privilege has negatively influenced the writer's interpretations of the
world. Referring to the opponents to Freedom Summer, the student says:

> If these people who are not so different from me, who are perhaps similar in
> age and upbringing to my grandparents, were incapable of seeing the injus-
> tice in what they were doing, what is it that my generation, that I, cannot
> see? ...I would not want to be the snarling face on the documentary for my
> grandchildren to see in school. ...what cause, what ideal, do I hold strongly
> enough that I would willingly put up with what these others did to uphold
> it?... Am I willing to risk anything to find out and then risk more to chal-
> lenge it?... I do not think that racism could happen again in quite the same
> way...so perhaps each person's purpose is a more individual one today...
> Now what is left is the more difficult job of changing minds, opinions, and
> habits. These things only change on an individual basis, and so it seems that
> this is the basis on which we must deal and it takes no less will to do this job
> than it did to challenge things 40 years ago.

While attempting to change both individuals and structures of oppression was
an important element of Freedom Summer's strategy, this student falls back
on the question of individual change without acknowledging the relationship
of individuals to structures. However, the student's recognition of powerful
forces that prevent him/her from seeing oppression gestures to a willingness
to consider an entire shift in paradigm that might make change possible.

A response from a different student similarly recognizes how the student is
implicated within the events of Freedom Summer.

> Forty years is not that long ago! When I learned about this previously, it
> seemed so distant and removed. However, really, my parents were both
> alive during the time! My grandparents were adults. One thing that I never
> thought about before is the effect this had on their lives. It seems like a big
> deal that would influence them a lot. However, I have never heard any of
> my grandparents (or parents) discuss any memories of this time. Was there a

> lack of publicity?... Did it just not have a huge role in their lives? After all,
> they all lived in Ohio... However, I have never discussed it with any of
> them so I have no idea [if] it changed them or their attitudes at all. I cannot
> wait to discuss this with my family!

While still not quite connecting history to the present power structure, the
student's contagious enthusiasm launches a productive line of questions that
will perhaps move towards an understanding of his or her family's implicat-
edness within the history.

Questions such as "why didn't my grandparents [or parents] participate?"
appear in several other student responses. This questioning resonates with a
sense of responsibility and historical awareness that goes beyond the question
of "would I have gone?" Instead, it dares to acknowledge the possibility that
they are part of the structures of oppression that created the problem. Not surprisingly, it is a queer student who comes closest to acknowledging a sense of
"implicature": "Before students can change the unjust political and social structures, however, victims of the injustice and non-victims must mutually understand each other, and realize that at the most fundamental level, *everyone* is
affected by the structures of social injustice simply because we live in the same
environment."

INSTITUTIONAL CHANGE, FEMINIST PEDAGOGY, AND PERFORMANCE

One of the strengths and limitations of performance is its temporary and
ephemeral nature. Audiences, like communities and coalitions, exist only in
time and space, and the effectiveness of community-based performance is
determined by the extent to which it is embedded within its community, working in concert with other forces and voices that sustain it, and providing a space
to envision action for social change. The summer of 1964 was just such a fleet-
ing moment in which a "beloved community" was performed and imagined
through a comprehensive plan of activism that included at its center song,
drama, storytelling, and photography.

The arts become an important medium through which we may continue to
trace Freedom Summer's reverberations. With this in mind, the performance
"Walk with Me" is only one small component of a larger interdisciplinary project at Miami University called "Finding Freedom Summer" that has included:
(1) a conference/re-union of historic participants in Freedom Summer; (2) a lecture series and co-curricular programming around civil rights and Freedom
Summer; (3) curricula surrounding Freedom Summer; (4) development of an
archive that includes oral histories from Freedom Summer; and (5) the development of a full-length play about the Freedom Summer training at Western
College for Women.[28] This multi-year, multi-phased project capitalizes on the
arts as a catalyst for discussion, a space for reflection, and as a tangible process
that can guide our explorations. But will it also, for example, lead to significant
changes in minority recruiting practices, scholarships for minority students, and

changes to the social structures of campus life that make it a hostile environment for minority students? I am haunted by Ella Baker's admonition: "Anytime you continue to carry on the same kind of organization that you say you are fighting against, you can't prove to me that you have made any change in your thinking" (qtd. in Ransby 369). Our project, "Finding Freedom Summer," is fraught with many of the same issues of identity politics that overwhelmed participants of Freedom Summer, albeit in a different context. The philosophical premises of SNCC leadership was non-hierarchical, and it was based upon the need to empower black leadership, specifically at the grassroots so that people would participate in their own struggles. This project, in a predominantly white institution, under white leadership,[29] can't aim to truly create cross-racial dialogue or coalitions with the very few minorities that are present. Can we, however, create an atmosphere that values social justice? What are the dangers of confronting white privilege without consistently and regularly also engaging in cross-racial dialogue?

If my university can't immediately transform our economic and ideological structures that keep it segregated, what is the value of imagining the possibility of cross-racial dialogue through dramatizing this history? Does it become wishful thinking? The appropriation of other's histories/narratives? Does it merely placate the white guilt of this institution? How can the experience of the historical story of Freedom Summer generate emotion, dialogue, and sustain itself to turn into real action, social justice, and reverberate as institutional change? I ask these questions while the project is in progress, mid-stream, and during an enormous sea of change in the institution's leadership. How can introspection and retrospection through historical narrative help us see the self within systems of oppression? Perhaps the role of the project is to foreground such questions. However, another role of the project is to break down barriers that create the illusion that we are isolated. Can new relationships tear down those barriers? For example, in one tangible measure, a scholarship program for students in Bob Moses' Algebra Project has been created by the university.[30] Perhaps such relationships between the university and organizations outside it provide further impetus in a movement toward real institutional change.[31]

In asking how an emotional outcry can reverberate to change an institution, I have etched in my memory the September 2004 conference/reunion of Freedom Summer participants. I was viscerally moved by the convergence of people, place, and history as I watched the veterans of Freedom Summer passionately challenge students to embrace the struggles of the present. In a memorial service, a middle-aged white man timidly asked, "Can we sing 'We Shall Overcome' now?" Without a reply, all of the veterans of Freedom Summer in the audience responded, jumping to their feet to cross arms and exuberantly sing. The experiences of singing freedom songs was a fundamental part of the Freedom Summer training that occurred at Western College, and an important ritual that invited white students into the movement. The experiences of singing with each other and in the black churches in Mississippi instilled a profound "communitas" that dissolved boundaries and became the emotional engine of the movement. It is significant that despite the heated battles and debates of the SNCC meetings, the ritual of singing that ended each gathering sustained activists and their relationships with each other for a period of time.

Though I reflect upon Minnie Bruce Pratt's description and the dangers of losing sight of one's self in the moment, it is clear that much of the movement's success rested upon this collective vision to be a part of something much larger than one's self. Chude Pam Parker Allen, a Freedom Summer volunteer, returned to the Miami campus for a lecture series in September 2005. She shared the deep pain that she had experienced when she returned to her white suburban community after Freedom Summer and struggled in isolation to find her path towards social justice. Allen conjured the experience of singing in Mississippi, "...the thin brown-skinned man at the front of the church has told the audience, 'If you can't reach the note, sing louder!' and I am singing, 'Oh, freedom!' At the top of my lungs" (Allen). And with the passion of a twenty year old, the sixty-year-old Allen embraces the song in all of her awkwardness, missing every single note of the tune, but completely at ease with her white identity as she challenges students to embrace the struggle for social justice with her. Allen performs with a consciousness of her own identity, inviting other white students to join her. Calling a full connection between spirit, mind, and body, the performance reverberates into passionate conversation that engages past, present, and future. The "truth telling" spaces begin to multiply as such connections become realized.

I would like to thank my Miami University colleagues Mark McPhail, Tom Dutton, Mary Jane Berman, and Paul Jackson for their significant support and insights in the development of this article.

NOTES

[1] Palmer, "The Quest for Community" 187.

[2] Starhawk 9.

[3] Ransby 369.

[4] See, for example, Martin; Howell and Tuitt; and McLaren for discussions of how such trends impact both policy and pedagogy.

[5] For this insight, I want to thank my colleague in the Architecture Department, Tom Dutton, who noted how this pedagogy complements other efforts to physically get students out of familiar territory and encounter difference. Jill Dolan makes a similar observation: "University theater, in particular, has the potential to teach spectators how to be moved by difference, to encourage them to experience emotion not as acquiescent, but as passionate, and motivating toward social change" (*Geographies* 84).

[6] John O'Neal is currently the artistic director of Junebug Productions, Inc., a theatre company that works with community organizers and uses story circle methods to advance community activism. For more about John O'Neal's methods and work, see Cohen Cruz's *Local Acts: Community-Based Theatre in the Unites States* and Bean's *A Sourcebook for African-American Performance.*

[7] Ransby traces Baker's work as an "organic intellectual" who fostered her philosophies first within a community of black women in her father's church and later encountered socialist philosophies in her work as an educator and union organizer (74-75). Though Baker's educational and activist philosophies share much in common with Freire and Gramsci's work (which is influenced by a Marxist tradition that combines education with activism to create a bottom-up approach to knowledge and which emphasized the collective over individual leadership [359]), it is important to underline the African American origin of Baker's work.

[8] Doug McAdam notes that Kathie Sarachild, a Mississippi Summer Project volunteer, is widely credited with promulgating methods of "consciousness raising" (185), and Kathy Weiler specifically looks at the connection between Sarachild's formulation of consciousness-raising and feminist pedagogy. McAdam also writes that the premise of Freedom Schools (created in response to Ella Baker's philosophies) influenced the feminist consciousness of many of the women working on the Mississippi Summer project (185). Recent scholarship by Jean Wyatt and Wine Breines further traces these important links between civil rights and feminism.

[9] Michael Schwerner, James Chaney, and Andrew Goodman left the training session at the campus in Oxford, Ohio, earlier than other volunteers in order to investigate a church burning in Neshoba County, Mississippi. They were arrested for speeding by local police and were held until the Klu Klux Klan assembled a lynch party. Once released from jail, the three were brutally murdered and buried in an earthen dam, where their bodies were found later that summer.

[10] Doug McAdam has documented the specific connections between Freedom Summer and the New Left, the Free Speech Movement, Vietnam protests, and feminism.

[11] John Lewis articulates the objective to "…let people live alongside each other, and in the process, educate not only ourselves and the volunteers, but, perhaps more importantly, the whole nation" (Marsh 108).

[12] bell hooks similarly notes how "[w]hite students learning to think more critically about questions of race and racism may go home for the holidays and suddenly see their parents in a different light…it may hurt them that new ways of knowing may create estrangement where there was none" (*Teaching to Transgress* 43).

[13] Like many women's colleges, Western suffered financial setbacks in the 1970s, giving the larger university, Miami, the opportunity to purchase its facilities. Miami's appropriation of Western's campus and history is complicated by a lack of continuity in institutional history and the marginalization of Western College's successor, Miami's Western College Program for Interdisciplinary Studies, within the university.

[14] Charles Marsh calls this spiritual dimension a "theology for radicals" (89) and Victoria Gray has called it the "enfleshened church" (qtd. in Marsh 89).

[15] A group of six students worked with me in September 2004 through an independent study to conceive the script. I am grateful to Aisha Allen, Andrew Beal, Sam Britton, Amy Foster Munoz, Annie Perry, Vashon Williams, and other walking tour guides for their inspired work on the project.

[16] The continuation of the tour is largely due to support from the Ohio Humanities Council, the W.E. Smith Family Charitable Trust for Local History, the Department of Theatre, and the Center for American and World Cultures at Miami Universtiy.

[17] The reading of the cards was inspired by two sources. First, the United States Holocaust Museum in Washington, D.C. (see Patraka), where visitors are given notecards that allow them to follow and identify with the narrative of an individual's experience of the Holocaust, a technique that encourages individual empathy while maintaining the focus on the collective memory of the Holocaust. The second inspiration comes from Jo Carson and Jules Corriere of Community Performance, Inc. (www.comperf.com), who frequently use the exercise of "I come from…" as a way of drawing a connection to place through vivid images and of creating bonding among members of community-based theatre projects.

[18] See, for example, Fishman and McCarthy, Howell and Tuitt, Maher and Tetreault, McLaren, McPhail and Dace, and Stucky and Wimmer.

[19] This is reminiscent of cultural critic Raymond Williams' "structure of feeling,"which he described as

"the distilled residue of the organization of the lived experience of a community over and above the institutional and ideological organization of the society" (*Johns Hopkins Guide to Literary Theory.* "Raymond Williams" www.press.jhu.edu/books/hopkins_guide_to_literary_theory/ raymond_williams.html). Bruce McConachie has explored the significant potential of this concept in interpreting audience response in community-based theatre. He elaborates on how a "structure of feel-ing" in community-based theatre helps construct boundaries that separate the "...ethical 'us' from an immoral 'them'...to examine who 'we' are" (42). In terms of the walking tour, we can imagine the col-lege students of 1964 and 2005 as existing within a community across historical boundaries. In this respect, we begin to see how spectators negotiate the materiality of images and create emotional reac-tions that symbolically construct structures of community, imagining ethical futures, and creating a "structure of feeling."

[20] For example, cultural critics like Judith Butler and Richard Dyer have noted the significant element of performance in the construction of these identity categories.

[21] Many have speculated on the role of sex, particularly between African American men and white women, during the Civil Rights Movement. Some have even gone as far as saying that these relation-ships directly lead to the radicalization of consciousness that became second wave feminism. See McAdam, Wyatt, and Brienes.

[22] Elin Diamond's work *Unmaking Mimesis: Essays in Feminism and Theater* breaks down these issues around identification, catharsis, and spectator response.

[23] The singing of freedom songs in the Mississippi Summer Project was an important ritual that perhaps at times led to a dangerous lapse in boundaries like the one Pratt describes. However, as I analyze later in the essay, singing also became a significant entry point for white students into the already close-knit group of activists. In *The Art of Protest,* T.V. Reed explores the many dimensions of singing in the civil rights movement and its strategic deployment (1-39). Although singing in the movement had some religious undertones, it was essentially a different context from the one described by Pratt.

[24] Spry takes her inspiration from Starhawk's terms: "power-over," "power-with," and "power-within."

[25] Some scholars in dialogue studies, such as McPhail, have noted the vast misinterpretations between blacks and whites as to what constitutes action (213). Frequently whites consider dialogue action in and of itself, while black participants wait around for real action (which never seems to occur) that will impact economic and material issues (214).

[26] Certainly the professors of students who take the tour deserve significant credit for students' increased consciousness, since they make unique contributions to students' preparation for, and subsequent dis-cussion of, the tour. Some professors have shown video documentaries such as *Freedom on my Mind* (Clarity Films, 1994); in one case, a professor had been a SNCC field secretary who participated in the 1964 training session.

[27] Robert Putnam discusses the idea of social capital in his book: "Whereas physical capital refers to physical objects and human capital refers to the properties of individuals, social capital refers to con-nections among individuals–social networks and the norms of reciprocity and trustworthiness that arise from them. ...'social capital'...is most powerful when embedded in a sense network of reciprocal social relations" (19). Putnam goes on to explain how this reciprocity creates trust, which assists in col-lective problem solving.

[28] Further information about the "Finding Freedom Summer" project can be found at: www.cas.muohio.edu/freedomsummer/home.html

[29] I am co-directing the project with Dr. Mary Jane Berman, the director of the Center for American and World Cultures, a Jewish woman.

[30] Bob Moses founded the Algebra Project as a math literacy project in rural and inner-city schools. The project was conceived as a continuation of the civil rights struggle: "in which transforming math edu-cation in our schools is as urgent in today's world as was winning the right to vote in the Jim Crow South in the early 60s" (www.algebra.org).

[31] See Parker Palmer's "The Quest for Community," in which he cites the important example of Princeton's alumni, who brought pressure to bear on the university administration and created a serv-ice learning program.

WORKS CITED

Allen, Chude Pam Parker. "Why Struggle? Why Care?" September 2005. Western College Program for Interdisciplinary Studies Lecture Series.

Armstrong, Ann Elizabeth. "Paradoxes in Community-based Pedagogy: De-Centering Students through Oral History Performance." *Theatre Topics.* 10.2 (September 2000): 113-129.

Ayvazian, Andrea. "Interrupting the Cycle of Oppression through the Role of the Ally." *Race, Class, and Gender in the United States,* Sixth Edition. Ed. Rothenberg, P. S. New York: Worth Publishers, 2004. 598-604

Bean, Annemarie, ed. *A Sourcebook for African-American Performance.* London and New York: Routledge, 1999.

Belfrage, Sally. *Freedom Summer.* Charlottesville: Virginia University Press, 1965.

Boler, Megan. *Feeling Power: Emotions and Education.* New York and London: Routledge, 1999.

Breines, Wini. "What's Love Got to Do with It? White Women, Black Women, and Feminism in the Movement Years." *Signs: Journal of Women in Culture and Society.* 27.4 (2002): 1095-1133.

Butterwick, Shauna and Jan Selman. "Telling Stories and Creating Participatory Audience: Deep Listening in a Feminist Popular Theatre Project." 2000. *Proceedings of the 41st Adult Education Research Conference.* 1 October 2005. <http://www.edst.educ.ubc.ca/aerc/2000/butterwicks&selmanj-final.PDF>.

Clayborne, Carson. *In the Struggle: SNCC and the Black Awakening of the 1960's.* 2nd Ed. Cambridge: Harvard University Press, 1995.

Cohen-Cruz, Jan. *Local Acts: Community-based Performance in the United States.* New Brunswick: Rutgers University Press, 2005.

Diamond, Elin. *Unmaking Mimesis: Essays on Feminism and Theater.* London and New York: Routledge, 1997.

"Diversity Facts: Multicultural Enrollment: Oxford Campus" 2004, Miami University of Ohio. 5 February 2006. <http://www.miami.muohio.edu/documents_and_policies/diversity_facts/table_oxford.cfm>.

Dolan, Jill. *Geographies of Learning: Theory and Practice, Activism and Performance.* Middletown, CT: Wesleyan University Press, 2001.

Dyer, Richard. *White.* New York: Routledge, 2001.

Fishman, Stephen M. and Lucille McCarthy. "Talk About Race: When Student Stories and Multicultural Curricula Are Not Enough." *Race Ethnicity and Education.* 8.4 (2005): 347-364.

hooks, bell. *Teaching Community: A Pedagy of Hope.* New York and London: Routledge, 2003.

hooks, bell. *Teaching to Transgress: Education as the Practice of Freedom.* New York and London: Routledge, 1994.

Howell, Annie and Frank Tuitt, eds. *Race and Higher Education: Rethinking Pedagogy in Diverse College Classrooms.* Cambridge, MA: Harvard University Press, 2003.

Maher, Frances and Mary Kay Thompson Tetreault. "Learning in the Dark: How Assumptions of Whiteness Shape Classroom Knowledge." *Race and Higher Education: Rethinking Pedagogy in Diverse College Classrooms.* Eds. Annie Howell and Frank Tuitt. Cambridge, MA: Harvard University Press (2003). 321-49.

Marsh, Charles. *The Beloved Community: How Faith Shapes Social Justice, From the Civil Rights Movement to Today.* New York: Basic Books, 2005.

McAdam, Doug. *Freedom Summer.* New York and Oxford: Oxford UP, 1988.

McConachie, Bruce. "Approaching 'Structure of Feeling' in Grassroots Theatre." *Performing Democracy.* Eds. Susan C. Haedicke and Tobin Nelhaus. Ann Arbor: U of Michigan P, 2000. 29-57.

McLaren, Peter. "Developing a Pedagogy of Whiteness in the Context of Postcolonial Hybridity." *Dismantling White Privilege: Pedagogy, Politics, and Whiteness. Counterpoints: Studies in the Postmodern Theory of Education.* Eds. Nelson M. Rodriguez and Leila E. Villaverde. New York: Peter Lang, 2000: 150-157.

McPhail, Mark L. and Karen L. Dace. "Crossing the Color Line: From Empathy to Implicature In Intercultural Communication." *Readings in Cultural Contexts.* Eds. Judith Martin, Thomas K. Nakayama, and Lisa Flores. Mountainview, CA: Mayfield, 1998. 434-442.

McPhail, Mark L. "Race and the (Im)possibility of Dialogue." *Dialogue: Theorizing Difference in Communication Studies.* Eds. RobAnderson, Leslie A. Baxter, Kenneth N. Cissna. Thousand Oaks, CA: Sage, 2004. 209-224.

Palmer, Parker J. "Forward: The Quest for Community in Higher Education." *Creating Campus Community: In Search of Ernest Boyer's Legacy.* Ed. William M. McDonald and Associates. San Francisco: Jossey-Bass, 2002. ix-xvi.

Palmer, Parker J. "The New Professional: On Thinking and Acting Like a Community Organizer." Lilly Conference for Teaching and Learning. Oxford, Ohio. 17 November 2005.

Patraka, Vicki. *Spectacular Suffering: Performing Presence, Absence, and Witness at U.S. Holocaust Museums.* Bloomington: Indiana UP, 1999.

Pratt, Minnie Bruce. *Identity: Skin, Blood, Heart.* Ithaca, NY: Firebrand Books, 1984.

Putnam, Robert. *Bowling Alone: The Collapse and Revival of American Community.* New York: Simon and Schuster, 2000.

Ransby, Barbara. *Ella Baker & the Black Freedom Movement: A Radical Democratic Vision.* Chapel Hill and London: U of North Carolina P, 2003.

Reed, T.V. *The Art of Protest: Culture and Activism from the Civil Rights Movement to the Streets of Seattle.* Minneapolis: Minnesota UP, 2005.

Rolland Martin, Jane. *Coming of Age in Academe: Rekindling Women's Hopes and Reforming the Academy.* London and New York: Routledge, 2000.

Spry, Lib. "Structures of Power: Towards a Theatre of Liberation." *Playing Boal: Theatre, Therapy, Activism.* Eds. Mady Schutzman and Jan Cohen Cruz. London and New York: Routledge, 1994: 171-184.

Starhawk. *Truth or Dare.* San Francisco: Harper & Row, 1987.

Stucky, Nathan and Cynthia Wimmer, eds. *Teaching Performance Studies.* Carbondale: Southern Illinois UP, 2002.

"Walk With Me: Freedom Summer Training at Western College Campus." Unpublished Manuscript, January 2005.

Warren, John T and Deanna Fassett. "Subverting Whiteness: Pedagogy at the Crossroads of Performance, Culture, and Politics." *Theatre Topics.* 14.2 (September 2004): 411-430.

Weiler, Kathleen. "Freire and Feminist Pedagogy of Difference." *Race and Higher Education: Rethinking Pedagogy in Diverse College Classrooms.* Eds. Annie Howell and Frank Tuitt. Cambridge, MA: Harvard UP, 2003. 215-241.

Wyatt, Jean. "Toward Cross-race Dialogue: Identification, Misrecognition, and Difference in Feminist Multicultural Community." *Signs: Journal of Women in Culture and Society.* 29.3 (2004): 880-993.

PERFORMING SPELMAN
THEATRE, WARRIOR WOMEN, AND A DRAMATURGY OF LIBERATION
Paul K. Bryant-Jackson with Joan McCarty

PROLOGUE: VOICES

> *...I ask the men and women who are teachers and co-workers for the highest interests of the race, that they give the girls a chance!... Let us insist then on special encouragement for the education of our women and special care in their training. Let our girls feel that we expect something more of them than that they merely look pretty and appear well in society. Teach them that there is a race with special needs which they and only they can help; that the world needs and is already asking for their trained, efficient forces. Finally, if there is an ambitious girl with pluck and brain to take the higher education, encourage her to make the most of it... To be plain, I mean let money be raised and scholarships be founded in our colleges and universities for self-supporting, worthy young women.... I claim that at the present stage of our development in the South she is even more important and necessary.*

> —Anna Julia Cooper, *A Voice from the South*

> *It never occurred to me that the fact that I was a head of a theatre or head of a department was anything other than it should be. Being a woman, I wasn't that woman-minded. I was interested in getting certain jobs done and having my chance at it. When I wanted a fellowship and I wanted money, I wanted it. I didn't care whether I was white, Black male, female, or neuter. I never fought that battle as a female. Women do have to get together to fight, but evaluating a problem or a situation in terms of sex is not my first item.*

> —Anne Cooke Reid, unpublished interview

> *Suzanne (Present): The fall of my sophomore year my major became elementary education. After I received a "C" in the trial course on Wilde and Shaw, I was told by the secretary in the English Department that I could take no further English courses. My professor had been a man called Hodgson, a tall man in his fifties. He was*

accompanied often by his assistant. He smiled a great deal but seldom talked to anyone. He gave me "C's" on every paper. When I told the secretary I'd like to talk to him she said Professor Hodgson wasn't able to see anymore students that quarter...

So in the fall I declared elementary education and began taking courses on teaching children. How I missed the imagery, the marvel, the narratives, the language of the English courses.

The new courses made me depressed. I hated them.

—Adrienne Kennedy, *The Ohio State Murders*

The most influential institution [for girls] within [some African] societ[ies] is the Sande School, a select group of initiates led by a preceptor and her assistants. For young girls Sande School is a school of initiation where they are trained in matters designed to enhance their potential as wives, mothers and full-fledged members of the community, Sande School is...a music school emphasizing singing and dancing as life enriching arts that bring refinement to the individual, grace to the community, and recognition and prestige to gifted, serious performers. Sande School functions as a "university of the forest" with an advanced curriculum: myth, history, ethics, herbal medicine: all is self consciously intellectual: all is graded and ranked...[It also] intersects with national government-sponsored campaigns to introduce modernization. Thus, social welfare and community development extension officers teach health and hygiene, childcare, and literacy at Sande convocations. Furthermore, in the rural areas, where 95 to 100 percent of the women are Sande members, only those who are themselves Sande initiates are accepted as government representatives.

—Sylvia Boone, *Radiance from the Waters*

The Project for Transforming thru Performing: re/placing Black womanly images began in 2000 at the University of Michigan with a generous grant from the Ford Foundation. The original goal of The Project was to enter the Black woman's performing voice into the scholarly discourse surrounding gendered.... By using the kitchen as the central metaphor for this work, we (re)create a space in which Black women are made central and shift scholarly attention to the experiences of "ordinary," easily forgotten women. After 9/11, while keeping the Black woman's performing voice at center, we tried to capture and reflect the global impact of war and terror on women around the world.

—Glenda Dickerson, *Transforming thru Performing: (re)Placing Black Womanly Images*

I began teaching at Spelman in the fall of 1986.[1] During that period of Spelman's history, there was great anticipation. Dr. Donald Stewart, the current president, had announced his resignation and, although it was by no means certain, it was generally accepted and expected that Spelman would appoint her first African American woman president. Spelman, like many smaller private institutions, carries rich historical traditions, and markers of that history are located throughout the campus. Joan McCarty, a colleague and assistant professor of drama at Spelman from 1994 until 2006, who assisted me greatly with this article, would often talk about the "living presences" at Spelman. As I reflect, I now see how Spelman College can configure its institutional history upon a body, becoming a site from which we call forth history: "Here is where Sophia Packard stood," "Here is where Dr. King laid in state," and "Here is where the birth of the Atlanta University Center Summer Theatre began."

It was therefore quite propitious that Dr. Johnnetta Cole, a cultural anthropologist whose scholarly work centered on West African retentions within certain African American religious/performance practices, would be appointed president. Dr. Cole would, from time to time, enact and perform various women in her public addresses, including Ida B. Wells, Anna Julia Cooper, and Lorraine Hansberry. At public functions, she would also draw gendered parallels between the given activity at Spelman and West African traditions such as the importance of the orixa, the Sande Society, the process of coming of age, or the importance of being a leader, a Soweii, within the community. It is therefore not surprising that African drumming, literally a voice of history, would be a constant presence at Spelman functions.

In this essay, I will attempt to braid several historical voices into a narrative that "performs" the development and importance of theatre at Spelman College. The essay begins with a discussion of the performative form of the essay, then moves to a brief history of Spelman, and the development of theatre at the college. The final section is the "talking essay" in practice, which articulates the development of theatre within an historical context of twentieth-century progressions of race, gender, sexuality, representative consciousnesses, and political movements. The talking essay includes additional "asides" that complete the drama. The essay concludes with a look at activities of recent graduates from Spelman's theatre program.

THE "TALKING ESSAY" IN THEORY

Spelman College, a historically Black college for women, self-locates upon the various sites mentioned and described in the quotations/voices that open this "talking essay." These many voices, representing locations and discourses of history, theatre, and performance; the interlocking systems of race, gender, and by necessity, class; West African cultural retentions embedded within African American societies; and "prayers" for the future, are all performed and heard daily among the intellectual, dramaturgical, and cultural enterprises of African American women at Spelman College. The Department of Drama, presently the Department of Drama and Dance, mirrors those same actions.[2]

This article is creatively conceived as a "talking essay," an historical, annotated, performative, and transcribed meditation.[3] Compositionally, a "talking essay" incorporates selected "voices," present and past, from a variety of sources, and organically places them within an intertextual context in which they might dialogue. The talking essay draws upon given histories within the African American and/or national consciousness in order to re-vision those voices in a given dramaturgical construct. Ultimately, it is a format transhistorically rooted in forms and practices such as naming, sistertalk, reading, and call and response. It therefore reflects a cultural and experiential worldview rooted in aspects of a circular, ancestor-present cosmology, and offers a discursive, open form and forum of analysis, reflective of orality. Ideally, a talking essay might "enact" a more organic portrait of Spelman, theatre, its "warrior women," and her dramaturgy of liberation. Such an approach is therefore necessarily culturally grounded and speaks to the various unique relationships that surround African Americans, "theatre," and, by extension, performance. This essay will also illumine how the Department of Drama (later the Department of Drama and Dance) weathered and fostered change through pedagogy, the most important element being an approach of consciousness-raising, interdisciplinarity, performance, and history. In doing so the department mirrored, to a large extent, the roles of African American women in society in general and in theatre in particular.

SPELMAN: THE BRIEF HISTORY

The economic, political, and social status of the newly-emancipated African American community after the Civil War was both tenuous and precarious. Suddenly bereft of food, shelter, and other essentials, and often denied opportunities to obtain the skills needed to acquire these essentials, Black families were in turmoil. Black women fared particularly badly.

Sophia B. Packard and Harriet Giles were white missionaries from Boston. In 1880 Packard toured areas of the South as a representative of the Women's American Baptist Home Missionary Society. She was extremely saddened at the status of Blacks in general: "She was particularly appalled at the plight of the Black female ex-slave in the South, and the seemingly prevalent perception that the status of these women was equivalent to that of the lowliest member in the American social hierarchy, a perception that she herself did not accept" (Watson and Gregory 7). Giles had witnessed the struggles of ex-slaves firsthand during her visit to the South, and both missionaries adopted a revolutionary, religious-based zeal to prepare Black women for service in the uplifting of the Black community. Declaring that "we do not feel that this is our work; it is God's work," (Watson and Gregory 7) Giles and Packard raised funds and moved to Atlanta to begin the arduous task of educating Black women ex-slaves. On April 11, 1881, in the basement of Friendship Baptist Church in Atlanta, Georgia, on a "site that had been used as barracks and drill grounds for federal troops during the Civil War," they held the first class of the Atlanta

Baptist Female Seminary. This site would later become Spelman Seminary and eventually Spelman College.

The founding of Spelman was historically situated in a most dynamic and contentious period for African Americans. The college was founded less than twenty years after the end of the Civil War (1865) and the Emancipation Proclamation (1863), during a period when society was engaged in discourses of Social Darwinism and eugenics, only two years before the infamous "Berlin Conference"(1884-85) that would usher in twentieth-century colonialism in Africa, and fifteen years before Plessey vs. Ferguson. It was also almost thirty years before the Niagara Movement and two years before a young Ida B. Wells would refuse to give up her seat in a train car. In 1928, some forty years later, Anna Julia Cooper, ex-slave, educator, intellectual, and "warrior woman" (who would influence major African American thinkers of the twentieth century) ver-bally constructed a gendered bridge with her now famous observation, "Only the black woman can say 'when and where I enter, in the quiet, undisputed dig-nity of my womanhood, without violence and without suing or special patron-age, then and there the whole...race enters with me" (Lemert and Ghan 892).

Drama came formally to Spelman College in 1928 with the hiring of Anne Cooke Reid, an English teacher whose interests and experience were in theatre.[4] Cooke Reid received her B.A. from Oberlin and was later one of the first women to receive a Ph.D. from Yale. Her doctorate was in theatre. When she joined the faculty in 1928, she distinguished herself by writing and directing the fiftieth-anniversary college pageant, performed at Sisters Chapel. Under her aegis, the dramatic talents of students at Spelman, Morehouse, and Atlanta University (now Clark Atlanta University) were merged under the name University Players, an organization whose purpose was "to promote better dra-matics, to train more thoroughly the persons participating, and to procure the best materials to train" (Spelman Messenger 3). The "classics," including *Macbeth* and *Antigone,* comprised much of Cooke Reid's production work at Spelman. Owen Dodson, another Yale graduate, would follow Anne in 1939.[5]

Baldwin Burroughs came to Spelman in 1942 but left for the war in 1943. During the war, the college hired three women to staff the department, Mrs. Francis Perkins and later, to assist her, Dr. Henrietta McMillan and Spelman faculty member Mrs. Billie Geter Thomas. Dr. Burroughs returned in 1950 and continued an illustrious career at Spelman, eventually becoming the Chair of the Department of Drama for twenty-five years. He was crucial in designing and garnering support for the building of the Rockefeller Fine Arts Building, which was dedicated in 1964. During his tenure, the performing ensemble for the department became the Spelman-Morehouse Players. Upon his death, he bequeathed one of the largest collections of African plays in the U.S. to the school.

The progression and development of the department mirrored theatre departments at small liberal arts colleges throughout the U.S. Theatre began in the Department of English, which then became the Department of English and Speech. Later, separating from English, it became the Department of Speech and Drama, the Department of Drama, and finally and presently the Department of Drama and Dance.

During the 1940s, students were required to take Development of Drama, Play Directing, Acting, and Play Production Methods. A minor in drama was initiated in 1950. Students were also required to produce one-act plays and take part in technical/design work, including building, painting, costume construction, and lighting. Embedded within the curriculum were the following goals: effective self-expression; personal poise; intensive speech training; pleasure through cooperative endeavor; an awareness of social and political history, music, and art; and an acquaintance with the technical and histrionic techniques of theatre arts.

During segregation, Spelman students were not allowed to witness professional theatre productions in Atlanta. Nonetheless, touring companies visited the school and luminaries such as Howard Thurman, Randolph Edmonds, and Langston Hughes visited the campus on a regular basis. Baldwin Burroughs speaks about the bitter and absurd irony of developing African American theatre artists for an art form that would have little to do with them:

> The place of blacks in the professional theatre, if any, was a momentary one. There were practically no roles written for them.... Abbie Mitchell, that gracious, talented and dynamic personality, brightened the scene for a moment as a maid in *The Little Foxes* and, except for a few jobs outside the theatre, was forgotten and died on relief. At the production and technical levels the situation for blacks was even worse.
>
> The facts illustrate that the study of drama and theatre in the early days at Spelman was an anachronism, for it introduced the students to an activity in which there was no place for them in the professional world. Serious students of the theatre facing impossible barriers in the professional world and subsequent to disappointment and starvation accepted a more practical approach. They pursued those positions that were opened to them; mostly, they went into high school teaching. Having participated in and been exposed to theatre, they were assigned or accepted the extracurricular duty of supervising dramatic activities. They enriched this field by their presence and, concomitantly, the communities to which they lived. Likewise, most producing groups in black college theatre have been influenced by personnel trained by or who, at some time have passed through the Spelman complex. (15-16)

In a 1993 interview with Anne Cooke Reid, Shauneille Perry, a noted African American playwright and director, further observes that such discriminatory practices continued in the 1950s during her residence at Spelman, even given the rise of Black theatres and other potential opportunities:

> As a former student, going to Howard and Spelman, those were the only places that we Black students could play those parts at all. When we left and

went to graduate school in other places, that's when we found out, we were not allowed to play them. Things have not changed completely today. It was important to be able to do them.... I remember sitting around and saying, "Well, what do we know?" I remember Anne Cooke said, "My dears, I'm not sure." Zaida went to the American Negro Theatre in New York. Roxie [Roker] had to petition the Urban League to get a job at NBC as a secretary. I went the teaching route. This drama thing was a part of us without thinking. It was pure. (Reid and Perry 99-100)

There are probably many observations that must be made in regard to this brief history. Within the context of a Jim Crow South and Plessey vs. Ferguson, both Spelman and the Department of Drama were active agents of resistance. Spelman theatre artists were and are presently educated by graduates from premier institutions of theatre study. The first four faculty members had graduate degrees from Yale! Presently at Spelman College, and as part of the liberal arts experience, drama and dance exist, flourish, and continue to engender conversations and negotiations among all members of the community in the areas of gender, race, sexuality, equity, agency, subjectivity, and representation. Given these social conditions, the study of drama for women (and men) of color was, and perhaps continues to be, an act of freedom, activism, and faith.

THE TALKING ESSAY IN PRACTICE: PERFORMING SPELMAN

On January 18, 2006, I had the opportunity to interview Dr. Beverly Guy-Sheftall, the Anna Julia Cooper Professor of English and Women's Studies and Director of Women's Studies at Spelman College, and Dr. Cheryl Johnson, Associate Professor of English and Director of Women's Studies at Miami University, both graduates of Spelman College. This talking essay traces the ways in which their individual subjectivities developed and were influenced by both theatrical representation and the performativity of Spelman's institutional rituals. Furthermore, as Women's Studies faculty, Beverly and Cheryl provide a broad interdisciplinary lens through which to view the role of the arts in the emerging intellectual life of Black women. Particularly at Spelman, theatre has always served a significant function, as a means of enriching and enhancing community identity. This function offers important insights into the theatre department's evolving pedagogy and is just as significant as the numerous successful professional theatre artists who have emerged from the program. Tracing this evolving pedagogy through the eyes of audience members/community members, we begin to see how a theatre department can influence the personal subjectivities of young women, how it is deeply embedded within its institutional environment, and how it can encourage and respond to social change within that environment. Beverly and Cheryl are also agents within the historical narratives they explore. At Spelman, Beverly, in her role as Director of Women's Studies, has assisted many departments in integrating Women's Studies across the curriculum, and Cheryl, also a Director of Women's Studies, was a student at Spelman during the Black Arts Movement.

Interspersed throughout the essay are a number of asides. These "talking moments" are either direct quotes solicited for this essay or are short essays from a variety of primary and secondary sources. Expanding the conversation, these voices further actualize, illumine, graph, and critique Spelman and the theatre experience she engenders.

PAUL: Cheryl and Beverly, you are both graduates of Spelman and are now directors of Women's Studies programs. Would you each talk about your unique paths and how Spelman informed that path?

BEVERLY GUY-SHEFTALL: Having gone to Spelman between 1962 and 1966, before the development of Black Studies or Women's Studies, I actually had a Eurocentric, male-focused education at Spelman. Even though I was an English major, I had courses that focused on race at some point but no gen-der-inclusive or Women's Studies courses while I was an undergraduate at Spelman. So, I should say that I left Spelman like most students leaving any college in 1966–with no courses having been Women's Studies-oriented. Even when I had a few courses that might have been Black studies-oriented, they focused on male life; for example, there might have been Richard Wright's *Native Son,* but there would not have been any women writers. I left Spelman and went to Wellesley for a fifth year, and that is where I actually had my first Women's Studies course, although I did not realize that that was what I was having. I had a course called "Women in Drama;" however, it was focused all on white situations. I came back to Atlanta University to work on my M.A. in English and, literally, this is where my journey to femi-nism and my involvement in Women's Studies began. I decided to do a the-sis on Faulkner's treatment of women; this was in 1969…I started reading what were those first texts in what we would now call feminist literary criti-cism. I started to read those texts in order to prepare me to start writing this thesis on Faulkner's treatment of women. Like most African American women in the academy, I started doing Women's Studies on my own. I started reading feminist literature.

When I came back to Spelman to work in 1971, I noticed, and this was not surprising to me because I would have been in the same category, that my students did not know anything about Black women intellectuals…[or] Black women's literature. Alice [Walker] talks about being at Spelman for two years and not knowing Zora Neale Hurston. So I was very clear in what I wanted to do, to make sure that our students at Spelman didn't have the kind of Eurocentric, phallocentric curriculum that I had. So I started, in the context of my courses at Spelman, trying to infuse what we would now call Black Women's Studies. I started teaching the first two Black Women's Studies courses at Spelman: "Images of Black Women in Literature" and "Images of Women in the Media." I also…with Roseanne Bell started doing this anthology *Sturdy Black Bridges: Visions of Black Women in Literature* and that was a direct response to my...students; I wanted Spelman students to leave there with some notion that there had been a Black female literary...[and] intellectual tradition. So, being at Spelman, actually for reasons that might not be on the surface, I wanted my students not to have the kind of, what we would call "missed education" that I would have had or any student would have had going to any college between 1962 and 1966. I would say [it was] my desire to have Black women students at Spelman have something other than a Eurocentric, male-centered education that motivated me to start doing Women's Studies in English at Spelman.

PAUL: [*to Cheryl*] You came to Spelman in what year?

CHERYL: Johnson 1968.

PAUL: And what was your experience?

CHERYL: I took a course in African American literature and I don't remember reading one woman writer at that time.

BEVERLY: Were you an English major too?

CHERYL: Yes. When I heard Beverly in my class today, it reminded me of the context in which I came of age or started to come of age intellectually. [It was] a time when we had been through discrimination. We actually saw racism. So it was not something that you just read about, it was something that you actually saw. This kind of knowledge was not knowledge for knowledge's sake. It does something else, and we have a responsibility to that knowledge... [*to Beverly*] [T]hat is why it was so good hearing you say you can "re-question" yourself as to what you are doing as an intellectual. What kinds of things influenced me? So hearing you today, I started going back. What happened for me in terms of Women's Studies was reading *The Bluest Eye* back in the late 70s. It changed my life. I never encountered a text that talked to me so intimately–

BEVERLY: –Right.

CHERYL: –about skin color and community and trying to find a place for yourself in this world. So I saw literature as a way to cure you, and I still think that literature has that power. So I think that what I try to do in the classroom is to get my students to see how literature gives us so many ways of looking at reality, so many different windows. Knowing that at some point our students will need to look through a window. They will encounter a death of a mother. They might encounter a rape. They might encounter driving down the street and hitting someone. They will encounter, finally, understanding what love is all about, and it is not that romanticized notion that they see on television. So that is what it is about for me, and so sometimes I think that my critical distance is a little fuzzy. [*Laughs.*] Because I do see myself involved with language and literature in very profound ways.

PAUL: Theatre does that. It empowers students. In performance, theatre allows the audience to reflect upon and enter into an imagined world.

CHERYL: So what Spelman did for me, even though I didn't have access to Zora Neale Hurston or Anna Julia Cooper, was to make me incredibly confident about myself. It made me say to myself, I am smart, and that I have a place in the world, and I am surrounded by all of these other beautiful Black men and women, and we were sassy and with our 'fros and our sense of pride. So Spelman did make me stop to think—so I am supposed to be different. I never stopped to think that I had to get married and have children. Spelman did provide for me an atmosphere that made me feel like, yeah. I have a place in the world. So maybe by the time I came to Women's Studies, I was ready, I was inclined anyway, but when I got there I had kind of a lot of preparation for it.

BEVERLY: Let me say something here because this is very interesting. Actually, my confidence eroded when I came to Spelman College. I had been a very smart student all of my life. I had skipped two grades. However, when I got to Spelman, I had the opposite experience. I took math and almost flunked. I had a white racist English teacher who gave me a C in freshman English. I had been an A student. I had an English teacher who was giving me Cs, and one time a C over a D on an English paper. I wrote about that. There was a time when I was at a gathering and she [the English professor] was there; she wrote me a letter of apology about that experience. Most of my teachers were white when I came there in 1962. At the end of my freshman year, I had to say to myself, am I as smart as I think I am? [*Chuckles.*] So, I did not have a first-year experience that reinforced my sense that I was smart, I had to gather that back up over time. I was extremely shocked. I didn't talk in class. I did not have a surge in confidence as a result of my being at Spelman until Richard Carroll came into the department, and I started to take his English classes and started doing exceptionally well...that was the point at which my confidence came back in terms of my smarts.

CHERYL: That is amazing.

BEVERLY: ...People had very different experiences and it depended on what their major was, who their professors were, and if you had a lot of white professors as I did. [If you] were basically a humanities person taking those math and science courses, you could feel like a little dummy. I was actually much more confident when I came to Spelman than when I actually left, and in 1966, when I came back, it had changed.

CHERYL: In just a few years.

BEVERLY: I would say that to the extent that you had more Black professors, and I am not saying that my experience was representative, because students who were taking Anne Reid and, later, Baldwin Burroughs probably had a very different theatre experience because they would have had mostly Black professors.

PAUL: They were all first generation Yale Drama School graduates and–

BEVERLY: –and they were also...what we would call progressive...[however, many of] the Black professors at that time were not progressive. [They were] stiff, doctrinaire, and so I think that if you would talk to Spelman students who were in drama you would get a very different perspective. You should talk to them.

AUTHOR'S ASIDE

I later talked with Pearl Cleage, playwright, performance artist, novelist, and Spelman graduate, and asked her about her experiences at Spelman in the late 1960s. Pearl's works for the stage include Bourbon at the Border, Flying West, *and* Blues for an Alabama Sky. *Her novel,* What Looks Like Crazy on an Ordinary Day, *was a featured Oprah Winfrey Book Club selection.*

PEARL: I think the thing that struck me most about the theatre program when I arrived at Spelman after three years at Howard was that the department had a campus-wide reputation for being both excellent and provocative. Carlton and Barbara Molette were both teaching in the department at the time and they were encouraging students to tackle difficult political issues in their work. Baldwin Burroughs never censored any of us for writing politically charged material. He demanded only that whatever you created be excellent. He had no respect for people who were using the revolution to excuse sloppy writing–he even allowed me to stage Jimmy Garrett's revolutionary black theatre piece And We Own the Night *for my directing final! The department's standards were so high that it made you want to work hard to be sure you measured up to those who had come just before you. Andrea Frye was already working with some other Black actors to create Black Image Theatre, a highly political band that performed in the nearby projects and in whatever other spaces they could "liberate," and she had been a student at Spelman just a few years before. A production of [Genet's]* The Blacks *that had been done before I arrived was still talked about in reverential tones as being an amazing pro-duction.*

The important thing about all of this for me was that it reinforced the possibility that Black folks could be energized and excited by good theatre. I could see evidence all around me. That gave me great confidence, which is, of course, essential to working in the theatre. I came to Spelman from a great program at Howard, where I had been taught by Owen Dodson, Ted Shine, and Paul Carter Harrison. Spelman had to meet my high expectations about what a drama department could be and how playwrights could be developed. They did not disappoint me.[7]

PAUL: How would you talk about Spelman today in relation to transformative pedagogy–is it because there is a Women's Studies Center? You mentioned that Spelman today is very different. One sees in the literary work of Pearl Cleage an ability to create feminist/womanist literature that foregrounds social issues. In her work she tackles issues such as Black women and AIDS, homophobia, and family planning. She is a guest faculty at Spelman.

BEVERLY: Yes. The curriculum is totally different, loads of Women's Studies classes, loads of Black Studies classes. The students take "African Diaspora and the World" the first two semesters of their Spelman experience. The curriculum is just totally transformed. You even have some curricular offerings that deal with issues related to sexuality, and that would have never been the case with us. So you are talking about a sea change. You really have to talk about the impact of Johnnetta Cole and her tenure. Women's Studies was already there, but what it meant to have Johnnetta Cole, a progressive academic president coming out of Black Studies and the Civil Rights movement–

PAUL: –and a cultural anthropologist as well whose work reflects connections and retentions throughout the Black Atlantic.

BEVERLY: I think it is hard to imagine the curriculum has changed so dramatically. We also offer more global courses. So I think that students learn much more now about cultures outside of the U.S., so I think that there has been a real profound change.

PAUL: …[There exists] a kind of fearlessness, [a] refusal to be reticent the way, quite frankly, some White students are. Spelman students are much more focused and verbal.

BEVERLY: Unlike my generation, they are much more verbally savvy. They are not shy. I didn't really start being assertive until after I got into graduate school. So I think that the students have much stronger sense of themselves as competent Black women.

CHERYL: [To Beverly] I think I want to ask you this question, because it is something that I struggle with here with my students. I remember that while I was at Spelman that, although I learned a whole lot, I saw that learning as something that would help me get a job. I never thought of myself as a thinker, as an intellectual. Even though I did take some classes that really got my mind going, right? It seems to me that with the different courses and the way that the curriculum has changed that there is a difference now, a whole new intellectual climate at Spelman.

BEVERLY: I agree with that. I think I saw myself as a person who was getting things for a job. I also did not have much activism. I did not see myself as a person who would be doing things in the world, to change things. Did you have much activism when you were there?

CHERYL: Not really. The first year and a half we were going to chapel and all with the white dresses. Then the Black Power movement took hold, and I was there when Samuel Jackson took over Harkness Hall. I wore the natural, and I saw Black Power and Black Pride and that kind of set me on the way. By the time I left Spelman in 1972, I was deeply into Black Aesthetics, Black Power, and that sort of thing. I never joined the Panthers or anything like that but some of my peers did. So you see there was all of that kind of talk going around and all of a sudden we were picking up Africa in different kinds of ways, thinking about what Fanon had to say. [Although] I still was not taking it in the way that I should have, I was surrounded by it. I think it made a difference.

PAUL: As a contemporary Black feminist, do you ever reflect on that period in terms of its misogyny and its heterosexism?

CHERYL: That period for me was one of personal revolution. It clearly planted the seeds for what was to come. Yes there was misogyny and homophobia, but I wasn't about to give up my body for the revolution, nor was I going to embrace any form of hate. Having grown up in the South, I knew that text too well.

PAUL: Would it be fair to say that there was a shift from a colonial framework to a framework of liberation?

CHERYL: Yes.

BEVERLY: Black Studies and the Movement really did have an impact. It really did. I left in '66 and things really began to shift in '68.

CHERYL: At least in '69. It really did start to shift.

BEVERLY: When we were there, it was in a way much more colonial. A professor was fired. A tenured professor was fired just because he was involved in a student demonstration. A faculty member could get fired. So the environment shifts dramatically in a few years.[8]

CHERYL: In my first year, I had pressed hair; by my sophomore year I was wearing a natural. And my mother screamed, "I did not send you there so that you would do that! You were supposed to be a young lady." I started to speak out a lot more too; there was something about [those times]. I saw my body differently, my hair differently, and that shift did occur in those four years. In my first year it was clear that [college] was a continuation of Catholic high school–young ladies [that] are demure, are deferential, are religious, and this is what would make you a good girl. I was supposed to be this "good girl" not to shame the family. A year later, my mother did not recognize me. I had on this miniskirt, white go-go boots, and a big natural. She didn't know what [that meant] and my mind was changed, and instead of me saying "colored" I was saying "Black," and, well, that had been an insult. During those years I just experienced those changes. Black pride was both performed and performative.

BEVERLY: It's also important not to forget that Baldwin Burroughs was also bringing those African plays.

AUTHOR'S ASIDE: THE EMERGENCE OF AFRICAN THEATRE AT SPELMAN

The Spelman Department of Theatre was a large part of the cultural shift toward what Cheryl describes, and this shift included not only Black Aesthetics but a global awareness. In The Aspects of Theatre at Spelman College, *Burroughs notes that as a result of a 1968 Non-Western Studies grant, he was able to travel through thirteen African countries during the summer of 1968 for the purpose of collecting playscripts by African playwrights. In addition to this trip, he also notes that he would make "several more trips at his own expense" (81), and as a result of his "year's tenure at the University of Ghana working with drama students"(81) he would amass more than five hundred catalogues and bound African plays. It is important to bring this aspect of the-atre into the discussion of Spelman for many reasons. Baldwin remembers,*

> *This adventure into African Theatre has been of great benefit to The Players at Spelman for the simple reason that in the sixties the emphasis in most things shifted to black and areas of black relevance. In the Department of Drama we were faced with somewhat of a dilemma. We could not disregard completely the basic Western drama on which our core depends, for students would be faced with Western drama in graduate schools. We felt a reluctance to turn to the profuse new Afro American drama for production because of its insistence...on depicting dope addicts and prostitution, and the obscene language.... Certainly no censorship prevailed concerning the new Afro American drama and we have produced some very good plays in this category, but we felt that in a school for young women too much of such controversial matter would be inappropriate. Therefore we turned in some degree to African plays.*

> *African Plays, in the main, are written by black African playwrights and deal with subjects that could be considered relevant to black Americans, since the latter could share in the historical perspective if not the emotional one. (81-82)*

Baldwin's perspective is both important and troubling. Like many African American artists at the time, "Dr. B." saw the value of a pan-African theatre experience. In that regard he is to be applauded for bringing global diversity to the Department of Drama. It is equally important to note that Baldwin saw as troubling those aspects of the "new Black revolutionary" theatre that, in relation to gender (and, though not mentioned here, in regard to sexuality) had originally warranted (and continue to warrant) critique. Nonetheless, Baldwin was apparently not immobile: in addition to Pearl's production, Sonia Sanchez's 1968 play Sister Sonji, *a one-woman play about the role, or lack thereof, of women in the Black revolution, was also produced during the 1970-71 season.*

Baldwin's observations are important because we see operating an active practice of a DuBoisian "double consciousness" applied within the context of theatre. Baldwin, the

Yale and Case Western graduate, wants the Spelman and Morehouse students to be versed in both African and European worlds. Conversely, it is perhaps this desire to be versed in both worlds that can also be problematic. What is missing or is at best only obliquely hinted at is the notion of a Black female agency and subjectivity. Clearly the objectification of Black women as prostitutes, so evident in many of those early plays, is reason and cause for concern, and Baldwin, like others of that period, is right to question and condemn that practice. However, it is also important to recognize that during this era there would be no such enlightenment, especially in terms of Black female subjectivity, found within the Western canon!

In 1991, Spelman College introduced "African Diaspora and the World" (ADW) into its curriculum. Mentioned earlier in this essay, ADW, a two-semester course, is required of all first-year students. ADW developed from a series of campus-wide and interdisciplinary discussions about recentering the curriculum. Virtually all of the disciplines of the arts and the humanities, and to some extent the sciences, were involved in the discussions. An edited two-volume reader, African Diaspora and the World, *was prepared for the course. In addition, film, concerts, lectures, plays, field trips, and other activities regularly compose aspects of learning within the course. From its inception and continuing to the present day, the course is gender-informed and gender-sensitive. Its first director, noted African historian Michael Gomez, worked closely with Beverly Guy-Sheftall and other faculty at Spelman to ensure the primacy of gender in the development of the course and course materials. Theatre has always been an integral part of ADW. The roots of ADW might be said to be found in Baldwin's early insertion of African plays into the drama curriculum, as well as the efforts of other faculty members throughout the college, who sought a more Afro-centric approach to education and learning.*

BEVERLY: I went to all of the plays. [Tennessee Williams'] *Summer and Smoke* [was] my first introduction to the theatre. You see, we did not have plays in high school and so Spelman was my first introduction to theatre and they were very fine.

CHERYL: Oh yeah.

BEVERLY: When I was there, they were mostly not Black plays.

PAUL: Yes, I saw that in the season. They were mostly European plays.

BEVERLY: I saw [Ibsen's] *A Doll's House.*

PAUL: The Atlanta University Center also had a summer theatre. It produced those plays, and it was nationally known. It really becomes one of the few places where there is a sustained theatre activity for professionals doing those kinds of work for a Black audience.

AUTHOR'S ASIDE: THE ORIGINS OF ATLANTA UNIVERSITY SUMMER THEATRE: ANNE COOKE REID IN AN UNPUBLISHED INTERVIEW WITH JAMES HATCH

> *Anne: Atlanta University Summer theatre began in 1934. [There was] no summer theatre in Georgia for anyone; they were not the vogue. I gave the idea to the presi-*

*dent of Atlanta University, John Hope, who sold the idea to my immediate boss,
Florence Reed, president of Spelman.*[9]

*We did five plays in eight weeks, and each ran for one week. The company was subsidized. Four years later I met Owen [Dodson] at Yale. It was my job to get a staff
together for the summer. I knew that there were enough blacks around the states that
had no place to perform.*

*[It's] 1938, summer's coming and I am in New Haven. I said to Owen, "Can't you
do anything but talk? You could help me." He said, "I don't have a job; I'll do anything, anything." Well, we produced Medea at once. He went to the summer theatre
for three years after and made quite a contribution...*

*When I decided to leave, I recommended that Owen take over the head [of the theatre
department] and they were more than happy to have him. There was a Department
of Drama. This summer theatre may be the oldest continuing summer theatre in
America.*

*Atlanta had little theatre and little cultural intermingling. White and Black came [to
our theatre] from all around; it was a calm and quiet and pleasant affair. No air
conditioning, no smoking; without planning that, it developed into a fine social relationship for the arts in Atlanta. I wanted a place where young people who loved the
theatre could get out of the academic regime and enjoy theatre. (Hatch and Reid 1)*

The Atlanta University Summer Theatre (AUST) flourished until 1975. Like many
African American cultural institutions rooted within the African American community,
the Atlanta University Summer Theatre perhaps fell victim to both integration and
related economic concerns. Although Dr. Oseloka Osadebe, Chair of the Drama Department from 1985 to 1989, attempted to revive AUST for two summers (1985-86) using
funds primarily from the Fulton County Arts Council, it did not continue after 1986.

BEVERLY: Those productions were stunning. I can still remember those presentations. I can remember those presentations more than I can remember the
Glee Club, even the Christmas Carol Concert. I remember the plays as some
of the most memorable moments of my four years at Spelman College.

CHERYL: I had some friends who were in some of those plays. I would go and
see them.

PAUL: Could you put your finger on what made them memorable?

BEVERLY: The acting. The acting was just amazing.

CHERYL: For me it was how they were participating in that kind of revolutionary moment. So it was a way of contributing to a sense of revolution, and
Blackness, and interrogating all of those kinds of things. Then came Barbara
and Carlton Molette.

BEVERLY: Who did *For colored girls?*

PAUL: I think that was the Molettes.

BEVERLY: You know that LaTanya Richardson [Jackson] starred in it. Barbara Molette directed it.

PAUL: Carlton only wanted to do Black plays and he and his wife have published a book, *Black Theatre: Premise and Presentation.* He refused to do anything in the European canon. They left Spelman in 1975.

Beverly: So when I came back as a faculty member, he did the plays of LeRoi Jones. In 1971…

CHERYL: I was there in '71.

BEVERLY: So that was my introduction to Black Theatre, also at Spelman.

BEVERLY: Let me say that I do remember, that I perceive, the arts at Spelman as a place where people were wilder.

CHERYL: Oh yes.

BEVERLY: I was there when Baldwin and [James Preston] Cochran were there.[10] We did have a sense that people in the arts were on a different trajectory. I don't know if we had a sense if they were gay, but we kind of did. I do not know if we would have ever said that they were gay.

PAUL: Or labeled that they were gay.

BEVERLY: We knew that they were very different and very flamboyant. We would hear about these wild parties after the shows. I think that there was a sense that there was this space on campus, where the students who were "wild"…

PAUL: I think for many of them…there was, perhaps, another social reality.

AUTHOR'S ASIDE: QUEERING SPELMAN

The question of being gay, and/or one's sexual practice and how it is performed at Spelman College and within the Department of Drama/Department of Drama and Dance warrants discussion. Johnnetta Cole and Beverly Guy-Sheftall's chapter "Black Lesbian and Gay: Speaking the Unspeakable" in their work Gender Talk: The Struggle for Women's Equality in African American Communities *provides an important framework. Drawing upon a broad range of queer and straight African American intellectuals and activists, and "intellectual/activists," the chapter does a nice job of surveying a broad range of opinion and fact regarding the topic of homosexuality within the African American community. Included within the discussion is an historical overview that addresses Black homophobia, its manifestations, and, however specious, historical and political reasons for that homophobia. Broadly addressed, their discussion might be summed up as: there exists perhaps five tropes, practices, or perspectives that operate within the community in relation to being gay or lesbian: homophobia, "don't ask don't tell," "everybody's got a place," "being closeted," and "being queer." There also exists a broad social activist perspective that relates to activism, including AIDS-related charities and social justice. It is perhaps fair to state that Spelman, and the Spelman Department of Drama, mirror the larger African American community.*

Historically, there have obviously been gay and lesbian professors and students within the Department of Theatre. However, for the most part they have operated within the framework(s) of "the closet," "don't ask don't tell," and/or "everybody's got a place." James V. Hatch's biography, Sorrow Is the Only Faithful One: The Life of Owen Dodson, *chronicles and articulates the complex negotiations and manipulations that often took place for Dodson, a gay theatre artist who worked at Spelman.*

Being queer and out at Spelman, or in the Department of Drama and Dance, really developed under the tenure of Dr. Cole. Proving that her administration would be an open one, Dr. Cole addressed the college in 1993 in the following letter, in which she demonstrated her support for the newly-founded Lesbian and Bisexual Alliance (LBA), her commitment to diversity, and her desire to foster a "beloved community" at Spelman (Cole and Sheftall 22):

> *Each member of the community has the right to work, to study, to live, and to learn without interference to their well being, their safety and their piece of mind. We must have as our cardinal rule that our own individual beliefs and values do not give us license to dictate those beliefs and values to others. Most importantly, our own individual beliefs and values do not give us license to discriminate against those whose beliefs and values are different, not to impede in any way their ability to participate fully in campus life. (22)*

The LBA students later changed the name of their organization to Afrekete. Being queer and Spelman could mean that you were under negative scrutiny. LBA students found strength in the life and work of "Sister Outsider" Audre Lorde; therefore, to honor Lorde and give focus to their struggle, they changed the name for the Lesbian Bisexual Alliance to Afrekete.

I served as an advisor to LBA from 1996 until 1998. During that period, LBA sponsored events that highlighted their activism and educated the community. One such forum, "Gays and the Bible," was especially spirited. It is important to remember that this panel took place during the rise of religious conservatism, and at a school whose "nineteenth century, missionary-conceived" motto is "Our Whole School for Christ." Additionally, during this period, LBA would be visible at the Atlanta AIDS Walk, and the more queerly polemic annual Atlanta Gay Pride March.

From the period of Johnnetta's letter until 1997, the Department of Drama and Dance, under Glenda Dickerson, maintained an active agenda in relation to plays that dealt with issues of sexuality. The department produced Cheryl West's Before It Hits Home, *a play about AIDS, bisexuality, and the Black family, directed by Paul (Bryant) Jackson; Kia Cothorn's* Cage Rhythm, *a play that addresses sexuality in the context of Black women in prison, directed by Joan McCarty; and* Zora and Lorraine and Their Signifying Tongues, *a "PraiseSong" that focused on two "Sister Outsiders," Zora Neale Hurston and Lorraine Hansberry, written and directed by Glenda Dickerson. These works marked a clear commitment by the department to support works that centered questions of sexuality and gender.*

In 2004, Joan McCarty's production of Stop Kiss, *a lesbian love story, included a supportive visit from the current president of Spelman, Beverly Tatum, and included queer sponsored panels.*

BEVERLY: Who was chair when you came? The department had always been male-dominated.

PAUL: When I came, Oseloka Osadebe was the Chair and the department was all men. Feminism did not play that large a role in the department or in the production season at that time. I remember my production of Alex DeVeaux's *Tapestry* and the kind of responses that I received. They were mostly negative, from the old guard. The students valued the work. I remember an early conversation with Johnnetta, who personally knew Alexis. Johnnetta encouraged me to "bring on the trilogy"–*Tapestry* had three parts. Dr. Cole said something like "this womanist-centered work is what it is about." She then added a faculty line allowing us to bring on an African American woman faculty member.

CHERYL: Well, Johnnetta–

BEVERLY: –was the first Black woman president.

PAUL: That begins the real shift, the Alice Childress plays, the one-woman performances, Adrienne Kennedy, Glenda's new plays and deconstructions, and on and on. Ruth Simmons' presence as Provost was another encouraging step. It was her encouragement that allowed us to bring on Glenda Dickerson as professor and Chairwoman.

AUTHOR'S ASIDE: GLENDA DICKERSON, PRAISESINGER AT SPELMAN

Glenda Dickerson's arrival at Spelman College as the Chair of the Department of Drama in 1992 heralded a significant change in the tone and direction of the department. An accomplished director, writer, and adaptor of works for the stage, Professor Dickerson was deeply rooted in the idea that Spelman College should be in the forefront in examining, critiquing, nurturing, and producing works of women in general, and particularly the works of African American women drama and dance artists.

Professor Dickerson chaired the Department of Drama for five years. Chairwoman Dickerson believed strongly that students learned from the presence of the arts, and from the words of the living ancestors/artists. She sought to fuse the Department of Drama and the Department of Dance, and, to this end, she facilitated guest artist residencies and performances with noted African American women choreographers Blondell Cummings, Dianne McIntyre, and Debbie Allen. She also brought in noted male choreographers Otis Salid and Charles Augins. She organized, along with other faculty, workshops, performance roundtables and visits from theatre artists Rhodessa Jones, Phylicia Rashad, Kenneth

Daugherty, Samuel Jackson, and Denzel Washington.

Professor Dickerson emphasized that the women of Spelman should be at the center of their own discourse and encouraged student writing and performance pieces that explored the lives and struggles of Black women. She also encouraged the production of works by Adrienne Kennedy, Lisa Jones, Kia Corthron, Ntozake Shange, Josefina Lopez, and others. The Trojan Women, *set in war-torn Rwanda, was her final production at the college.*

In 1994, under Dickerson's direction, the Maya Angelou Practice Theatre was dedicated. A donation from Ms. Angelou allowed an outdated classroom space in the Rockefeller Fine Arts Building to be re-structured as a flexible black box theatre. The Baldwin Burroughs Theatre, the mainstage proscenium theatre with seating for three hundred, was also re-dedicated and updated with a new grand drape, light board, and seats. Professor Dickerson left Spelman in 1997. Dr. Veta Goler, a choreographer and dance historian with a focus on autobiography and African American women choreographers, became (and is at the time of this writing) the Chair of the Department of Drama and Dance.

FINALE: VOICES

But with the black slave woman, there is a strange twist of affairs; in the infinite anguish of ministering to the needs of the men and children around her (who were not necessarily members of her immediate family), she was performing the *only* labor of the slave community which could not be directly and immediately claimed by the oppressor....the black woman in chains could help to lay the foundation for some degree of autonomy for herself and her men.... She was therefore essential to the *survival* of the community. Not all people have survived enslavement; hence her survival oriented activities were themselves a form of resistance. Survival moreover was the prerequisite of all higher levels of struggle.

—Angela Davis, *Reflections on the Black Women's Role in the Community of Slaves*

Living life as an African American woman is a necessary prerequisite for producing Black Feminist thought because within Black women's communities thought is validated and produced with reference to a particular set of historical, material, and epistemological conditions. African American women who adhere to the idea that claims about Black women must be substantiated by Black women's sense of our own experiences and who anchor our knowledge claims in an Afrocentric feminist epistemology have produced a rich tradition of feminist thought.

Traditionally such women were blues singers, poets, autobiographers, *storytellers,* and orators validated by everyday Black women as experts on a Black women's standpoint.

—Patricia Hill Collins, *Black Feminist Thought: Knowledge, Consciousness, and the Power of Empowerment* [emphasis ours]

Anne Cooke stood waiting [for Owen Dodson] in the bright sunlight,
dressed up so everyone would know that she knew about good deportment.... The complete segregation of Atlanta startled Owen. 'I had been to
Harlem and seen black people, but as we approached the college, I had
never seen such a coverage of black people–not one white person! When
we reached the campus, I felt like I had come into an oasis. [Owen] had
been assigned two roommates "Mac" Ross, a theatre director who had
attended Yale, and actor Thomas Pawley, and a recent graduate from the
University of Iowa.

At Yale, Owen had partied, but he had not bent elbows with the members
of the black bourgeoisie of Atlanta who had partied in the wider world.
Heading the hierarchy was W.E.B. Dubois.... From Paris, two black artists
had been lured home to build an art department–Hale Woodruff and
Elizabeth Prophet.... The white desert of self-segregation that ringed the university had created a rich intellectual black oasis.

–James Hatch, *Sorrow Is the Only Faithful One: The Life of Owen Dodson*

There is one aspect that continues throughout this "talking essay," the literature, and the many interviews about Spelman and the Department of
Drama and Dance: Place. "Place" not only in terms of Spelman, but also in
terms of Atlanta, represents evolving concepts of race, gender, and identity.
Spelman can be seen as a physical oasis, an alternative freedom space in a town
defined by Jim Crow. It also represents a performative oasis, an evolving epistemological space in which transformations in social thought and performance
were manifested in all aspects of the body politic.

The Department of Drama and Dance at Spelman becomes a place where
such change is instigated and reflected. Over the years, survival and performance have marked symbols of both resistance and change. Whereas Adrienne
Kennedy's imagined Suzanne Alexander could not study English at Ohio State,
at Spelman College, the Department of Drama, during those post-war years,
produced Shakespeare, Molie_re, Casey, Zola, Saroyan, Mowatt, and whomso-
ever she pleased. As the focus shifted away from the Western canon to
Afrocentricity, race consciousness, and gender empowerment, the Department
of Drama and the Department of Drama and Dance would mirror those shifts
as well.

It is possible, necessary, and important to talk about the development of
theatre at Spelman using terms representative of postcolonial studies. In doing
so, it is important to see those earlier periods, those periods of deportment,
poise, and white dresses as more representative of a colonial framework.
Language–and here language is used much like postmodern readings of "text"
and must therefore be envisioned in the broadest sense–is central to any reading of a dramaturgy of liberation, and language figures centrally in the case of
Spelman and theatre. Ngugi wa Thiong'o's articulatation of the centrality of lan-

guage and the process of freedom in the context of colonialism is also apt here: "language was the most important vehicle through which that power fascinated and held the soul prisoner. The bullet was the means of the physical subjugation. Language was the means of the spiritual subjugation.… Language, any language has a dual character: it is both a means of communication and a carrier of culture." (437)

Therefore, those "deconstructions" of Shakespeare, with all-Black casts, the collection and presentation of African scripts, the presence of the Black Arts movement that saw both systemic and "cosmetic" change, the Women's Center, the arrival of Sista' Prez Cole, and the Chairwoman/PraiseSinger Glenda Dickerson, Afrekete, and the transformation of the curriculum and the programs that they would engender, created, and continues to create, a new language, a dramaturgy of liberation at Spelman.[11]

ACKNOWLEDGEMENTS/CURTAIN CALLS

The authors would like to thank the amazing people, past and present, at Spelman College, including Dr. Beverly Guy-Sheftall, Dr. Cheryl Johnson, Pearl Cleage, Glenda Dickerson, and Ruby Byrom.

Paul K. Bryant-Jackson would also like to thank Camille Billops and James Hatch, founders of the Hatch-Billops Collection, for their great assistance on this project. The time was well spent. Special thanks to Dr. Alma Jean Billingslea-Brown, Dr. Johnnetta Cole, Dr. William Doan, James D. Engstrom, Dr. Michael Gomez, Kenneth Green, Dr. E. Patrick Johnson, and Dr. Jacqueline Jones-Royster, Dr. Ruth Simmons, Dr. Daryl White, and the students at Spelman and Morehouse for teaching me. Mama, this one is for you.

Joan McCarty would like to acknowledge/thank her husband Anthony Sanchez and the magnificent women of Spelman College, past and present.

NOTES

[1] I worked at Spelman College from 1986 until 1998 and chaired the Department of Theatre from 1989 until 1992. During my tenure at Spelman I attended a series of Ford Foundation-sponsored workshops specifically aimed at integrating race and gender into the curriculum.

[2] The Spelman College Department of Drama was the original name of the academic unit. In 1993, the college joined the dance program with the Drama Department, creating the Department of Drama and Dance, which has a theatre major and a dance concentration. Therefore, in speaking about the Department, we will refer to the "Department of Drama" to indicate those activities before 1993 and the "Department of Drama and Dance" to signify later activities.

[3] The "talking essay" has many close and distant foremothers. They include West African orality, elements of what Henry Louis Gates, Jr. calls "speakerly texts"–imaginatively reminiscent and playfully indebted to "talking books" (1988), African American enslavement autobiographies, what Patricia Hills-Collins calls "situated knowledge" (1990), and acts of "talking back," a term that bell hooks borrows and further empowers in the context of African American women refuting hegemonic systems of power (1988).

[4] In an unpublished memoir/record of drama at Spelman, *Aspects of Drama at Spelman College,* Baldwin Burroughs notes that the earliest record of theatre on the Atlanta campuses is 1905, a production of

Shakespeare at Morehouse College. The dates used in this essay in constructing Spelman's history are from Burroughs's manuscript and from other sources at the college.

[5] Owen Dodson would have a short career at Spelman, leaving in 1942, but would have a long and illustrious theatre career at Howard University and beyond. See James Hatch's book, *Sorrow is the Only Faithful One: The Life of Owen Dodson.*

[6] Most recently, in honor of Mozel Spriggs, a warrior woman in dance, administrator, professor and choreographer at Spelman, and reflecting both an interdisciplinary spirit, as well as a gender-sensitive and informed naming, the theatre majors and dance concentrators have become the Spriggs-Burroughs players.

[7] Jimmy Garrettt's play, *And We Own the Night,* is a classic in Black revolutionary theatre. The play includes much profanity, violence, and ultimately matricide, when mama impedes the revolution. For a complete description of Pearl Cleage and her work see www.pearlcleage.net.

[8] The professor that Beverly is referring to is Howard Zinn, who mentored young students including Marian Wright Edelman and Alice Walker in the area of social activism. He was fired in 1963 for going against "the grain" of the college which at that time focused on "turning out young ladies."

[9] At that time there were six distinct institutions: Spelman, Morehouse, Clark, Atlanta University, Morris Brown, and the Interdenominational Theological Seminary. At the present time, Clark and Atlanta University have joined together, and they all exist under the Atlanta University Complex.

[10] James Preston Cochran was professor of theatre at Spelman from 1957 to 1965. He had a Ph.D. from the University of Iowa.

[11] Under the Spell Productions, a professional theatre company, is one such product of that dramaturgy of liberation. Teresa Michelle Lasley, Spelman B.A. in Theatre and English, and Rhonney Greene, Morehouse B.A. in Theatre, founded and developed Under the Spell Productions, which is currently in residence at UCLA. Under the Spell Production creates theatre with the following mission statement:

'The Way Makers'

Under the Spell Productions provides trained theatre artists with the opportunity to perform in main stage productions. The primary purpose of Under the Spell Productions is to provide those artists with artistic outlets. In addition, the focus of Under the Spell Productions is to produce a variety of new and proven artists' works that capture the plight of women today and throughout history.

Specific Goals of Under the Spell Productions:

* To provide opportunities for beginning professional theatre artists to perform and to network with working professionals in the theatre industry.

* To provide income support to beginning professional theatre artists who are pursuing a career in the performing arts.

* To provide opportunities for working professional theatre artists to train and to work with beginning professional theatre artists.

* To provide www.underthespellproductions.com as an information and resource website for beginning theatre artists.

There are many others who also work in the tradition of a "dramaturgy of liberation," but Lasley and Greene reincarnate the moment described in Hatch's biography of Owen Dodson, when Ann Cooke Reid is waiting at the train station for Dodson, and for so many others, to arrive in order to change and "dream" a world.

WORKS CITED

Burroughs, Baldwin. *The Aspects of Theatre at Spelman College.* Unpublished Manuscript, 1976.

Cole, Johnnetta Betsch and Beverly Guy-Sheftall. *Gender Talk: The Struggle for Women's Equality in African American Communities.* New York: Ballantine, 2003.

Collins, Patricia Hill. *Black Feminist Thought: Knowledge, Consciousness, and the Politics of Empowerment.* New York: Routledge, 1990

Davis, Angela. "Reflections on the Black Woman's Role in the Community of Slaves." *Black Scholar,* 12:6 (1981): 2-15.

Dickerson, Glenda. "Transforming thru Performing (re) Placing Black Womanly Images." <http://www.umich.edu/news/index.html?Releases/2004/Oct04/r100804>.

Gates, Jr., Henry Louis. *The Signifying Monkey: A Theory of Afro American Literary Criticism.* New York: Oxford University Press, 1988.

Greene Rhonney and Teresa Michelle Lasley. "Mission Statement; Under The Spell Productions," <http://www.underthespell.org/home.html>.

Hatch, James. *Sorrow is the Only Faithful One: The Life of Owen Dodson.* Urbana: Illinois University Press, 1995.

hooks, bell. "Men: Comrades in Struggle," *Feminist Theory: From Margin to Center.* Cambridge: South End Press, 1984: 68-83.

hooks, bell. *Talking Back: Thinking Feminist, Thinking Black.* Cambridge: South End Press, 1989.

Kennedy, Adrienne. *The Ohio State Murders. The Alexander Plays.* Minneapolis: University of Minnesota Press, 1992: 25-64 .

Lemert, Charles and Esme Bhan, Ed. *The Voice of Anna Julia Cooper: Including A Voice from the South and Other Important Essays, Papers and Letters.* Lanham, MD: Rowan and Littlefield, 1998.

Lorde, Audre, *Sister Outsider: Essays and Speeches by Audre Lorde.* Berkely: Crossing, 1984.

Reid, Anne Cooke with James Hatch. Unpublished Interview. New York: Hatch-Billops Collection, 4 Feb. 1984.

Reid, Anne Cooke with Shauneille Perry. Interview. *Artist and Influence.* Vol. 12, (1993) 94-104.

The Spelman Messenger. Vol. XLVIII. Atlanta, GA: Spelman College, 1937: 3.

Thiong'o, Ngugi Wa. "The Language of African Literature." *Colonial Discourse and Post-Colonial Theory: A Reader.* Ed. Patrick Williams and Laura Chrisman. New York: Columbia University Press. 1994: 435-456.

Watson, Yolanda L. and Sheila T. Gregory. *Daring to Educate: The Legacy of Early Spelman College President.* Sterling: Stylus, 2005.

PLAYING IT STREET
TALES FROM THREE INSTITUTIONS
Rebecca Schneider

Author's Note: This text is a palimpsest. Layers of it are almost as old, now, as my current undergraduate students. Different tales represent different times and changing approaches to teaching gender and sexuality issues in the classroom, but throughout, my impulse to try to listen to my students, as much as to invite them to think outside of sedimented identity categories, has remained strong. I first began compiling these "tales" in the early 1990s and have kept adding to them and tinkering with them until 1998. I've returned to them only recently, and added a brief postscript. Some of the references to figures from popular culture are outmoded now, while others arguably remain relevant, but outmodedness and cross-generational exchange are important to grapple with as we try to keep our teaching fresh. I offer these "palimpsestuous" tales here in the spirit of "temporal drag," as recently theorized by Elizabeth Freeman (2000).

MADONNA IN WASHINGTON SQUARE

I'm teaching my first class ever. It's 1989 and it's Feminism and Performance. I have five students, five young white women. I myself am a young white woman. It's New York University and it's summer. It's hot. I'm doing the best I can.

The summer session meets four days a week for six weeks and we're a little over halfway through. We've parsed the feminisms using Jill Dolan's guidelines; we've discussed performative strategies; we've looked at videos and attended live shows. The students have been assigned papers and performances. Deb Margolin is scheduled to visit. All seems in order. Everything's moving right along.

When you're in charge for the first time, there's an odd sense of getting away with something–or of not quite getting away with something. Wasn't I a student yesterday? Won't I be a student tomorrow? When class ends and a new teacher puts her lecture notes back in her backpack and thinks about leaving the room, the milling about of her students is intriguing, even inviting. What are they really thinking? Am I one of them? Am I pulling this off? This summer, this first time, I begin to notice that after class the students stick around. I take more time putting my materials away.

What I realize is that the students are hanging out with each other and talking about Madonna. (Remember, it's 1989.) This happens several classes in a row and I begin to throw a comment or two into the discussion. The "is she or isn't she feminist" question was quite compelling–these were the days when grabbing one's own female genitals on the cover of trendy magazines could cause a stir, and when "blond ambition" had resonance as an oxymoron. These were the days when "candle-in-the-wind" Marilyn could be reincarnated as a blowtorch in the doldrums. In any case, the women are drawn together, partly by the fact that one student is such an avid Madonna fan that I imagine her dorm room resembles a shrine. Certainly her fashion makes her a walking billboard. She wears "Blond Ambition Tour" t-shirts to class–big and baggy and bright. The discussion goes this way: Madonna's a feminist saint. No, Madonna's a total sham. She's in it for the money. She's using her body to get what she wants. No, she's in it for the political statement. She's using her body to get what she wants. At least no one disagrees about the body.

The interesting thing to me at the time was that none of these students were indifferent. Passion infused their conversation, and the way they tried to apply everything to HER as example led me to try (like so many of us did then) to use these discussions in class, to tie them in with questions of performance strategy–what's at stake in siding one way or the other with Madonna? What's so horrible about a woman who is "after money"? This was a good moment for Madonna discussions. These were the days when students brought her up, not teachers. The undergraduates I teach now were in elementary school or junior high in '89 [*NOW, the students I teach were in diapers then*]. Now they turn to Courtney Love, the Spice Girls, Hole, No Doubt's "Spiderwebs" or Garbage's "Stupid Girl" [*and NOW they debate Christina Aguilera and 'Lil Kim or Paris Hilton*].

But it's still 1989, and Madonna's on the burner. Madonna is the burner. While the Madonna fan wears baggy tour t-shirts, another woman in the class dresses like Madonna herself. This student's skirts are always tight and short and often vinyl. Her lipstick always thick, sometimes black, sometimes green, and sometimes even red. Her hair is dyed jet black (most days), long and chaotically piled. She's ahead of her time, on the margins of the heroine death look that would overtake tabloid Madonna mascots in the early nineties as ad campaigns copied Cindy Sherman copying ad campaigns. Not dead yet, and closer to a fleshy Madonna than Evita's embalmed corpse, the Madonna dress-alike imagines herself defiant at all times. Before class begins she's angry. After class ends, she's angry. And she revels each day in the same story: "Today they whistled at me on the street. They made comments and leered. I hate them. Today I gave them the finger, but I want to kill them."

Her classmates get annoyed–especially the baggy-shirted "blond ambition" Madonna fan: "Don't dress like that if you don't want comments."

"I want to dress the way I want to dress!" the look-alike declares, self-righteous. "But I don't want to be leered at." Veterans of undergrad feminist classes (at least from the 1980s and early '90s) will recognize her argument: I should be free to wield whatever iconography of the body I wish, without repercussion. The woman with the ambition tee broadcasts the slogan, but won't walk the walk—and she's the one who is most virulent about her classmate's outfits. It becomes clear that what's okay for Madonna—that is, for the stage, for the public "show"—does not translate to the personal, to the "real" world, to the everyday street.

Of course, this seeming space between the "show" and the everyday "real" will become a heated site for productive inquiry in the 90s as cultural critical inquiry, enthralled with the "performative," will intersect with queer theory to further unsettle the ground on which the "real" world is erected as distinct from representation. Indeed in 1989, psychoanalytic and postmodern theorists (in distinct ways) already encouraged my students to ditch the "real" as a reliable or even applicable category. But despite the pages of rhetoric, when these women left the classroom for the street they were hit squarely in the face with the reality of representation's effects. "They jeered at me." "You asked for it." How, the question became, to deal?

I thought about what I'd asked them to read: Cixous, Dolan, de Beauvoir, Case, Irigaray, Frye, de Lauretis, Russo on the carnivalesque. They discussed it. We turned it around. Margolin came and led a great class. We did Finley's *Constant State of Desire.* And still their conversations turned, every chance they got, to their lives and the streets they negotiated on their ways to and from the class.

One day two women came in with a story about how they began to talk back to men who were ogling them in the subway very late one night. They seemed thrilled by the danger they were courting: the slippage we'd been romancing between representation and the real had given them some uncanny courage. At this point, at the threshold of my teaching, I began to be afraid of what I was giving them. "Please, don't talk back late at night on the subway," I remember saying. "Sometimes just ride quietly and get off. You can publish somewhere, or make a performance. But on the street, on the subway—get through the night safely."

I felt their disappointment in me.

I realized I needed some more profound ways to teach the space between the stage, the page, and the street. I made an intersection in the syllabus and assigned Augusto Boal.

Perhaps not surprisingly, with hindsight, the Madonna look-alike in the tight skirts got particularly inspired. She made a sudden change in plans about her performance project. She would, she declared, make a performance piece using Boal's techniques of Invisible Theatre (see Boal 1990—as managing editor of *The Drama Review* at the time, I had access to the galleys. See also Boal 1985). Could we all go to Washington Square Park and participate with her? I paused.

If you get class consent to participate…you can do it.

Everyone agreed. The Madonna look-alike (I'll call her Mary) would ask a male friend to come with us to Washington Square. We would station ourselves around and about, pretending not to know each other. Mary would then walk through the park, and at a point just southeast of the central circle, the man she asked to participate would make a loud comment: Hey Babe, Nice Tits. She would stop him and begin an altercation. Don't say that to me! How dare you, etc., etc., etc. Another woman from the class would join in as if she were a passerby and defend the guy, saying stuff like, "Yeah if you dress like that you're asking for it." The hope was that people just happening by or hanging out in the park would, as Boal describes his aim for Invisible Theatre, get involved in the discussion and debate the issues. Okay–it was a plan. The main thing, as Boal reminded us, was not to let the people in the park know that ours was "only an act." We must bear the cloak of "reality" at all times.

The day came. I was nervous. We assembled in the classroom first. Everyone was there. Mary was dressed as usual in an extremely provocative outfit–tight tight and short short, ripped ripped and skin skin. The male friend was with her, and when I saw that he was African American I had one of those flashes of the enormity of my unpreparedness–we had discussed race but only marginally, reading Lorde, but not taking it very far, shying away from it, mentioning it as an "of course" and noting that we were all white, berating white liberal feminists in predictable ways and then going on about our topic: gender. But here we were heading off to the park to provoke an altercation…about…gender? Suddenly, gender ceased to signify itself alone and I realized how much the whitewashed walls of the academy had, to this point, insulated me, and all the theory we had buttressed ourselves with appeared full of holes. Of course, Lorde had already told us there were holes, but now the holes were closing in on us *as the street itself.* If we were all white in the class, it was not the case that we were all white the minute we left the classroom. I wondered–should we have left the classroom long before this moment? The mantra "too bad we are all white here" became particularly bogus.

I gathered them together and said: Okay, we are not as prepared for this as we should be. We have not discussed the imbrications of race, class, and gender to the degree that we should have. Heading into the street, race would become a factor. Of course, *race was already a factor, and would have been a factor in any case*–if she had brought a white friend it would have been a factor too, but the fact that we did not address this in depth loomed now as our particular blindness. At this point…it was too late to prepare. We were heading out. A black man would "accost" a white woman, a scene would be provoked, and we would see how far our theories took us.

In the park we fanned out. I sat under a tree to the northeast of where the action would take place. I could see the other students sitting here and there. We were each aware of where the others were. At this point a completely unex-

pected scene began to unfold. A large black man came and sat down beside *me.*
He began to talk to me, very nicely, but clearly with a somewhat "come-on"
kind of attention. I could see my students watching me. He sidled closer beside
me. If my students hadn't been watching, and if the subject of the day weren't
about unsolicited male attention, I might have simply had a nice conversation,
or moved on, but the frame around the whole thing was twisted. My students'
eyes on me, my need to pay attention to what Mary was about to do, this man's
efforts to engross me in conversation, my concerns to keep my eyes on the
scene—just all made his attentions particularly fraught, particularly unwanted. I
wanted to be left alone to WATCH, I wanted the comfort of a spectator in a
planned performance, disembodied, removed—I was not prepared to be the
"spectactor" Boal called for. But here I was, an actor in an accidental sideshow.
I could see several students begin to laugh at my apparent confusion.

I couldn't tell this man—who was actually quite nice—what was up. I
couldn't say "Look I'm a professor here and I can't talk because my students
are engaged in a performance about a black man accosting a white woman."
And I didn't want to say "Get lost" when he wasn't being rude, just trying to
talk. Ultimately, he was so persistent in talking that I tried to get him interested
in the scene that was starting to unfold. "Look at that," I said to him. "That
woman over there is getting very pissed at that guy. Seems like he said something to her she didn't like." He didn't want to talk about that. I didn't want to
get up and leave, because this was my appointed spot as lookout—I could keep
an eye out from here, watch the policeman in case we needed him. I finally
told this man to leave me alone, but I blurted out the very thing I had vowed
not to say: I whispered quickly, "Look this is all an act. I can't talk to you. I'm
teaching at NYU and my students are engaged in a performance. I have to sit
here and observe this scene." When the man looked up, saw the white woman
shouting at the black man, he looked at me with a look I'll never forget. It was
akin to disgust, but it was wiser than that. He shook his head. He moved away.

Meanwhile, Mary and the students who jumped in to defend her or the
man had actually managed to gather a crowd. Mary was shining in her anger as
if she'd lived her life for this moment. She was defiant and her assembly was
increasing. I was somehow surprised that it was working. People were jumping
in and arguing all sides. The man who had "accosted" her was listening to other
men talk about "respecting women." He countered, I *was* respecting her.
Others joined in to agree—he was respecting her. Fascinatingly, the only women
involved were four of the women from my class (one of the women and myself
remained relatively silent on the sidelines, watching). No women from the
street stopped to get involved. People would come and go, and over the course
of twenty minutes there were probably twenty-five people involved—all of them
men, more than half of them men of color. Many of them seemed to be park
regulars, but some seemed to be on lunch or were passing through. Women in
the park either stopped briefly at the outskirts or simply walked on by. I whis-

pered to one of the students that this was the case and she tried to get women to stop and engage, but none would. A white male Jehovah's Witness joined the crowd and began passing out literature, raising his voice about Christ and Salvation. Mary-cum-Madonna kept it up.

It became quite a scene. It was hard, keeping an eye on it all, to figure out the terms of the debate. It didn't seem like anyone was talking about race overtly. Most of the men were talking about how Mary was dressed and whether commenting on "sex" was insulting or complimenting. They talked about what they would do to another man if their woman was hassled and didn't like it. I think someone actually asked if Jesus would have said "nice tits" and someone replied, "if the tits were nice," while Mary was holding forth on how they were her tits and not to be leered at–ironically drawing more and more attention to them with every word.

But Mary was impressive. She got some discussion fitfully turned to how it would be different if sex weren't used to delimit women, if there weren't a glass ceiling, if there were equal pay, etc. One of the women from the class also impressed me by mentioning that Mary didn't look like she was hurting for money, what did she have to complain about? Mary said she was a struggling student and she had her share of worries. Yeah but you have opportunity, privilege, you make your choices, you have options. And Mary replied, even if I were the richest woman in the world I wouldn't want "hey babes" in my way, they bring me down. I don't want to be defined by the tired patriarchal habit of making me an infant to be exchanged between men. Some women like it, someone said. It's a sign of respect. Why do you hate the fact that you're a turn-on? Mary tried to answer. How would you like it if women ogled you?! Oh, I like it when women think I'm sexy. The men were clearly enjoying this parlay. Yes, but it's different, it's different–on the street you're a man, you don't face rape and sexual harassment. Not true, said someone. Okay, Okay, another student raised her voice, how would you like it if men ogled you? Oooooh, they said, and laughed. This was not safe territory. Someone returned the conversation to where it had been: My woman likes it that I appreciate her, but don't you grab her ass.

The talk went this way, round and round. Race was never mentioned. Sexual preference was skirted. Religion oddly hung in the air. And class privilege was only obliquely touched on. It seemed that talking about scantily clad women was well rehearsed. These facts in themselves would provide intensive material for later discussion in class.

When we broke away, one by one, people were still talking. I was impressed that a core of about eight appeared to remain, continuing to talk even after we left. When we got back to the room, class was over. We would have to talk about it during the next session. And as I recall, we talked about it quite a bit, turned it over and over, and wondered how, if we were to do such a thing again, we could get more women involved. Why hadn't the women joined in? Why had I been concerned about "race" and was it of concern? Did anyone hear anyone talking about it? Why not? If we had brought race into the discussion how would we have done it? How might the discussion have changed? What were the privilege issues involved? The preference issues? How did they impact the gender ones? These kinds of questions, even without answers, proved to be the best thing that happened in that class.

But I have to say that what provoked the most thought in me was the degree to which it both was and was not "performance"–that delicate line that Boal so gracefully puncturing between "art" and "life," that line so many performance artists, from Dadaists to Montano to the Guerrilla Girls, have been interested in disrupting or making apparent. We did not leave there as a pack of actors, but as a group of women with a lot on our plates to discuss–and many of the students were very keen to have me discuss the sideshow they witnessed as I was, as they put it, "hit on" in the park. Sadly, I was too embarrassed to tell them that in order to handle the situation I had blurted out the "truth," that I had rallied on my authority as a professor conducting an experiment, that all of it had been a "show." I didn't tell them about the look my attendant cast me– the sorrow in it, the affront he seemed to feel, the dismissal. I should have told them. It would have been an excellent way to talk about the frame of "performativity" in relation to the frame of "the real." It was becoming apparent to me how important it was to approach performativity in the frame of the "real," and the real in the frame of "performativity." How to do that in the classroom became a recurrent concern.

From that time on I have tried to teach performance as always in the context of the street. While contextual analysis is a staple of much feminist theory and of performance theories from New Historicism to queer theory, the question of how to make the street present in the classroom leads to interesting teaching techniques. One way, of course, is to pull out the Erving Goffman and discuss the classroom as ritual performance space, discuss the issue of appropriate role behavior on the street, in the class, and in any social context. Another way is to always locate the frameworks of the venue in which any performative act occurs–what does the frame of the classroom require in terms of appropriate performance? What does the street require? What does a theatre, a church, a protest assume? How does the frame dictate the reception of any given behavior? What is "inappropriate" and how does any "inappropriate" performance talk back to the frame–such as "porn" content in the frame of "art"? Is the body itself a frame, a venue, a stage? And if the body is a stage across which dramas get enacted (dramas of fashion, dramas of physical markings, ghosted by precedent dramas of how those markings are read), what would a subversive performance on the bodily stage entail? What are reception theories of the bodily stage? How does the venue dictate the reception of the drama of the body? How can venues be made apparent? How can the body as performance space be made apparent, and what is at stake in approaching the body *as* a perform-ance space?

JEZEBEL IN NEW HAVEN

Five years after the Washington Square event, I was teaching at Yale as a lecturer. Students in a class on "Theories and Techniques of 20th-Century Performance" were each assigned to mount a performance project in the style of a theorist or of a particular practice or movement as we made our way through the century. On the day that concerns this story, a student had been assigned Environmental Theatre. This student (I'll call her Teresa) decided to stage a Bible story on the grounds of a local Catholic Church. She had gotten verbal permission from the priest so everything was set–though I knew nothing of this before the day of her project. On that day we trooped out of the class-room and convened in front of a neighboring apartment building. We heard shouting from a window and then Teresa emerged, her dress torn and her head down. She was bound at the hands and waist by ropes, held by a group of three men and one woman. The gang began to drag her through the street–literally down the middle of the road–shouting "whore," "slut," "cunt," and other sexual slurs. "Jezebel." Accidental passersby looked momentarily worried, then almost immediately curious. Some would stop for a moment and, after deciding the scene was a performance (at least I assume that's what they surmised), they would move on. A few hung around and watched us process up the street. The "actors" dragged Teresa past a campus police station in an old storefront a few doors up from the apartment, a few doors down from the church. We could see a few cops inside at desks. I was amazed that the officers took no notice–how were they so sure this scene was harmless?

Finally the actors dragged Teresa into a small courtyard at the side of the church where a stone table memorial to a church father stood inside a high wall. Teresa was placed on the table, lying on her back. Now the voices of the actors were low, almost whispering, and in order to get the gist of the scene we had to press close. Were they speaking words straight from the Bible? At this point, a church secretary burst out of a side door. You have to leave, she said. You are desecrating our memorial.

Thinking that Teresa should handle this, I said nothing. But Teresa would not break character. She lay unmoving. "This is a class project," another stu-dent finally said. "We called ahead and got permission. We were told we could perform by a priest." The secretary immediately went and got a priest. While she was gone, the performance resumed. When the secretary emerged again with the priest, she was still very upset. So was he. "If I gave you permission," he said, "I wasn't clear on what you were going to do."

I still did not take over from the students. This was their project and I wanted them to handle it. But they were not moving, and the priest and secre-tary were obviously disturbed. Students looked at me, and at each other. Teresa still lay motionless on the table. "But it's the story of Jezebel," someone said. "A Bible story." " Well, you can't do it here."

Still no one moved. This was a hard moment, filled with the kind of tension only silence can produce. As the teacher, I knew that I was in a mediating role. But I also felt that the awkwardness of the situation, even the silent stand-off, was part of the lesson. The demarcation of "performance" and "reality," or "theater" and "ritual," like the borders of public and private, were here coming into a bold relief across Teresa's body, across the Father's memorial. Finally, I had to open my mouth. "We'll have to leave," I said. "But think about whether or not you want to stop the performance."

Without stopping to plan, the actors dragged Teresa back into the street. As if of one mind, they went directly to the front steps of the church. They stretched her out half on the steps, half on the sidewalk, and proceeded with the performance. The blatant abuse/sacrifice of a woman on the street as spectacle, or in a church as theater, raised serious questions about performance and complicity—our complicity as well as the church's—and we talked about all of this at length when back in the classroom. Because Jezebel (Teresa) would use a particularly quiet voice whenever she spoke, we had had to gather in close to her bound body if we wanted to hear her defense and counter-accusation. If one didn't press in close to her (a disturbing choice, as it made one feel particularly complicit), one would only see and not hear—another kind of troubled complicity. The pressure of such choices focused us, as spectators, on the question of participation. Why did the priest stop the show? Why hadn't we, the "spectators," stepped in to stop the "show"? When onlookers saw that it was "just" performance, what did they see? Were those of us who were spectating class members as much a part of the show (to the street onlookers) as the actors? To what degree, then, are spectators always participant? Is a performance ever "just" a performance? Clearly the church workers didn't think so, but did we think so? To get to the church the actors had dragged Teresa past the campus police office—no one had emerged to query why a woman was being dragged through the street in bondage. What if it hadn't been "just" a performance? Performing on the street, to what degree did we recapitulate violence? To what degree did we critique it? What did the frame of the street do to the performativity of the actions?

As a result of this experience, and in light of an upcoming class on performance art, I asked students to spend some time walking the streets outside the classroom as if everything they saw were a performance. (This was in part possible because the class met for three full hours at a time.) When we came back to talk about this exercise, they were either awestruck or disturbed. One man was upset. "I went up to a drunk, apparently homeless person who was collapsed in a corner and watched. I went right up and stood there as if it weren't really happening—as if it were performance. It felt wrong. Then I realized that it's what I do every day—I look at him and I walk by, as if he weren't there." Approaching the street as spectacle made this young man confused. On the one hand, approaching the real as performance seemed to separate the everyday from "reality," and made him feel removed. But on the other hand, paradoxically, it allowed him to see, in a new way, the *reality* of his *performance* every day–his everyday habit of removal, even of spectaclization. Again, by virtue of leaving the classroom, we had amassed a considerable amount of unknown territory to navigate by way of discussion–even if we had managed to disturb ourselves in the process!

INVISIBLE AVENUES IN HANOVER: SOME INDOOR ACTIVITIES

The situation is different in Hanover, New Hampshire, where I taught as a Visiting Assistant Professor in the Drama Department at Dartmouth between l994 and l997. If the line between representation and "real life" can be explored by leaving the classroom for the street, I found myself faced with an interesting challenge. In this small New Hampshire town, the line between the classroom and the street is far from distinct. In fact, the Dartmouth campus envelops the street, takes it in in every way, dominates it, and appears to color coordinate everything in the school colors, green and white–even other private businesses. The Gap looks like the college, and so the college looks like the Gap. Everyday life in Hanover seems wrapped up in Dartmouth, which is perched at the apex of the town and appears to exceed it in size. Taking to the street in Hanover was not necessarily to leave the purview of the institution, not necessarily to feel the privilege of the institution–its blind spots and insights, its inclusions and exclusions–reflected against a broader framework. There was no broader framework in Hanover–or, at least, it was more neatly managed, harder to access.

Interested in getting students to explore the frameworks around perform-ance as well as the ideological investments in any performative action, includ-ing everyday rituals of identity, I found myself in an interesting quandary at Dartmouth. The teaching challenge I encountered had more acutely to do with how to make the invisible visible. Privilege, for instance, was largely invisible because of the absence, removal, or veiling of the signs of its opposite. If asked to discuss privilege, for example, it was not beyond the realm of believability that an undergrad might honestly ask "What is privilege?" While this is an excellent question, it is more difficult to discuss when distinctions to privilege are not near at hand. (Indeed I should not have been as surprised as I was to find that those students who have firsthand knowledge of disprivilege often actively secreted their experience, trying to "pass" in the general milieu.) While there is a potentially disturbing irony in the fact that a homeless person in New Haven became an unwitting pedagogical aide–and while I wouldn't wish Hanover a population on the street (though one only need drive a few miles to experience poverty in neighboring New Hampshire towns)–I was a bit stymied as to how to continue "playing it street" in this quintessential New England college town.

I took to indoor activities. What follows are three exercises which provoked interesting discussion.

On the first day of a performance theory class I passed out two slips of paper to each student. The first slip gave them instructions on how they were to present themselves, such as, Speak only in third person; Stand up and turn around before every sentence; Talk directly to your hand; Use nonsense words only; Exaggerate femininity; Exaggerate masculinity. The second slip of paper had the same phrase for each student: You can at any time rebel.

I told students that they must follow the instructions on the first slip. I said nothing about the second slip. They were to introduce themselves and say why they were in the class. Almost everyone followed the instructions of the first paper. Some of them were embarrassed, confused, uncomfortable. Some seemed to enjoy it. Some ostensibly "rebelled" by using normative behavior and not altering the way they presented at all. We went around again, this time finishing the sentence: "I'm performing when I..." One student stood up and slammed her book on the table, as if to rebel by an exaggerated performance of frustration before refusing to finish the sentence. One student almost walked out of the room, but turned around at the door. We went on to the next student, who continued following the directions of the first paper and said, "I'm performing when I sit quietly and do as I'm told." Others offered other endings with other gestures–trying on rebellion (which proved very difficult in the context of its sanctioning), or carrying out directions.

I then said, Okay, let's talk about what just happened. This exercise worked very well. The students basically said, We understood the first instructions on how to behave, but not the second. What does it mean, You can at any time rebel? We were able to talk about performance codes, complicity, and resistance in the present context of their own performance *choices* where normative became apparent as a performance choice and rebellion bore the flavor, by way of instruction, of normativity.

The second exercise I inherited from Silvia Spitta, a colleague in the Spanish Department at Dartmouth. This assignment concerns a strategy to make whiteness, which is often invisible to whites who consider themselves "unmarked" by race, apparent in terms of codes of performance. In a class which happened to be one-third Anglo/white, one-third African American, and one-third Latino/a, Spitta assigned her students a three-page paper on how they each *perform* their ethnicities. Interestingly, every single white student came to her office hours in dismay, with no idea of what to write. On the contrary, the African American and the Latino/a students only had trouble keeping the assignment to three pages. This difficulty on the part of the white students was, actually, the lesson. In this context, the privileges of invisibility and the invisibility of privilege (whiteness as unaware of its markings and ritual performances) could be discussed in class, as well as some of the ramifications of performance.

The third exercise, one of my favorites, was also discovered at Dartmouth. This one has to do with tricking a group into acknowledging their cultural biases on the level of basic assumptions. In the context of some broader discussion, I'll ask the class: "What do we know for sure? What is something we can say is completely true?" Because an answer is never offered to the above (partly because I only pause for a moment or two), I suggest: "How many of you are sure, for instance, that you have a body? Raise your hand if you know you have a body." Without fail (every time I've tried it anyway) everyone will raise their hands. "Now look around you at the raised hands. Is it safe to say, then, that everyone here has a body?" They laugh, as if they didn't need to look around. They bring their hands down. I say, "Raise your hand if you feel certain that everyone here has a body." Again, almost invariably, everyone raises their hand. Here is where the trick comes in. I say, "Are you quite sure that everyone here has a body? Are you certain there's no one here who does not have a body?" At this point, interestingly, a few people begin to "get it." And I've been fascinated to see that persons of cultural heritages other than Euro-American are sometimes right with me—occasionally not raising their hands the second time. "Is there anyone here who does not have a body? Can you imagine a cultural context in which ancestors, no longer with body, might still be considered to be present? They might not have a body, but might they be *here*?"

At Dartmouth, where more than one classroom is adorned with oil paintings of the busts of distinguished gray-haired Dartmouth ancestors, this question can lead to humorous comments on partially embodied presences, etc., and certainly we are on the track of scouting out sociocultural and political investments in representation beyond the transcendent "beauty" of art for art's sake, or the favorite undergraduate mantra of "just" performance. The partial bodies of the Dartmouth forefathers are present for a purpose. Are other "partial" or "invisible" bodies present as well? What is at stake in making the visible the measure of presence? The point of the exercise is to make the invisible visible by unpacking cultural assumptions, to make apparent the cultural construction of seeming absolutes (everyone here has a body), and to open the door to discussing their cultural orientations, as well as others.

The goals of the above indoor activities, while not about "playing the street," are certainly in tune with the street in that they have the potential to upset the comfort level of assumed frameworks of knowledge, such as assumed lines of demarcation between "just" performance and a seemingly nonperformative reality. I am sure that, had I been blessed with greater creativity, I could have found a way to access the actual street in Hanover, but these exercises did some of the trick. And "trick" is the right word, as part of the pedagogical point is to challenge ourselves to explore avenues which are at least partially beyond our control, which can surprise us at any turn—avenues which will raise more questions than answers.

Postscript, 2006

Over ten years have passed since the story told above. I have since taught at Cornell University, and now I hold a tenured position at Brown University. I could expand the telling to five institutions, but will resist that impulse. Instead, I'll briefly tell a story that happened in a class not overtly concerned with gender. I was teaching a seminar on performance and photography, and I was showing some images of historical reenactments as the class was discussing the tangled histories involved in temporal play. I showed one picture of a Civil War soldier and I said that this particular reenactor was a woman cross-dressed as a male soldier. I was trying to get at issues of cross-temporality and I was hoping that we could think, together, about Freeman's notion of "temporal drag." But a hand almost immediately shot up in class and a student (whom I will refrain from categorizing by sex—I'll call him/her Lion) asked why I said that the photo showed a "woman" and why I said that "she" was "cross-dressed." Why was the person in the photograph not just dressed?

I did not deal with the question well, as I felt the time pressure educators often feel in teaching a class full of material. I said something like: "Well, I took the picture and, honestly, talking with the person, looking at the person, I thought that the person was a woman dressed as a man." I could sense Lion's disappointment in me. As an activist for transgendered people, Lion no doubt encounters this problem all the time, but I think this student was hoping for better from me. Though I heard in Lion's comment that I was replicating gender in normative ways, it was honestly the case that I did not yet know how to discuss "women" and "feminism" without replicating gender. Instead of taking the time then, in class, to discuss the issue, I made the mistake of moving on. Later, Lion came to my office and we had an honest and difficult discussion. Lion made very articulate points, and in the process I learned a great deal. I have begun to further my inquiry into whether in fact *temporality, reenactment,* and the *outmoded* are not precisely where we should be thinking; can there be a *past tense* to gender that haunts the present, that, when cited as anachronistic, allows a move into a future less shackled by binary gender codes? It was Virginia Woolf, after all, who wrote in *A Room of One's Own* in 1929 that someday "woman" will be outmoded:

> All assumptions founded on the facts observed when women were the protected sex will have disappeared—as, for example, (here a squad of soldiers marched down the street), that women and clergymen and gardeners live longer than other people. Remove that protection, expose them to the same exertions and activities, make them soldiers and sailors and engine-drivers and dock laboureres, and will not women die off so much younger, so much quicker, than men that one will say, "I saw a woman today," as one used to

say, "I saw an aeroplane." Anything may happen when womanhood has ceased to be a protected occupation, I thought, opening the door. (Woolf 40)

The mention of "aeroplane" invites one last comment. Since the decades of the tales offered before this postscript, we have entered a time categorized by "terror," promoted by the U.S. government and the interests of multinational capital. After 9/11, in the few days that airplanes did not fly, I thought about Wolf's comment a great deal.

I do think that fear is an underestimated ingredient in what keeps us habitually playing out old patterns of gender and race and ethnic identification in heteronormative tropes of behavior. And fear can have a major place in the classroom—on the part of teachers as well as students. Lion (who reminded me in some interesting ways of the Madonna look-alike from 1989) wanted to push the class into arenas that opened out blind spots for discussion and further opened the door, as it were, to the disappearance of gender as an overdetermined way of knowing. Of course, Lion's issues are ones I was (and am) sympathetic with, and I was willing to learn. But what if a student wanted to take up class time with conservative platforms designed to subjugate persons via gender? Should all "positions" be engaged? If yes (and the answer must be yes), is the trick to insist on argument and an articulate engagement with the issues of fear—assuming that fear attends to any positioning, whether so-called progressive or so-called conservative? A student or a teacher following a line of questioning about gender should always be able to articulate—or attempt to articulate—these questions: *What is at stake?* and, *What might I (or we) fear in thinking otherwise?* An argument that in the end devolves to prejudice is often designed to harbor a fear of difference, and in every case that fear is something our classrooms should be designed to explore, always in the interest of opening doors.

WORKS CITED

Boal, Augusto. *Theatre of the Oppressed.* New York: Theater Communications Group, 1985.

_____. "Invisible Theater." *TDR: The Drama Review.* 34:3 (1990): 24-42.

Freeman, Elizabeth. "Packing History, Count(er)ing Generations." *New Literary History* 31.4 (2000): 727-744.

Woolf, Virginia. *A Room of One's Own.* New York: Harvest Books, 1989.

NAVIGATING DANGEROUS WATERS
TEENS, PLAYS, AND THE "FEMINIST WAY" IN A TRADITIONAL HIGH SCHOOL SETTING

Jo Beth Gonzalez

Several years ago I designed a high school course that I now teach one semester every other year; it is titled, simply, "Play Production." The course offers students an opportunity to write and stage vignettes that address issues that matter to them. Because the process of writing about such issues encourages students to be vulnerably honest, risk-taking is a characteristic of the course. The culminating goal of Play Production, a public performance that is typically attended by parents, siblings, and friends, keeps the energy level high throughout the semester. Having taught this course several times now, I expect the turbulence that arises from risk-taking, and recognize that "dangerous waters" are a quality of feminist teaching.

Issues important to youth make their way into theatre classrooms when students have license to create dramatic work that reflects their lives. The risk-taking associated with original artistic expression by youth in public schools is often accompanied by administrative pressure and parent scrutiny. Administrators in some school districts enforce a censorship policy that makes teachers accountable for their risk-taking choices, but this policy can likewise protect teachers from repercussions of those risks if parents disapprove of a controversial class topic and seek some sort of disciplinary action.[1]

This essay presents ways that feminist education can operate in the public high school theatre classroom, using anecdotes from the first Play Production performance, *Anything Else Would Be Substandard* (1998) and the most recent, *Seeing Eye to Eye; A Glimpse of Reality* (2005). I consider a feminist classroom to be, as Susan Stanford Friedman describes, a non-hierarchical place where personal narrative is both validated and integrated into the curriculum ("Authority"). In addition, a feminist pedagogy must be committed to changing students' attitudes toward women and girls, while also attending to the emotional well-being of men and boys. A feminist theatre classroom can become one of few safe locations for boys to express genuine emotion. Establishing a space where boys and girls share power as they devise and act in scenes that speak to issues important to them is the foundation of my feminist pedagogy.

Theatre can be a dynamic force for change, but it can be dangerous in public education when it invites a redefinition of power structures. I believe that power is not something that teachers hold over students. Rather, teachers exercise power in relation to students, who exercise power in relation to the course, the classroom learning environment, and the climate of the school (Gonzalez "Temporary Stages" 17). This essay will discuss a feminist pedagogy in the context of the high school classroom that includes: personal narrative and self-disclosure; consciousness-raising; shared authority; ownership over material and self-censorship; and transgression and censorship. Against a backdrop of traditional secondary education, the Play Production course promotes student voice and artistic expression.

PLAY PRODUCTION'S BACKDROP

Play Production is an elective course for students in grades nine through twelve that meets for fifty minutes a day, five days a week. The course is divided into two sections. During the first nine weeks, students write a script; the second nine weeks is spent casting, staging, rehearsing, performing, and reflecting. In the first several classes, students write brief, two-minute responses to a set of twenty open-ended statements. These initial explorations will eventually evolve into scenes that students revise several times. I have found that themes such as teen incarceration, suicide, agnosticism, high school stereotypes, and death tend to appear in every class. References to masturbation and "faggots," and use of the word *fuck*–never used in plays that the high school's co-curricular drama club produces–occasionally pepper the vignettes. The open-ended prompts that inspire these vignettes include:

- The question that people older than myself ask me that bugs me the most is…

- A discovery I made about someone who I once ignored was…

- The person I see on TV or in films today who I most respect is…

  Next, students attend to narrative voice and dramatic conflict as they shape three of their prompts into scripted scenes. I provide format options to help in this step, such as:

- Consider the subject from two different perspectives and write a debate. One voice is an adult or authority, the other is the voice of the teen.

- Imagine you had five minutes to broadcast anything you wanted to say over the radio to an audience of teens, adults, or both. What would you say?

  The goal in this phase is for each student to write on three topics until they gain enough confidence to share what they've written with their peers. When students complete first drafts, they form groups. Each writer reads his/her draft aloud and receives feedback. I am an observer to their small group discussions and interact only when asked for assistance. After this first reading, students revise their writings, share them with classmates, receive feedback, and then revise a third and fourth time, receiving feedback each time, until every student in the class has completed at least one vignette for the production. By the time a student's vignette is ready to be staged, the entire class holds ownership in it because they have contributed to its development. Sharing ownership in this way builds students' trust for one another.

The collaborative, honest projects that evolve from the Play Production course stand in stark contrast to other performances at the school, most notably, the "pep rally." Our high school holds two pep rallies each year that honor fall and winter athletes. Like all community performance rituals, the typical high school pep rally celebrates common beliefs and ways of seeing, and heightens generally accepted notions of patriarchy. Because performance rituals break down barriers between art and life, spectators caught up in them may unknowingly reinforce stereotypes and tacit norms.

The first pep rally, in October, is part of a week of festivities related to Homecoming. Like most high schools and colleges, students elect a Homecoming Queen, who is crowned during the football game. At our school, she is flanked by four female attendants, representing the freshman, sophomore, junior, and senior classes. The second pep rally, in February, is part of a week-long set of festivities celebrating "Cominghome." Cominghome has roots in the old-fashioned Sadie Hawkins Day, when girls could invite boys to a dance. Students elect a senior boy to be Cominghome King, who is crowned during a basketball game and flanked by four male attendants.

The Cominghome pep rally that took place when students were devising *Anything Else Would Be Substandard* was unique because of the extent to which it complicated the concept of gender. The rally, held in the gymnasium, was mandatory for students, open to parents, organized by students leaders, and sanctioned by administrators. It began with a seriously performed, flashy set of moves to music that the school's dance team was taking to regional dance team competitions: twenty-five girls in spandex leotards and very short skirts swung their rear ends, kicked their legs, and smiled wide-eyed. Not surprisingly, boys feverishly whooped each time the girls bent over.

Next came a "Mr. Swimsuit" competition. Ten boys dressed comically in swim trunks, Hawaiian shirts, beach hats, and flip-flops extended carnations and gave their best "pick-up lines" to mystery "lovely ladies" from the audience, each of whom was a female teacher who had agreed to participate. The last "lovely lady" was a well-liked male math teacher (and grandfather). The "reigning" king, wearing a Burger King crown, was played by another male math teacher (and golf coach). Sentimentally wiping away mock tears, he handed a large bouquet of flowers to the new king. The nine "runners-up" raised the new king onto their shoulders as a male student in the bleachers spontaneously shouted, "Take a victory lap!"

The audience laughed at, cheered, and applauded this farcical presentation, whose origins stem as far back as Aristophanes, the ancient Greek playwright whose comedies jabbed political, social, and cultural norms. Similarly, ridicule of the familiar beauty pageant pleased the high school audience. Yet this skit disturbed me, a few of my colleagues, and I'm guessing many students who lacked the confidence to speak out. What if the gender inversions were reversed? Would this scene have been as funny if the girls had staged the parody rather than the boys? Who would have benefitted? The girls? The guys who were struggling with their sexuality? What if the dance team had entered the gym with layers of bulging muscle pads and gigantic athletic supporters strapped over their crotches?

This "spirit-generating" school-wide performance ritual purported good will and unity, but denied students' individual voices and perpetuated stereotypes. Against this backdrop of competing tensions–the dynamic potential for classroom playwrights to stage vignettes that speak to their peers' lived experiences versus stereotype-perpetuating rituals–the Play Production course and the Cominghome rally co-exist in my high school, albeit unequally.

PERSONAL NARRATIVE AND SELF-DISCLOSURE

My feminist classroom is a place where personal narrative is both validated and integrated into the curriculum. Nearly half of the vignettes in *Anything Else Would Be Substandard* and *Seeing Eye to Eye; A Glimpse of Reality* stemmed directly from the personal experiences of the student authors. Autobiographical dramatization is a means of self-expression that can empower young women and men to communicate insights about their lives they might otherwise keep to themselves, and is a means of self-disclosure that involves vulnerability. Teachers who employ a feminist pedagogy that encourages such self-disclosure must be vigilant about not coercing it. Students may become dangerously vulnerable if they feel pressured by teachers to write in ways that are emotionally unsafe for them. However, guided by a protecting teacher, journeying through that "vulnerable space" can lead students to increased self-confidence.

I always make a point of telling students to avoid topics that they are too emotionally close to, although some students select topics such as friends' deaths, their own depression, or thoughts of suicide. Those students who find a balance between the riskiness of the subject matter and enough emotional distance to keep them safe can come to grips with the issue, often finding empowerment and growth in the process.

Self-disclosure is an important element in the process of transformation, a quality of a feminist classroom that many education theorists consider a source of power (Aronowitz 1994, Behar 1996).[2] Transformation refers to the ongoing influence that a class can make on a student, even after the course is over. In the classroom, the "transgression" that can lead to transformation can be dangerous because it often requires students to step beyond the boundary of expectation (hooks 1994, Hessford 1999). I contend that stepping beyond expectation is dangerous because students can risk being so honest with themselves that they may discover a tacit truth. Students can become unsettled when they recognize that a self-disclosing statement they have made in the course of public dialogue uncovers a previously unconsidered truth. As Basil Bernstein writes, "transgression can become its own source of power, which generates instability but also its own processes of resolution" (as qtd. in Wallace 111). For my students, transformation is an influence that can lead to change—in self-esteem, in behavior, even in ideology.

One student, Sue,[3] wrote an autobiographical scene she called "Oppression," in which demon voices told her she was worthless, ugly, and unloved. Sue tried to block out the voices, which represented failure in friendships, school, and communication with parents, but was successful only after cutting her wrist with the point of a compass until she bled. The stage lights pulsated red as Sue asked the audience, "Sometimes I wish this was over. Don't you?"

The process of writing and performing "Oppression" helped Sue gain self-agency. Three years after she wrote it, Sue commented on the script she had written when she was sixteen:

> Sharing what I did in my play opened so many floodgates of healing....
> That "oppression" made me realize what can happen to a human soul. I
> know that if I forget what happened to me, it will be so much easier for it to
> happen to me again. There are ways out of it, though I wanted...to show
> that I had become strong, and conquered the depression in my own way.
> (personal interview 5 April 2002)

While Sue's increased self-confidence demonstrates the positive influence of feminist pedagogy, some student-empowering methodologies still adhere to traditional, manipulative teaching strategies that reinforce dominant ideologies. Wendy Hesford asserts that autobiographies can reinforce dominant assumptions by demonstrating "the ways that teachers and students have been disciplined and stylized to produce certain narratives of the self" (35). In the case of "Oppression," Sue was expected to observe a standardized writing format and rules for correct grammar, punctuation, and spelling. I surmise that without the entrenched writing conventions that Sue followed, her empowered self-disclosure and publicly dramatized personal narratives would have developed in complexity.

Oppressed individuals are disadvantages by traditional classroom power relationships. The language and terms of Sue's discourse reflected dominant patters of expression, and the monologue focused solely on the individual rather than speaking more broadly of social change (Maher and Tetreault 218). But in a classroom, discourse can easily flow from the individual to the collective, as students recognize their own experiences in those of their peers. While Sue communicated her struggle with depression through drama, her monologue remained focused on herself. But on the other hand, this collaborative, cooperative process of the monologue's creation built trust among students and led to discussions that raised student consciousness about bullying, stereotypes, and mental health.

RAISING CONSCIOUSNESS

Critical theorists believe that consciousness-raising is a pedagogical goal that can ultimately lead to change (hooks 1994, Britzman 1991). Paulo Freire asserts that challenging students to think beyond the reality they know can help them broaden their understanding of the larger world because they will see themselves against the backdrop of history (Shor and Freire 175). The process of changing attitudes and perceptions takes time, and it begins with dialogue. Unlike discussion, which serves to seek consensus, dialogue is a complex, more layered form of conversation that invites extended participant engagement in critically conscious thinking. Dialogue is an intense, incomplete process wherein the engaged voice is never "fixed and absolute but always changing, always evolving in dialogue with a world beyond itself" (hooks, *Teaching* 11).

Deep dialogue can be moderated by an expert on the topic or an objective third party, or it can be free-flowing, as is usually the case in the high school classroom. For example, a talk-back between audience and actors following a play such as *'Night Mother* (about a daughter who informs her mother at the beginning of the play that she is going to commit suicide) might be formally guided by an invited mental health expert. Likewise, students and teacher in a classroom, deciding whether or not to include a play about suicide for their student body which has recently become victim to suicide might seriously talk among themselves, but their dialogue would be more casual because the group is smaller and knows one another. Opposition to a feminist perspective will, and should, be allowed to emerge in free-flowing dialogue that takes place in a feminist classroom because dialogue engages all who have opinions to share. However, a feminist teacher should not coerce a class into accepting her or his own point of view. If dialogue is free, eventually one or more students will communicate the teacher's point of view, which will then become one of many that students leave the class pondering. Participants leave a dialogue thinking because dialogue does not seek closure; continued thinking raises consciousness, which in turn increases potential for change.

Berenice Fisher claims that the process of dialogue in the classroom provides students with an "opportunity to learn from and teach each other, collectively address problems of social injustice, and imagine and think through alternative responses" (32). In the midst of dialogue, questions will emerge that guide students toward recognizing difference as well as an emerging sense of self. The bonding that can occur when classroom dialogue raises students' consciousness of social issues can "pla[y] an especially valuable role in feminist discourse that invites emotional forthrightness" (70).

During the Play Production course, discussions develop throughout the process and raise students' awareness of themselves in relation to each other. Some of these are formal, where we pull chairs into a circle and discuss current newspaper and magazine articles that resonate with issues similar to those the students are writing about; many other discussions are impromptu. Reflecting after the production of *Anything Else Would Be Substandard,* both boys and girls remarked that the course broke preconceived notions they had held of one another. One student commented, "I gained a perspective of other people's experiences, ranging from religious beliefs to misinterpretations of sexual identity" (post-performance reflection 4 June 1999). Raising consciousness about one another includes awareness of gendered stereotypes. A girl wrote, "I used to think any [girl] with the 'in-crowd' was a mindless zombie, without any individuality or intelligence. Leslie showed me that she and many others have a wit and intelligence that makes them a joy to be around."

As a teacher in a co-ed public school, I try to help boys express themselves, and I try to foster communication between boys, and between boys and girls. Boys need this support. Norah Vincent observes in her memoir *Self-Made Man*:

> So much of what happens emotionally between men isn't spoken aloud, and so the outsider, especially the female outsider who is used to emotional life being overt and spoken (often over-spoken), tends to assume that what isn't said isn't there. But it is there… (46).

Part of the process of girls establishing their social identity involves recognizing that boys' emotions exist, though often they appear buried. The feminist high school classroom can foster interactive communication and dialogue so that girls encourage boys, and boys encourage boys, to bring more of their emotions to the surface.

This was brought to life for me during the rehearsals of *Seeing Eye to Eye; A Glimpse of Reality.* In one vignette, the male author, Tom, composed seven different reasons why a teenage boy would consider killing himself by driving suicidally fast down a flat, open country road. Male actors conveyed each perspective in short monologues. Confused, angry, depressed, sarcastic, each character was intent upon testing the limits of his control behind the wheel. Part way through the rehearsal process, Tom decided to add a laugh track to underscore the piece. My initial reaction, which I kept to myself, was, "That would destroy the poignancy of every moment Tom has created!" But I chose to remain silent, and let the class discuss the idea.

After the actors staged the scene in rehearsal, I asked, "What do you think of the addition?" Some students were unsure why it had been included, but others commented that it added humor to the scene. Near the end of the conversation, one senior girl, Jane, commented, "I think it's cool the way you guys show your emotions onstage relating to such a serious topic. I think the laugh track takes all the honesty away." Later, Tom reflected in his journal, "I didn't want my scene to come off looking stupid. What Jane said made me think, so I took the laugh track out. But I still think it would've been funny" (6 June 2005).

How truly humorous he thought the laugh track was, or whether the laugh track was a cover-up for real thoughts of suicide, I can only guess. What I do know is that at our high school over the past two years, four young men have committed suicide. Because class dialogue focused on topics that genuinely mattered to teens, Tom listened to the opinion of a female peer who wanted to see boys express emotions with sincerity and simplicity. Jane appreciated Tom's public expression of emotions, an observation that contrasts sharply with the Cominghome parody where a man's mock tears ridiculed a newly-crowned beauty queen. Carol Gilligan, attending to today's "boy-crisis," asserts that the mental health of boys would increase if they gained comfort expressing themselves emotionally:

> Emotions and relationships, once associated with women and therefore with limitation, are now understood to enhance intelligence and the self, and have become desirable attributes of manhood. ...an effective strategy for preventing boys' psychological difficulties and educational problems would involve recognizing their sensitivities, building honest relationships and strengthening a healthy capacity for resistance (53). [4]

The consciousness-raising precept of feminist pedagogy that shapes the Play Production course also provides an opportunity for boys and girls to challenge accepted notions of masculinity. In our culture, few spaces permit boys to show a variety of emotions. A feminist theatre classroom is one of them. During class discussions, none of the students overtly questioned how the fight for male superiority festers into violence in our culture. Yet student writers wrestled personally with the "Tough Guise," a term Jackson Katz coined to refer to the gendered image of masculinity which links power, control, threats, violence, homophobia, and the glamorization of drugs and alcohol to "real" manhood (2000). Some male students critiqued their self-images. One student, Blake, wrote and delivered a monologue entitled "Guys Like Me." His monologue questioned whether or not men attract women more successfully through bravado rather than by demonstrating vulnerabilities, passion, and caring:

> I've been hearing all my life from the opposite sex that they're looking for...a guy who isn't selfish, who is in tune with what he's feeling, who isn't looking for "wham-bam-thank you-ma'am," but rather a meaningful relationship. "I need a guy like you, but not you because" (and here are the words which haunt my nightmares), "you're my best friend." Apparently I'm everyone's best friend these days. Apparently that nice guy crap goes out the window when the thinker clicks off and the simian instinct takes over. Apparently nice guys aren't chic. Apparently, Bad-to-the-Bone George Thorogoods are the real winners (*Anything Else Would Be Substandard*).

Blake's monologue made visible the connection between male image and brute force by suggesting an alternative construct of masculinity that celebrates intellect and sensitivity. His re-vision of masculinity became a consciousness-raising opportunity because it allowed Blake to present another construct of the male teen, although it remained safely within the boundaries of male/female pairing.

Dialogue can also foster stronger interpersonal relationships. Students in the Play Production classes hold in-depth conversations about their individual vignettes, but they integrate current events topics that aren't directly related to their writing as well. Because the feminist classroom fosters emotional expression in girls and boys, the course helps students center their personal experiences within the context of a broader community consciousness.

A significant national event, the Columbine shootings, occurred in April 1999, right before we performed *Anything Else Would Be Substandard.* At that time in the rehearsal process, students' writings were solidly scripted and they were deeply involved in rehearsals. But references to the tragedy peppered many discussions. In particular, the class talked extensively about the "Trench Coat Mafia" and Marilyn Manson, both topics that the news media centered on as investigators tried to understand the Columbine killers' motivation.[5] It was during one of these talks that a visibly upset male student shared with his peers that he'd been sent to the office that week and interrogated because he often wore a long black coat and goth-like chain around his neck to school.

That student's comfort in sharing something he could have kept to himself demonstrates how a classroom environment that invites genuine dialogue can help students connect through personal experience and increase their abilities to critically analyze national events. In post-performance reflection, some students, without prompting, referred to the Columbine shooting. One student, noting that the discussions we had about the Columbine shooting were a memorable element of the class, recalled that "not only did [the discussions] help all of us deal with the whole ordeal, but it made us really think–What can we do to help prevent it from happening to us?" (post-performance reflection 4 June 1999). The class provided an outlet for students to share their thoughts on the tragedy, demonstrating that the issues with which students were dealing raised their consciousness both of themselves and the nation at large.

SHARED AUTHORITY

A primary component of a feminist pedagogy is creating opportunities for students to engage in extended dialogue that aims to raise critical consciousness. Decentering teacher authority is a crucial step toward accomplishing this goal. When the teacher is not constantly standing "front and center," class space opens up, giving students more freedom to speak out during discussions. However, it is imperative that a teacher cautiously moderates the discussion because an atmosphere in which students are free to speak out can prompt some students to say hurtful comments to others. Decentering authority can be especially challenging for the high school teacher, whose students have been ingrained to view their teacher as "the authority."

An example of such decentering occurred in the Play Production class when a boy, Kip, wrote a vignette for *Seeing Eye to Eye; A Glimpse of Reality* that made fun of our high school's hockey players. During rehearsal, Kip had directed a peer, Carl, to skip offstage, and when Carl rehearsed in front of the class, he embellished the action by pointing his toes and flaunting a limp wrist. After Kip explained that some hockey players are "flamboyant," I asked the class if Carl's exit made a statement about hockey players. For two days, the class shared opinions about whether or not Kip's scene represented gay stereotyping.

At no time during class discussions did I instruct the boys to downplay Carl's body language. Because the class did not know whether or not I would allow the limp wrist interpretation, tension increased, and this tension sustained the conversation among students. After these discussions, students rehearsed their scenes for another two weeks; by performance time, Carl's flamboyant skipping remained, but the limp wrist and pointed toes had disappeared. As a feminist teacher, I want my authority to stem from shared experience and be based upon cooperation among and between the students and me. Thus I chose to remain silent, and my silence extended student dialogue.

A playwriting/performance classroom in which students freely discuss subjects and share perspectives that connect to their personal lives is one in which teacher and students share power. Power-sharing fosters a critical perspective that enables students to discern between the discourses of dominant school culture and the layers of meaning pressed into their daily experience. But a power-sharing classroom environment is not risk-free. Effective leadership in a feminist classroom requires an awareness of the contradiction embedded in the role of teacher. Henry Giroux states:

> On the one hand, teacher voice represents a basis in authority that can provide knowledge and forms of self-understanding allowing students to develop the power of critical consciousness. At the same time, regardless of how politically or ideologically correct a teacher may be, his or her "voice" can be destructive for students if it is imposed on them or if it is used to silence them (142).

Not only can power-sharing be dangerous when teachers misuse it and manipulate students, but it can also lack effect. Jennifer Gore observes that decentering teacher authority doesn't prevent students from looking to teachers for approval, guidance, and assessment and that the "progressive pedagogical practice of 'negotiating' with students is frequently much less open than we pretend or believe" (143).

Thus, apprehension is a component of a feminist theatre class within the cultural milieu of a traditional American high school. When I teach, the experience often feels clandestine because I am apprehensive that my motives might be misinterpreted by other faculty and administrators. I am concerned about students whose vulnerabilities indicate a need for help that I can't provide. And I wonder if students perceive that the negotiating that takes place among us is just a game; if they know that as a high school teacher, it is my hired responsibility to uphold the position of ultimate authority in my classroom. The students live with apprehension as well, for they know that the perspectives they express in their vignettes often contradict the dominant culture of their peers and their school.

Despite these cautions, it is important to practice techniques that enable students to exert authority in the classroom. In the Play Production course, I organize rehearsal sequences for students, but they are responsible for blocking and running scenes and providing notes to one another. I make a point to give my notes only after they share theirs. As the production date approaches, however, I have to force myself to let the students run the rehearsals. Usually–for the sake of the art and the audience–the creative process must give way to polishing the product, but "letting go" is critical in a student-empowered theatre learning community where a production is the goal. Furthermore, students learn that my continued withdrawal means that they have to discipline themselves in order to focus on details and manage their time.

During the last week of rehearsals for *Anything Else Would Be Substandard*, Leslie revised a dramatic scene into a monologue, changes that encouraged peers to contemplate the typical characterization of young high school girls, constructed in part by the widely-accepted view that men are aggressive. The performance was scheduled for Thursday evening. It was 9:15 Thursday morning. Leslie asked to revamp the blocking of her scene with nine non-speaking actors since it was now a monologue. "What?!" my director's brain screamed at her. I looked at the clock. "Sure," I replied calmly. "You have until 9:34. You better get going." Her actors worked intensely for fourteen minutes and the changes made the scene the most direct critique of high school culture in the production. Leslie's characterization of a freshman girl revealed a behavior she believed to be tacitly true, and because she was publicly critical of her peers, her self-image was up for public scrutiny as well.

Entitled "The Cycle," the vignette was set at a weekend party in a friend's home, and characterized the perpetual "victimization" of freshmen girls by senior guys at high school parties:

> Leslie: God these parties get more and more disgusting each year. The same
> old people drinking the same old beer, having the same old drunken con-
> versations. The only thing different about this year's upcoming parties are
> the new freshman girls. Poor things, after tonight, their reputations are
> gonna be shot to hell. There's nothing I hate more than watching people do
> things I know they'll regret later, and not having any control over the situa-
> tion. (*Anything Else Would Be Substandard*)

The next day, when the last minute staging of her scene came up in discussion, Leslie said to me, "I knew you would freak out at that." Leslie recognized the risk she was taking, and that I was not going to hinder her from taking that risk. This remark illustrates the shift in student/teacher power that can occur in a feminist classroom, and also how it can be inherently dangerous to students whose self-images are on the line, and to the teacher whose judgment–if risks in content or language go too far–may be questioned by parents or administrators.

Yet this danger is the fuel that propels consciousness-raising. For example, one of the changes that Leslie and her actors made during this final rehearsal reinforced the healthy view of masculinity purported by Blake's vignette "Guys Like Me," which preceded "The Cycle" in performance. And at the end of Leslie's reworked scene, she described the "stoner" clique's perspective of girls:

> Ah, and here are our final Romeos, the stoner table. Their whole theory revolves around the idea that if you get a girl high, she becomes so horny that she can't keep her hands off you. Of course this has never actually worked, but I guess in La La Land anything is possible. (*Anything Would Be Substandard*)

At the last moment, Blake and Leslie decided that the monologue should end when Blake appears and stands next to Leslie, facing the audience. Leslie stated, "But here in the real world I'm lost." Then together Blake and Leslie asked, "Where are all the nice guys?"

While Sue's monologue empowered her personally, Leslie's insistence on re-working her scene and coordinating it with Blake's demonstrates a more complex response to the class' pedagogy because they recognized their ability to raise consciousness collectively. Rather than validating the "macho" identity that equates "real manhood" with popular culture's glamorization of alcohol and drugs, Leslie showed that girls "are looking for more in men than 'bad guy' posturing" (Katz video).

A feminist classroom fosters a rapport between the teacher and students that helps students express the perceptions of their realities, and discover links between differing perceptions. As students saw how their individual vignettes connected to one another, their ownership of the project continued to increase. The confidence with which they owned the production sharpened their perception when self-censorship became an issue.

OWNERSHIP AND SELF-CENSORSHIP

The trust we were developing was tested one morning. We were holding a formal discussion about an article I had seen in an issue of *Newsweek* entitled "High School Confidential."[6] The article described the upcoming summer's movies aimed at teens, all of which were rated R, and it included detailed descriptions of the sexual activities of some of the films' characters. I was concerned about sharing this with students, who spanned all four grade levels, and sought advice from our media center specialist. I decided to use the article, but prefaced our reading of it by reiterating why it was relevant to our class, and warned students about its content. (That in itself intrigued them!) I mentioned that ours was a non-traditional kind of classroom, and that the conversations would stay in the classroom, to be used for the development of the play. I told them that we could talk frankly about issues that might not be discussed in other classes because we wanted to generate honest reflection about teen views on life for the creation of our play.

We read the article and as students began to discuss it with animation, a knock on the door interrupted us. I opened the door and to find a professional, studio-type television camera staring at us. Behind it was a technician who explained that he was taping a program for the local university television station. Could he come in and record a typical classroom? After a moment of stunned silence, the class broke out in nervous laughter. The technician reassured us that there would be no sound recording. There was a long pause. The students looked at me, I nodded to the technician, they breathed a sigh of relief, and we continued our conversation–albeit more stilted–as the camera operator filmed us for a minute.

Within the traditional educational system in which I work, the Play Production class is a fragile bubble. Revelations of vulnerabilities, risk-taking autobiographical dramatizations, and teacher-guided forays that lead students into discussions about controversial issues create tensions within that bubble. Students can see through it to the outside, and they are searching for signs of approval from other teachers, their friends, and their parents; they likewise seek approval of themselves via images reflected in the media. As a teacher, I am simultaneously aware that at any moment the bubble can collapse from the inside, due to administrative pressure, or burst from outside elements poking in. Thus, two energies affect students' impulses to self-censor: concern for parental and audience approval of their ideas, and tacit-yet-nonetheless-palpable tensions emitted by a cautious teacher.

Constantly aware of the outside, students expressed reservations about their parents' reactions to the truths their scenes would present. Before the performance of *Anything Else Would Be Substandard*, Blake, who'd written another vignette that comically examined agnosticism, doubted a supportive response from his father, who was a Methodist minister. Another student felt she knew her parents would balk, so she planned not to invite them. At some point during formal discussions, I read the school's policy on inappropriate language and asked students to think about their vignettes in terms of the policy.[7] After a lively dialogue, they often decided that individual writers should eliminate what they considered to be extraneous use of PG-13 language.[8]

I felt especially vulnerable as *Anything Else Would Be Substandard* loomed closer because my inexperience treading the "dangerous waters" of the course increased my reservations about the content of the play. These reservations, in turn, diminished my confidence in the students' scripts. I had received responses from elementary school teachers and their principals regarding a children's play that my students were touring to the district's elementary schools that same month, and this contributed to my vulnerability. The play, *The Noodle Doodle Box* by Paul Maar, depicted three clownish characters who exerted power over one another. Although students prefaced the production with individual classroom theatre workshops on bullying (informed by Augusto Boal's Theatre of the Oppressed techniques), teachers complained that their students left the production spitting at one another; ultimately three out of seven schools canceled their performances. Teachers and principals didn't embrace this play for the opportunity it presented, on the heels of Columbine, to address why boys spit and why bullies push. Instead, teachers were generally appalled that we brought the play; their principals responded to the staff's reaction with deep concern.

The response of these educators points to a divide between the dramatic presentation of controversial issues and the kind of preview and follow-up they demand. If educators (in this case the elementary school teachers) do not significantly engage with their students on the topic, the presentation risks reinforcing the very notions it is critiquing. Contrary to this, the work of students in the Play Production class, coupled with an audience of parents and peers who cared about the performers on a personal level, helped establish everyone's deep investment with the controversial content.

Nonetheless, I was on edge, particularly nervous about a scene which mentioned masturbation. About three weeks before the students performed, I explained the elementary teachers' reactions to the children's play, and brought up for discussion the possibility that we write letters to the students' parents, "warning" them of the content of the play. By this time, students held such confident ownership of the production that this suggestion insulted them. Ironically, the student who was not inviting her parents to the play contended, "I don't understand why we've done all this [writing and staging] and now we have to question it…. Why was it OK then and just now we're getting worried because of the reaction to the *Noodle Doodle Box?*" In this moment, I was tempted to take authority in an effort to circumvent a second set of potentially damaging criticisms directed at the content of my high school theatre program. To withdraw any vignette because of last minute reservations would have dishonored my students and proven me a hypocrite, but I cannot deny the very real fear I was wrestling with. In *Teaching Positions*, Elizabeth Ellsworth notes, "My pedagogical relation to 'the community' (it teaches me who it thinks I already am) is put at risk by the *performativity* of my self-conscious self-monitoring" (111). For me, it is often difficult to resist reiterating authoritarian teaching methods. While the feminist classroom environment nurtures students' abilities to take risks and self-censor, institutional rules dictate behaviors the students and I must adhere to.

The authority figure I present at school is a persona that changes shape

depending upon the situations I'm in, the course I'm teaching, and the chem-
istry among the students in my classes at any given moment. I change this persona at various times to encourage the needs of my students, to meet the
requirements of my job, and to explore my pedagogy. Because I encourage students to produce original work in Play Production, I must acknowledge and
respect the policies established by my school district that govern controversial
topics. Many high schools have banned the use of guns in plays, and plays produced in high schools of the more conservative districts are forbidden to mention rape or homosexuality ("Censorship"). Simply, artist/educators working
within the confines of traditional high school settings face censorship. Thus,
while students write plays in the public school classroom that deal with "sensitive" issues, their teachers are often contemplating job security. At the 2000
International Drama in Education Research Institute (IDIERI) conference in
Columbus, Ohio, Kathleen Gallagher asked, "At what junctures can teachers
give up power and still work within the institutional setting?"

Yet drama is an effective strategy for infusing adolescents with the confidence and skill to communicate insights and experiences about issues important to them with clarity, wit, and poignancy. When teen voices speak words or
teenage bodies enact images that school officials, parents, or community members consider off-limits, teacher and students enter a pedagogical danger zone.
In the high school theatre classroom, the personal becomes political. hooks
warns, "Fear of painful confrontation often leads women and men active in
feminist movement to avoid rigorous critical encounter, yet if we cannot engage
dialectically in a committed, rigorous, humanizing manner, we cannot hope to
change the world" (*Talking Back* 25). It is my hope that students will gain skills
in my feminist classroom that fortify them to become self-agents for positive
social change. One of those skills is articulating the purpose for change to others. Play Production students practice this skill by preparing their audiences for
the content they are about to see.

I cannot be sure that the parents of the students in my community will
accept the content of the Play Production scenes, so to fortify our production
we become pro-active. For example, prior to the performance of *Anything Else
Would Be Substandard*, I informed my principal of the evolving content of the
play and she suggested writing a statement in the program, and perhaps giving
a pre-show introduction. Much of my work as an artist/educator today integrates techniques and philosophies of Augusto Boal and Michael Rohd, with
whom my students and I have had the opportunity to train. Excerpts from the
program note reflect their influence:

> What you see in this presentation are not answers...because no single
> answer can apply to all. Rather, these scenes offer insight into what teens in
> this particular class are thinking, and how they interpret the media's percep-
> tions of contemporary American teens. For students to voice themselves
> honestly, it was important that they felt free to write about a multitude of

issues. Several of the scenes are serious in subject matter and some stem from personal experience. Realistic expressions pepper the performance. The students in Play Production invite you to listen, for listening is the first step toward dialogue, and dialogue can lead to understanding.

Blake volunteered to explain to the audience before the show that we decided to rate the play PG-13, and that none of what they might hear was intended for gratuitous effect, but rather to communicate messages the students wanted to express. I had a conversation some time later with Blake's father, and he asked me how I was able to get the kids to open up. (He was teaching a college writing class and was encouraging his students to self-disclose, but sensed their reluctance.) This casual conversation affirmed for me that the students succeeded in communicating to their parents. Blake's doubts about his father's disapproval did not manifest, and in fact his mother contemplated aloud after the show, "If only more parents would listen to their kids..." (author's notes 28 May 1999).

Since I've been teaching the Play Production course, class presentations have generated positive audience feedback. However, this does not negate the reality of the risks students take in writing and staging these scenes in our conservative institutional setting. Denigrated self-images, bruised friendships, displeased parents, and authority censure are at stake when teens write, stage, and perform points of view about controversial issues that are important to them. The success of the Play Production performances is due in great part to the efforts students and I take to inform and prepare our audience for the vignettes presented before them.

But why didn't anyone prepare the audience of the Cominghome rally for what they were about to see? Because the goal of the event was to treat students to an entertaining assembly that recognized the achievements of winter athletes (boys and girls), not to provide an opportunity for students to re-think accepted notions of gender and class bias in our school. The greatest danger of the Cominghome rally is that it sanctions a public display of stereotypical behaviors, and embeds those images into the mass consciousness of the student body. The Cominghome pep assembly is an example of how an educational institution promotes "normal" males celebrating dominance by disrespecting women. Transformation in a public high school cannot take place in a forty-five minute athletic pep assembly for eleven hundred teenagers. But face-to-face dialogue about issues important to teenagers, and time for listening, reflecting and revising a creative work in an atmosphere of trust, can. Contending that small groups effectively nurture critical consciousness, hooks explains, "Small groups of people coming together to engage in feminist discussion, in dialectical struggle make a space where the 'personal is political' is a starting point for education for critical consciousness..." ("Feminism: A Transformation Politic" 495).

So what helps me navigate my feminist ship through the hallways of my high school? I've learned that the principal is the drawbridge. If the principal is informed every step of the way as a classroom of students explores topics that "press buttons," he/she is more likely to support the teacher if a parent or other administrator questions the content. When my drama club produced *Simply Maria, or, the American Dream* by Josefina López, a parent of a female cast member stepped into the rehearsal of a scene where the protagonist Maria is captivated by her dawning sexuality; Maria looks at herself in a full-length mirror and runs her hands along the curves of her body. Maria's mother enters, notices her daughter's activity and scolds, "Maria, what are you doing? Sex is dirty!" The next day the parent called the principal and complained that the drama club was producing a play that contained masturbation. Because my principal had read the play and because she and I had discussed the content, she was aware that the scene was not about masturbation, but about an adolescent girl's emerging sexuality. My principal told the parent, "High school theatre isn't what it used to be."

In this situation, the scene and reality simultaneously mirrored one another. The drama parent's uncontextualized judgment of a moment in a scene demonstrates the same powerful fear of teen girls' sexuality as the central character's mother expressed. The comments of both the fictional and the real parent reinforce the notion that girls' bodies are off-limits, even to themselves. This resistance contradicts the advice of psychotherapist Virginia Beane Rutter, who asserts that "Her body is the seat of a girl's self-esteem. If she feels comfortable in her body, she will be able to speak out about her feelings, and she will know when her feelings are affecting her body" (53).

Another step that teachers and students can take to ward off potential negative feedback by parents or administrators when a production involves sensitive issues is to provide a brief pre-show introduction that identifies the themes and rates the production "PG-13." In the talk, students can mention the seriousness with which they explored the topics and the importance that examining the issue(s) has had in their lives; students must explain that the process of writing/producing the play *mattered* to them.

hooks contends that the feminist effort seeks transformation of self ("Feminism" 493); individual change is the basis for social change. I have been able to resist dominant norms in my institution by presenting issues to the public slowly while remaining acutely sensitive to the limitations of my resistance within the institution that employs me. I work to create a trusting environment where students contemplate introspectively, then engage in dialogue, and finally own their dramatized perspectives with the confidence to present them in public performances. As I position my pedagogy and frame my work as a feminist educator, I recognize the importance of negotiating the context of events that occur both in school, like the Cominghome rally, and outside of school, like the Columbine shootings. Events like these provide the material from which students gain experience developing points of view and practicing skills that can help them effect social change. Social studies teacher Al Levie observes that teachers who connect with students on issues that matter, help them organize, and stand with them, have the power to alter school dynamics and generate student leaders. He asserts, "By engaging students in real-life issues and encouraging them to act on a political level, we will transform schools into places where authentic learning takes place" (64).

The style and structure of feminist pedagogy fosters a dynamic relationship among students, teachers, and the primary school administrators. This relationship transfers power from adult to teen; the power transfer enables student voice; listening to student voice leads to dialogue; dialogue can lead to partial understanding; and emerging understanding can lead to change. Leslie reflected:

> Having real discussions is so much better than being talked at. It's really broken the monotony of daily classes; it was such a better environment to work in. Through our discussions on the media, I learned so much about my peers and how they see the world. We all became so close that we were completely comfortable speaking freely without feeling self-conscious. My mind has opened up so much to people who appear to be different. I also learned that my peers can teach me more about life, and emotions, and important issues than any teacher could (personal interview 3 June 1999).

High school theatre isn't what it used to be.

NOTES

[1] Many students value their parents' opinion. Students' desire for parental approval to address a controversial subject in class may result from feelings of vulnerability, fear of reprisal, lack of self-confidence or other dynamics between them and their parents (Gonzalez 2006 12-14).

[2] The following classroom approaches to build trust all demand honest communication between the students (I credit the first two activities to Michael Rohd, who demonstrated them in a week-long summer workshop he conducted in Bowling Green, Ohio, in 1998): 1) Students sit in a circle on the floor. I ask students to tell a short (one minute) story about any given topic that makes them think about that topic. The story may be about them, or about someone they know. Each student concludes his/her story with: "And it made me think." Speakers do not explain what their stories meant to them, only that the story made them think. Sometimes, I ask students to write down on a sticky note what each person's story made them think about, or a question they want to ask the speaker. Then we post the notes so that the speakers can silently read the comments they have made to one another. This silent dialogue often validates students' experiences, and/or helps them recognize that others have encountered similar circumstances. 2) Sometimes after the "It Made Me Think" activity, I ask students to form tableaux depicting an image that a particular story they heard evoked in their minds. Image-making, or "sculpting" as Michael Rohd describes in *Hope is Vital*, is a silent activity wherein students take random turns manipulating the bodies of peers in the center of a circle into formations that depict concrete relationships and abstract impressions. After ten or fifteen minutes of sculpting, I ask students to observe what they saw in various images. I do not ask students to explain what they were attempting to communicate. This exercise enables students to communicate without words, and to realize that what they communicate may be interpreted differently by their peers. Students also learn to trust their peers when they observe that they can share multiple, but nonetheless serious and reflective, interpretations of a single image. 3) After any students present work before their peers—in written or staged form—I ask the presenters to sit down in front of their peers. Then I ask the class to provide the presenters with feedback. The feedback must always begin with compliments first, before we move into constructive criticism.

[3] All student names have been changed.

[4] Increased suicide risk is a concern among students who are lesbian, bisexual, gay, or transgendered. See James Lock and Hans Stiener, "Gay, Lesbian, and Bisexual Youths' Risks for Emotional, Physical, and Social Problems: Results from a Community-Based Survey," *Journal of Child and Adolescent Psychiatry*, 1 (1999): 297-301.

[5] As psychologists, parents, and other adults tried to make sense of the Columbine shootings, some suggested that the music of rocker Marilyn Manson, whose dress promoted the "goth" image and whose lyrics contain references to shooting and death, might have influenced the boys' killing of their classmates. See Manson, Marilyn. "Columbine: Whose Fault Is It?" *Rolling Stone,* June 24, 1999, 23+.

[6] Chambers, Veronica and Yahlin Chang. "High School Confidential." *Newsweek.* March 1, 1999. 62+.

[7] The regulation regarding student speech in the school's student handbook states: "School authorities have the right to determine what constitutes lewd and inappropriate speech (verbal or written) inconsistent with the educational process."

[8] For a different description of how students negotiated potentially controversial content in a Play Production course, see pp. 11-12 in *Temporary Stages: Departing From Tradition in High School Theatre Education* by Jo Beth Gonzalez, Portsmouth, NH: Heinemann Press, 2006.

WORKS CITED

Anonymous, postperformance reflections, 1999.

Anything Would Be Substandard. Unpublished script, 1998.

Arnot, Madeleine. "Bernstein's Sociology of Pedagogy: Female Dialogues and Feminist Elaborations." *Feminist Engagements.* Ed. Kathleen Weiler. NY: Routledge, 2001. 109-140

Aronowitz, Stanley. Dead Artists, Live Theories, and Other Cultural Problems. New York: Routledge (1994).

Behar, Ruth. The Vulnerable Observer. Boston: Beacon Press (1998).

"Censorship vs. Freedom of Artistic Expression." *Ohio Marquee.* Winter Issue. Diana E. Vance, ed. <http://www.ohioedta.org/cen.htm> (accessed December 22, 2004).

Chambers, Veronica and Yahlin Chang. "High School Confidential." *Newsweek.* March 1, 1999. 62+.

Ellsworth, Elizabeth. *Teaching Positions.* New York: Teachers College Press, 1997.

Fisher, Bernice M. *No Angel in the Classroom: Teaching Through Feminist Discourse.* Lanham, MD: Rowman & Littlefield Publishers, 2001.

Friedman, Susan Stanford. "Authority in the Feminist Classroom: A Contradition in Terms?" *Gendered Subjects.* Eds. Margo Culley and Catherine Potruges. Boston: Routledtge and Kegan Paul, 1985.

Gallagher, Kathleen. Personal Comment. 6th Annual IDIERI Conference. Columbus, OH, July 24, 2000.

Gilligan, Carol. "Mommy, I Know You." *Newsweek.* January 30, 2006. (53).

Giroux, Henry A. *Pedagogy and the Politics of Hope.* Boulder, CO: Westview P, 1997.

Gonzalez, Jo Beth. *Temporary Stages: Departing From Tradition in High School Theatre Education.* Portsmouth, NH: Heinemann Press, 2006.

Gonzalez, Jo Beth. Unpublished production notes and journal. 1998-1999.

Gore, Jennifer. *The Struggle for Pedagogies.* New York: Routledge, 1993.

Hesford, Wendy. *Framing Identities: Autobiography and the Politics of Pedagogy.* Minneapolis: University of Minnesota Press, 1999.

hooks, bell. *Talking Back.* Boston: South End, 1989.

_____. *Teaching to Transgress: Education as the Practice of Freedom.* New York: Routledge, 1994.

_____. "Feminism: A Transformation Politic." *Race, Class and Gender in the United States.* Ed. Paula S. Rothenberg. New York: St. Martin's Press, 1998.

Jhally, Sut. Campus lecture at Southwestern University, Georgetown, TX, March 2002.

Katz, Jackson. Tough Guise. Videocassette. Produced by Sut Jhally through the Media Education Foundation, 2000

Levie, Al. "Don't Scold, organize!" *NEA Today.* Vol 25, No. 3 November 2006. (64).

López, Josefina. *Simply Maria, or, the American Dream.* Woodstock, IL: Dramatic Publishing Company, 1996.

Maar, Paul. *The Noodle Doodle Box. Theatre for Youth: Twelve Plays with Mature Themes.* Ed. Coleman A. Jennings and Gretta Berghammer. Austin: University of Texas Press, 1986. 122-157.

Maher, Frances A. and Mary Kay Thompson Tetreault. *The Feminist Classroom.* Lanham, MD: Rowman & Littlefield Publishers, 2001.

Mandell, Jan and Jennifer Lynn Wolf. *Acting, Learning, and Change.* Portsmouth, NH: Heniemann, 2003.

Manson, Marilyn. "Columbine: Whose Fault Is It?" *Rolling Stone,* June 24, 1999. Issue 8115, 23+.

Rohd, Michael. *Hope is Vital: Theatre for Community, Conflict and Dialogue.* Portsmouth, NH: Heinemann, 1998.

Rutter, Virginia Beane. *Celebrating Girls Nurturing and Empowering Our Daughters.* Berkeley, CA: Conari Press, 1996.

Seeing Eye to Eye; A Glimpse of Reality, Unpublished script, 2005.

Shor, Ira and Paulo Freire. *A Pedagogy for Liberation.* Westport, CT: Bergin & Garvey, 1987.

Vincent, Norah. *Self-Made Man.* NY: Viking P, 2006.

THE *ACTUAL LIVES* PERFORMANCE PROJECT
A PEDAGOGY OF DIFFERENCE
Chris Strickling

In August of 2000, the *Actual Lives* Performance Project of Austin, Texas, gave its first public performance at the Vortex Theater, an alternative theatre space, and one of the few in the area equipped to host an ensemble of disabled performers in the area.[1] We titled that show "Cripples in the House," suggesting that our presence there was in no way apologetic, and perhaps to make people laugh in the process. *Actual Lives* was the brainstorm of deaf performance artist Terry Galloway, who has used a similar page-to-stage format in various community contexts since 1993. The Austin version of *Actual Lives*, which focused Galloway's model on disabled performers, came to life through a tight collaboration between Galloway, myself, and Celia Hughes, executive director of Access Arts Austin, a local non-profit organization dedicated to making the arts accessible to people with disability.

I met Galloway in the fall of 1998, when I participated in an *Actual Lives* workshop she taught at the University of Texas. Both of us were interested in applying her workshop strategies to a group of adults with disability in order to give voice and presence to people for whom disability is a daily reality. Galloway, a deaf woman who has worked hard to establish herself as a performance artist, understood firsthand how important these narratives could be, both personally and culturally. My motivation for pursuing the project arose from twenty years of daily interactions with disabled people as an occupational therapist. I knew stories that most people never hear, stories that kept me up at night, and wanted to see what such a collaboration with disabled adults might produce. Galloway traveled back and forth between her home in Tallahassee, Florida, and Austin to be an active part of *Actual Lives* from August of 2000 through June of 2004, when the ensemble performed at the H Street Theatre in Washington, D.C., as part of the 2004 VSA International Arts Festival.

Now under my direction, *Actual Lives* continues to critique cultural and medical attitudes toward disability, reassert the sexuality of disabled people, trouble the reduction of disability to metaphor, worry the binary of "normal"/"Other," and engage the imagination of audiences in re-envisioning what it means to live with disability. This activist agenda is accomplished through conscious efforts to maintain diversity, practice an ethic of accommodation, and create and sustain a deep collaboration between all participants. Each of these integral practices has roots in a disability awareness informed by feminist principles–what Rosemarie Garland-Thomson (2002) has identified as "feminist disability studies," an area of inquiry that seeks to integrate issues of disability into feminist theory and praxis.

Actual Lives is predicated on what I refer to as a "pedagogy of difference": the intersections of feminist and disability theory and practice in relation to facilitators' principal strategies of diversity, accommodation, and collaboration. Much like the mainstream feminist movement in the United States, the disability rights movement and disability scholars have gradually moved away from an essentialized notion of a single or unified disability identity and toward valuing the diversity of embodiment and experience among those who claim disability as an identity. Accommodation, for purposes of this discussion, is reflected in the practice of "positional pedagogies" which assume that "people are not defined in terms of fixed identities, but by their location within shifting networks of relationships, which can be analyzed and changed (Enns, et al. 415). Such a view includes goals of re-imagining power dynamics (based on differences in privilege, race, class, gender, ability) and how they impact learning, and the development of flexible ways of seeing each other that are based on recognition of specific ways that we are all embodied (415). Working in theatre from a standpoint of feminist and disability awareness allows these goals to be realized in particular ways; collaboration is one such practice. Feminist collaboration, according to Shauna Butterwick (2003), requires that a group come into coalition around common concerns without obliterating the separate identities of all participants.[2] In our *Actual Lives* collaboration, we struggled to achieve group cohesion without obscuring individual identity, while continually questioning the assumed value of fixed, autonomous identity and "independence."

As a prelude to a discussion of the feminist pedagogy of *Actual Lives*, I want to acknowledge the impact of popular culture as a form of public pedagogy. In her essay "The Pedagogy of Shame," Sandra Lee Bartky includes as "particular pedagogies" the teaching strategies of institutions such as the mainstream media, workplace, school, church, and even family. She posits that each of these institutions "has its characteristic kind of teaching" (227) aimed at demonstrating what female social destinies should rightfully be, and that, through these insidious systems of power, women are encouraged to internalize shame about the ways in which their bodies fail to live up to an imagined ideal of womanhood, both physical and social. She defines shame succinctly as "the distressed apprehension of the self as inadequate or diminished" and adds that the production of shame develops through a (false) recognition that "I am, in some important sense, what I am seen to be" (227). In her discussion of how shame functions in the college classroom, Bartky notes several specific ways in which shame is taught unwittingly to female students by faculty and students alike. For example, female students are more often interrupted when speaking than their male counterparts (by peers and by instructors), are addressed by professors less formally than male students, and receive less engaged attention when they speak in class (233). She cites research evidence that "men's success generally is viewed as deserved, women's as due to luck or to the easiness of the task" (233). Having catalogued a series of "microbehaviors" that diminish women's achievement in the classroom and in theorizing the cumulative effect of the teaching of shame, Bartky admits to being "tempted to regard the shaming behavior visited upon women in the modern classroom as the moral equivalent of the dunce-cap of old" (234).

Disabled people are familiar with that "dunce cap of old." Interrupted, ignored, patronized, and still expected to be "overcomers," disabled people have traditionally faced the shaming behaviors that Bartky locates as gendered, regardless of their gender. Petra Kuppers, in *Disability and Contemporary Performance: Bodies on Edge*, discusses this marginalization as a negotiation between invisibility and hypervisibility: disabled performers, "relegated to borderlands, far outside the central area of cultural activity, by the discourses of medicine [are also] hypervisible, instantly defined by their physicality" (49). Kuppers resists the notion that "people who are defined by their bodies are trapped by them" (53), and theorizes disabled performance as a way to destabilize cultural knowledges of disability. She notes that for disabled performers there is always a tension between "being" disabled onstage and "performing" as performance. To "be" onstage is considered therapeutic for the performer: the focus is inward, "authentic," and connected to the "true being" of the performer. "On the other side, disabled performance can be seen as performance: challenging dominant notions about suitable bodies," constituting a critical political intervention. Through this tension, according to Kuppers, "a split can be created between performer and performance, body and representation: the 'truth' of the bodily expression is manipulated, cited and rewritten" (56).

As Garland-Thomson asserts, disability, on and off the stage, is "a culturally fabricated narrative of the body, similar to what we understand as the fictions of race and gender" ("Staring" 334). Garland-Thomson asserts that the goal of feminist disability studies is "to augment the terms and confront the limits of the ways we understand human diversity, the materiality of the body, multiculturalism, and the social formations that interpret bodily difference" ("Integrating" 75). By foregrounding the bodies and narratives of the disabled, *Actual Lives* radically "claims disability" (Linton), always questioning the construction of normalcy (Davis) to contest definitions of disability and work toward a more fully realized disabled subjectivity.

Galloway began using the *Actual Lives* format to work with non-traditional performers (untrained community citizens with little or no theatre experience) in the production of theatricalized personal narratives in 1993. She was touring a solo piece with the PS 122 Field Trips in Manchester, England, when she was asked to conduct a theatre workshop for disabled participants. It was assumed, even by Galloway, that her deafness somehow qualified her to work with a group of disabled adults. However, when confronted with twenty-five adults with many different kinds of disability, she knew instantly that her standard approach would never work. She could not assume that every participant could write, or that participants would be able to communicate with each other, or that their shared experience of disability would be enough to knit them together into a cohesive group. All of those commonalities and boundaries had to be acknowledged, accommodated, and integrated into the group process. That first encounter with an ensemble group of adults with disability produced in Galloway the desire to "create a writing and performance workshop geared for people with disabilities; people who, like me, were not standard theatre material" (NCA).

Galloway uses her own performance work as a way to critique and participate in a hearing culture that has shaped her experience. She sees performance as a way "to achieve through truth, through art, work, communion, that amazing state of recognition and understanding" (Interview) that is the highest function of art, an understanding that is absolutely essential to the recognition of viable, visible, vocal, complicated public selves for people with disability. We envisioned *Actual Lives* as a way to offer that same opportunity to others. If we were going to engage Galloway's formula for achieving effective performance by striving for "truth" and making art from it by working together in "communion" with each other and our audiences in order to achieve new understanding, what strategies would we need, and to what material realities did we need to attend?

First, Galloway and I understood that the success of *Actual Lives* would hinge on our ability to facilitate the production of personal narratives. It was our responsibility to convince participants that they had something to write about, help them envision their stories as performance, and support them at their varying individual literacy levels. Second, we needed to create a situation that was safe enough that participants would be willing to explore the potentials and limitations of their personal movement repertoires. After hearing a particular narrative and beginning to think how that story might take shape onstage as performance, we would often ask "How high can you raise your arm? How fast? Can you do it three times in a row?" or "How fast can you turn your wheelchair?" Watching their bodies, and the bodies of others, as we experimented with the movement possibilities, performers began to see the "art" in their bodies, to experience their movements as contributions to an artistic expression that needed the body in concert with the narrative. And third, we had to create "communion," a situation where communication flowed freely among participants, and between the participants and Galloway and me as leaders. Communication and collaboration depended on the elimination of as many obstacles as possible, both technical and personal, and forming alliances that could prompt and sustain self-revelation.

Actual Lives takes from feminist practice the idea that the personal is political, that events of daily life both reflect and shape social practice and policy. We also acknowledge that things political have real material outcomes on the personal level. *Actual Lives* has both a private and a public face; it deals with personal experiences that reflect political realities, and creates art in the activist tradition of theatre for social change. The tangible result of the workshop process is the public presence of an actively engaged group of performers, all with varying types of disability, whose mission is to use the personal as a political tool for increasing disability awareness and effecting change. As a celebratory, hopefully liberatory pedagogy of difference, these self-representations of life with disability participate in and constitute a public discourse about ability and disability, primarily from a materialist standpoint. Performing in venues as diverse as church basements, schools, local alternative theaters, university campuses, and the H Street Theatre in Washington, D.C., *Actual Lives* can be seen as comprising what Nancy Fraser has called a "subaltern counterpublic sphere" which creates and sustains a discursive arena where disabled subjects "invent and circulate counter discourses to formulate oppositional interpretations of their identities, interests, needs" (123), and functions as "bases and training grounds for agitational activities directed toward wider publics" (124). [3]

It is especially challenging to try to encapsulate the messy, complicated, and never predictable stew of events, attitudes, and narrative that inform this work. In an effort to convey a sense of both the structure and the heart of our work, I want to further examine the pedagogical continuum of diversity-accommodation-collaboration in order to illuminate pedagogy's role in the production of the autobiographical narrative and performance in *Actual Lives*. I conclude with a discussion of pedagogical outcomes as they impact community theatre.

RECOGNIZING THE VALUE OF DIVERSITY

"Diversity" is always situated and contextual. Our commitment to diversity within the ensemble rests on an ability to recognize and respond to the characteristics of the local community, which is always, at best, a difficult undertaking. Galloway and I wanted to establish a diversity of disability for *Actual Lives*. Just as there is no identifiable "African American," no monolithic "feminist" (or even "woman"), and no easily defined "queer" subjectivity, there is no static, all-encompassing definition of disability. As Kuppers explains, the notion of disability "is structurally similar to gender and race—they are all defined by a mythologized physical difference" (58). The simple discursive act of creating the category "people with disability" is fraught with social and political tensions. Despite those tensions, we acknowledged an interest in working with people whose bodies would visibly demonstrate difference (from an able-bodied, normative ideal) in order to confront an aesthetic tradition that has refused space and presence to the disabled subject onstage. We realized that foregrounding visible bodily difference might also be suspect, as it so often has been with feminism's highlighting of gender difference, since such an emphasis potentially essentializes the disabled person, reducing the complex person to the corporeal character of the body. It also risked erasure of the experience of people with less visible disability. Yet we were convinced of the efficacy of assembling a disability-identified performance group to speak for and represent themselves, and we imagined *Actual Lives* as having the potential to effectively complicate the cultural meaning of disability by adding privileged personal narratives to the visible presence of disabled bodies.

Additionally, we agreed that disability cannot be legitimately located in the individual disabled body or adequately defined as a personal or medical pathology. Rather, disability is produced by the material realities of a world quite literally constructed to render deviations from an assumption of physical normativity as disabling. Galloway asserted recently in an address to the National Communication Association that disability is not simply "a medical diagnosis such as paraplegia or blindness" (NCA), but arises from the pervasive intrusion of obstacles in the physical environment. Our culture "disables" a person who lives with an atypical body by building a physical environment that assumes normative physical capacities and failing to provide accommodation for those whose embodiments are different. In the same way that early feminist theatre confronted issues of women's oppression and challenged gender assumptions, we wanted *Actual Lives* to resist and challenge common assumptions that shape the lives of people with disability, such as language that denies or denigrates disabled subjectivity, physical barriers that limit access, taboos on disabled sexuality, and a range of practices and policies that shape day-to-day experience.

In their article "Res(Crip)ting feminist theater through disability theater: Selections from the DisAbility Project," disability scholar Ann Fox and activist director Joan Lipkin of *The Uppity Theatre Company* in Saint Louis refer to early feminist theater as seeking "to effect social change through questioning the traditional apparatus of theatrical representation, and by extension, calling attention to the social construction of identities upon which privilege is based" (77). Our project was similar. By creating a performance ensemble of non-actors who self-represent from a position of cultural otherness, formulating the group without a defined selection process (anyone who wanted to participate could do so), by working collaboratively from an egalitarian assumption instead of through a more typical hierarchy, we were upending the apparatus of representational privilege, which would allow us the opportunity to confront the social practices that have such important impact on the daily lives of disabled people.

A true commitment to diversity required that we assemble a group of participants with several types of disability to form an ensemble inclusive of people of color, people whose identities would complicate an assumption of heterosexuality, and whose socio-economic positions in society would help our work confront the economic and social difficulties that many people with disability face. We also wanted to examine different relationships to disability, and hoped to explore the ways in which social positionings impact disability itself and disability identity. For example, one member who came to *Actual Lives* shortly after being diagnosed with rheumatoid arthritis experienced herself as living with a disability but had not assumed disability as an identity marker. Despite a slow, labored, and unsteady gait, she refused to use a wheelchair for mobility, which caused a prolonged and eventually productive discussion within the group (several members of the group are wheelchair users) about the difference between "having" a disability and "being" disabled, and also produced an interesting non-narrative movement performance piece. One of our African-American performers had multiple physical disabilities, but her primary identity markers were race and poverty. A white performer with a visible physical disability acknowledged his limitations but identified primarily as a "Southern intellectual." We wanted all of those intersecting identities to find expression in *Actual Lives*.

In terms of recruitment during that first year, the participants who self-selected (responding independently to print material announcing the opportunity) were primarily white, heterosexual, physically disabled adults with a history of disability activism.[4] We knew *Actual Lives* needed to be a broader, more complicated mix, and since single-issue, identity-based performance work has already enjoyed wide success, notably in work by the National Theatre of the Deaf and New York City's Theatre by the Blind, we also knew that there was cultural room for our project. I actively recruited performers with hearing and visual impairments in order to ensure a mixed ensemble. To work with performers with hearing impairments, I had to locate and recruit volunteer American Sign Language (ASL) interpreters, a task which was, and continues to be, a major time consumer. Having worked with blind students at the Texas School for the Blind for several years, I was familiar with the concerns of blind adults and used my experience as an occupational therapist as a vehicle for approaching social groups and agencies with services for both blind and deaf adults in Austin (the state capitol, and home to myriad state agencies).

Race was another story. Despite its claims to liberalism, Austin is still a racially segregated urban space, with white and black cultural spaces literally divided by a major highway. Issues of class and economic disparity complicate the experience of disability for people of color, and recruiting people of color as participants made the reality of their conditions all too real. Additionally, the lack of racial diversity in the disability activist community and in disabled arts became obvious as I looked for (and failed to find) examples of conscious diversity in other performance ensemble work by people with disability. The unmarked whiteness of disabled academia and the disability rights movement has been a topic of much concern and conversation over the past several years, and it was evident in the recruitment process.[5]

Recruitment aimed at increasing racial diversity in the group was difficult and time-consuming, perhaps at least partially because of my embodiment as white and non-disabled. I generated printed promotional material and disseminated it to many of my personal community contacts with support from VSA arts of Texas, the non-profit through which our project was sponsored.[6] Recruitment required repeated phone contact with prospective participants, home visits, and initial and follow-up interviews. I interviewed four African Americans and three Mexican Americans with disability for the first show, but was only able to recruit one African American woman and one Mexican American man. My social positioning as a lesbian also provided contacts within the active and engaged gay and lesbian community of Austin and made it relatively easy to recruit participants from that community. The queer performer who joined *Actual Lives* in its first year was a white woman who understood the activism of the project from a background of lesbian feminist activism. Later, an African American woman who identified as bisexual, and performed pieces from that perspective, joined the group for two seasons, based more on her desire to perform than on any impetus toward activism. Yet another motivator for potential queer participants was the chance to meet and work with Galloway, who enjoys a significant local reputation as a successful queer performer. The group was evenly divided between men and women, without any conscious effort on our part to effect that dynamic.

Representing disability in American culture, in any broad sense, mandates an engagement with issues of income, employment, and availability of resources. Household income for people with disabilities is approximately half that of the non-disabled population. Roughly thirty percent of working-age adults with disabilities work, versus about ninety percent of adults without disabilities (Loprest). In our group, less than half of the fifteen members had adequate incomes, and less than a third had meaningful employment. This would not be theatre as usual. If we assumed and demanded that each participant make it to the rehearsal space on time and on their own, or assumed that every participant could manage personal care like toileting and eating unassisted during rehearsal, we would limit participation to the usual few. We did not want to miss the voice of a fifty-four-year-old African American woman with a college education who lived in poverty because of her long history of complications from diabetes, so we would need to provide transportation, and sometimes meals, to enable her to attend rehearsals regularly. We could not afford to exclude the voice of a thirty-five-year-old ex-carpenter whose life had been completely turned around by a closed head injury solely because he had difficulty finding the rehearsal site. Aware that there had to be some balance between requiring commitment and recognizing different levels of ability, we began to realize that the results of our conscious attention to diversity would require us to implement a level of accommodation that we had not seen modeled elsewhere

THE ETHIC OF ACCOMMODATION

The diversity of ability within the group required an emphasis on accommodation and collaboration in an exercise of what Galloway has termed "the ethic of accommodation" (interview). The ethic of accommodation recognizes a fundamental disjuncture between disabled bodies and "mainstream" environments, and provides a model for moving through obstacles in both the physical and social environments to ensure the fullest inclusion possible. Speaking about the ethic of accommodation as it applies to her work with "The Mickee Faust Club," a "community theatre for alternative communities" which she directs in Tallahassee, Florida, Galloway asserted recently in an address to the National Communication Association that "genuine inclusiveness requires a willingness to make changes to one's core beliefs and in some cases a willingness to spend time and money to change fundamental structures of an organization" (2003). For us, accommodation was both a strategy that helped us accomplish the generation of narratives and their transformation into performance pieces, and a commitment to the performers to make it possible for everyone to participate in whatever way they could.

One of the most basic accommodations had to do with technological mediations that would allow participation by people with a variety of disabilities. The workshop process of *Actual Lives* requires "writing" (in whatever form is possible) from memory, "speaking" (whether in actual voice or through sign, movement, or augmentative communication device), reading or otherwise delivering your personal narrative to the group, and later performing, either solo or with others, before an audience. Each of these acts brings a set of challenges when working with a mixed ability group. For those who could speak but were unable to physically write their narratives, we offered two kinds of accommodation. We used tape recorders and word processing software for one participant, and we provided a personal assistant who acted as scribe for another. We have not had any performers who could not "speak" once these accommodations were made, but we have had performers who chose to chronicle their experiences nonverbally, and for those people we accept and welcome movement or other forms of expression.

Accommodations also had to be made for Galloway, who is deaf but can read lips in one-on-one conversations. We used real-time captioning (customarily used to make conversations, performances, or presentations accessible for those who cannot hear well but do not know ASL) projected onto a screen, so that she could keep up with group discussions. This made it possible for her—and, later, audience members—to understand people whose speech patterns are difficult to understand. It also allowed us to privilege the sometimes labored speech of performers who are often silenced by audience members' unwillingness to listen to their ways of speaking.

In addition to these kinds of technological aids, our commitment to accommodation extends to the ways in which the workshop and rehearsal schedules are established and the manner in which responsibilities are shared. Some *Actual Lives* participants work during the day, which requires that all of our group meetings be held in the evening. Some participants have de facto curfews because of attendant care schedules, which makes it necessary to end meetings relatively early in the evening (before nine p.m.). I rehearse individually with participants who have daytime availability. Physical and mental fatigue is a factor for all of our participants, so rehearsals and other meetings are held to no more than three hours each, with at least one half-hour break. We cannot rehearse a movement piece for more than twenty to thirty minutes at a time because the physical demands are too great, and for some participants, rehearsal time comes to an abrupt end because breath support for voice volume is exhausted. Each participant's particular skills (cognitive, physical, artistic) are taken into account when duties are assigned, and sometimes this means that two people are assigned to a job that one non-disabled person might be able to handle alone (i.e., two people assigned to produce a flyer because one has the computer capabilities and the other can drive to get the flyers reproduced).

Accommodation also includes providing basic personal services not usually required in such settings. Several cast members need assistance at mealtimes, which was often part of our workshop time, or with wheelchair transfers in restrooms, or with organizing materials due to physical limitations. We use volunteers and, at times, more able-bodied cast members to perform these services for their colleagues. On the organizational level, all of these accommodations produced a sense of give and take between the cast members and a respect for each other's needs and abilities.

CONSCIOUS COLLABORATION

Collaboration has long been one of the radical strategies employed by feminist writers and academics, partly as a mechanism for surviving in a masculinist pedagogical tradition in which their minority status worked against them. In feminist theatre, too, much of the early work was collaborative in nature. Engaging an ethic of accommodation became a key point of our collaboration, since without the many necessary accommodations there could be no collaborative effort to produce performance. The most basic level of collaboration was between Galloway, Celia Hughes of VSA arts of Texas, and me. We developed the model for the Austin workshop together, planned for and arranged the details of individual accommodation for performers, and publicized and promoted the work through a process of frequent communication, role release, and cooperation. None of us had sufficient skills to bring the work to life single-handedly, and we were motivated to work together as equals. Galloway had considerable expertise in solo performance and as a director, but lacked exposure to the range of disability encountered in *Actual Lives.* I brought more than twenty years of experience accommodating to physical and cognitive disability in my work as a therapist, as well as four years of writing facilitation with disabled and non-disabled students at the University of Texas in Austin, but was a novice in terms of theatre and performance art. As producer, Hughes used her twenty-plus years of experience in community theatre, much of it in Austin, to help with early aesthetic decisions, and she brought the non-profit apparatus to support our work.

In order to make the process work, both pragmatically and artistically, all three of us had to acknowledge our relative strengths and weaknesses, and each other's. Our work was enriched, and somewhat bogged down at times, by the need to receive and process feedback from each other, and to resolve differences of opinion. Yet, together we could work through disappointments (such as having to change the show when we discovered our funding for lighting had vanished), anger (over personal or aesthetic boundary violations), and worry (about exhaustion, or attributions of credit for the work), or push forward with exciting changes because we were there to listen to and think with each other.

The multiple ways in which we deploy a strategy of collaboration can best be elaborated through an example of our work. Gene Rodgers, a man in his fifties who became a quadriplegic at the age of seventeen, wrote a humorous account of his attempts to open and prepare a package of microwave popcorn, a piece that came to be known as "Popcorn Predator." The piece, which was transcribed by an assistant because Rodgers is unable to physically write, is constructed with a voice-over narrative that interprets the physical actions of the piece as if he were a "mighty hunter," and the popcorn his prey. On first reading, the piece was not easily understandable, so he gathered feedback from the workshop participants and directors and revised it, with help from his assistant. His original intention for performing the piece was to modulate his voice in order to serve as his own voice-over narrator and speak the lines of the Rodgers/self character in a lower register while enacting the demise of the popcorn. He took direction about staging and movement from Galloway, and performed it by himself with some success. During rehearsals for our next performance, he asked for suggestions about improving the piece, at which time several cast members suggested that he might allow someone else to be the voice-over narrator. The second time he performed the piece, another cast member read the voice-over from offstage, and he was then free to concentrate on his lines and movements.

In preparation for our Washington, D.C., show in June of 2004, Galloway and her partner, Donna Nudd, returned to Austin to rehearse with the ensemble. The three of us were faced with the need to reduce the length of the show from fifty-five minutes to the allotted forty-five minutes, which would mean reshaping, shortening, and tightening several pieces. "Popcorn Predator" was included in the show lineup. We talked with Rodgers about the possibility of shortening the piece and still maintaining its integrity, then marked the script and showed him how it might work. He initially resisted the changes, and began to call the piece "Popcorn Predator Lite," a humorous way to disagree with the edits. As co-directors, we took his hesitation seriously, yet asked him to try it the way it was edited, in front of the ensemble, and get feedback from them about whether the piece still held together. Galloway asked Rodgers to concentrate more on his physical movements, and less on the text, just for that one run-through. "It was difficult," Rodgers admits, "to let Terry push me so hard for movement. I wasn't used to that" (interview), but he tried it out on the cast, and there was general consensus that the piece worked well with more emphasis on movement. Watching a man with quadriplegia go through the painstaking act of opening a sealed package with his teeth, of retrieving a fork and placing it into an adaptive cuff on his wrist, seeing the substitution of neck muscles for absent arm muscles–these elements of the piece carried as much weight as the clever narrative. Listening to him "growl" as he moved his power wheelchair said almost as much as his vocal intonation. Rodgers was able to collaborate with the directors and other cast members to restructure the piece, and performed it to near perfection in that show, and several later ones. "It turned out to be a pretty good piece," Rodgers admitted, smiling, "even if you did help" (interview).

Collaboration in this piece, and in many others, took the form of producing the narrative with assistance, editing with the directors, revising scripts based on feedback and suggestions from ensemble members, as well as taking and using direction that pushed past established physical comfort zones. Because of their disabilities and their inexperience with theatre, all of the performers needed and received some sort of assistance in order to participate. Providing such assistance is central to the ethic of accommodation. Collaboration and accommodation, though, have different aims. Accommodation is a way to guarantee an individual's ability to participate, while collaboration asks that enabled individual to bring their creative energy into a partnership with others in order to produce the best theatre possible.

We taught collaboration between performers as well as collaboration between the leaders and performers. Offstage, we asked performers to help each other practice during rehearsal periods and encouraged them to add ideas to a piece after a reading (with the agreement that feedback could be freely accepted or rejected). From that initial structured collaboration, performers developed a sense of group commitment. They began to give each other rides to and from meetings, rehearse with each other outside of our regular meeting times, and offered support to each other when the tensions in the group got high. Onstage, for solo and ensemble pieces, we also encouraged collaboration between performers. Autobiographical writing tends to produce solo pieces, but solo pieces in succession can easily become tedious. To alleviate this, we urged cast members to think of ways to incorporate others into their work. For example, in our most recent show, Laura Griebel wrote a story about "Girls Night Out," depicting an embarrassing encounter with "hotties" in the parking lot as she and her friend left a bar one night. Instead of using the piece as a monologue, we revised the narrative into a two-part conversational piece and added another performer to play the friend character, which made it easier (and more humorous) to visualize the moment when Griebel, whose shortened limbs prevent her from retrieving any fallen item, drops the keys to the van. She does not compromise her voice in the piece, but by collaborating with another performer, her story takes on new dimensions.

Galloway was instrumental in modeling methods for transforming a collection of responses to a single writing prompt into a collaborative group piece. For example, asked to respond to the question "What do people expect from you when you're disabled?" workshop participants generated a litany of complaints about unreasonable expectations for disabled people. Terri Stellar, a performer with cerebral palsy who uses a wheelchair for mobility, complained that people didn't think she should have to go to the bathroom in a public place because it was too inconvenient. Joby Dixon, a doctoral candidate at the time he participated in *Actual Lives*, who uses two crutches (or "sticks," as he calls them) for walking, commented that people "think I can't do anything for myself." Danny Saenz, a long-time disability rights activist and excellent humorous writer noted that "people think I'm supposed to be funny all the time. It's like I took an oath." And with that, the seed for "Good Cripples' Oath" was planted. Each participant raises the right hand or "whatever else you can raise," then "promises, on my honor, to be a good cripple," and takes her own oath. "I promise," says Stellar, "to never have to pee in a public place." Saenz says, sarcastically, "I promise to always be an inspiration to others." Each promise is an act of resistance to the social expectations the performers confront daily. The lines of text change with each new cast, but "Good Cripples' Oath" has become a signature piece that reflects the kind of crip-with-attitude energy for which *Actual Lives* is known.

In and beyond the workshops and performances, *Actual Lives* has been (and continues to be) sustained through collaboration with many people in the community, who have generously provided a wealth of skills and assistance to the project. Olivia Whitmer, a graduate student in the Theatre As Public Practice program at the University of Texas, and a specialist in contact improvisational dance with disabled adults, served as sound designer and movement coach for three years. In her unpaid position, she taught everything from warm-up exercises to diction and enabled the ensemble to take physical presence onstage. Others have acted as guest directors and script developers, instructing the group in the Alexander Technique, providing free ASL interpreting, building ramps (and supplying materials), hanging lights and staying to strike them, providing food, and housing rehearsals and performances for free. These types of collaborations are as crucial to our success as those that occur among the performers and directors.[7]

AUTOBIOGRAPHY'S RELATIONSHIP TO *ACTUAL LIVES*

In *Actual Lives*, strategies of maintaining diversity, providing accommodation, and fostering collaboration create the material and social circumstances that enable autobiographical writing and performance by disabled people. Still a relatively rare event in American theatre, autobiographical performance by disabled artists talks back to a long tradition of misrepresentation. According to Victoria Ann Lewis, founder of the Mark Taper Forum's *Other Voices* project, the problem of disability representation in theatre is not that disability is under-represented, but that most depictions of disability reinscribe an outdated "dominant narrative of disability" that rarely attempts to portray disability as a real lived experience (93). Instead, traditional theatre uses disability to signify everything from moral depravity (as in Shakespeare's *Richard III*) to saintly innocence. Lewis identifies the equation of physical difference with evil or moral shortcoming and/or with saintliness as "dramaturgically useful," which partially explains why "the twisted body, twisted mind" approach to characterization has become a stable element in American theatre (94).[8]

Unfortunately, feminist theatre is no exception to this trend. Disabled theatre scholar Carrie Sandahl has pointed out that many feminist plays, otherwise noteworthy for championing feminist sensibilities, "ignore the actual material conditions of the disabled people portrayed," preferring to use disability as "narrative prosthesis" in which "the use of disability as a dramaturgical device tends to ease the particularities of lived disability experiences" (15), in order to serve the narrative trajectory.[9] Fox and Lipkin, who draw on Sandahl's work, seek to put feminist theatre practice into dialogue with disability theatre practice in order to produce cultural work that moves beyond the conceptual frameworks of gender and disability as we know them and "calls attention to the social construction of identities upon which privilege is based" (79).

The material constraints on the production of autobiography by people with disability are considerable, yet because of its engagement with individual and collective identity, autobiographical performance has the potential to accomplish the dialogue between feminist and disability theater that Fox and Lipkin call for.[10] In the act of combining autobiographical narrative with the physically available disabled body in performance, two important effects are achieved. First, the voice and presence of the "real person," speaking from the disabled point of view, presents a radical alternative to stereotypical images of the disabled. In the introduction to *O Solo Homo*, lesbian performance artist Holly Hughes discusses the fact that in solo performance work, the audience knows that the performer is also the writer, and that what happens onstage is likely to have "really happened" (4). This "realness," which is an aspect of both solo and ensemble autobiographical performance, decreases the emotional distance between performer and audience, and a certain level of safety is lost to the audience, since they "can't hide behind 'It's only art'" (4). I would posit that this also is at work in ensemble performance that is autobiographically based. The increased intimacy works to the advantage of the disabled performer(s) by reducing the already substantial social distance that must be negotiated in encounters between disabled and non-disabled people. And, just as significantly, performers have the opportunity to own their disability in a situation of relative empowerment, instead of denigration.

Despite the name "Actual Lives," the project treats autobiographical writing and performance not as mimetic reproductions of lived experience, but as conscious processes of revisionary self-narrating, or, as disability scholar Michael Berube suggests, instances of "performative utterance."[11] In the daily act of self-narration (i.e., the making of a narrative or the constructing of a "story" from the events or feelings of the day) people form identities—making meaning out of the random (and not so random) events of everyday life.[12] Identity takes shape in the purposeful inclusions and exclusions of that story-making, and allows us to present ourselves to others, exchanging identity narratives as a way of knowing each other. Self-narration seemingly confirms that identity is in working order and produces an "autobiographical self." In autobiographical performance by people with disability, the self as constructed through narrative competes for recognition with the visually available marked body and offers the possibility of responding to cultural meanings assigned to it.

In the work of *Actual Lives*, this reconstruction of lived experience takes shape in four distinct ways. First, writers reconstruct and re-narrate an encounter in order to critique it. Jeff Marsh, a performer with spina bifida, in a piece entitled "Trial and Error," recounts several of the thirty-two surgeries he had before he was twenty years old. Though humorously presented, the simple details of "bladder surgeries numbers 1-5," none of which were successful, and of "hip tendon transfer numbers 1 and 2," which did nothing to improve his chances for ambulation, are enough to indict the medical system for abuse. Marsh ends by making his point in a powerfully didactic way: "Take a child, lock him up, tie him down, stick needles in his body, rubber hoses up his ass, and worse. Poison him unconscious, cut him open, sew him up a few hundred times. They would give you the death penalty for that, but doctors and nurses do it all the time" (*Actual Lives* 2004). Marsh wrote the piece in collaboration with another cast member with a similar disability, who helped him formulate his thoughts, incorporated stage directions and movement coaching into his presentation, and performs it as a solo work.

Second, performers re-narrate scenarios to reverse power dynamics or highlight power differentiations. Many of these pieces recreate scenes in doctor's offices or rehabilitation facilities, places where people with disability are "evaluated," "catalogued," "treated," and otherwise diminished. Others expose the ways in which disabled people are caught between expectations of "overcoming" and the material realities of their lived experiences, addressing work situations or uncomfortable encounters with non-disabled people in public spaces. "Mop Boy," performed by Mike Burns, illustrates the experiential roller coaster of his life after a closed head injury more than thirty years ago. Burns is a visual artist who has had a modicum of commercial success as a visual artist and has been performing with *Actual Lives* for four years. "Mop Boy" describes his day job as a janitor and all of the humility of that work in contrast to his success in the arts. He enters from stage left, faces the audience as he rolls a mop bucket toward center stage, and says, "Some days I'm an artist and performer. Other days I'm the mop boy." He excitedly describes a trip to New Orleans for a gallery exhibit of his work, recounting his sale of three paintings in one day, and "eating food on Bourbon Street–food like you wouldn't believe!" only to return home and back to his job as a mop boy. Burns dances with the mop handle as he describes the high he experienced performing "Clothes" in an *Actual Lives* show as "a fifty-four-year-old fat man, brain injured, dancing to striptease music wearing black-and-white pajama bottoms and rockin' the house" and his return, the following morning, to "the SHAC, a self-help advocacy center, where I clean bathrooms, empty trash, and of course, mop." "Life's a roller coaster," he says as he gathers his cleaning supplies to leave the stage, "and I'm on it." In this piece, also, accommodation and collaboration are at work. Burns, whose head injury makes it difficult for him to organize his thoughts, usually does not write out his work. He speaks it, and I transcribe. For this piece, in his natural speech, he kept repeating, "I go back to the mop boy job." I developed the internal rhythm of the final narrative for him, though all the words were his, directed his movement and staging, and coached him on diction. For Burns, the result of accommodation and collaboration is a well-crafted and well-delivered resistance to a system of power to which he cannot otherwise respond from a position of power.

Third, in the *Actual Lives* process, we sometimes re-narrate experiences, transforming them from tragedy to humor in order to change the emotional trajectory of a piece and maximize its effect. People who are unfamiliar with disabled performance often expect it to reiterate the themes of loss, personal tragedy, and limitation most often associated with disability. *Actual Lives* consciously resists portraying disability as tragic, striving to achieve a balance between recognizing the profound impact that disability has on identity and creating work from fresh perspectives. Galloway does this often in her own solo work, making mental illness and deafness the objects of humorous, yet still serious, inquiry in *Out All Night and Lost My Shoes*, or comically confronting issues of fat subjectivity in *Lardo Weeping*, as a way to seduce audiences into considering these issues. One *Actual Lives* piece in particular provides an example of how this collaborative re-narration impacts the work. Meg Barnett uses most of her performances to explain the links between her multiple disabilities and a childhood of poverty and neglect. In her piece "Dignity," Barnett chronicles her stay in a rehabilitation hospital after a total knee replacement at the age of forty-six. Menstruating and incapacitated in a hospital unit where most of the patients were over eighty, Barnett had trouble finding anyone who could help her insert a tampon. In the workshop process, she wrote the piece as a comment on the loss of dignity, as a sincere and eloquent lament. Though we could see that the issues Barnett's piece was raising had social and emotional power, Galloway and I also recognized its sentimentality and wondered if it would work onstage as written. Galloway approached Barnett about the possibility of revising the piece to make it comical, imagining that comedy here might be more effective than tragedy. A complicated conversation ensued between Galloway, me, and Barnett, a conversation which caused us all to shift our opinions, and eventually come to agreement. Galloway directed the "Dignity" so far toward farce that instead of being a lament, the piece became a hilarious jaunt through the "horrors" of rehabilitation, complete with an almost burlesque re-enactment of the tampon insertion by two of Barnet's fellow cast members playing the roles of "nurse." "Dignity," the product of a conscious collaboration between writer, director, and cast, has become one of our most celebrated pieces precisely because it turns a painful experience of disempowerment into an irreverently comic piece that makes essentially the same point: "Sometimes all we have left is our dignity; sometimes we have to redefine what that means" (*Actual Lives* 2004).

Fourth, sidestepping the constraints of traditional autobiographical performance, we re-narrate experience from both the individual perspective and from a collective identity that unites disparate subject positions into a more cohesive message. According to disability scholar David Mitchell, disabled autobiography and solo disabled autobiographical performance is susceptible to an "ethos of rugged individualism" and to "narcissistic self-revelation... served up as an isolated affair of overcompensation and confessional self-reckoning with bodily limitation" (312). Though *Actual Lives* is an ensemble group, solo pieces are common in our productions. All of us wanted to steer clear of the kind of individualist work Mitchell describes, work that denies community or over-emphasizes individual identity. In our June 2004 performance at the H Street Theatre in Washington, D.C., the ensemble performed a closing piece entitled "Crip Ward Tango." Based loosely on "Cell Block Tango" from the musical *Chicago*, "Crip Ward Tango" put four individual statements in dialogue with each other, both musically and textually, and backed up the four solo spots with a group chorus, just as "Cell Block Tango" does. The four solos embedded in the group piece address four different disabilities and cultural responses to them: head-injury or other cognitive impairment ("If you can't talk, you must be stupid"), congenital birth defects ("If only we'd known, the pregnancy could have been terminated"), acquired disability ("Have you tried Jesus?"), and long-term illness ("I won't get better, this is the best I'll ever be"). The piece establishes the shared concerns of ensemble members and creates a visually and vocally united group identity while still celebrating individual difference.

PEDAGOGY'S PRODUCTS

In our experience with *Actual Lives*, a focus on diversity, accommodation, and collaboration has fostered the development of a group of performers whose resistive voices and active critiques are a much-needed contribution to the ongoing dialogue about disability. They recognize the events of their daily lives as opportunities for self-narration and for performance, and make time to record them whether or not the group is preparing for a show. They have become artists in a community where six years ago there were no disabled performers. Participant interviews indicate that their motivations are clear: they perform for the thrill of being in front of an audience, for the opportunity to get their urgent message across, to have a voice, for the fun of participating in the process, and because they recognize the impact their work has on the community (everything from attitude changes to ramps that are built to accommodate us).

Actual Lives has broadened the wider audience for disability-related performance to include an eclectic mix of professionals, academicians, medical and social service providers, educators, church groups, and disabled and non-disabled family members—all of diverse races, ethnicities, religions, sexual orientations, and socio-economic classes. Audience surveys consistently indicate that *Actual Lives* is the first performance ensemble they have seen comprised of disabled adults, and that they would attend more shows if we could produce more. Audience members report changes in attitudes as varied as "The next time I get on the elevator with that guy at work who's in a wheelchair, I think I'll talk to him," and "I was moved by the anger in some of these pieces."

And finally, our work has begun redefining what "access" means. More than fifteen years ago, the Americans with Disability Act (ADA) required that accommodations be made to allow disabled people full access to public buildings, modes of transportation, and services. Though the ADA requires that any facility that receives city, state, or federal support monies must make its physical facilities accessible to disabled people, because the burden of enforcement relies on the disabled plaintiff bringing suit against a facility, many (and in some communities, most) local theatre venues remain inadequately accessible. Over the past five years, as we have performed in local venues in Austin, the physical demands of our company have literally restructured the physical landscape. When we make our initial inquiries regarding space to rent for performance, we ask if the space is accessible. Predictably, managers usually mention that there is ramp access to the seating area (though often the ramp is in poor condition, or does not meet minimum ADA safety standards). Also, there is rarely mention of whether restrooms are wheelchair accessible from the audience area, or from the stage. When we ask whether or not the sound booth is wheelchair accessible, whether the backstage area and the stage itself can be accessed in a wheelchair, or if light boards are available in a location suitable for someone in a wheelchair, we often discover that the theater is only "accessible" if the disabled person is a patron (who does not mind sitting at the back of the room and does not need an adapted public restroom). Location is also an access issue for us. Since many of our performers travel in power wheelchairs and do not have personal vans with lifts, they use public transportation. Theaters that are located more than four or five blocks from a bus stop are not accessible to those performers, or to many of our audience members, without considerable advance planning.

In order to make the venues we want to perform in accessible enough for us to use, we engage in a series of dialogues with theater managers and we compromise whenever we can. We have constructed wooden ramps to give us access to too-tall stages and left them with the theater to use again. We have adapted restrooms by removing exterior doors, installing grab bars and rearranging the location of soap and towel dispensers so that wheelchair users can have safe access. We have made makeshift sound and light booths in order to accommodate disabled technical assistants. And the response from local theater staff has been overwhelmingly positive. In one venue to which we return regularly in order to participate in a fringe performance festival, we made temporary modifications to the plant for our performance, at our own expense the first year, and after that, the management took responsibility for making the adaptations more permanent and for providing ASL interpretation for the show. In another, we requested changes to the green room area, and they were made before we got there. The simple fact of our presence in a space educates those who are unfamiliar with disability in a pragmatic and non-judgmental way, and makes it possible for us to "advocate" just by occupying a space.

Since its inception in 2000, *Actual Lives* has drawn together a fiercely devoted cadre of more than thirty disabled people who make theatre from the raw material of their daily lives. the work is hard, physically and emotionally, and there are no financial incentives. What keeps performers coming back show after show, despite the difficulties, is that *Actual Lives* is a place where their lives become stories–stories that they construct and reconstruct at will, and a space in which their abilities take precedence over their disabilities. Engaging a pedagogy of difference that focuses on diversity, practices the ethic of accommodation, and honors collaboration has empowered disabled performers to create and sustain this activist theatre project for which they have created a loyal and expanding audience.

NOTES

[1] I consciously choose the terms "disabled people" and "disabled performers," instead of the politically correct formulation "people with disability" or "performers with disability." I am influenced in this

decision by my colleagues in Disability Studies who consider these examples of "person-first language" to be euphemistic devices employed by professionals who are uncomfortable foregrounding disability as it relates to identity. For a discussion of the issue, see "People-First Language: An Unholy Crusade," by C. E. Vaughan, http://www.blind.net/bpg00006.htm, accessed 6 October 2006.

[2] Butterwick's article presents the results of a research project designed to explore feminist coalition and collaboration in the context of community theatre. Her essay is a thoughtful examination of the tensions within and creative potential for collaborative feminist theatre work.

[3] Fraser's work on public spheres and the possibility of producing counterdiscourses is especially applicable to cultural production by people with disability, who always, already, constitute something of a counterpublic.

[4] For a thoughtful analysis of sexism in the disability rights movement and in disability studies, including the construction of the "mythic disabled man" who became the exemplar and visible symbol of the disability rights movement, see "The Sexist Inheritance of the Disability Movement," written by lesbian disability activist Corbett O'Toole in *Gendering Disability*, edited by Bonnie Smith and Beth Hutchison (Rutgers University, 2004) 294-300.

[5] At the 2002 Queer Disability Conference in San Francisco, the planned final plenary addresses were displaced by a spontaneous and somewhat rowdy town hall meeting in which disabled queers of color and people with psychiatric diagnoses/differences challenged the mostly white and physically disabled conference participants to a discussion of racism and the hierarchy of disability.

[6] Access Arts Austin affiliated with VSA arts in 2000, to become VSA arts of Texas. VSA arts (formerly Very Special Arts), an affiliate of the John F. Kennedy Center for the Performing Arts, is an international non-profit organization founded in 1974 by Ambassador Jean Kennedy Smith with the mission to create a society where all people with disabilities learn through, participate in, and enjoy the arts.

[7] Kathleen Juhl, longtime feminist and a member of the theatre faculty at Southwestern University in Georgetown, Texas, gave us a large portion of her sabbatical to work as guest director and instruct the group in the Alexander Technique. Practicing both collaboration and accommodation, she worked with some of our most physically involved performers to bring them into intelligible voice, performed alongside them when the piece called for that, and developed and directed a piece entitled "Panties," an homage to the long-surrendered lace panties of a young woman who now requires Depends. Lucy Wood, Jill Arechiga, Terri Littlejohn, Lauren Kinsler, and Sharon Ploeger gave us free ASL interpreting when we had to have it. Local food vendors have fed us, and the Texas School for the Blind and the Austin Groups for the Elderly have housed rehearsals and performances for free.

[8] As well as outlining specific dramaturgical strategies for disabled theatre, Lewis provides a useful short history of plays and performances by disabled people in her essay.

[9] "Narrative prosthesis" is a term coined by Sharon Snyder and David Mitchell in their book *Narrative Prosthesis: Disability and the Dependencies of Discourse* (U of Michigan 2001). They formulate disability as "a character-making trope in the writer's and filmmaker's arsenal, as a social category of deviance, as a symbolic vehicle for meaning-making and cultural critique, and as an option in the narrative negotiation of disable subjectivity" (1) and use their idea of narrative prosthesis to examine literature and theater, as well as film and visual arts.

[10] Thomas Couser, in his introduction to "The Empire of the Normal: A Forum on Disability and Self-Representation," discusses the material and cultural constraints on the production of autobiography by disabled writers and performers. For an in-depth discussion, see his *Recovering Bodies: Illness, Disability and Life Writing.*

[11] Berube's essay, "Autobiography as Performative Utterance," addresses issues of production and dissemination of autobiographical writing by people with physical and cognitive disabilities.

[12] See *How Our Lives Become Stories*, by Paul John Eakin, for a thorough discussion of the ways in which self-narration by an assumed autobiographical self comes into play in the formation of identity.

[13] Antonio Damasio, in his *The Feeling of What Happens: Body and Emotion in the Making of Consciousness*, develops a neurobiological account of selfhood that hinges on the creation and deployment of an "autobiographical self." In Damasio's model, the autobiographical self is the self linked to identity, and

it consists of awareness of relatively stable "facts" of an individual's life: who you were born to, where, and when; likes and dislikes; usual reactions to a problem; etc. (17). Damasio's autobiographical self mediates between the lived past (through memory) and the anticipated future (by constructing expectations for the future from memories), helping us decide how to respond to the present (224). It is this autobiographical self, mediated through the body, that makes decisions in the moment, evaluates previous actions and events, and allows us to imagine new possibilities, onstage or off.

[14] For more information on the ADA access guidelines for theatres, contact Celia Hughes, VSA arts of Texas, www.vsatx.org.

WORKS CITED

Actual Lives Theatre Company. *The Road Show.* Unpublished playscript. May 2004.

Actual Lives Theatre Company. *Inside Out.* Unpublished playscript. March 2006.

Anzaldúa, Gloria and Moraga, Cherrie. Eds. *This Bridge Called My Back: Writings by Radical Women of Color.* New York: Kitchen Table Press, 1983.

Berube, Michael. "Autobiography as Performative Utterance." *American Quarterly.* 52.2 (June 2000): 339-343.

Bartky, Sandra Lee. "The Pedagogy of Shame." *Feminisms and Pedagogies of Everyday Life.* Ed. Carmen Luke. Albany: State University of New York Press, 1996. 225-241.

Butterwick, Shauna. "Re/searching Speaking and Listening across Difference: Exploring Feminist Coalition Politics through Participatory Theatre." *International Journal of Qualitative Studies in Education.* 16.3 (May-June 2003): 449- 465.

Couser, Thomas. "The Empire of the 'Normal': A Forum on Disability and Self-Representation." *American Quarterly.* 52.2 (2000): 305-310.

Davis, Lennard. *Enforcing Normalcy: Disability, Deafness, and the Body.* New York: Verso, 1995

Eakin, Paul John. *How Our Lives Become Stories: Making Selves.* Ithaca, NY: Cornell University Press, 1999.

Enns, Carolyn, Sinacore, Ada, Ancis, Julie, Phillips, Julia. "Toward Integrating Feminist and Multicultural Pedagogies." *Journal of Multicultural Counseling and Development.* Vol. 32 (2004): 414-427

Fox, Ann M. and Lipkin, Joan. "Res(Crip)ting Feminist Theater through Disability Theater: Selections from the Disability Project." *NWSA Journal.* 14.3 (Fall 2002): 77-99.

Fraser, Nancy. "Rethinking the Public Sphere: A Contribution to the Critique of Actually Existing Democracy." *Social Text.* No. 25/26 (1990): 56-80

Galloway, Terry. Unpublished lecture transcript. National Communication Association, November, 2003.

—-. Personal Interview. August 2002.

Garland-Thomson, Rosemarie. "Staring Back: Self-Representations of Disabled Performance Artists." *American Quarterly* 52.2 (2000): 334-338.

—-. "Integrating Disability, Transforming Feminist Theory." *NWSA Journal.* 14.3 (2002): 1-32.

Hughes, Holly. "Clit Notes." *O Solo Homo: The New Queer Performance.* Eds. Holly Hughes and David Román. New York: Grove Press, 1998. 411-440.

Kuppers, Petra. *Disability and Contemporary Performance: Bodies on Edge.* New York; London: Routledge, 2003.

Linton, Simi. *Claiming Disability: Knowledge and Identity.* New York: New York University Press, 1998.

Lewis, Victoria Ann. "The Dramaturgy of Disability." Ed. Susan Crutchfield and Marcy Epstein. *Points of Contact: Disability, Art and Culture.* Ann Arbor: University of Michigan Press, 2000. 93-108.

Loprest, Patricia and Maag, Elaine. "The Relationship between Early Disability Onset and Education and Employment." *The Urban Institute.* 1 Sept 2003. http://www.urban.org/url.cfm?ID=410992>.6 Dec, 2005.

Mitchell, David. "Body Solitaire: The Singular Subject of Disability Autobiography." *American Quarterly.* 52. 2 (June 2000): 311-315.

Rodgers, Gene. Unpublished Interview. 14 February 2006.

Sandahl, Carrie. "Ahhhh Freak Out! Metaphors of Disability and Femaleness in Performance." *Theatre Topics.* 9.1 (March 1999): 11-30.

Scott, Ellen K. "Beyond Tokenism: The Making of Racially Diverse Feminist Organizations." *Social Problems.* 52.2 (May 2005): 232-255.

OKAY, PRINCESSES, LET'S GIRD UP OUR LOINS!
GRAPPLING WITH THE RULES OF ENGAGEMENT FOR THEATRE ACTIVISM
AN INTERVIEW WITH NORMA BOWLES

Ann Elizabeth Armstrong

INTRODUCTION

After having known Norma Bowles and her work with Fringe Benefits Theatre for more than six years, I had the opportunity to invite Fringe Benefits to lead a Theatre for Social Justice (TSJ) Institute at Miami University in April 2005. One of the many offerings of Fringe Benefits, the TSJ Institute is a one-week residency in which company members collaborate with student and community groups to create a short play based on their experiences, with the goal of raising social and political awareness about a specific discrimination issue. Our institute was responding to Ohio's recent ban on same-sex marriage and the impact this was having on our community.

The institute began after we had collected some research. Then, once Bowles and fellow Fringe Benefits teaching artist Cristina Nava arrived, stories were gathered, scenes were improvised, and students worked with them to script a play that resonated with sincerity, passion, and urgency. An important element of the process was the way in which students took complete ownership over the play and have continued to revise it in relationship to changing audiences and issues on our campus.

Bowles calls her process a "Dramaturgical Quilting Bee" (Bowles, "Why Devise?" 16). What is most unique about this approach is the way in which the focus on a well-defined goal can bring together and utilize an incredible diversity of perspectives. The process oscillates between concrete, focused, and creative strategizing and "branching out" to include increasingly more diverse perspectives that enrich the artistic work and its ability to make social change. In the case of our project, this meant developing a strong LGBTQ-straight alliance among students, reaching across generations to include faculty and community voices, and building relationships with school administrators and advocacy organizations. Our play, *A More Perfect Union*, has been performed for more than a thousand students in classrooms, theatres, and diversity programs throughout the university.

During this residency process, most remarkable was Norma's vision as an activist/artist and how this vision extended to the many logistical details, from permission forms and legal advice to the post-show questionnaire and organizational sustainability. As Bowles explains in the interview, her unique combination of a "Martha Stewart"-like attention to details, logistics, and outcomes is balanced by her "Richard Simmons"-like queer aesthetic, which activates others to play, have fun, and take risks. How else could a theatre company sustain itself for more than fifteen years on grants, and manage to reach diverse groups of people, ranging from "Mr. Richardson's fifth-grade class...to the Korean Immigrant Workers Association, from Families to Amend California's Three Strikes to homeless lesbian, gay, bisexual, and transgendered (LGBT) youth, and from Latina parent groups to college students and community members." (Bowles, "Why Devise?" 16)? Bowles' ability to reach young audiences through schools and other organizations, and the way in which she harnesses the creative process to advocate for and allow people to articulate their own needs, are crucial to the success of the company. Because she goes beyond logistics to carefully design programs, curricula, and performances that engage the multiple dimensions of students, parents, teachers, administrators, and community, the work is carried through all levels of the community or institution.

Many times, Fringe Benefits' work hits barriers of resistance. These may be moments in which identities or agendas come into conflict, or moments in which extremely conservative groups feel threatened by such work. Whatever the case may be, this is a good indication that the work reaches places where it is most needed. Able to enter into institutions and confront the "isms" within them, Bowles also works the system as she assists organizations in using theatre to reach their activist goals. As became clear in our interview, many times this requires a delicate balancing act of flexibility and structure, and an acknowledgment that organizations and rules can both constrain and enable the work.

Bowles maintains a wide-ranging vision that deploys different theatre methods and techniques in many different situations. The full range of Fringe Benefits' offerings includes: 1) touring performances to schools; 2) Theatre for Social Justice Institutes and Workshops that take place around country to create performances specific to an organization's goals; 3) Common Ground Workshops, which use theatre techniques to educate all ages about kinds of discrimination and ways to counter it; 4) long-term residencies in the Southern California area that educate participants about the history of various civil rights movements and the role of the arts in those movements, as well as develop ongoing creative processes that include plays, guest speakers, and workshops; and 5) Theatre and Activism Community Skills Sharing Workshops that bring together artists, activists, educators, and students to enrich the growing community of those working for social change through the arts.

Bowles' teaching takes place on many different levels. In this interview I wanted to explore how the planning, the collaborative partnering, the structures of time and space, and the issues of community have all come to bear on Bowles' methods of teaching and facilitation. Only because Bowles remains on the cutting edge of understanding legal issues and techniques of activism is she able to step up to the line and do innovative work within these structures. Preferring not to wave a banner of feminism in most communities within which she works, she does a complicated dance between creating work narrowly focused on a particular activist goal or identity issue and work that takes a comprehensive, multiculturalist/humanist view of various "isms" and the interplay between them. This relationship between concrete details and global vision is an important one that I've tried to focus on in this interview, which is a compilation of conversations that took place between 2005 and 2006.

INTERVIEW

ANN ELIZABETH: When did you begin to realize that you could use theatre towards activism and education?

NORMA: As far back as seventh grade and all the way through college, I was scared to death that people would find out I was gay. That held me back in numerous ways–socially, creatively, and politically. I even tried to hide behind anti-gay humor! In my third year of graduate school, however, I began to see how I might channel my ongoing interest in doing political, socially-relevant theatre to address the impact of homophobia on youth. As I began to try to think about what I could do, I thought, "Hmmm…theatre's fun. Theatre's engaging. Theatre can open minds and hearts. Maybe what I can do is use theatre as a way to raise awareness about these issues. I should work with LGBT youth, find out exactly what kind of impact homophobia and heterosexism are having on their lives." So that's why I started working with LGBT street youth. Back in 1991, the only place that I could find a critical mass of out gay and lesbian youth was in these group homes for kids who'd been kicked out of their homes for being lesbian, gay, bisexual, or transgender. So that's where it started–doing workshops and plays with those youth. At first we did our shows at Highways Performance Space [Los Angeles], a venue with hip, liberal, largely gay audiences. Then in 1993, our third year of doing those projects, the L.A. Festival and A.S.K. Theatre Projects commissioned a play from us, but stipulated in their grant that, following our Highways premiere, we tour Los Angeles high schools. That nudge, and their institutional and financial support, made it possible for us to make this crucial leap in our work–to reach beyond the choir, to reach peers, parents, and teachers in school settings, to help stop the anti-LGBT discrimination that propels youth to drop out of school, leave home, even attempt suicide.

ANN ELIZABETH: Since the 1990s, your work has exploded to encompass more than just LGBTQ issues, though that's still an important focus for you. And what fascinates me more are the different kinds of methods you've developed to work in different contexts to achieve different goals. Can we talk about some of these methods you use and how they relate to different goals for different groups?

NORMA: When I am facilitating the development of a play, the collaborative development of a play, the overarching goal is to come up with the text of a play that can successfully be produced by the group for the audience they feel they need to reach in order to effect the change they want to achieve. For instance, our Spanish-language documentary *Mitos, Ritos y Tontería*, was initiated after we presented *Cootie Shots: Theatrical Inoculations Against Bigotry* at two Pacoima, California, elementary schools. After observing *Cootie Shots'* positive impact on their children, a group of thirty-some mothers from two school-based parent groups asked us to work with them to create a show to help the Latino community understand how harmful gender bias and homophobia are to all children. The mothers had observed that children exposed to this kind of demeaning speech and behavior experienced low self-esteem, were afraid to pursue curricular or extracurricular interests outside of very narrowly-defined gender norms, and often engaged in discriminatory, destructive, and self-destructive behavior. During our first collaborative script-development workshop, after several hours of story sharing about the homophobia and gender bias they had witnessed, we asked the women, "What's the best way to reach your husbands, uncles, grandfathers about this problem? What kind of play will be most effective with them? Which stories should we use? What tone? Does it need to be funny, serious, very realistic, very abstract? What? How do we reach them?" There was sobering silence, then giggles, and then someone said, "They aren't going to come and watch a play. My husband isn't going to come and watch a play. I can't get him to come to the school for anything!" And someone else said, "Yes, it would have to be something he could watch on TV!" So, we decided to come up with a show that the husbands could watch on television. That was the group consensus: the most effective way to reach our target audience is through a video—not a play, not a stand-up comic act, but an educational and entertaining video that could be enjoyed at home.

ANN ELIZABETH: Yes, so the audience had to have a comfort level with that medium. Once you decided on TV as your format, how did you generate the material?

NORMA: Through several months of theatre workshops, Fringe Benefits worked with mothers to transform their real-life experiences into a series of fictionalized scenes using humor, parody, and highly stylized, Teatro Campesino-like techniques.[1] We taped their stories and re-enactments. They told us about their daughters not being allowed to cut their hair, their sons being called "*joto*" or "*maricón*" for helping with household chores like ironing, and the countless cruel ways they'd seen stereotypical gender behavior enforced in their families. The video we are creating interweaves these scenes with documentary interviews with families, educators, and religious and community leaders, as well as with experts in LGBT issues and Latino culture. A celebrity narrator–à la Cantinflas–will introduce and conclude the film and provide additional material through pop-ups and voiceovers. We are including parodies of *Lucha Libre* and *Epoca de Oro* shows, and PSAs, and advertisements. We structured the haircut story as a mock-*telenovela*, and the ironing story like an episode of *Placas* ("*Badges*," a COPS-like TV show in Spanish). We were even able to get the actual host of *Placas* to play the host for our *Planchas* ("*Irons*")!

ANN ELIZABETH: That's fabulous how the video format also allows you to pull in all of these various perspectives, from kids, moms, school administrators, and celebrity spokespersons. Having their actual presence would be harder to do in live theatre.

NORMA: My ideal arts activism organization would have the flexibility to go with whatever approach a group decides will be the most effective way to reach their target audience: a hip-hop opera; an informal, interactive play; a Robbie Conal-like poster campaign; or even an underwater ballet!

ANN ELIZABETH: In our TSJ institute, I really appreciated all the time we spent talking about our target audience, and how you conceived it as a "moveable middle" kind of group.[2] It's interesting how we moved from more stereotypical notions of our audience, like "typical sorority girl" or "frat boy," to more defined ideas like "the person who thinks it's okay for others to be LGBTQ but not for them to have marriage rights." Really zeroing in on that contradiction, like what you are doing with the Latina moms, and then refining *how* to really reach their audience. For our TSJ Institute on marriage equality, we spent a lot of time capturing the local references to campus culture, but also prioritizing the themes these college students seemed most focused on: friendships, romance, and religion. Now tell me about projects that use theatre techniques for general education against discrimination and are less focused on specific activist goals.

NORMA: Okay. Our Common Ground Workshop is a single three-hour session. Here, our goal is to use improvisation in order to equip the participants with tools for handling discrimination. We briefly discuss the concepts of stereotype, prejudice, and discrimination, and then invite the participants to share stories about the discriminatory behavior they've witnessed or experienced. We structure this discussion by using a "Social and Physical Traits" chart that we've created. We go through the list one item at a time, eventually covering–depending on the age of the participants–about twelve traits, from age, ability, and socio-economic status to gender identity, nationality, and beliefs: religious, spiritual, and secular, etc. As we go through the list, we briefly define each trait, give examples of appropriate, respectful terminology and discriminatory, disrespectful put-downs, and invite the participants to share relevant stories. Oh, and one of the guidelines we set as a matter of course is that the names need to be changed, unless the people involved in the story agree to have their names used, and/or if the story is already in the public record. Following the story sharing, we dramatize one of the stories, and use devices such as freeze frames, inner monologues, and flashbacks to explore the characters' motivations. For example, we might unpack a story involving sexist behavior by re-enacting the events through improvisation, then freezing the action periodically to allow observers to shout out what they think the characters might be thinking but not saying, and/or sound bites from the characters' past experiences–at home, in school or church, watching television, etc.–that might be influencing their current behavior. Then we might even develop some of these sound bites into flashback scenes–five minutes, five days, five years before the incident with which we started. This gives us an opportunity to further explore possible psychological, social, and/or political factors that might be influencing the actions (or inaction) of the person discriminating, the bystander[s], and the person targeted. We use "flash-forwards" to look at possible consequences–what might happen five minutes, five days, five years from now if no one intervenes to stop the discriminatory behavior. Through engaging in these improvisations, the participants can develop a better understanding about what discrimination looks, sounds, and feels like, how and why it happens, and what's at stake if it isn't stopped. Finally, we use Forum Theatre to give the participants an opportunity to practice what they could do if they were bystanders facing a similar situation.[3]

ANN ELIZABETH: The focus on the role of the bystander is also a very interesting position that you emphasize. With my students, I've also been using Theatre of the Oppressed to really transform the role of the bystander into one of an ally. What age groups do you do these workshops with?

NORMA: Kindergarten through graduate school…and beyond. Of course we adjust the content, structure, and tone of the workshop to fit the specific group. For example, we encourage older, more mature groups not just to settle for Forum interventions that seem well-intended, but instead to subject each strategy to a thorough interrogation: "Were the Intervener's actions and the Antagonist's responses realistic? What risks are there? Did the intervention provide a long-term solution to the problem or only a stopgap solution?" If a proposed intervention might exacerbate the problem, we want to make that visible.

ANN ELIZABETH: Yes, and that can be a big ethical problem. You don't want to use theatre to give kids a false sense of security when they could get themselves into situations in real life that are too dangerous for them to skillfully handle. Like much of your work, this involves certain risk taking. Are there ways that you educate folks on how to handle such ethical dilemmas in theatre and social change?

NORMA: One of the things we do is a Theatre and Activism Community Skills Sharing Workshop series that we co-sponsor with Center for Theatre of the Oppressed and Applied Theatre Arts, Los Angeles (CTO/ATA/LA).[4] My primary role in the process involves helping conceive and shape workshops, writing and sending out the email invitations, and making sure the leader[s] and participants all have what they need for the workshop to go well. One of the main goals of the series is to build and cultivate a community of people interested in theatre and activism.

ANN ELIZABETH: Wow, this is so important to grow and nourish our networks. So who are some of your guest speakers and what are some themes you've explored?

NORMA: One of my favorites was "Theatre Activism and the Law," which was co-led by theatre activist and scholar Mady Schutzman and ACLU lawyer Martha Matthews. Martha created a really great outline, a sort of First Amendment primer for theatre activists. So, we started off the session with this killer, you know, rip through the First Amendment and how it applies to everything from demonstrations to Shakespeare in the park. Then Mady talked about Invisible Theater[5] and a variety of public and street theatre actions in recent years. They then invited us to stand and speak very briefly about the particular issues that we wanted to address. Small groups formed around shared concerns—from harassment in schools to incinerators in low-income neighborhoods—and developed actions and work plans including everything from scripts, props, signage, and amplification systems to protest permits and "observers" armed with cameras, video cameras, and cell phones. When the groups reported back in the last section of the workshop, Mady and Martha gave really thorough feedback regarding how effective they thought each action might be and additional things to take into account if you didn't want to end up in jail. I remember Martha Matthews responding to one proposal, "Great idea, great project...really smart and well thought out! Good stuff, but you're going to have to find someone to watch your dog for a week because you are without a doubt going to go to jail if you do that." In response to another idea, both Martha and Mady agreed: "That's within the law and it's fine, but you might want to push the envelope further."

ANN ELIZABETH: Yes, because if you end up in jail, you might not get a chance to make your statement, right? But if you're not shaking up conventional representations, you're not going to be controversial enough to make it on the six o'clock news either.

NORMA: Yep. And it's crucial to inform everybody what risks they might be taking. Sometimes the parameters are pretty self-evident...sometimes almost counterintuitive. For instance, shortly before hosting that workshop, I learned from a group called Soul Force that going limp when an officer arrests you is now considered resisting arrest. Soul Force does thorough training with people before they do any kind of public action.

ANN ELIZABETH: Yes, I've been thinking about this a lot when I look at non violent training used during Freedom Summer in the Civil Rights movement. The different methods and techniques of direct action–we have so much to learn from them. Okay...so now, have we at least touched on each of the different programs Fringe Benefits offers?

NORMA: I think so.

ANN ELIZABETH: I'd like to switch gears and talk about pedagogy. How would you describe the difference between the way you work as a facilitator from the way you work as a teacher?

NORMA: Well, first, there are the really product-oriented processes, the TSJ workshops and institutes, where I'm facilitating collaboration in order to create the best, the most effective, play possible to help resolve a specific problem. On several occasions, I've worked with groups of LGBT high school students to create plays dramatizing the harassment they experience at school. It's really sobering to know that they will be performing the play *themselves*, for their peers, some of whom participated in the harassment, and others who watched or laughed along. When I'm leading TSJ projects, I often feel overwhelmed by the gravity of the issue and the risk involved for the collaborators. So, those kinds of facilitations challenge me the most–in every possible way. Then, there's the job I have of training people to lead Fringe Benefits workshops. When I'm doing that I feel horribly pedantic, anxious, and boring. Oy! Finally, there are the Think Tanks and the Common Ground and Skills Sharing workshops. Facilitating those is almost like teaching–except there's still a bit too much emphasis on immediate results, and definitely not enough time for research, reflection, dialogue, and experimentation. My ego and my zealous fervor get in the way too much for me to completely enjoy product-driven projects.

I feel so much more at home, more in my element, when I'm really teaching. For instance, when I'm teaching acting, I may have as many as three pairs of students who all want to work on the "wooing scene" from *The Taming of the Shrew*. One pair might want to set their scene in the "Wild, Wild West," another on the moon, and the third might say they want to do the scene "the way Shakespeare would have done it." I can joyously, completely, throw myself into helping them do the best possible Western, lunar, or "traditional" version of the scene. It doesn't matter if I like their idea or not. It doesn't even matter if I like the play or if I think it's an important play to perform now, in our current socio-political climate. My focus, my passion, is to help them develop their skills as theatre artists! This coming fall, I'm looking forward to teaching Theatre for Social Justice in a process rather than product-oriented manner. With Intercollegiate Women's Studies of the Claremont Colleges, I'm going to be able to take a semester to carefully lay the groundwork through reading, class discussions, and theatre and diversity awareness exercises, and then to mentor the students as they develop and implement t*heir own* projects. Ah...bliss!

ANN ELIZABETH: I don't think your joyous teaching and your zealous facilitating are that unconnected. I know that the creative spirit you describe in teaching oozes into your activist facilitating. Would you say that yours is a feminist or a queer pedagogy? Or both?

NORMA: Hmm...I'm still trying to figure that out. I was in my hotel room at the Association for Theatre in Higher Education conference last summer, getting ready to speak on a "Queer Pedagogy" panel.[6] And as I was getting dressed and trying to de-Bride of Frankenstein my hair, I was half-watching *Martha Stewart Living* on the tube. She was "crafting." She was crafting and her guest was Richard Simmons. They were making tiaras. I kid you not.

ANN ELIZABETH: Genius.

NORMA: Sooo, Richard Simmons is jumping around, twirling, and giggling...totally in his element: "*Ooooh!* Martha, if you put some of these jewels on your face, I'll put some on mine!" She does not take him up on this. She does not even appear to have heard him. She is soldiering on...perky soldier, but a soldier nonetheless. "Now, you'll need to thread the pipe cleaners through like this," she demonstrates. Richard is undaunted, "*Ooooh! Ooooh!*" He's scooped up a couple of the flimsy cardboard tiara forms, and is running around Martha, flapping them around her blonde tresses, "Caw! Caw! I'm Tippy Hedren in *The Birds!* Heeeeeeelp me!!!" She is unflappable. "Now, you can have a lot of fun with this! Use *any* color that feels right!" Ohmygod, she is being a most ungracious hostess and a dud of a "straight man"! Doesn't she know who Richard Simmons is? Didn't she know what he was going to do? I mean, he's giving her *classic* Richard Simmons—work with it, girl! But nooo. Now he's grabbed the glue guns and he's voguing, "Hey, Martha! Hey, Martha! Let's play *Charlie's Angels*! I wanna be Drew Barrymore! You wanna be Lucy Liu?!" At this point, she has so completely frozen him out that I'm not even sure she sees him anymore. Martha is *hell bent* on showing us how to make those damn tiaras! I mean, *Hello!* This is what people want to see, Martha! You and Richard Simmons— Dean Martin and Jerry Lewis, Abbott and Costello, *The Honeymooners*—doing schtick! She's almost got the straight man thing down, but she's so uptight that it's not funny. And so, although I get the sense I'm watching history being made, I have to turn off the TV. It's just too painful to watch.

I gather my pile of notes. I have to speak for ten minutes about Queer Pedagogy. Ugh. I either have three hours of material or none. I mean, I create plays with various LGBT communities, and address LGBT issues, but is my pedagogy queer? Oy. Finally, the panel member right before me states the obvious, "Of course pedagogy isn't what we teach, it's *how* we teach." It hits me like a brick. *Ohmygod*! My pedagogical approach is *definitely* queer. It is queerer than queer!⁷ I am a cross between Martha Stewart and Richard Simmons. Not an integrated, edges-softened version. No. A schizophrenic, lurching from one extreme to the other version: "Okay, princesses, *focus*! We're seven minutes behind schedule, and we still need to cover stereotype-busting stories, okay! So… [*grabs her crotch like a Major League player*] let's gird up our loins and tear the roof off the sucker!"

ANN ELIZABETH: [*laughter*] You're scaring me! And you definitely channel Martha when you're in planning mode. So let me get this right: the goal-oriented, product-driven facilitator persona is Martha. She is perhaps the activist side of your pedagogy that wants results. And then Richard Simmons is your queer teaching persona, the one who makes everyone feel like they can build their fantasy world and take some risks. Of course, this is exactly what you do! Let's talk a bit more about this Martha-Richard complex of yours.

NORMA: Ya, ya. Dr. Freud…danke schöen.

ANN ELIZABETH: Let's start with the Martha tendencies first and how you plan and facilitate all those details.

NORMA: One of the big things I believe, especially the more I do this social justice work, is the importance of dealing with things proactively. This comes partly from my experience working with social service organizations where a lot of the rules weren't laid out very clearly. I often found out about the landmines only when I tripped them. I really like, like, *like* to have ground rules and everything laid out very clearly and very early in the game.

ANN ELIZABETH: Both when you are partnering with an organization and when you are facilitating a group process?

NORMA: Yes. For instance, waiting until young students call each other names in class is problematic in so many ways. I prefer to lay it out at the beginning, "We all need to treat each other with respect." And then spell out what that looks like, "No side conversations, no put-downs, arrive on time and prepared, etc." And it's exponentially more important to set safe parameters when working in the socially, politically, emotionally, and often physically challenging terrain of theatre for social justice. I find that guidelines such as "Change the names of the people in your stories, no physical contact, you can pass or call 'Uncle' any time you need to," actually allow people to feel more comfortable taking risks. I know that a lot of my colleagues really disagree with this approach. Michael Rohd, for example, has said that he actually prefers pedagogically to play a game fairly loosely in the beginning, allowing the participants to discover the rules as they go, when they make mistakes, or when something doesn't work, at which point he might offer, "Well, it sometimes works better if everyone stays in a circle," or "It tends to work better if you keep your eyes closed." His philosophy is that if you stumble over something, you learn it more deeply than if you were told it ahead of time.

ANN ELIZABETH: So you're saying you disagree with that? It seems that for Rohd it's about discovering an exercise together.

NORMA: Yep. Y'know, for one thing I think there's *plenty* to discover. If someone's already figured out how to make a wheel, let's learn from that person and build on what they've discovered…start working our way towards solar-powered cars! If someone's discovered that the road is icy or that the bridge is out, please put up a sign! There are plenty of adventures to be had on the ride without people needlessly taking risks. Also, as you know, I'm a pretty wild gal in some ways—

ANN ELIZABETH: Richard Simmons!

NORMA: Painfully true! So, I want to make sure people know that, while I might be pushing and cajoling, Martha and Richard-ing them, within an inch of their lives, that I want them to say "Whoa!" whenever they need to. One of the reasons I'm so careful about setting up boundaries when I teach is that when I'm a student or participant, I really want the teacher or facilitator to set up really clear guidelines. I remember one teacher asking us to do an improvisation and to "Pursue your objective by any means necessary. Your partner will come up with an opposing objective. Go!" In that situation, I started inhibiting and protecting myself, perhaps unnecessarily, because I didn't want to offend or hurt the person I was working with, or get hurt myself. I wanted the teacher to set physical limits, to say, "You may not touch your partner's breasts," or "You may not throw your partner against the wall!"

ANN ELIZABETH: I see, so Martha's rules create the safe space for Richard to allow everyone to get crazy?

NORMA: Yes!

ANN ELIZABETH: So this tells me about how you are proactive as a teacher and facilitator. But when you are working with an organization, they might have rules and they forget to tell you, rules that are unwritten. How do you remain proactive in this situation? What are you looking for in planning a partnership?

NORMA: Well, basically, I impose the Martha modality on everyone! We have lots of planning meetings, during which we discuss expectations vis-à-vis outcomes and procedures, share our organizations' "Rules of Engagement," and create detailed schedules and contracts. Nevertheless, some things don't get spelled out, because what might seem like common sense to one organization may seem completely counterintuitive to another. Assumptions are made. Mistakes happen. So, I do my best to develop a context in which people feel comfortable saying when something is a problem, giving each other the benefit of the doubt, and figuring out mutually agreeable solutions.

ANN ELIZABETH: Let's go back to facilitating in the workshop. What are other teaching skills you work on?

NORMA: I'll boil it down to one instance. I'm pretty transparent in my reactions to other people's comments, pretty much out there. Well, I was co-leading one of the institutes, and at one point, when somebody was sharing a personal story, my co-facilitator exclaimed, "Oh, my God!" I started meditating on that one and thinking, "Wow, y'know, that could have come off in a number of problematic ways." The person who shared the story might now be feeling that her story is qualitatively freakier than everybody else's story. Or, other people in the workshop might feel that their stories weren't as cool or exciting. Or they might think, "Wow, hasn't that facilitator dealt with these issues long enough to know that that's what's going on in the world? How naïve is she?" Then, I thought, "God, I do that all the time!" I'm constantly sighing, grunting, "Alright, Girl"-ing my responses to everything! I need to get somebody in to work with us–someone who's a trained facilitator–to really help us understand the rules about effective, compassionate listening. We're not trying to lead therapy sessions, so we've got to make sure that we're not inviting people to think of us as therapists. And even though the stories are being shared as part of an artistic process, and we'll eventually all need to decide which stories to include in the play and which to leave out, the moment when someone is sharing can be very, very delicate–not the time to pass judgment, but not the time to be completely detached either. It's really challenging for me; I can "do" the same thing in response to each speaker, treat them equally, smile, and nod and say "Thank you," but I'm so transparent, right? I just reek of whatever I'm really thinking…like a smoker, you know?!

ANN ELIZABETH: You don't have a good poker face, in other words.

NORMA: I do not have a poker face!

ANN ELIZABETH: Ah, Richard again. He's a bit too impulsive, isn't he? So has Richard gotten you into any other trouble when you're facilitating?

NORMA: We were creating a play with students and community members to address discrimination based on socioeconomic status. On day five of this institute, during our final "Dramaturgical Quilting Bee," after we'd read through the play, one of the students across the circle from me raised her hand. Instead of passing the tape recorder around the circle to her, I got up, crossed the circle and knelt down in front of her, and held up the tape recorder for her to speak into. She pointed to a line, a line that really disturbed her, in which a transgender woman says, "This is practically the only charity that doesn't turn me away. I was at X faith-based food service and I blew this guy a kiss and they kicked me out–blacklisted me! At Y (another faith-based food service) they make you pray to Jesus before they'll let you have a meal, and I was raised Jewish! And they won't even let me in the door at Z (a faith-based shelter) 'cuz they don't see me as a woman! I just wish people would accept me for who I am!" The student framed her discomfort with lines such as "This will be offensive to our audience, and we've already said that we should focus exclusively on discrimination based on socioeconomic status and not get into another bunch of other issues. So I don't think this line should be in the play." Then, I heard a guffaw from the other side of the circle behind me, and probably because the guffaw was reflecting my discomfort with what this woman had said, I just simply stood up and went over to the other side of the circle with my tape recorder to get the input from him: "What do you think?"

ANN ELIZABETH: The guffaw person?

NORMA: Yes. I also think that I didn't call the guffaw person on breaking the workshop guidelines regarding "not passing judgment" and "no put-downs" because he was one of the homeless community members in the project, a wise, well-educated elder, whose experiences in this area and understanding of the issues I valued highly. However, if I'd been following my own workshop guidelines, I would not have gone across the circle, knelt in front of the student with my back to everyone else in the first place. And, in response to the guffaw, I would have said something like, "Okay, let's remember that we need to treat everyone with respect, and to articulate our opinions respectfully, so that it's a safe space for people to put their ideas out." Instead, I ended up ping-ponging around the circle for about forty-five minutes, taking the tape recorder to all of the people who wanted to share their diverse opinions about the line. My mistake cost us priceless editing time–forty-five minutes of the two hours allotted to edit a fifty-minute play–and, more importantly, group cohesion and support for the play. Several of the students who had been excited about the project became quite disheartened at this point in the process. I could see them shutting down, and their feedback forms reflected their disappointment and anger.

ANN ELIZABETH: It's always a balancing act when we're trying to decide these things in the moment of facilitation. When do we enforce the rules and when does the context require us to break the rules so we can pursue a larger goal?

This is a really interesting example to me because I'm noticing how it's not easy for a group to isolate a topic, goal, or identity issue—or rather, it's not easy to *keep* that idea isolated from other issues because, inevitably, the diversity of the group's perspectives will create such conflicts. An artistic process can really reveal all the contradictions within the group, and that can be dangerous. I know that the rules allow us to commit to respecting each other as we pursue our goal, but these conflicts can be so dangerous and deep that the rules can't always protect the participants. Obviously, you just can't let certain statements go unchallenged.

NORMA: It's really tricky to set up the context so that it's truly respectful, inclusive, and productive. I'm usually the champion for more thorough, stricter guidelines, but recently I ran into a situation in which our partnering organization had such strict guidelines that we could not complete our play development collaboration. They were primarily a support group, and they were adamant that each and every time someone took issue with something someone else said—or a line in a draft of the play—we needed to stop and process the problem for as long as the participants wished. Process had to trump product every step of the way.

ANN ELIZABETH: What was this group's goal for the collaboration?

NORMA: I should have figured out early in our planning that both their organization and their project goals were primarily about empowerment, and not sufficiently activist to be a good fit for a collaboration with us.

ANN ELIZABETH: Do people usually have a goal when they contact you about a Theatre for Social Justice Institute or do you ever lead them through a process of trying to understand and discover that goal?

NORMA: Some groups have a really clear theatre activism goal when they contact us, like y'all: "We want to create a play promoting marriage equality in Ohio!" In other cases, university theatre departments have been motivated more by educational goals—because they want their students to learn our process, or get to work with our organization, or because they want their students to do something with the community. Maybe there's a particular town/gown divide they want to address. Grassroots community organizations have approached us with goals ranging from changing discriminatory behavior, policies, or laws to finding emergency housing for homeless youth. We work hard to understand each other's organizations, methodologies, and goals; we then focus on clarifying and defining the specific goals of our collaboration, and devising measurable outcomes. Then we put our heads together to come up with a plan to accomplish our shared goals.

ANN ELIZABETH: How does the process differ when you're invited by a community organization instead of a theatre group?

NORMA: We ask them to find a local university or theatre to co-sponsor the institute. And when universities or theatres invite us, we ask them to partner with a local community group that works on the issues they want to address in their play. Community group participation in the institutes is crucial, because their stories provide the primary material from which the plays are made, and their knowledge about the issues and their activism experience guide the decision-making process regarding the target audience and how best to reach them. The participation of theatre department students and faculty in the institutes helps ensure that improvisations—which are the source of all the dialogue in the plays—and the dramatic structure of the play are as theatrical, powerful, and lively as possible. Their expertise in guiding the production process following the institute is also invaluable!

ANN ELIZABETH: It's always tricky to come in from the outside of an organization to create an artistic product and then pull out without it collapsing, causing the project to lose momentum and focus. You have to have that commitment up front or be able to really cultivate both the artistic and organizational skills that sustain the work and keep it going. Let's go back and talk more about the question of goals. How do you figure out what they are?

NORMA: Lots and lots of phone calls and emails! And we use a sample "Measurable Outcomes" outline. I know we developed this after working with y'all, because we use the Miami U project as a model!

ANN ELIZABETH: Tell me about these measurable outcomes. This makes me think about some of the bureaucratic rhetoric we hear as teachers about accountability and assessment, but, on a more positive note, I really do want to be able to measure how theatre is effecting social change.

NORMA: We start with very basic questions: "What's the problem you're addressing? What's the audience you want to reach? What results do you want to see? What is your organization's capacity?" An organization may want to produce a show on the scale of *Fiddler on the Roof* and tour it throughout the South East, but do they have the capacity—the funds, personnel, time, experience, connections, space, etc.—to accomplish this? Would it be better for them to create something that can be performed successfully by a cast of five community members with no professional acting training? What desired outcomes can be reasonably anticipated and measured? Perhaps, say, a twenty percent change of attitude? Something like that could be measured by including in a post-show audience questionnaire a pair of questions like, "How did you vote on Issue One in November 2004?" and "If a ban on same-sex marriage were to appear on our ballots again, would you vote for or against it?"

ANN ELIZABETH: That's pretty precise, Norma…can we really measure those outcomes with things like post-show questionnaires though? Aren't some of these attitudes more complicated than that?

NORMA: I've heard on-the-spot feedback sheets referred to as "smile sheets"–basically worthless. Often audience members in a hurry to leave dash off quick, superficial comments such as "Great show! Keep up the good work!" or "Interesting," or "I don't know." But, actually, I have found that post-show questionnaires can be pretty useful.

ANN ELIZABETH: You think the forms are useful and are worth the effort?

NORMA: Yes, depending on what questions one asks.

ANN ELIZABETH: How have you been using them? Are you making changes to the show based on them? Or just getting new insights into the audience?

NORMA: We use participant feedback forms to refine our workshops, residencies, and institutes. Post-show audience surveys are a crucial element in our seemingly endless pursuit of dramaturgical perfection–affecting not only the script, but also acting, staging, even costume choices. After about a year of touring *Cootie Shots*, we received some feedback from an audience member. She pointed out to us that in the short play *Doing the Right Thing*, two men–a father and a teacher–who stood on either side of the mother, literally talked to each other over her head and then shook hands right in front of her face. Furthermore, the woman did not have a single line of dialogue in the scene! As the parents were Latino, the audience member pointed out, the scene perpetuated racist and cultural as well as sexist stereotypes! A definite, embarrassing, "Aha!" moment. For some strange reason, though we'd all felt uncomfortable with the moment, we couldn't put our finger on either what the problem was or how to resolve it. We'd been so eager to foreground the actions of the father–a Latino, Catholic, working-class man who was standing up for his gay son, and for his younger daughter, who was being subjected to homophobic harassment by her classmates–that we didn't notice that the mother was being excluded from the conversation. I think the fact that the play was based on actual events, and the scene was only a couple lines long, had also obscured our thinking. After reading that survey response, we adjusted the blocking and gave half of the father's lines to the mother. So, questionnaires help with this kind of practical stuff, but they also help with marketing, and with reaching foundations and individual donors.

ANN ELIZABETH: Yes, it really is important for grants and fundraising, but it's frustrating at the same time to have to try to prove something so concrete about changing people's minds. Especially when we might want to complicate issues around identity sometimes. Contradictory feelings are hard to measure in a questionnaire.

NORMA: And it's frustrating to have to conclude a show by making the audience fill out questionnaires. It's not the feeling that I want to leave an audience with. I want to leave the play kind of humming in them. But, it's just not practical–and perhaps not very fair–to ask people to fill in questionnaires several days after they've seen a show, especially if it takes up class time.

ANN ELIZABETH: Right, but I think part of what I'm doing with the Freedom Summer Walking Tour,[8] and what you do when you go into schools, is working with teachers to effectively prolong the discussion and remind students about how it connects to other things. I mean, you really do need someone like that, a teacher or a professor who can sort of sustain the reflection and help students see their own role in the struggle as empowering. Do you have any thoughts on that?

NORMA: I love your thinking on that. But, I can also sympathize with teachers who have a hard time fitting post-show discussions and surveys into their lesson plans. I know I plan my class time so tightly that I'd have trouble adding new content mid-semester. Here's the thing: Since it's so uncertain what anyone will do after they leave the theatre, I think we need to help them see the connections while we're all together, in the play itself and/or in the post-show discussion. I think, for instance, that y'all did a great job connecting the dots in *A More Perfect Union.* You made good, thought-provoking connections between ideas and emotions, between homophobia and racism, and between historical facts, the experiences of fictional characters, and choices the audience members can make.

ANN ELIZABETH: What is interesting to me is: how do you work with the restrictions that are placed upon you in schools, and what are the things that can potentially go wrong and be misinterpreted?

NORMA: We have two basic strategies. First, our basic modus operandi: in the play development process, we include diverse members of the community for whom we are going to be performing. Let's say it's a school piece dealing with discrimination issues among youth. Involving administrators and people with legal expertise helps us to really, really understand the parameters within which we need to work. What's acceptable within the school? What's protected by state and national law? To get the stories and the diction accurate, we make sure that a diverse group of students are involved in the play development process. We also include parents and therapists who help ensure that the process, the play, and the post-show discussions will provide safe structures for delving into complex issues. For instance, in our *Clothes Minded?* middle school play, we dramatized a Columbine-like situation. In an early draft of the play, one of the young characters says he feels guilty when he realizes that the kid who has done all the shooting is a boy he often ridiculed. A psychiatrist with a specialization in treating adolescents told us that the way we'd worded and placed that line might trigger too much anxiety in some of our young audience members, so, we reworked the line accordingly. By involving teachers, we see how to connect the issues with the curriculum. Finally, we also include in the process experts on various relevant diversity issues—representatives from the NAACP, the Anti-Defamation

League, the Muslim Public Affairs Council, etc. When writing a piece addressing racism, we want to avoid being homophobic, or vice versa—as happened in that final scene of *Doing the Right Thing.*

ANN ELIZABETH: It's so hard to bridge communities if you don't have diversity of connections represented throughout the entire process. Those perspectives also help you maintain the organizational support needed to move it forward.

NORMA: Yes and once we feel the script is really solid, we send it out for one more vetting before starting rehearsals. This final vetting is generally done with school district officials and a battalion of law, education, and diversity experts. We ask them to give us their feedback in writing, and to write us a letter of support, and/or to be available for phone calls from concerned administrators and parents.

The second major strategy concerns our communications with the schools interested in hosting our work. When we book a show, workshop, or residency, we are very clear in our verbal and written communications about what subject matter will be covered. Finally, and perhaps most importantly, our written contracts include two important sections. First, an authorized representative of the school needs to sign off on the following statement: "From my conversations with Fringe Benefits and from the literature they have sent me, I understand that this [play, workshop, or residency] addresses a broad range of diversity issues, including ethnicity, age, size, gender, sexual orientation, religion, class, appearance, and ability, and I agree that it is appropriate for my school. And, second, the contract also stipulates that after X date, the school cannot make any changes in dates, times, location, or content, including postponements or cancellations, for any reason. If a school that is scheduled to receive a free, fully grant-supported show violates the contract, they have to pay the full price of the show.

ANN ELIZABETH: It's not free if it's not on these terms...

NORMA: Right. In fact, we pull the show if they insist on content changes, and/or on logistical changes that could compromise the work. Back in 2001, a radical religious right organization in Northern California sued a school district, two schools, and two principals for bringing in our show. They acknowledged to the press that what they were really upset about was state law AB-537, the School Safety and Violence Prevention Act of 2000, which makes it illegal for public schools to discriminate on the basis of actual or perceived sexual orientation or gender identity.[9] The plaintiffs also made it clear that they were objecting to our play as a way to challenge and overturn AB-537. When we heard that this lawsuit was afoot, even though our organization wasn't being sued, we approached a number of different legal organizations to help us out. But they all said, basically, "The lawsuit is completely spurious. Don't worry, it'll go away." Still, the suit remained unresolved for almost two years, and it was starting to make other California schools even more nervous about addressing anti-LGBT discrimination. Finally, the ACLU, along with a group of progressive parents in Northern California and the National Council for Lesbian Rights decided to intervene in the case, and they invited us to join them. We all felt it was imperative to intervene so that the radical religious right organization wouldn't triumph either by this suit continuing to linger in the courts and continuing, thereby, to intimidate other schools, or by the Northern California schools agreeing to a legal settlement requiring them to give away some of their rights to present tolerance-promoting curricula and presentations. It really helped our case that our contract was very clear, and that we had created the play with a lot of administrative and legal input. We knew we were working within the law.

ANN ELIZABETH: If you hadn't done such thorough partnering, you could have been more vulnerable. When you're working with so many partners and collaborators, are there ever difficult moments where collaborations fall apart?

NORMA: In the course of one of our Think Tank sessions, one of our regular participants, whom I will call Jenna, began talking about two historical characters and the parallels in their stories. I pointed out that by dramatizing their stories, especially for parent groups, we could create a powerful, bridge-building play that might help people appreciate some of the connections between racism and homophobia. I then asked, "Who would like to work on this?" Jenna said she would, and so did one other person. As Jenna began working, it gradually became clear that she wanted to work on it on her own. She didn't seem interested in developing it collaboratively. Nevertheless, I continued to express a strong interest in collaborating, and even in producing the play.

Over a period of about eighteen months, Jenna and I continued to have discussions about the play, outside of the context of the Think Tank. It seemed as if we were slowly developing a way to work together on the project. Fringe Benefits sponsored four public readings of the play during that time period. The first two readings involved performances of excerpts, edited by the actors and me, for community celebrations. I felt encouraged by the fact that the playwright let us make the decisions about what to present on those occasions, and by the fact that she seemed to like what we'd done. Then she hosted a reading in her apartment, mostly for her own friends and colleagues. This time I felt discouraged because she didn't seem interested in listening to their feedback. She wasn't even writing down what they were saying! Still, I continued to hold out hope–the concept was brilliant, and her writing in some sections was luminous! Then, in the summer of 2004, Fringe Benefits put together two more readings of the full piece for theatre colleagues, conducted for the purpose of getting dramaturgical feedback before our scheduled fall tour of the show. The playwright was unable to attend, as the readings were in Canada and Ohio. I shared the feedback with her–feedback that included lots of praise, but also strong, strong recommendations that some significant rewriting needed to be done. I also told her that, as we needed to start rehearsals in two weeks, and as eighteen months had already passed without her being able to complete the play, I wanted to bring in a ghostwriter, a talented, nationally-recognized playwright who had offered to help get the play ready for production with only a "with additional contributions by" credit. I proposed that, although we needed his help to get the play ready for this tour, she could elect to use his edits or not in any future productions of the play. She got very, very upset, and we couldn't go forward with the project.

ANN ELIZABETH: So there was no willingness to collaborate, and no way to get through to her.

NORMA: It was a nightmare, but I'm completely responsible. What did I say earlier about putting up a sign if the bridge is out? Hell, I ignored dozens of "Bridge Out" signs along the way, and just kept barreling on forward...I'm lucky it didn't turn out any worse. I found ways to justify it all to myself because I was so, so excited about the play I was picturing in my mind's eye. I kept thinking, "I guess we don't need a contract, because I'm not going to want to tour a play that she doesn't feel comfortable with. And she understands that we can't tour the play unless it's got approval from the communities that have to vet it." But, hello! I knew better. Fringe Benefits always does contracts. We used contracts back in 1991when we first started working with LGBT street youth. We asked them to tell us in writing how they wished to be credited, and if there were any segments where they needed us to edit content or change names, etc. It's crucial for people to understand that when they contribute stories, ideas, or suggestions to a collaboratively developed play, it's as if they're contributing tomatoes to a community feast! Depending on the group's dramaturgical decisions regarding the form and content of the play or community feast, your "tomato" might appear in a salad and be quite clearly recognized as your tomato, or it might be pureed and become an indistinguishable element of a soup, gumbo, or ratatouille...what's yours and what's someone else's may not be apparent at all.

ANN ELIZABETH: I love the analogy...you're making me hungry.

NORMA: It's also like contributing eggs to a cake–once the eggs are cracked and the batter's in the oven rising, it's pretty hard to get that egg back. That's another reason why it's important to make sure that collaborators know that they're always welcome in the kitchen! That their input is welcome throughout the entire play development process. That they know how long the writing and editing process will be and how it will be structured.

ANN ELIZABETH: So there are never too many chefs in the kitchen?

NORMA: As long as everyone is clear about the process and the goal.

ANN ELIZABETH: So, what are we making today, ratatouille, cake or tiaras?

NORMA: (*laughs*) Don't matter to me—as long as I get to be Lucy Liu!

NOTES

[1] Teatro Campesino, a theatre company founded in 1965 by Luis Valdez, has developed techniques from Chicano cultural traditions towards the community-based and agit-prop goals of their theatre company. Their early traditions included the use of improvisation, masks, and other Brechtian devices that highlight the political messages in plays performed by and for farm workers or others in La Raza.

[2] In "Why Devise? Why Now? 'Houston, we have a problem,'" Bowles explains how she borrows from persuasive speaking: "20% of your audience ('The Choir') probably already agrees with you; 20% of your audience may well be unreachable; the remaining 60% are the 'Moveable Middle.'" (18-19) *Theatre Topics*. 15.1 (2005): 15-21.

[3] Forum Theatre is one of Augusto Boal's Theatre of the Oppressed techniques, which "begins with the enactment of a scene…in which a protagonist tries, unsuccessfully, to overcome an oppression relevant to that particular audience. The joker [facilitator] then invites the spectators to replace the protagonist at any point in the scene that they can imagine an alternative action that could lead to a solution. The scene is replayed numerous times with different interventions. This results in a dialogue about the oppression, an examination of alternatives, and a 'rehearsal' for real situations." Schutzman, Mady and Jan Cohen-Cruz, eds. *Playing Boal: Theatre, Therapy, Activism.* New York: Routledge, 1994. 236-237.

[4] See http://www.ctoatala.org/ for more information.

[5] Invisible Theatre, another of Augusto Boal's Theatre of the Oppressed techniques, "is a rehearsed sequence of events that is enacted in a public, nontheatrical space, capturing the attention of people who do not know they are watching a planned performance. It is at once theater and real life, for although rehearsed, it happens in real time and space and the 'actors' must take responsibility for the consequences of the 'show.' The goal is to bring attention to a social problem for the purpose of stimulating public dialogue" (Schutzman and Cohen-Cruz 237).

[6] Special thanks to Daniel Nadon for organizing this panel.

[7] In this context, queer pedagogy refers to "queer" in the broadest sense of the word. Bowles refers to a pedagogy of non-normative practices, but does not evoke the post-structuralist connotations from queer theory that radically destabilize identity categories.

[8] For more on the Freedom Summer Walking Tour, See Armstrong's "In Search of the Beloved Community: Engaging Agents of Change through Freedom Summer 1964" in this volume.

[9] This state law makes it illegal for public schools to discriminate against students and education employees on the basis of actual or perceived sexual orientation or gender identity, or to allow the school environment to become so hostile for students who are, or are perceived to be, lesbian, gay, bisexual or transgender, that they are, in effect, denied equal access to an education. The State of California must afford all persons in public schools equal rights and opportunities. Regulations for implementing this law state that: no person shall be subjected to discrimination, or any form of illegal bias, including harassment. No person shall be excluded from participation in or denied the benefits of any program or activity on the basis of sex, actual or perceived sexual orientation or gender, ethnic group identification, race, ancestry, national origin, religion, color, or mental or physical disability. For more information about this California law see the Gay Straight Alliance Network at: http://www.gsanetwork.org/resources/ab537.html

CONTRIBUTORS

Ann Elizabeth Armstrong holds an M.F.A. in directing and a Ph.D. in theatre from University of Hawaii at Manoa. She is an Associate Professor of Theatre at Miami University in Oxford, OH where she co-directs the "Finding Freedom Summer" project. She is currently developing a play about Freedom Summer 1964 with playwright Carlyle Brown. Ann Elizabeth has trained and collaborated with theatre companies such as Split Britches, Fringe Benefits, Los Angeles Poverty Department, and Community Performance, Inc., and she has published articles such as "Building Coalitional Spaces in Lois Weaver's Performance Pedagogy" and "Paradoxes in Community-based Pedagogy," both in *Theatre Topics*. Her article "Negotiating Feminist Identities and Theatre of the Oppressed" appears in *A Boal Companion* (Routledge, 2006).

Kate Bornstein is an author, playwright and performance artist whose latest book is *Hello, Cruel World: 101 Alternatives To Suicide For Teens, Freaks, and Other Outlaws*. Other published works include the books *Gender Outlaw: On Men, Women and the Rest of Us* and *My Gender Workbook*. Kate's books are taught in over 120 colleges and universities around the world; , and she has performed her work live on college campuses, and in theaters and performance spaces across North America, Europe, and Australia. Her new solo show, *Kate Bornstein Is A Queer and Pleasant Danger* premieres in May 2007.

Norma Bowles is Founder and Artistic Director of Fringe Benefits theatre since 1991. She leads many of the company's "Theatre for Social Justice" workshops and institutes. She edited both *Cootie Shots: Theatrical Inoculations Against Bigotry* and *Friendly Fire*, two Fringe Benefits' play anthologies. Norma has conducted acting, commedia dell'arte and new play development residencies at theatres and universities throughout the United States—including South Coast Repertory (for nine years) and CalArts—as well as in Spain and Canada. She holds a B.A. from Princeton, and an M.F.A. from CalArts, and studied with Philippe Gaulier in Paris, France. Norma is also a recipient of PFLAG/LA's 2003 "Oscar Wilde Award" and Cornerstone Theater Company's 2002 "Bridge Award" for her work building bridges within and between communities.

Sharon Bridgforth is a touring artist and widely anthologized and produced writer. She is the author of the performance/novels *the bull-jean stories* and *love conjure/blues*, (RedBone Press). She is also a recipient of the Lambda Literary Award, Theatre Communications Group/National Endowment for the Arts Playwrights Award, Rockefeller Foundation Multi-Arts Production Fund Award; and Funding Exchange/The Paul Robeson Fund for Independent Media. She is the Anchor Artist for The Austin Project (sponsored by The Center for African and African American Studies at the University of Texas at Austin).

Paul K. Bryant-Jackson received his Ph.D. from the University of Wisconsin-Madison and is Professor of Theatre at Miami University in Oxford Ohio. He is co-editor of *Intersecting Boundaries: The Theatre of Adrienne Kennedy* and editor of *Blackstream*, a journal that publishes the conference proceedings of the Black Theatre Association. He has published articles in *Theatre Journal, Black Comedy* (Applause*), Black Theatre: Ritual Performance in the African Diaspora* (Temple University Press), *ItaliAfrica: Bridging Continents and Cultures* (Forum Italicum Press). He regularly directs at Miami University and is often an invited speaker on the works of Adrienne Kennedy. He was formerly Associate Professor and Chair of Theatre at Spelman College.

Laurie Carlos has been an original player in the New York avant-garde performance scene for more than thirty years. She has created shows such as *White Chocolate, The Cooking Show,* and *Organdy Falsetto*. Laurie is an Obie Award-winning actress for the role of the lady in blue in Ntozake Shange's *for colored girls who have considered suicide/when the rainbow is enuf* and is a two-time Bessie Award-winning choreographer and has worked with Urban Bush Women. She has also directed the work of award-winning writers Sharon Bridgforth, Carl Hancock Rux, Luis Alfaro, Rebecca Rice, Daniel Alexander Jones, Florinda Bryant, and Zell Miller III. She is currently working on the performance novel *The Pork Chop Wars*. For six years, Carlos served as Artistic Fellow at Penumbra Theatre Company in St. Paul, Minnesota. She curates the Pillsbury House Theatre's performance series *Non-English Speaking Spoken Here*. Laurie has received awards from the New York Foundation for the Arts, the National Endowment for the Arts, the Theatre Communication Group, the McKnight Foundation, and the Bush Fellowship for Performance.

Barbara Carrellas is an author, sex educator, and theatre artist. She is the author of *Urban Tantra: Sacred Sex for the Twenty-First Century* and *Luxurious Loving: Tantric Inspirations for Passion and Pleasure*. She directed *Kate Bornstein is a Queer and Pleasant Danger* and *Annie Sprinkle: Post Porn Modernist* (Australian National Tour), and also collaborated with Annie Sprinkle on *MetamorphoSex*. She has been a Guest Lecturer at Harvard University, Brown University, Vassar College, Barnard College, the Chicago Art Institute, and Yale University.

Lisa Jo Epstein received her Ph.D. from the University of Texas at Austin. She is a theatre educator, director, scholar and community-based artist. She is founder and Artistic Director of Gas & Electric Arts, a socially-engaged theatre company in Philadelphia with an education program focused on transformational theatre. Lisa Jo worked as assistant to Ariane Mnouchkine at the Theatre du Soleil, trained at the Boal Center for the Theatre of the Oppressed, and in Bataclown techniques in Paris, France. She has published in *Theatre InSight, The Journal of Beckett Studies* and is the author of "Flexing Images, Changing Visions: The Twin Poles of Contemporary French Political Theatre" in *Staging Resistance: Essays on Political Theatre* (University of Michigan Press, 1998).

Jo Beth Gonzales received her Ph.D. from Bowling Green State University and her M.F.A. from the University of Minnesota. She is a teacher and the Drama Director at Bowling Green High School. Her book, *Temporary Stages: Departing From Tradition in High School Theatre Education* was published by Heinemann in 2006. Jo Beth has also published in *Youth Theatre Journal* and *Communication Quarterly*. She is the winner of the 2005 Research Award and the 1998 Distinguished Dissertation Award from the American Alliance for Theatre and Education and the 2002 Wilson National Mentor's Award to a High School Drama Teacher from the Children's Theatre Association of America.

Beverly Guy-Sheftall has a B.A. in English from Spelman College and a Ph.D. from Emory University. She is founding director of the Women's Research and Resource Center and is the Anna Julia Cooper Professor of Women's Studies at Spelman College. Guy-Sheftall published the first anthology on Black women's literature, *Sturdy Black Bridges: Visions of Black Women in Literature* (Doubleday, 1979). Her most recent publications are an anthology co-edited with Rudolph P. Byrd entitled *Traps: African American Men on Gender and Sexuality* (Indiana University Press, 2001 and *Gender Talk: The Struggle for Equality in African American Communities* with Johnetta Cole (Random House, 2003.) Guy-Sheftall is the recipient of a National Kellogg Fellowship, a Woodrow Wilson Fellowship, and Spelman's Presidential Faculty Award for outstanding scholarship.

Cheryl L. Johnson has a B.A. in English from Spelman College and an M.A. and Ph.D. from the University of Michigan. She is currently director of Women's Studies and Associate Professor of English at Miami University of Ohio. She has published articles in *Signs, College English*, and various anthologies. In 2002, she had a Fulbright teaching and research fellowship at the University of the Western Cape and the University of Stellenbosch in South Africa. She is working on a book length manuscript about the narratives of deference and resistance in Black women's novels.

Joni L. Jones/Omi Osun Olomo received her Ph.D. from New York University and is Associate Professor of Performance Studies and Associate Director of the Center for African and African American Studies at the University of Texas at Austin. Omi has published in *Theatre Topics*; *Teaching Performance Studies* (Southern Illinois University Press 2002*,*),; *Teaching Theatre Today* (Palgrave 2004); *Centering Ourselves: African American Feminist and Womanist Studies of Discourse* (Hampton Press 2002); and *The Color of Theatre* (Continuum 2002). She is the recipient of a Fulbright Fellowship to Nigeria 1997-98.

Kathleen Juhl received her M.F.A. in Acting and Directing from University of North Carolina at Greensboro and her Ph.D. in Performance Studies at the University of Texas at Austin. She is Associate Professor of Theatre and former Chair of Feminist Studies at Southwestern University in Georgetown, Texas. Juhl was Brown Distinguished Teaching Professor at Southwestern University, 2001-2004. She is the author of "Everyday Life Performance, 'the Method,' and the Acting Classroom," *Text and Performance Quarterly* and "Arts In London: The Intersection of Performance Studies and Intercultural Learning," *Theatre Topics*. She is an actor, director, voice and movement specialist, and Alexander Technique teacher. She edited the Women and Theatre Program Newsletter from 1997-2003. She recently directed and toured to high schools *As Seen on TV*, a play about racism which was developed in collaboration with Norma Bowles and the Fringe Benefits Theatre Company.

Joan Lipkin is the artistic director of That Uppity Theatre Company in St. Louis, Missouri where she founded the Alternate Currents/Direct Currents and Women Centerstage Series, the DisAbility Project, the Louies, Inner Vision, Democracy on Stage, and As American As Apple Pie among other projects. Joan specializes in creating original theatrical work, facilitating dialogue for corporations and social service agencies, and in making work with marginalized populations including people with disabilities, lesbian, gay, bisexual, transgendered youth and adults, blind teenagers, women with breast cancer, and adults with Alzheimer's and early stage dementia. She has taught at Washington, Lindenwood, and Webster Universities and the Community Arts Training Institute. Joan's work has been anthologized and presented throughout North America, Great Britain, and Asia. She has received Visionary, Human Rights Equality, Focus for Improving Racial Equality, Fredrick H. Laas, Arts for Life Lifetime Achievement, and James F. Hornback Ethical Humanist of the Year awards.

Deb Margolin is a playwright, performance artist, and founding member of Split Britches Theater Company. She is currently an Associate Professor in Theater Studies at Yale University. Deb is the author of eight full-length solo performance pieces including *Index to Idioms* (2004) and is the recipient of a 1999-2000 OBIE Award for Sustained Excellence of Performance and the 2005 Kesselring Prize for her play *Three Seconds in the Key*. She has been an Artist in Residence at Hampshire College, the University of Hawaii, and Zale writer-in-residence at Tulane University. Deb's work has been widely published, including an anthology of her solo performance pieces entitled *Of All The Nerve: Deb Margolin SOLO* edited by Lynda Hart (Cassell/Continuum Press 1999).

Ellen Margolis received her Ph.D. from the University of California Santa Barbara and her MFA from the University of California Davis. She is Associate Professor and Director of Theatre at Pacific University, Forest Grove, Oregon. Ellen was also Literary Manager for the International Center for Women Playwrights and is a member of the Dramatists Guild of America. She is an actor, director, playwright, and voice and dialect coach. She is author of the award-winning play *How to Draw Mystical Creatures* and several other plays which have been produced throughout the U.S. Her current project is co-editing a book on the politics of U.S. actor training with Dr. Lissa Tyler Renaud.

Joan McCarty is the author of the plays, *A Time to Dance* and *Last Bus to Stateville*. She has also written a collection of short stories entitled *Through My Windows*. She is a contributor to the *Greenwood Encyclopedia of African American Literature*, *This day in the Life—Diaries from Women across America*, *the Greenwood Encyclopedia of African American Women Writers*, and *Life Spices from Seasoned Sisters*, an anthology of life stories. She received the first place short story award from the Georgia Writer's Association in 2003. She is a member of both Actors' Equity Association and the American Federation of Radio and Television Artists. Formerly a faculty member at Spelman College, she is currently an Assistant Professor at Savannah State University and a professional stage manager.

Cherríe Moraga is a poet, playwright, and essayist and co-editor of *This Bridge Called My Back: Writings by Radical Women of Color*. She is the author of numerous plays including *Shadow of a Man* and *Watsonville: Some Place Not Here*, (Fund for New American Plays Awards, 1991 and 1995) and *Heroes and Saints* (Pen West Award for Drama, 1992). Her collected non-fiction writings include *The Last Generation*; *Waiting in the Wings: Portrait of a Queer Motherhood)*, and an expanded edition of the now-classic, *Loving in the War Years*. Cherríe is the recipient of the National Endowment for the Arts' Theatre Playwrights' Fellowship. She has been Artist-in-Residence in the Department of Drama at Stanford University since 1996. She recently completed *A Xicana Codex of Changing Consciousness: Essays Turn into a Century* and a memoir of her mother's dying from Alzheimer's, *Send Them Flying Home*.

Donmica Radulescu received her Ph.D. from the University of Chicago and is Professor of Romance Languages and Chair of the Women's Studies Program at Washington and Lee University. She is co-editor of *The Theater of Teaching and the Lessons of Theater* (Rowman and Littlefield Publishing, 2005) and *Vampirettes, Wretches and Amazons: Western Representations of East European Women* (Eastern European Monographs, Columbia University Press, 2004). She edited *Realms of Exile: Nomadism, Diasporas, and Eastern European Voices* (Rowman and Littlefield Publishing, 2002) and is the author of *Sisters of Medea: The Tragic Heroine across Cultures* (University Press of the South, 2002). Domnica is founding Director of the National Symposium of Theater in Academe.

Corinne Rusch-Drutz received her Ph.D. from the University of Toronto. She is currently the Director of Advocacy and Communications for the YWCA of Toronto, the city's only multi-service organization by, for, and about women and girls. Prior to joining the YWCA, Corinne was on faculty at York University in the Department of Theatre. In addition to writing for various academic journals, television documentaries and lifestyle series, Corinne has worked on a number of government sponsored programs, most recently, "Equity in Canadian Theatre: The Women's Initiative," and the 2006 Status of Women in Canadian Theatre study. Recent publications include: "Stage Mothers: A Qualitative Analysis of Women's Work Experiences as Mothers in Toronto Theatre" and "Performing the Good Mother: Maternal Identity, Professional Persona and Theatre Practice," both in *The Journal for the Association for Research on Mothering*.

Amy Seham received her M.F.A. from Northwestern University and her Ph.D. from the University of Wisconsin- Madison. She is Associate Professor and Chair of Theatre and Dance at Gustavus Adolphus College. Amy is the author of *Whose Improv is it Anyway?* (University of Mississippi 2001) and has published in *The Drama Review* and *Theatre Insight*. She is playwright, director, and co-founding artistic director of Performance Studio Theatre and Free Shakespeare on the Green in New Haven, Connecticut. She created and conducted workshops investigating race, gender and power in improv performance at Second City-Toronto, the Funny Woman Festival in Chicago, the University of California-Santa Cruz, DePauw University, Miami University, the Playwrights' Center, and with Fringe Benefits of Los Angeles along with a multi-year series of "Stereotype-busting Improv" sessions at the Association for Theatre in Higher

Education. Amy developed social justice theatre workshops with the Visthar Outreach Program in Bangalore, India and currently mentors social justice theatre troupe *I Am, We Are* in Minnesota.

Rebecca Schneider received her Ph.D. from New York University and is Director of the Doctoral Program in Theatre and Performance Studies at Brown University. She is the author of *The Explicit Body in Performance* (Routledge 1997) and co-editor of a book on 20th-century directing practice and theory titled *Re:Direction* (also with Routledge). She has written numerous essays, among them "Hello Dolly Well Hello Dolly: The Double and Its Theatre" in *Psychoanalysis and Performance,* "Solo Solo Solo" in *After Criticism: New Responses to Art and Performance,* and "Performance Remains" in *Performance Research.* Schneider is a contributing editor to *The Drama Review* and on the board of *Theatre Survey.* She is co-editor (with David Krasner) of the book series Theatre: Theory/Text/Performance with the University of Michigan Press.

Chris Strickling received her Ph.D. in English from the University of Texas at Austin. She is an independent writer and theatre artist/producer. She is the author of "Actual Lives: Cripples in the House," *Theatre Topics,* September 2002. Chris is also the producer and co-director of the Actual Lives Performance Project in Austin, Texas, a project comprised of adults with disability who write and perform original, autobiographical works.

Stacy Wolf received her Ph.D. from the University of Wisconsin-Madison and is Associate Professor in the Performance as Public Practice Program in the Department of Theatre and Dance at the University of Texas at Austin. She is the author of *A Problem Like Maria: Gender and Sexuality in the American Musical* (University of Michigan Press, 2002) and other essays on musical theatre. She is the former editor of *Theatre Topics,* a journal of pedagogy and praxis.

Aunt Lute Books is a multicultural women's press that has been committed to publishing high quality, culturally diverse literature since 1982. In 1990, the Aunt Lute Foundation was formed as a non-profit corporation to publish and distribute books that reflect the complex truths of women's lives and to present voices that are underrepresented in mainstream publishing. We seek work that explores the specificities of the very different histories from which we come, and the possibilities for personal and social change.

Please contact us if you would like a free catalog of our books or if you wish to be on our mailing list for news of future titles. You may buy books from our website, by phoning in a credit card order, or by mailing a check with the catalog order form.

Aunt Lute Books
P.O. Box 410687
San Francisco, CA 94141
415.826.1300
www.auntlute.com
books@auntlute.com

This book would not have been possible without the kind contributions of the Aunt Lute Founding Friends:

Anonymous Donor
Anonymous Donor
Rusty Barcelo
Marian Bremer
Marta Drury
Diane Goldstein

Diana Harris
Phoebe Robins Hunter
Diane Mosbacher, M.D., Ph.D.
Sara Paretsky
William Preston, Jr.
Elise Rymer Turner